THE INSIDER

THE INSIDER

Malcolm Cowley and the
Triumph of American Literature

GERALD HOWARD

PENGUIN PRESS
NEW YORK
2025

PENGUIN PRESS
An imprint of Penguin Random House LLC
1745 Broadway, New York, NY 10019
penguinrandomhouse.com

Designed by Christina Nguyen

LIBRARY OF CONGRESS CATALOGING-IN-PUBLICATION DATA
Names: Howard, Gerald author
Title: The insider : Malcolm Cowley and the triumph of
American literature / Gerald Howard.
Description: New York : Penguin Press, 2025. | Includes bibliographical references and index.
Identifiers: LCCN 2024061549 (print) | LCCN 2024061550 (ebook) |
ISBN 9780525522058 hardcover | ISBN 9780525522065 ebook
Subjects: LCSH: Cowley, Malcolm, 1898–1989 | Authors, American—20th century—Biography
| Critics—United States—Biography | Editors—United States—Biography |
Literature publishing—United States—History—20th century | LCGFT: Biographies
Classification: LCC PS3505.O956 Z67 2025 (print) |
LCC PS3505.O956 (ebook) | DDC 818/.5209 [B]—dc23/eng/20250327
LC record available at https://lccn.loc.gov/2024061549
LC ebook record available at https://lccn.loc.gov/2024061550

Printed in the United States of America
1st Printing

The authorized representative in the EU for product safety and compliance
is Penguin Random House Ireland, Morrison Chambers, 32 Nassau Street,
Dublin D02 YH68, Ireland, https://eu-contact.penguin.ie.

To my beloved wife, Susanne—
"Walking through life with you, my dear,
has been a very gracious thing"

To five good friends, gone too soon:
James Atlas, Charlie Conrad, Dan Frank,
Duncan Hannah, Peter Kaldheim

"You are one of the people I count on for the future. See that you do not disappoint me."

—Amy Lowell to Malcolm Cowley, May 10, 1921

—

"One must be an inventor to read well. . . . There is then creative reading as well as creative writing."

—Ralph Waldo Emerson, "The American Scholar"

—

"A good critic—we cannot help seeing, when we look back at any other age—is a much rarer thing than a good poet or a good novelist."

—Randall Jarrell, "Poets, Critics, and Readers"

CONTENTS

———

INTRODUCTION:

THE COWLEY ERA

———

In 1944 the careers of two of the most important American literary figures of the past century were at a low ebb.

The more famous of the two was the novelist William Faulkner. Since the early thirties he'd produced an astonishing string of Modernist masterpieces dealing with the tragic and haunted aspects of Southern history, including *The Sound and the Fury*, *As I Lay Dying*, *Light in August*, *Absalom, Absalom!*, *Go Down, Moses*, and the immortal novella "The Bear." His work had attracted positive and even passionate critical attention, but also a great deal of hostility regarding its difficulties in syntax and narrative structure and its often lurid subject matter. As a result, his sales had been meager, and by 1944 every one of his seventeen books to date was out of print and nearly impossible to find, aside from *Sanctuary*, a crime shocker that he claimed he'd written in 1931 for a quick payday. His publisher had even donated the printing plates for some of the books to be recycled for the war effort. Faulkner had to spend part of every year in Hollywood as a scriptwriter to support himself, his extended family, and his farm in Oxford, Mississippi, under contracts so draconian that he was not so much employed by Warner Bros. as indentured to them.

Faulkner and his work seemed destined for oblivion. The great

Scribner's editor Maxwell Perkins had declared that "Faulkner is finished." But one person refused to accept Perkins's verdict and was determined to do something to prove him wrong. That person was the critic and editor Malcolm Cowley. Cowley was not famous exactly, but in the literary world, he had been a figure of considerable stature. He'd been in Paris in the twenties as a participant-observer at the birth of the Lost Generation, and as the literary editor of *The New Republic*, he'd held what was then one of the real power seats in American letters. Then, like so many other American writers, he'd become radicalized by the Great Depression in the thirties and taken a hard left turn politically, becoming an all too visible fellow traveler of the Communist Party. As a result, in 1941 he'd been shunted aside from his editorial responsibilities at the magazine and reduced to mere contributor status, a humiliating demotion that had serious financial consequences. Even worse, in 1942 he'd been very publicly forced to resign from his job in the Office of Facts and Figures in Washington after being hounded by the Dies Committee, Whittaker Chambers at *Time*, and the right-wing columnist for the Hearst papers, Westbrook Pegler. Banished to rural purdah in Sherman, Connecticut, he was faced with the problem of supporting himself, his wife, Muriel, and son, Robert, and of reviving a literary career in almost terminal disrepair.

Luckily, he was thrown a financial lifeline by the Mellon Foundation: a so-called living grant of five years of income sufficient to live on. Relieved of the pressure of having to churn out freelance articles and reviews, Cowley turned to doing what he always did best: reading. And what he was reading was American literature in all its periods, including the twentieth century, in a quest to grasp its inner nature and its commonalities. One of the writers who attracted his attention most strongly was William Faulkner. It seemed to him that a very great literary injustice had been perpetrated. The critics had really only read Faulkner's books one by one, and no one had fully grasped that each of his books was part of a much larger project, that of creating the myth and legend of the American South and its guilt-stained history. So Malcolm Cowley began to write a long critical essay to try to correct this injustice, and at a certain point he wrote to William Faulkner in Oxford to resolve some questions he had . . .

What happened next was arguably the most successful rescue mission in American literary history, one that would reverse Faulkner's drift into obscurity and lead to his recognition, well into his lifetime, as not just an American classic but a writer of world stature worthy of the Nobel Prize in Literature.

That was hardly the only service Malcolm Cowley performed for American literature. In 1934 he wrote the first, and many feel the best, of the raft of Lost Generation memoirs, *Exile's Return*. It set forth the durable template of revolt and reintegration of the artistic Americans who flocked to the Left Bank in the twenties to escape their country's cultural limitations, only to rediscover the virtues of the country they'd fled. The critical introduction to a 1944 anthology he edited, *The Portable Hemingway*, proposed an entirely new way of looking at the writer and his work as the product of wartime trauma and with hidden depths that complicated and enriched the way we think of Hemingway for good. He played an important role in the Fitzgerald revival of the fifties—yes, F. Scott Fitzgerald needed reviving as well—as the editor of his short stories and a new edition of *Tender Is the Night*. As a consulting editor for the Viking Press he worked tirelessly and shrewdly for years to get his reluctant employer to publish Jack Kerouac's *On the Road*, the book that can be said to have ignited the counterculture. At *The New Republic* in 1930 he'd published "Expelled," an unsolicited first story from the eighteen-year-old John Cheever about being booted from Thayer Academy; later, Cowley would take Cheever under his wing and help him to get published in

The New Yorker, where he would become that magazine's signature fiction writer.

Malcolm Cowley's life story from 1898 to 1989 spanned most of what we still call the American Century, and he would be involved with just about everything and everybody of literary consequence during those years. That is not hyperbole; a list would include Faulkner, Hemingway, Fitzgerald, Kerouac, and Cheever, as well as John Dos Passos, Ezra Pound, Hart Crane, Eugene O'Neill, E. E. Cummings, Ken Kesey, Thornton Wilder, Edmund Wilson, Archibald MacLeish, Alfred Kazin, Mary McCarthy, Lionel Trilling, James T. Farrell, Alexander Calder, Dwight Macdonald, Dawn Powell, John Updike, Kenneth Burke, Allen Tate, Conrad Aiken, Marianne Moore, Van Wyck Brooks, Wallace Stegner, Larry McMurtry, Dorothy Day, Mike Gold, Robert Penn Warren, John Berryman, Saul Bellow, and Eudora Welty. These were friends and working colleagues and students and sometimes bitter adversaries, whose work he'd reviewed and edited and championed and published, whom he'd made common cause and feuded with. He'd been with them on the battlefields of France as a volunteer driver during the Great War, in the tearooms and tenement apartments and low bars of bohemian Greenwich Village, in the cafés and boîtes of Montparnasse, fighting the little magazine wars of the twenties and the pitched ideological battles of the thirties, and later, after World War II had ended, creating the American literary canon and taking stock of how far our writing had come. With his passionate commitment to the cause of American literature and his instinct for what was fresh and valuable and likely to last, Cowley was in the thick of it, for longer and with greater influence than just about anybody else.

Malcolm Cowley's life also provides a vehicle for the larger story that this book tells, that of the triumph of American literature. At the time of his birth, it was considered to be a body of work of minor interest or importance. Certain of our nineteenth-century writers had been taken up enthusiastically in Europe—Cooper in Germany, Poe in France, Whitman in England—but they were thought to be isolated geniuses, not the flowers of a vigorous national literature. To be an American writer was to be regarded as provincial, backward, lacking in artistic polish or value. No one thought it odd when Henry James felt that he had to betake himself to Europe to realize himself as a novelist.

By the time Malcolm Cowley died in 1989, all that had changed, spectacularly. Beginning with Sinclair Lewis in 1930, seven Americans had been awarded the Nobel Prize in Literature, eight if you include T. S. Eliot, which you probably should. There were departments of American literature in universities around the country and across the globe. Writers everywhere looked to America for inspiration. Cowley played a central role in helping this come about.

Malcolm Cowley was generally known as a critic and sometimes as an editor, but he was also an accomplished poet, a skilled translator from the French, a memoirist, a literary historian, a university teacher of writing and literature, and a skilled administrator and all-round operator. The term for this sort of person used to be "man of letters," a phrase that now has an archaic ring to it, and which is also, with a nod to Mary McCarthy, Hannah Arendt, Joan Didion, Elizabeth Hardwick, et al., sexist. But becoming a person of letters was Cowley's real ambition as a young writer, and a perfectly reasonable one. There were plenty of these learned and versatile people around for most of his life and he would succeed in turning himself into an admirable example of the type. Also, in his quiet way, a powerful one. Persons of letters used to be influential tastemakers, proposing standards of judgment and applying those standards to the established and the aspiring, the living and the dead. Cowley's story demonstrates how the system of literary reputation and canon formation worked, and how one determined actor bent it to his tastes and convictions.

The authors and their novels and stories and poems and plays and essays that fill the literary textbooks and anthologies and college reading lists can seem to arrive with the solidity and inevitability of almost papal authority and tautological reasoning. They are in the anthologies because they are great, and they are great because they are in the anthologies. In point of fact, a literary career and a posthumous reputation are unpredictable, dependent on accident and timing and broader shifts in taste. A change can arrive in a moment with just the right (or the wrong) essay in just the right publication, or slowly, the way the tides can either build up or erode a beach over decades. Malcolm Cowley was a player who understood this system as well as anyone ever has. His career is a master class in how the literary Game of Thrones was played in the twentieth century, and, to a certain extent, to this day.

This book has been gestating for a long time. In the early seventies I had newly graduated from college and was suffering from an acute case of the English major blues. It was the dispiriting Watergate/post-Vietnam era; the country was low in the water and so was I. At the end of my college education, I had contracted a passion for American literature and was now reading as much of the stuff on my own as I could manage. I suppose I was, like the American literary intellectuals of the forties, searching for "a usable past" as solace for the squalid national estate and my own frustrations and perplexities.

At just this moment—on Sunday, May 6, 1973, to be precise—I came upon a long and perfectly gorgeous review in *The New York Times Book Review* by William Styron of *A Second Flowering: Works and Days of the Lost Generation* by a writer I had never heard of, Malcolm Cowley. So persuasive was Styron about that book's merits, and so in sync was its subject matter with my reading at the time, that I got myself to the Strand Bookstore to buy a half-price review copy, $7.95 full retail being way beyond my means. In writing so personally and at the same time with such critical acumen about the towering yet often flawed figures of the Lost Generation, this man Cowley acquainted me with a fact my otherwise excellent undergraduate English courses had failed to address: that *writers were actual people.* In my hero-worshipping frame of mind, this had never really occurred to me.

I was smitten, and in time I would read *Exile's Return* with equal avidity and admiration. By 1981, I had gotten myself together professionally and a happy providence arranged for me to begin a job as a trade paperback editor at Viking Penguin, the publisher where Malcolm Cowley was still employed as a consulting editor. One day he was in the office for a meeting and I was introduced to him, whereupon I experienced exactly the same feelings that Billy Crystal felt when he was introduced to Mickey Mantle. In shaking the hand of this deaf and elderly man, I was but one degree of separation from the giants of American literature he'd known and written about so movingly in *A Second Flowering.* I would meet him casually two or three more times, and a couple of years before his death, I actually became his last editor at Viking, seeing into print the monumental volume *The Selected Correspondence of Kenneth Burke and Malcolm Cowley* and commissioning *The Portable Malcolm Cowley.*

In 2014, I would review in *Bookforum* another, even more monumental volume, *The Long Voyage: Selected Letters of Malcolm Cowley, 1915–1987,* edited by the superb scholar of American literature Hans Bak. I tried my best to be as convincing on its merits and importance as William Styron had been. In my final paragraph I made the assertion that, as important as the book was, what was really needed was a biography that could do for Malcolm Cowley what A. Scott Berg's *Max Perkins* had done for its subject. Over the course of my career as a book editor, I'd actually been in search of an author to write that book, but no suitable candidate had ever emerged. And then one late afternoon, on a commuter bus heading north on the eastern spur of the

New Jersey Turnpike, the fatal thought entered my mind that *I* needed to write that book, or something like it. I did my level best to make that thought go away, but as you can see from the book you hold in your hand, I was unsuccessful.

Some final words about this book. If you are looking to find out what Malcolm Cowley was up to on any given day in his life, you are unlikely to do so in the pages that follow. I fly over large tracts of that life in order to focus on the consequential episodes that truly define his place in American letters. When I have described the book I was working on, I resorted to the inadequate descriptors "a biographical study" or sometimes "a sort-of-biography." No one seeking fame would be foolish enough to pursue it by becoming a literary critic, but even so, Malcolm Cowley's name recognition in comparison to his achievements is considerably lower than that of such comparable figures as Edmund Wilson, Alfred Kazin, or Lionel Trilling. When I tell my well-read friends that I have been working on a book about Malcolm Cowley, they usually think at first that I am writing about Malcolm *Lowry*. I wanted to reverse the polarity of his diminishing profile by writing a readable and lively book of digestible size that foregrounded his immense achievements on behalf of American writing, one that could draw an educated general reader into his life and career. A standard-issue biography seemed antithetical to my intentions. It is up to you to decide to what extent I may have succeeded.

I'll close with some cautions and caveats. There is a great deal of politics in this book, and I wish there could have been less. So, to be sure, would Malcolm Cowley himself. But the hyper-political thirties represented both the zenith of his influence and power and the nadir of his judgment, and they needed to be unpacked and considered, as did the long-term effects of his mistakes on his position in American literary history. I touch only glancingly on Malcolm Cowley's private life, to the extent that it is necessary to understand his character and inner wellsprings. And Malcolm Cowley's life and career and milieu were very white, very middle class and sometimes privileged, very male, and very heterosexual. He was a man of his era. He had a genuine feeling for ordinary American life, especially rural life, but his interest in the working class coincided with the brief vogue for the proletarian novel and waned after that. He was in no way a misogynist and he respected and worked with a great many women, but he was also capable of using the slighting term "lady novelist" in a review. He could also use the word "pansy" in the same fashion, even though he knew that two of his closest friends, the poet Hart Crane and the critic Newton Arvin, were gay. He evinced no particular interest in Black writing and writers from the Harlem Renaissance to the Black Arts period, a conspicuous lacuna in his portfolio. (He did cowrite a pioneering history of the Atlantic slave trade, *Black Cargoes*.) In short, it would be a mistake to try to present or judge Malcolm Cowley from our current-day perspective. He can't be fit into the mold and I don't try to do so.

Toward the end of his life, an excited woman, a Cowley superfan, came up to him after a lecture and gushed, "Oh, Mister Cowley, I love your era!" She almost certainly meant the high twenties, but the Cowley Era really extended over most of the twentieth century. During the course of engaging with his work and career for (and this is startling to contemplate) more than fifty years, I have come to love his era, and Malcolm Cowley himself, too. I hope *The Insider* can accomplish something similar for you.

ONE.

BOY IN SUNLIGHT

———

Although he wrote two memoirs, Malcolm Cowley would never produce a full-scale autobiography. He did, however, regard the 1968 edition of his more or less complete poems, *Blue Juniata: A Life*, as his real autobiography, the poems being arranged not chronologically but in a fashion meant to convey a sense of his inner and outer life over the decades. He chose to begin that book with his pastoral poem "Boy in Sunlight." Written in 1967, the poem reads very much like an update of that old American chestnut, once obligatory in all most-loved-poems anthologies, John Greenleaf Whittier's 1855 "The Barefoot Boy." ("Blessings on thee, little man, / Barefoot boy, with cheek of tan!," etc.) In contrast to Whittier, Cowley strips away the conventional sentiment from his memory of himself on a boyhood ramble through the Pennsylvania countryside, fishing pole in hand. Instead, he substitutes a kind of precisionist imagery, fitting for a poet who'd bumped up against most of the major poets of the twentieth century in one fashion or another.

The "boy in sunlight," the younger Cowley, has caught four small trout and now carries them in an old lard bucket. He finds a sunny spot above a pool in a burnt-down former stand of hemlock and sits down to eat his lunch of corn pone and to doze, half asleep but still alert, "like a snake on the stone." He takes everything in, the buzzing insects, a hovering hawk, the blue mountain sky, and then a kind of transmigration between boy and landscape happens. "The land absorbs him into itself, / as he absorbs the land, the ravaged woods, the pale sky, / not to be seen, but as a way of seeing; / not to be judged, but as a way of judgment; / not even to remember, but stamped in the bone." Sixty-plus years after the event, he would recall this moment as "a rite of initiation: the countryside marked me as its own, as if a surveyor had scarred a witness tree."

Cowley's feeling for the countryside of the town of Belsano in Cambria County, Pennsylvania, where he was born and where he spent long summers on his family's farm until he went away to college at the age of seventeen, indelibly marked what he would call "the essential me." For his entire adult life, he lived and worked at the highest level of American literary society, a place he felt comfortable and confident in. But in his innermost self he would always at some level be that footloose, barefoot boy—literally barefoot, as he would take off his city shoes in the middle of May and not have to put them on until the middle of October. It was a place he could always retreat to in his mind, and not just as a poet. He would think of Cambria County as "the real beginning of the Midwest," which helped him identify with those Midwestern writers like Anderson, Hemingway, and Fitzgerald. And Belsano represented something primordial to Malcolm Cowley, a distinctly American kind of freedom and community that he would lament the waning and then extinction of as progress made its inexorable inroads into an older, fragile, rural way of life.

Country existence influenced his outer manner as well as his inner life. "Look at the hands if you get a chance," the poet John Peale Bishop wrote to his Princeton classmate Edmund Wilson in the twenties. "The plowboy of the western world who has been to Paris." Alfred Kazin recalled that "whenever you crossed Malcolm directly, he would sidle into his familiar role of the slow-moving and slow-talking country boy." Kazin thought that Cowley was, as the saying goes, country-boying him, and maybe he was, a bit. But the slow-talking aspect of Malcolm Cowley was not an act he put on to gull the fast-talking urban intellectuals. He spoke slowly because he thought carefully, revising his words in his head before he said them. His mental metabolism was just that much more measured and unhurried than theirs, and it marked him as different.

Belsano was a rural community of a few hundred people on the tablelands west of the Allegheny mountain range, seventy miles due west of Pittsburgh and sixteen miles north of Johnstown, site of the tragic flood of 1889 that claimed thousands of lives. Malcolm Cowley was born there on August 24, 1898, in the farmhouse owned by his father William Cowley's family. It was an exceptionally difficult birth for his mother, Josephine Hutmacher Cowley. His father had been called away to Norfolk, Virginia, to care for his brother David Cowley, who had volunteered for service in Cuba during the Spanish-American War and was thought to be dying of typhus. His pregnant mother was left alone in Belsano with his aunt Margaret, who seems to have been ignorant of the physical facts of life and certainly was of little help in an emergency. Josephine went into labor and the terrified Margaret locked herself in a closet while her sister moaned in agony for two harrowing days. Someone finally heard the moans and rode his horse (there were no telephones or "horseless carriages") some miles to the nearest coal mining camp to summon a company doctor. He arrived in a thunderstorm just in time to save both the mother and the newborn infant.

Malcolm Cowley's mother was so shaken by the whole episode that she vowed never to have another child, a promise she kept. How she and her husband managed this is unknown. They were ignorant of even the rudimentary methods of birth control of the time, and

William Cowley's Swedenborgian faith regarded contraception of any kind as a sin against God's will. Their son believed that they abstained from sex for the next thirty-nine years of their marriage and that his mother may have directed all that pent-up celibate energy into her many offbeat ventures and activities.

The country Cowley was born in that August day was undergoing a world-shaping series of transformations. Military activity in the Spanish-American War, that "splendid little war," as John Hay dubbed it, had ceased, and the United States found itself in possession of overseas territory and launched on its path to global superpower status. Domestically the country was well on its way to its transformation from an agricultural to an industrial civilization and an economic juggernaut, dominated by all-powerful corporate trusts. That transformation created both previously unthinkable wealth and great domestic strife, as the gulf widened between hyper-prosperity at the top and exploited and immiserated farmers, laborers, and immigrants toward the bottom. The rise of a fervent populism and militant unionism, both sometimes prone to violence, created a counterreaction in progressivism, a movement of "the best people" to lessen and defang class strife with steady but incremental social, economic, and political reform. Few of these developments were evident in the sleepy life of Belsano, but they would shape the future of all of its inhabitants, including its newest arrival.

Josephine Cowley was thirty-four years of age when she had her only child. She'd been born Josephine Hutmacher in 1864 in Quincy, Illinois, on the east bank of the Mississippi River. She was the eldest daughter in a family of eleven children, five boys and six girls. Her father, Rudolph, had emigrated from Germany to avoid conscription into the Prussian army. Her mother, Rosa Josephina Stuckenberg, came from a family of German Catholic settlers in Louisville, Kentucky, and her children were raised Catholic. The family was prosperous. Rudolph ran a wholesale ice business whose source in Quincy Bay was prized for its purity; his chief customer was the Anheuser-Busch brewery in St. Louis, to which he shipped the ice on barges down the Mississippi. On the edge of town, he built a large brick house with a cupola, overlooking a cornfield, where he and Rosa raised their large family.

Josephine Hutmacher's education was truncated: five years in parochial school and one year of boarding at St. Mary's Academy in Nauvoo, sixty miles away. She learned from the nuns "to write a fine, legible hand," her son remembered, but "not how to punctuate." Then she was taken out of school and put to work by her mother as "a household slavey." Sentenced to unending domestic drudgery, she learned to sew, bake pies, launder and iron shirtwaists, and change diapers, and she performed these tasks and others year after year with no respite. Photos from this time show her to be a handsome young woman, with a nose that flared at the tip, a feature her son would inherit. She was not allowed to have suitors, and her mother constantly scolded her and made her feel unfit for a life outside the home. It was an oppressive existence with little prospect for happiness ahead, so when her younger sisters all got married and her older brothers left home to start their business careers, she did something bold for a single woman of the time: She left home. Like a character in one of the Naturalist novels that were beginning to be written by Dreiser and Crane, she struck out for the big city, in this case bustling Pittsburgh. She would find work as a seamstress for a dressmaking shop named Young Modiste. She was thirty-three and badly wanted to get married. And then Dr. William Cowley, a homeopathic physician of the same age and also conveniently in want of a mate, came along. They had vastly different backgrounds and Josephine was four inches taller than her prospective husband—they would never be photographed standing next to each other, only seated—but despite all that, they would marry.

The Cowleys were Scotch Irish Presbyterians who'd immigrated to Pittsburgh in the 1840s from the north of Ireland. They'd settled on Troy Hill, where their next-door neighbors were a family named the Carnegies. In fact, Malcolm Cowley's great-uncle William had been one of the original partners in the Carnegie Iron Works, but he died of fever during the Civil War in a Confederate prisoner-of-war camp and his share of the enterprise was sold. The idea that very great wealth had once been within their grasp may have given the Cowley family an exaggerated sense of stature that exceeded their actual worldly position. Cowley's grandfather David, who married his deceased brother's fiancée, threw over the family Presbyterianism to join a small Christian sect devoted to the writings of the eighteenth-century Swedish mystic Emanuel Swedenborg. He was a homeopathic physician, and his son William Cowley, Malcolm's father, followed him into that profession and was also a devout Swedenborgian.

Malcolm Cowley would describe his father, William, whom he called Popsie, as "an impractical, wholly lovable man." Both William Cowley's choice of profession and his religious affiliation placed him far outside the American mainstream. Homeopathy was an alternative form of medical practice that had been founded by a man named Samuel Hahnemann in Germany in the late eighteenth century. The central idea was that by giving a patient controlled amounts of drugs that would cause symptoms similar to the disease they suffered from, that disease could be cured. Today the word "quackery" is often used to characterize homeopathy, but it was fairly popular in the nineteenth century. And though some now see it as a forerunner of today's alternative medicine, it was regarded by the medical establishment—then and now—as unorthodox and unproven. It was certainly no path to prestige or prosperity.

Popsie's Swedenborgian religion was even more eccentric. While at no time did the Swedenborgian "New Church" have more than a few thousand adherents in this country, Swedenborg himself was taken seriously by many serious people as a religious figure; in *Representative Men*, Ralph Waldo Emerson wrote of this eighteenth-century Swedish mystic in the company of no less than Plato, Shakespeare, Napoleon, and Goethe, and called him "the Last Father of the Church . . . not likely to have a successor." Famous American Swedenborgians included John Chapman, aka Johnny Appleseed; Robert Frost, who was baptized in the Church; and Henry James Sr., the father of the writers William and Henry James. Church members would gather in small groups for hours to read Swedenborg's texts and discuss their meaning. Malcolm Cowley remembered having to sit through hours of this sort of thing on Sundays to please his father, fidgeting with extreme boredom, and being read the Bible before bedtime and at noon when not at school. The religion never took with him, disappointing his father. Josephine was baptized into the Swedenborgian Church of the New Jerusalem, but she, like her son, took no real interest in its doctrines or texts. The Cowley family, described by Cowley as "intellectuals of a sort, though impoverished," did, though, one of the reasons they rather looked down on his energetic and practical mother.

In Pittsburgh the Cowley family moved into the newly constructed three-story Wallace Building in the commercial East Liberty section, which Cowley described as "a generally prosperous, semi-suburban area." On the ground floor were shops, and above them were apartments and offices where music teachers and physicians not overly in demand, like William Cowley, practiced. It was an isolated place for the new family to live, as the area cleared out after business hours. Cowley remembered that after the janitor of the Wallace Building moved away with his two daughters, he had no other playmates. He would roam by himself around the East Liberty area and even farther afield, exploring vacant lots and sometimes getting into fights with local boys and returning home with a bloody nose.

Or he would read, that favorite activity of the only child with an active imagination. He learned at age six, and he never stopped. It was a big life change. "You learned to read and you weren't my boy any more. You lay on the floor reading a book, and I couldn't get a word out of you," his mother once told him. Josephine was in no way bookish, and he'd departed for a world she was unable to enter.

Another big change arrived when Cowley was nine years old. An economic panic had closed most of the Pittsburgh steel mills and Popsie's patients could no longer pay their bills—he was too diffident and kind to be much of a collector of overdue payments—and his income was cut in half. This was a period of serious financial difficulty and near-Dickensian shortages in the life of the family. He recalled, "The Cowleys were regarded as being quite strange, if harmless, and too poor to clothe themselves properly. In the Pittsburgh winters I didn't have an overcoat until I was fifteen." After three winters of this, his mother finally bought him a raincoat she found on sale.

Cowley grew up as a boy who had infrequent contact with his parents, who were content to allow him to go his own way with little or no supervision. Except for dinner he generally ate his meals alone, cooked for him by a local woman they paid a small amount for such domestic chores. In the summer that he was eleven, his mother was called back from Belsano to Pittsburgh by a family crisis and he was left alone in the country house for a whole month. He could charge groceries at the local general store, but he'd never learned how to cook. The upshot was that at the end of the month, he was suffering from sores on his legs, the result of malnutrition and scurvy. Cowley relates this story neutrally and without judgment, but the parental carelessness on display speaks for itself.

Even at the dawn of the last century, Belsano and the other towns in Cambria County were communities in economic and environmental decline. The area was dotted with coal mines and huge ovens that produced the coke needed to make steel. Cowley remembered one of them as "the God-awfulest mining camp in Pennsylvania; all the trees gone, all the houses squalid, and not even a company store." Many of the streams and creeks that had once teemed with trout now ran orange-yellow with sulfuric acid from the mine runoff. The worst destruction took place in 1907 when the Vintondale Lumber Company undertook to cut down the local hemlock forest, not for the timber but for the tree bark that was used for tanning leather. They left behind the birch and beech trees, and shortly after, devastating fires erupted, "turning," Cowley would remember, "thousands of acres into black meadows where ashes stirred in the breeze."

The young men began to drift away west and south to find work elsewhere in the steel mills and factories, and the area became a region for the old and the very young. Things went downhill socially and communally, an atomized every-man-for-himself condition evident in the bad roads, shabby churches, and forest fires that were allowed to rage. As a result, Cowley had a well-trained eye for the environmental damage and social decline that so often go hand in hand and took note of and wrote about it as he traveled about the country on journalistic assignments. Belsano and environs, its rural beauty, its relics of an older way of life, and its modern decline and decay, would provide the raw material for many of the finest poems in *Blue Juniata*, the collection that he would augment and revise for most of his adult life.

As a young boy, Cowley attended a one-room schoolhouse with about fifty students in Belsano, until October, when his family would close up the farmhouse and move back to Pittsburgh. This exposed him to an older American style of education. There were no formal grades but only so-called reader classes in various subjects, and the sole teacher, generally sturdy milkmaid types from the local normal school, allowed the students to progress at their own rate. For the most part, though, he was educated back in Pittsburgh, at the Shakespeare

School for his first seven years and then one year at the three-room Liberty School. For four months at age thirteen he attended a Swedenborgian school near Philadelphia, his father's last-ditch effort to interest his son in religion. He insisted on coming home.

Cowley would find in school both a cure to his loneliness and isolation and an arena where he could excel. His skill at reading and his ability to concentrate on tasks set before him meant that he was recognized by his teachers and classmates as an academic standout. The solitary boy had to wear shoes, but he found a place where he could be socialized and also praised for his achievements.

One of Cowley's classmates at Liberty School was Kenneth Burke, who would become his closest friend, an unbreakable association that would extend over his entire long life. As teenagers they would regularly meet up in the reading room of the big Carnegie Library in Pittsburgh. The library, like many others at the time, had certain books under restriction that were "not to be issued to minors," and those were, naturally, the books Cowley and Burke were keenest to read. Some of them, like the works of Arthur Schnitzler, were considered sexy and even borderline pornographic by the standards of the time, and some, like the plays of George Bernard Shaw, dealt with subversive ideas like socialism and the flaws of capitalism.

After the library closed at ten o'clock, they would walk the three miles home through the quiet residential streets back to East Liberty, conversing loudly on topics ranging from the problem of impressing girls despite their pimples to the books they'd just read and the ones they planned to write. Burke recalled, "We started out just talking back and forth, just talking, and then, by God, first thing you know we began to have something to talk about. . . . by that time, whenever I thought of something I thought I was talking about it to Malcolm." Cowley felt the same way. That conversation, carried on later via letters as well as in person, might have been interrupted at times, but it really never stopped.

After Liberty School, Cowley would attend the brand-new Peabody High School in Pittsburgh—a "big town high school," Cowley called it, of about eleven hundred pupils. It was one of the thousands of American public high schools in the earlier decades of the twentieth century that managed to impart a rigorous and demanding education at no cost to any student who wanted one and could handle the work. With rare exceptions, all the students were white and middle class, and they divided themselves into the usual cliques: the football crowd, the social crowd, and the literary crowd, toward which Cowley of course gravitated immediately. He remembers them, and himself, in *Exile's Return* as the boys who read books that had not been assigned and "were shy, noisy, ill-dressed and helped to edit the school magazine." These insecure and dreamy but also sometimes brilliant boys were familiar types, nursing alternating feelings of superiority and inferiority.

They had no American writer whom they felt they could model themselves on, "no one who spoke directly to our youth, no one for us to follow with a single heart." They didn't read Henry James, and William Dean Howells represented a literary establishment they disdained. Melville might have filled the bill, but he'd died in obscurity and his revival was some years in the future. There was no equivalent American writer who could do for them what Fitzgerald and Hemingway and then Kerouac and Salinger and Heller did in later years for the younger set. So they turned to the English authors: beginning with Kipling and Stevenson, then on to Hardy, Meredith, and Gissing and Conrad, and finally Wilde and Shaw, whose showy sense of paradox pleased them because it seemed so modern.

The one American periodical that genuinely captured the interest and devotion of the Peabody litterateurs was *The Smart Set*, which mixed metropolitan wit and chatter with the advanced fiction of the day. In 1913 its editor, Willard Huntington Wright, hired Ezra Pound as his talent scout for Europe and opened the spigot to the best writing then coming out of Europe. This landed like an alien spaceship in Peabody High: "It seemed that a new world was being revealed to us, that it was time to smash the Victorian gods, open all the windows, go floating off on a cloud of dream toward golden Vienna and Paris the City of Lights." Life, as always, was elsewhere to the young literary romantics, but *The Smart Set* gave them a powerful taste of the real thing until the subscribers revolted and Wright was cashiered. The magazine would later be taken over by H. L. Mencken and George Jean Nathan, and they helped to create the tone of the twenties. By senior year, though, Cowley would decide that Mencken's "perpetual mockery [was] a rather slender diet," and he was "the greatest existing menace to American letters."

Cowley's arrival at Peabody ignited his literary impulses and ambitions, which now had an outlet. The dreamy, ill-dressed, barefoot loner saw his opportunities and he took them. He wasn't an opportunist really, but he knew who was who and what was what in almost any situation and would position himself accordingly. That is what ambitious and talented people do. He also had a gift for leadership that isn't found all that often in the literarily inclined. Many years later he would claim in letters to Burke that both of them had assiduously avoided becoming famous until they were in their fifties and were able to handle it. This was disingenuous misremembering. Cowley's energy for achievement and need for approval were evident from the start and never flagged.

What was, to borrow the title of one of Cowley's later books, the literary situation facing a writer in the first decade and a half of the new century? Since the Civil War, something that was referred to as the Genteel Tradition had reigned largely unchallenged. Literature was meant to focus the reader's attention on the higher and finer things. The bare and vulgar facts of private and economic life were to be kept well away from the parlor. Cowley explained that "Victorianism, transplanted to America, had become intermingled with native characteristics, notably with New England Puritanism. This, in turn, had become the tendency to divide practical life from the life of the mind, just as Sunday was divided from the days of the week." Or as he also put it, "The whole territory of literature was thought to lie on the right side of the railroad tracks, in the chiefly feminine realm of beauty, art, religion, culture and the ideal." The result was that "culture" became something to be acquired as an accomplishment rather than being integrated into the larger life of the nation, and our official approved literature had become refined and bloodless. There were plenty of exceptions to this generalization—Whitman and Twain spring immediately to mind—but the stifling atmosphere of gentility, allied to the ingrained American hostility to intellectualism and the tendency to genuflect to England in matters of culture, had drained our native literary vitality.

The first revolt against gentility was mounted by a group of writers who became known as the Naturalists. American Naturalism was a literary movement that derived from earlier developments in Europe, chiefly that Darwin's idea of evolution meant that all life could be understood scientifically and was subject to natural laws. In his epic series of novels dissecting every level and sector of French civilization, Émile Zola put forth the idea that those laws were necessary to understand and apply in order to frame the behavior of literary characters. Zola's example galvanized the American Naturalists. Writers like Theodore Dreiser in *Sister Carrie* and *The Financier*, Frank Norris in *McTeague* and *The Octopus*, and Upton Sinclair in *The Jungle* were the literary allies of the muckraking journalists, placing before the reading public the unvarnished truths as they saw them of greed, sex, exploitation, corruption, and the drive for power in American life. If, as many critics have observed, they did so sometimes crudely and with a lack of literary polish, they nonetheless crashed into the house of gentility and set themselves down in the parlor to stay.

Something else was brewing in the background. Gertrude Stein, Ezra Pound, and T. S. Eliot, the prime exemplars of the twentieth-century literary movement that would be known as Modernism, were born in 1874, 1885, and 1888, respectively. They all felt they'd had to expatriate themselves to Europe to engineer their revolution, but the literature of the twentieth century had a distinct American accent as a result of their mentoring and writing and ideas.

Of equal significance was the extraordinary cluster of important American writers who were born just before or just after the turn of the century. They would include Dorothy Parker, born in 1893; E. E. Cummings, born in 1894; Edmund Wilson, born in 1895; John Dos Passos and F. Scott Fitzgerald, born in 1896; William Faulkner and Thornton Wilder, born in 1897; Ernest Hemingway and Hart Crane, born in 1899; Thomas Wolfe, born in 1900; Langston Hughes, born in 1902; and Nathanael West, born in 1904. These writers and others would form a literary generation that would in effect take ownership of the new century by sheer force of their talent and determination and, in the process, put paid to doubts that America could be the source and subject of great literature. Malcolm Cowley would devote most of his life to making it clear how and why this was so.

At Peabody, Cowley gravitated immediately to the Debating Club and the Literary Society, the two welcoming places for the verbally adept and literarily inclined, and made his mark quickly. He also wrote for the school paper and just missed becoming the editor in chief. As both a debater and a writer he would get his name in the local papers, *The Pittsburgh Press* and *The Pittsburgh Post*, fairly regularly.

And he made the list of honors students at Peabody, and would end up graduating second in his class.

Cowley's first real literary ambition was to be a poet, and his poems would appear regularly in the school's literary magazine, *The Peabody*. Elected the class poet, he wrote the class poem and read it at graduation: "Till the Journey Be Ended," which is overstuffed with hackneyed sea voyage imagery and rhymes. He also wrote short stories for the literary magazine.

Peabody High School was very good to, and for, Malcolm Cowley. He was so well educated that he was able to skip past the introductory English classes at the most demanding university in the country. It socialized a dreamy loner and prepared him to enter the wider world with some confidence. Belsano may have made him, but Peabody High School launched him.

Graduation broke up Cowley's old gang; Burke's family had moved to Weehawken and he was sad to be separated from his friend and literary foil. Cowley badly wanted to go to Harvard because he knew that that was where famous writers came from and that was what he planned to be himself. So he took the entrance exam, did well on it, and applied for a scholarship from the Harvard Club of Western Pennsylvania. While he awaited word, he went back to Belsano and fretted and wrote letters to Burke and got a job digging ditches. In late August, he finally got the news that he had been awarded a $150 scholarship to Harvard, which would cover the cost of a year's tuition. He was expected to arrive there on September 26.

Cowley's father was upset that his son would be attending a college not only a considerable distance away from Pittsburgh, but a Unitarian New England one at that. From the Swedenborgian point of view, Unitarians were not all that far removed from atheists. But he understood his son's ambitions and contributed to the cost of his schooling.

Malcolm Cowley and Popsie would always enjoy an uncomplicated and loving relationship, even as the son would eventually enter a world that made Unitarians look like Swedenborgians.

Matters were very different, and strained, between mother and son. It is not uncommon for a boy beloved by his mother to begin to pull back from her at a certain point in order to assert his independence. This is usually a phase, though, and after some period of time, son and mother can find their way back to each other. This never happened between Malcolm Cowley and his mother.

Late in life he would try to come to terms with this breach; he carried with him a burden of guilt over his own neglect and distance. In 1978 at the age of eighty he would publish a somber poem, "Prayer on All Saints' Day," that is directly addressed to his mother and reads like an unburdening and a settling of accounts. He finds things to place on the credit side of the ledger, like having lived a life of achievement and "not ever slipping a knife in the back" of his associates. But lines like "this I have failed to do" and "it is what I haven't done that tortures me at night" reveal an unquiet conscience. It is really a prayer seeking absolution, as the final line, "Forgive my absences," makes clear.

Someone looking at the broad scope of Malcolm Cowley's life cannot help but notice its contradictions. He grew up as an only child and a loner by instinct, happiest on long summer days rambling by himself in the countryside of Belsano when No Trespassing signs were nonexistent. Religiously, professionally, and temperamentally his parents lived well to one side from the muscular Christianity and go-getter/get ahead ethos that characterized the main currents of American culture in the first decades of the last century. They weren't in the least bohemian or politically oppositional; they were simply *different* and more than a little apart from the wider society. And yet, their son would become a highly public figure and a man of institutions, adept at both running them and working from within to bend them to his own ends. An insider. This only child and barefoot wanderer had a large gift for friendships, some of them lasting almost his lifetime, and he carried on correspondences with many dozens of people over the course of decades. He would find a way to balance the two sides of his being: the inward and solitary Boy in Sunlight and the outward-facing and shrewdly sociable Man in the Arena.

TWO.

SCHOLARSHIP BOY

———

Malcolm Cowley arrived at Harvard in late September of 1915, a very young seventeen years of age, eager and ambitious but acned and unsure of himself as well. Pittsburgh was five hundred miles from Boston and the train journey would have taken the better part of a day, with ample time to dream and to fret. But in Cambridge he would have to travel, in social and intellectual terms, a considerably longer distance, a treacherous passage full of pitfalls and subtle slights and humiliations. He was a "scholarship boy," and in those pre-meritocratic times the appellation carried with it a distinct social stigma, especially in the rigidly class-bound precincts of Harvard and Boston. Every year Harvard would publish a list of its students who had been awarded scholarships, and those whose awards came with stipends attached would be placed in their own category. It was not exactly the mark of Cain, but it sent a clear message that such students were there on a kind of sufferance. The more prosperous and socially advantaged Harvard students could, if they wished, slide through their college life on charm and connections and "gentleman's C's" or worse. But Cowley would need to be a scholarship boy during his years at Harvard to afford the tuition, which meant he had to apply himself academically and keep his grades high enough to renew his scholarship annually.

In the Harvard prestige ecosystem, the most prized asset was to have attended a very short list of socially approved prep schools, at the top of which ranked Milton Academy, St. Paul's, St. Mark's, Groton, Andover, and Exeter. Having attended a public high school was even more a deficit in this regard than needing scholarship funds. A Harvard historian once wrote, with appalling candor, that "a lad of Mayflower and Porcellian ancestry who entered from a high school was as much 'out of it' as a ghetto Jew." (The Porcellian was the most prestigious of Harvard's final clubs, so picky and exclusive that no less a figure than Franklin Roosevelt once said that not being "punched" for it was the greatest disappointment in his life.) These deficits meant that in the sprint for status that constituted much of undergraduate life at Harvard at that time, Malcolm Cowley was hobbled by two heavy ankle weights: the wrong kind of secondary school and not enough money. As he would explain to Kenneth Burke, "You don't know what it is to be an in here. It is a matter of birth, clothes, speech, training, and money." He would have to make his way on the strength of his own talents.

Luckily talent had recently become a more valuable currency in Cambridge. Six years earlier A. Lawrence Lowell—an intellectual aristocrat and the scion of the Boston Lowells—had ascended from the government department to the presidency of Harvard, succeeding Charles W. Eliot, who had served at that post for forty years. One of Lowell's fervent ambitions was to elevate Harvard's academic prestige to a level matching its social cachet. He disliked the then-prevailing culture of status and sought to replace it with a college aristocracy of talent and intellectual achievement. He pursued this goal by instituting undergraduate curriculum reforms designed to make course requirements more rigorous and focused, and adding a system of tutors and a so-called honors system modeled on that of Oxford and Cambridge. The aim was for Harvard to produce, as he said in his inaugural address, "not defective specialists, but men intellectually well rounded, of wide sympathies and unfettered judgment." His ideal was that of a demanding and well-rounded liberal education.

Despite the fact that Princeton's former President Woodrow Wilson now occupied the White House, Harvard's prestige and power at this time put its Ivy League competitors in the shade. Its most famous alumnus, Teddy Roosevelt (class of 1880), was a loyal and ever-visible "Harvard man" and still a potent force in American politics. His cousin Franklin (class of 1904) had been the editor of *The Harvard Crimson* and, as Wilson's assistant secretary of the Navy, was a rising man in the Democratic Party. Bliss Perry, an *Atlantic Monthly* editor turned literature instructor at Harvard, called Harvard "the Cockpit of Learning" and the faculty there "a brilliant array of prima donnas." It included such luminaries as the great Shakespeare scholar George Lyman Kittredge; the beloved composition instructor Charles T. Copeland, known to generations of Harvard students as "Copey" and one of the supreme mentor-teachers of his time; Irving Babbitt, the future proponent of something known as the New Humanism and a strong influence on his student T. S. Eliot; the aforementioned Bliss Perry, the great Americanist (one of the few) on the faculty; and the eminent scholar-teacher and gloomy Anglophile Barrett Wendell. Recent Harvard graduating classes had produced such figures as Eliot ('09), swashbuckling journalist John Reed ('10), political pundit and philosopher Walter Lippmann ('09), poets Conrad Aiken ('12) and E. E. Cummings ('15), the critic Van Wyck Brooks ('08), the legendary Scribner's editor Maxwell Perkins ('07), novelist John Dos Passos ('14), and the humorist Robert Benchley ('12). Harvard's high status was built on a solid foundation of scholarship and achievement.

By 1915 the Lowell-led Harvard had become a much more congenial place for someone like Malcolm Cowley. Still, he would have felt both unsure of himself and overawed. Cowley dealt with his insecurities by taking on the protective colorations of his new situation and identifying himself assiduously with Harvard College. Freshmen, almost by definition, are callow beings characterized by self-absorption. Most people are fortunate enough not to have the evidence of this vulnerable condition available for public examination, but Malcolm Cowley's is on full display in the letters he would write to Kenneth Burke. The letters on both sides are nakedly, if unconsciously, revealing and some of what is revealed is not very pretty.

He admitted to struggling to find his footing. He'd been assigned to a dorm suite in Gore Hall (now Winthrop House) facing the Charles River, one of the new freshman residences built by President Lowell in an attempt to break down some of the college's social barriers. He roomed with two Jewish students, John Rothschild and Jacob Davis, his friend from Peabody High. The implications of this fact would not have been lost on Cowley. As definitively documented by Jerome Karabel in his book *The Chosen*, Harvard's administration was by no means pleased by the increasing number of hardworking and quite clearly qualified Jewish applicants and had devised quotas and other barriers to keep these students either away entirely or at a low level of visibility in the college community. So-called genteel anti-Semitism was alive and well at Harvard.

In Cowley's letters to Burke from his freshman year, we see him striking a pose, one of premature worldliness and sophistication. He is all too pleased with Harvard and with himself for being at Harvard. Burke was taking a kind of gap year before deciding to attend either Ohio State or Columbia. He was justly annoyed by Cowley's air of superiority and his constant attempts to persuade him to come to Harvard himself, and would offer the tart riposte "Malcolm, how you college fops do abuse the channels of healthy good-fellowship!" Cowley's letters to him that academic year would offer Burke numerous opportunities to prick the balloon of his egotism and Ivy League self-regard, donned like an ill-fitting raccoon coat.

The anti-Semitism manifested itself in Cowley's very first letter to Burke from Harvard, in which he worried that Harvard might "some day be ruined by the damn Jews." He got this idea from another freshman, who had attended Andover. He thought that Jake Davis was a "fool" for joining the campus Menorah Society, thereby making his Judaism known. Apparently, if you had the misfortune to be Jewish, you should at least have the good grace to hide it. And in a letter to Burke in his second semester, Cowley unloads on his Jewish classmates as "mostly a race of ill-bred grinds," as well as chorus girl–chasing poker players (a difficult feat of multitasking, one would think), and not a real intellectual in the bunch.

It is a classic strategy for members of an out-group to adopt the attitudes and prejudices of the ruling clique as an antidote to and a cover for a sense of social anxiety and inferiority. Cowley's admirers might wish that he'd shown the strength of character to avoid this kind of upward class identification at the expense of other people, but he hadn't. Whether his anti-Semitism in particular was a disease he'd picked up after arriving at Harvard or the exacerbation of a preexisting condition is hard to know, but it was real. In no way can Malcolm Cowley be let off the hook for these comments. What can be said is that he grew out of his anti-Semitism fairly quickly. There is no evidence of such prejudices to be found after the early Harvard years, and in the future a number of his closest friends would be Jewish, and he would be employed by a publishing firm, Viking, all of whose principals were Jewish. More than half a century later he would correspond with his old roommate Jake Davis about the truth of a *Commentary* article on the institution of Jewish quotas by President Lowell, remarking, "I hadn't forgotten social anti-Semitism at Harvard."

The one area that Malcolm Cowley could feel entirely secure in was academics. He would flourish in the classroom, and his scholarship would be renewed each of the next three years, twice from the Harvard Club of Western Pennsylvania and in other years from Harvard itself. He would rank second academically in his freshman class of 685 students. Leery of being seen as a grind, he would do much of his studying "in secret" in out-of-the-way venues where he would not be noticed hitting the books.

Cowley knew what he was aiming for early. "I wanted to write poems. I wanted to write novels. I wanted to write plays and stories and biographies. I wanted, in short, to be a man of letters." This hits the ear now as cobwebby and antique, but at Harvard at that time, there were plenty of professors who fit the description, men who combined wide reading with scholarly attainment and intellectual versatility, as Barrett Wendell put it, "to discuss matters in which he makes no pretense to be expert." There were a great many recognized "men of letters," from the eminent magazine editor and novelist William Dean Howells on down, still holding forth in other universities and in the best-regarded magazines of opinion, and it is a bit startling to recall that in 1915 the current president, Woodrow Wilson, and the former President Theodore Roosevelt were skilled enough writers and thinkers to have fully qualified as the type. Cowley's literary generation would enter an altogether more contentious and unsettled literary sphere and would write and think considerably more against the grain than these people as they sought to achieve their high estate. But in the world where they started out, becoming a man of letters felt entirely doable and not eccentric in the least.

One striking aspect of Cowley's Harvard education is how completely free of any formal classroom encounter with American literature it was. The man who would become one of our finest advocates for classic American writing got through his four years there without being assigned a single work by Whitman or Irving or Hawthorne or

Poe or Emerson or Melville or Thoreau or Twain or James. One of the most stinging insults ever made against American authorship was delivered in 1820 by the English critic Sydney Smith when he asked patronizingly in *The Edinburgh Review*, "Who reads an American book?" Things had improved considerably in this area since then, but in respect to literary education at Harvard circa 1915–19, the answer still would have been "Almost nobody." English and European literature took up all the space and the scholarly oxygen. The only course fully devoted to American literature that one could find in the Harvard catalogues in those years was Bliss Perry's long-running graduate seminar on Emerson, who was of course a Harvard man and an inescapable New England sage. Even so, Perry had to struggle to get his course on Emerson grudgingly accepted and his colleagues remarked "that in their judgment Emerson was the only American author worthy of a course being devoted exclusively to him."

The same conspicuous absence of attention would have obtained in the course catalogues of most other prominent institutions of higher learning. American literature did not as yet have the prestige to attract widespread scholarly interest. It was the European critics—Baudelaire on Poe, Wilde on Whitman, Lawrence on Melville—who had experienced the shock of recognition upon encountering our native genius. In *Exile's Return*, Cowley would recall, "It seemed to us that America was beneath the level of great fiction; it seemed that literature in general, and art and learning, were things existing at an infinite distance from our daily lives."

Litterateurs in training like Malcolm Cowley would of course have been reading plenty of American literature on their own, especially the highly touted products of the moment, and aspiring to produce and publish some of the stuff themselves. One of the rituals of the first semester at Harvard was the series of so-called smokers put on by the various college publications and teams, where aspirants could be feted with free beer and cigarettes and looked over by the organizations they were aspiring to. Cowley first set his cap for *The Harvard Crimson*, launching pad for so many important journalistic careers, but he did not make the grade, proving less than satisfactory as a reporter. He spent a semester on the debating team, continuing his high school efforts in this arena, but did not continue. It was the two rival undergraduate literary magazines, *The Harvard Advocate* and *The Harvard Monthly*, that really beckoned to him as institutions where he might make a mark.

The *Advocate* was the older and more conservative and, arguably, the more prestigious of the two. Founded in 1866, it was, by the time of Cowley's freshman year, the oldest extant Harvard publication and it survives to this day, the longest continuously published literary magazine in the country. Despite the Latin motto it adopted, "Dulce est periculum" (Sweet is peril), the *Advocate* generally avoided controversy in the poetry, fiction, essays, and editorials it ran every fortnight during the school year. It was widely read and often heatedly discussed by the student body and faculty—at one time 90 percent of the student body subscribed to it. The fiftieth-anniversary celebration of the magazine's founding in the spring semester of Cowley's freshman year attracted almost four hundred alumni and was covered in *The New York Times*, which noted that "the clan includes many notable men— poets, dramatists, novelists, editors, statesmen, with a few businessmen sprinkled in here and there." Recent undergraduate contributors had included Edward Arlington Robinson, Wallace Stevens, T. S. Eliot, Conrad Aiken, E. E. Cummings, Maxwell Perkins, Van Wyck Brooks, John Reed, and Robert Benchley. Donald Hall would term the *Advocate* "the nursemaid of genius," with justification.

The Harvard Monthly, in contrast, was a younger, scrappier magazine with a smaller circulation, more in touch with the spirit of revolt and literary experimentation that was just beginning to make itself felt. It had been founded in 1885 by a group of undergraduates that included the future philosopher, novelist, and Harvard professor George Santayana with the intention to provide a literary and aesthetic counterbalance to the then-president Charles Eliot's program of practical, specialized education. And, of course, to the *Advocate*. Cowley would later recall, "From 1890 till 1916, Harvard was the most literary of American universities, and The Monthly was Harvard at its most literary. The Monthlies suspected that the board of The Advocate, which then appeared fortnightly, was composed of journalists, clubmen, athletes, and disciples of Teddy Roosevelt, a former editor, with not a man of letters among them. The Advocates suspected that the Monthlies were aesthetes (as indeed most of them came to be called), scruffy poets, socialists, pacifists, or worse." By the time of Cowley's arrival, the two most prominent *Monthly* contributors were E. E. Cummings, who while he was on its editorial staff continued to be published in the *Advocate* as well, and John Dos Passos.

Given his later activities as a literary insurgent, one might have expected Malcolm Cowley to gravitate toward the *Monthly*, especially since he had written to Burke, "The 'Advocate' is a remarkably poor magazine, publishing some good poetry. The 'Monthly' has a lot of good stuff in it." But by early spring of 1916 he would declare, "I am out for the *Advocate*. None of my stuff has been published yet, but some will be soon, I hope." And indeed his first poem, "To Certain Imagist Poets," would run in the March 31, 1916, issue, swiftly followed that semester by three more: "The Dilettantes," "On Re-reading Wordsworth," and "Execution." We cannot know whether he chose the *Advocate* to submit his work to in response to its prestige on campus, or whether the *Advocate* rather than the *Monthly* chose him by agreeing to publish his poems. But he was now a *Harvard Advocate* man, a distinct step up in social standing.

Cowley would publish eleven poems and four book reviews in the

Advocate and two vignette-length fictions before he left for France for volunteer service in May of 1917. He was elected to the editorial board at a celebratory banquet on March 20 of that year. He could justly feel that he had arrived. His association with the *Advocate* offered advantages besides the obvious one of being recognized as a big writer on campus. Chief among them was a built-in and enhanced social life. Donald Hall writes, "Wherever the *Advocate* had its sanctum . . . the members would gather, beer mugs in hand, for their various social affairs." The bibulous initiations of successful candidates were often accompanied by lighthearted playlets they'd written, and from time to time, parties to fete celebrities would be held, the first in 1907 for Theodore Roosevelt and two years later for a prominent actress.

Cowley's poems stood out from the start with their plainspokenness and distance from the conventional poetic style and sentimental subject matter of the time. His ear for language was never particularly musical or elegant, but the clarity of his writing, its directness of address and emotional frankness, would generally make up for that deficit. His better poems were sincere evocations of the rural life of his coming-of-age. Cowley may have been struggling to fit into an alien environment, but in his poetry he was following a path that was his own.

As a poet, Cowley stood out, but he was no rebel. What constituted an avant-garde on the literary scene of Harvard at the time was in chronological terms really an *arriere garde*, a loose retrograde association of like-minded Wilde worshippers who were known as the Aesthetes. Cowley captures them in this passage from *Exile's Return*:

> The Harvard Aesthetes of 1916 were trying to create in Cambridge, Massachusetts, an after-image of Oxford in the 1890s. They read the *Yellow Book*, they read Casanova's memoirs and *Les Liasons Dangereuses*, both in French, and

Petronius in Latin; they gathered at teatime in one another's rooms, or at punches in the office of the *Harvard Monthly*; they drank, instead of weak punch, seidels of straight gin topped with a maraschino cherry; they discussed the harmonies of Pater, the rhythms of Aubrey Beardsley and, growing louder, the voluptuousness of the Church, the essential virtue of prostitution. They had crucifixes in their bedrooms, and ticket stubs from last Saturday's burlesque show at the Old Howard. They wrote, too; dozens of them were prematurely decayed poets, each with his invocation to Antinoüs, his mournful descriptions of Venetian lagoons, his sonnets to a chorus girl in which he addressed her as "little painted poem of God." In spite of these beginnings, a few of them became good writers.

In 1913 several of the leading Aesthetes, including Cummings, Dos Passos, and the poets Robert Hillyer and S. Foster Damon, organized the Harvard Poetry Society, which would gather at the Harvard Union to read poems to one another and deliver and endure withering criticism, as well as invite noted poets such as Robert Frost and Amy Lowell to campus for readings and discussions. Most of its members were associated with *The Harvard Monthly*, but *Advocate* contributors were also welcome, and thus Malcolm Cowley became a frequent attendee at their events and, by sophomore year, a fully fledged member.

In December 1916, Cowley's attendance at a joint meeting of the Harvard Poetry Society and the New England Poetry Society brought him into the orbit of the poet Amy Lowell, who would become a mentor and a crucial champion in his career. After Ezra Pound, Lowell had become the most visible practitioner and theoretician of the poetic style of Imagism, the first true American literary movement of the century. In "The New Manner in Modern Poetry," she had pinpointed the quality of "externality" as the essence of Imagism, "the attitude of being interested in things for themselves and not because of the effect they have on oneself." The poets of "the new manner" eschewed introspection for objectivity, wrote poetry in the syntax of prose and in colloquial rather than florid language, and avoided anything smacking of the "noble thoughts" that poetry once was felt to convey. Imagists were also far more drawn to free verse, or vers libre, than to the use of meter, rhyme, and traditional forms. This essay moved the *Advocate* to sputtering that "the undisguised unwholesomeness of *The New Manner in Modern Poetry*, we reject without more ado as unfit for human consumption." But that did little to dissuade the Harvard Poetry Society.

Amy Lowell took more abuse from the students of her brother's university than just this. At one Harvard Poetry Society event, the poet John Brooks Wheelwright posed the question to her, "How do you write, Miss Lowell, when you have nothing to say?" That December meeting seems to have been a New England version of a poetry slam, with Cowley later bragging to Burke that "the poetry of the Harvard Poetry Club hopelessly outclassed that of the semi-professionals, except, I must admit, Amy." In his telling, Lowell said that he and the Harvard poet Royall Snow "were the only two poets who wrote modern verse among the members of the Harvard Poetry Society." This compliment got his attention, and as result, he reported, "I like Amy, and because I like her, I am beginning to like her poetry." He would remember the plus-size Lowell "puffing away at a Fatima, and looking very much like a volcanic mountain in eruption." He describes her "over in one corner, the mountain-queen . . . haranguing a half dozen subjects and enemies." Amy Lowell was formidable—"the commanding general of the new poets"—and she made a lasting impression on him as an artist sure of herself and her place in the literary firmament.

Soon enough he and Royall Snow and S. Foster Damon, his new friend from the Poetry Society, were calling on Miss Lowell at Sevenels, the expansive family estate in Brookline. In 1937, reviewing Damon's biography *Amy Lowell: A Chronicle*, he would evoke those visits, walking up a snowy driveway at night to the house, and "the warmth inside, the reading of manuscripts, the good laughter, the light brown Manila cigars dressed in tight robes of tinfoil and petticoats of tissue paper." Then and later she would offer him sound and helpful advice on his writing, gently but firmly steering him from the prosiness that sometimes left the poetry out of his poems, and she would, while he was still an undergraduate and later, end up serving as his informal agent, sending his work off to the editors of the most prestigious little magazines. Cowley was lastingly grateful to Amy Lowell for her friendship and support, and if he would never quite assent to her poetic genius, he had nothing but respect for her bottomless energy as a literary actor, alternately buttering up and bullying editors and reviewers and chivvying her publishers when they were failing to support her and her books vigorously enough. From watching Amy Lowell operate he got the sense that a literary career required not simply talent, but the force of will to shape the literary arena to one's desires.

As Malcolm Cowley was arriving in Cambridge in 1915 and settling into college life, the poet Alan Seeger, Harvard class of 1910, was settling into the encampment of his regiment of the French Foreign Legion, in which he'd enlisted, along with fifty other Americans, in August 1914. He was anxiously awaiting the start of a massive French attack on German lines that would be known as the Second Battle of

Champagne. This would be his first experience of combat on the Western Front, and he confided to his diary, "I am very confident and sanguine about the result and expect to march right up to the Aisne, borne on an irresistible *élan*. I have been waiting for this moment for more than a year. I shall take good care to live up to it."

Which Seeger did, surviving alive and intact, although the battle itself was reckoned a defeat for the French, who suffered 190,000 casualties, whom he would memorialize in his poem "Champagne 1914–1915." Alan Seeger was a romantic idealist of the sort that the Great War would render all but extinct, more than half in love with brave death in a noble cause. He'd edited *The Harvard Monthly* before taking up the life of a Bohemian poet, first in Greenwich Village and then in Paris. He gained a reputation as the American Rupert Brooke, in particular for his poem "I Have a Rendezvous with Death," a Keatsian chronicle of his own death foretold. On July 4, 1916, he was fatally shot in the stomach during an attack and was buried, grimly, unromantically, in a mass grave. He was posthumously awarded the Croix de Guerre.

Alan Seeger was one of the first of a number of Harvard graduates and students who would volunteer for service in France and on the Italian front, mostly in noncombatant capacities, before America entered the war and immediately after. Malcolm Cowley would become one of them in April of 1917, and he would serve in another battle along the Aisne front in Champagne, near where Seeger fought.

The war in Europe had been grinding along for a year and had settled into a strategic stalemate along the Western Front when Cowley entered Harvard. Despite the sinking of the British Cunard liner *Lusitania* by a German submarine on May 7, killing more than 1,000 civilians, including 128 Americans, neutrality in the conflict remained the steadfast policy of Woodrow Wilson up to his election the following year under the famous, and almost instantly ironic, campaign slogan "He kept us out of war." In a rambling speech in Philadelphia three days after the sinking, he had said, priggishly, "There is such a thing as a man being too proud to fight. There is such thing as a nation being so right that it does not need to convince others by force that it is right." This instantly attracted the scorn of the nation's most prominent Harvard man, Wilson's political enemy Theodore Roosevelt, who riposted, "We will do well to remember that there are things worse than war."

In a fire-breathing essay for the *Advocate* that December, "Harvard and Preparedness," Roosevelt would repeat that phrase in the course of thundering against "the milk-and-water doctrines of the professional pacifists" and going full-on TR: "The country needs to prepare itself materially against war. Even more it needs to prepare itself spiritually and morally, so that, if war be accepted as the alternative to dishonor or unrighteousness, it shall be accepted with stern readiness to do any duty and incur any hazard that the times demand." He suggested that Harvard needed immediately to institute a system of military training for undergraduates, which it did.

Well before Roosevelt's call to arms, students and recent graduates from Harvard and others of the elite tier of Northeastern universities had begun volunteering for noncombatant service in France in varying capacities, most often as ambulance drivers. Soon the trickle would swell into a small flood of young, high-minded, largely upper-class men overseas, channeled mainly through two organizations, both in a real sense made in Cambridge.

The first of these, which became known as the Norton–Harjes Ambulance Corps, was begun in 1914, soon after the war began, by Richard Norton, a Harvard graduate of the class of 1892 and the son of the famed Harvard professor Charles Eliot Norton. One of Norton's early supporters was none other than Henry James (not a graduate but extremely Harvard-adjacent), who wrote a twelve-page fundraising pamphlet for the enterprise in his late-period ruminative prose. By October 1915, Norton's corps had sixty vehicles and had carried twenty-eight thousand wounded; it would shortly merge with another volunteer ambulance service headed up by Herman Harjes, a senior partner of the Morgan–Harjes Bank in Paris.

An even larger institution in terms of ambulances and volunteers was the American Field Service, begun and run by A. Piatt Andrew, who'd taught economics at Harvard for ten years. Andrew had resigned from his government job with the Monetary Commission at the outset of the war and sailed to France, where he drove an ambulance for two months in Flanders and Dunkirk. Moved, like Norton, by the suffering he witnessed and with even greater organizational energy, he began a large-scale campaign to organize an exclusively American ambulance service and persuaded the French to attach it to their military. By early 1916 the AFS had hundreds of ambulances and drivers in nine Sections, as the groups were called, and had become an official part of the French military, subject to the same rules and regulations as French enlisted men, who served with them as clerks, cooks, and mechanics. AFS volunteers enlisted for six-month tours, which was a great boon to recruitment since a college student could resign for a term and resume his studies the next semester. This is what Malcolm Cowley would do in the spring of 1917.

Harvard became by far the dominant feeder school of volunteers to the American Field Service, leading the Ivies with 325 men. In October 1916, Andrew returned to Cambridge from France on a recruiting trip and was the subject of an admiring profile in the *Advocate*, "Piatt Andrew, Ambulance Driver." The writer hailed the volunteers as "strong men, doing a great work heroically," and proudly reported, "From Harvard one hundred and fourteen men have gone out now; some for adventure, some for love, some from a sense of duty, some seeking honor. And each of these men has found all of these things." Andrew himself stated, "We few college men have transported 700,000 wounded from the battlefields to relief hospitals in our 200 automobiles."

This gives a fair sense of the state of campus opinion on the war as Malcolm Cowley entered the second semester of his sophomore year. The state of *his* opinion is somewhat harder to pin down. He began a review of George Santayana's *Egotism in German Philosophy* for the *Advocate* by declaring, "That Germany, often called in the past the most civilized of nations, has murdered, plundered and turned pirate and broken all human obligations, is apparent to all observers." In letters to Burke he'd registered his intention to join the Harvard Regiment, a cadet corps for officers in training. But he signed up for the American Field Service shortly after Congress declared war on Germany on April 6, 1917, without much thought. The pro-war tide of opinion in the country and especially at Harvard clearly swept him along.

The quarrel at *The Harvard Monthly* between the pro-war and anti-war staffers was so bitter that it spelled the demise of the publication, but the *Advocate*, Cowley's new home, was all in on the war. Even many anti-war students were heading "over there." The avowed pacifists Cummings and Dos Passos had both volunteered for the Norton–Harjes Corps, ostensibly for humanitarian reasons, but Dos Passos much later admitted that "I was anxious to see what it [the war] was like . . . I wanted to go over before everything 'went belly-up.'"

Cowley basked for a bit in the approval he garnered. "Copey" presented him with a book inscribed in Latin "Solvitur ambulando"—"It is solved by walking"—implying that experience would resolve his student's doubts and quandaries. Another of his instructors, Frederic Schenck, wrote a fulsome letter of praise on his behalf to the head of the ambulance service and urged him to write letters about his experiences, which if they were good enough he would get published.

Before he sailed for France on April 27, 1917, on the *Touraine*, a French passenger liner, Cowley spent some days in New York with Kenneth Burke, who was enrolled at Columbia. Through Burke he would be introduced to his fellow student Matthew Josephson, a budding poet and a future noted journalist, biographer, and memoirist. Cowley and Josephson would become lifelong friends and, often along with Burke, collaborators in all sorts of scrappy literary enterprises and generalized mischief.

Cowley arrived in Paris two weeks later and reported to the American Field Service headquarters in a château in a five-acre park in Passy on loan from a French countess. The American Field Service was undergoing a reorganization at the time, so the delay in his assignment allowed Cowley and a friend, Bob Cunningham, to spend some time sampling the recreational activities still on offer in Paris, including the racy Folies Bergère and some French cabaret.

The organizational delay was due to the urgent French need for truck or camion drivers to transport war matériel, especially munitions, to the front. This need was communicated to A. Piatt Andrew of the American Field Service, and so was born the transport unit known as the Réserve Mallet, so named because it was under the leadership of one Commandant Mallet. Just like the ambulance sections, this unit was under the command of the French army. All of the volunteers acceded to their new assignment, and Andrew reported that in the spring and summer of 1917, more than eight hundred of them had joined the new transport unit and were soon carrying ammunition and trench supplies from railheads to the front in support of mass offensives.

Cowley and Cunningham were assigned to the new section T.M.U. 526 (Transports de Matériel États-Unis), consisting of forty men, and were sent to a camp close to Soisson, fifteen miles behind the front, to be acquainted with French military discipline and trained in driving their huge five-ton Pierce-Arrow trucks. This was a task calling for a fair amount of skill, as such automotive conveniences as power steering and automatic transmission were decades in the future, and the trucks required a considerable amount of daily maintenance. They were also driving those trucks not on paved highways but on muddy, rutted, debris-strewn country roads torn apart in places by artillery shells. At first, Cowley chafed at the strictures of military discipline and proved inept at his camion-driving duties. "Man, I was in for it at first," he wrote to Burke. "I was the perhaps the poorest driver in camp, and everybody came to regard me as a general nincompoop." He eventually became at least passably competent.

Relentlessly upbeat Allied propaganda to the contrary, the French soldiers with whom the volunteers lived were exhausted and demoralized by the seemingly endless and unwinnable war and the prospect of their own deaths. Cowley would inform his parents of several mutinies of French soldiers who had refused to march into the trenches. Some years later he would remember of the common soldiers: "Most of them served long enough to lose whatever exhilaration they may have felt in the beginning: there remained with them only a dead nausea."

By mid-June Cowley's camion-driving skills had progressed, and he was transferred to a camp east of Soisson to undertake his duties. In the afternoon the trucks would be loaded with artillery and gas shells, fuses, barbed wire, and trench flooring. Once it was dark, two drivers per truck, one to relieve the other, would drive, headlights off, within a mile or two of the front, and the supplies would be unloaded. Then they would drive back to camp. These trips were generally uneventful, as the cover of night protected the convoys from being spotted by the German observation balloons and targeted for shelling. In general, camion and ambulance service was reasonably safe, especially in comparison to frontline combat.

Cowley would recall his very first trip to the front with Bob Cunningham as the relief driver in a piece titled "On the Road with T. M. U. 526." For the most part it was uneventful, but they had to drive "in a dust-cloud thicker than a Sahara sandstorm" and the heavy traffic on the road of field batteries and staff cars and supply wagons and marching Senegalese Territorials and French chasseurs (light infantry) convinced the inexperienced new drivers that they were part of a huge offensive taking shape. But it was all just business as usual on the Aisne front. They passed the walls of the immense park of Château de Soupir, glimpsing inside the ruined splendor of the seventeenth-century manor house and grounds gutted by the Germans. They reached the depot at last and were unloaded, and then proceeded to return after midnight by a different route, which was unnerving, as was the constant sound of shelling from both sides. The French sentinel who directed the column of trucks urged them to get going "damn quick because they are knocking the hell out of the town." Little wonder that Cowley recalled his "tingling in useless fright." Useless, but not misplaced: As the trucks were delayed in crossing back over the river, a heavy *marmite*, trench slang for a huge artillery shell, burst in front of them. Unharmed, they proceeded, only to confront a final *memento mori*, the body of a middle-aged Territorial laborer lying on the road in a puddle of bloody mud, a fragment from that shelling having torn a great hole in his side. As Cowley drove over the river he would remember the brute fact of that dead man as the war's "immediate reality."

Not all the facts were brute, though. One of Cowley's fellow drivers along the Chemin des Dames, Henry C. Wolfe, recalled an act of great kindness on Cowley's part. Their unit was stopped at Pont Arcy, a town that had been obliterated by German shelling. Cowley heard some faint cries from beneath the rubble; investigating, he found two small kittens, which he put inside his shirt and brought back to the barracks. Fed and cared for, they became the unit's mascots and grew into healthy gray striped cats. Forty years later, Wolfe would remember Cowley as "one of the kindest men I've ever known."

A startling number of these American volunteer drivers went on to become writers of note. In the Norton–Harjes, there were Dos Passos, Cummings, Slater Brown, the poet Robert Hillyer, and the screenwriter John Howard Lawson. In the American Field Service, there were the novelists Louis Bromfield and Julien Green, the playwright Sidney Howard, the poet-sybarite Harry Crosby, the future editor of *The Atlantic Monthly* Edward Weeks, the journalist and coauthor of *Mutiny on the Bounty* Charles Nordhoff, and of course Cowley. Ernest Hemingway left his job as a reporter for *The Kansas City Star* to volunteer as an ambulance driver for the Red Cross on the Italian front. The literary critic Edmund Wilson enlisted in the U.S. Army Hospital Corps and served in France as an orderly and stretcher bearer; the poet and literary statesman Archibald MacLeish also served in the regular Army, initially as an ambulance driver and then as an artillery officer.

"One might almost say that the ambulance corps and the French military transport were college-extension courses for a generation of writers," Cowley would assert. What was on the curriculum? "They taught us courage, extravagance, fatalism, these being the virtues of men at war; they taught us to regard as vices the civilian virtues of thrift, caution and sobriety; they made us fear boredom more than death." It placed before them a vast spectacle with a global cast of millions; they were seeing a great show, and "there were moments in France when the senses were immeasurably sharpened by the thought of dying the next day. . . . danger made it possible to write once more about love, adventure, death."

His time in France gave Malcolm Cowley something of lasting importance to write about, and he made the most of it. He sent dispatches to the *American Field Service Bulletin*, the *Advocate*, and even sold a piece to his hometown paper, the *Pittsburgh Gazette Times*. "U.S Volunteer Tells of French Battle Front Visit—No Union Hours" was the headline, above the text and photos of the camions and of the local hero himself in uniform, holding a folded greatcoat. The piece earned him his first paycheck as a writer: five dollars. These pieces were coolly observant, anecdotally interesting, and free of the posturing tone that mars a lot of other student writing. Charles Fenton says that of the hundreds of pages of writing contributed by camion drivers to the AFS official volume of history, "[Cowley's] sketches and poems made him the most prolific and polished of the truck-driver writers."

Cowley's duties in the camion service settled into a routine. There was plenty of downtime in the camp and he filled it with copious reading: an anthology of French verse (Rimbaud, Verlaine, Baudelaire), a great deal of Dostoevsky, two novels by Arnold Bennett, Huysmans's decadent classic *Against Nature*. From this immersion in French poetry he began to discern the roots of Amy Lowell's theories of vers libre. He was unskilled at gambling and was soon shorn of the funds needed to participate. His French improved rapidly—on a week's leave in Paris he was delighted to find that he could carry on conversations—and this was a resource he would draw on all of his career. He found his American identity and national pride strengthening from the encounter with another civilization. And he began to grope his way to an understanding of the larger meaning of his experiences.

Cowley was scheduled to be released from camion service at the very end of October. For most of his time at the front, Cowley and the other drivers "had been hoping to see a real attack," as he would write in the *Advocate* in a piece titled "The History of a Push." That fall the real thing finally arrived, as the French made elaborate preparations on the Aisne front for an assault on the German-held fort at Malmaison.

Artillery of every size and description began arriving on every form of conveyance, and soon the air was filled with the deafening sound of their firing—which, it turned out, was only simple range-finding. Then the barrage, which the papers called the greatest artillery preparation for an attack on record, began in earnest: sixteen days and nights of it without rest. The camion drivers had to work from twelve to twenty hours a day, loading, driving, and then unloading their matériel over the rain-drenched roads to ruined villages behind the front. By the twenty-second of October, Cowley wrote, "every clump of trees, every bush, it seemed, concealed a battery." The next day the French troops went over the top, and by the twenty-seventh, they had captured Malmaison and the Chemin des Dames ridge. The push was successful, and Cowley and his fellow truck drivers had contributed to the victory. The next day he was released and he headed to a pension on the Left Bank of Paris to spend his soldier's pay on a month in Gallic bohemia.

One thing he accomplished was to equip himself with prophylactics against the very real danger of venereal disease and broaden his sexual experience with the women of Paris. In a letter to Burke, Cowley, an instant expert, confided that "beside the American street woman, French cocottes are such a superior type." One prostitute/artist's model by the name of Gaby had approved of his reading of Romain Rolland's massive roman-fleuve *Jean-Christophe* and suggested that they take in a production of *The Merchant of Venice*. The poules also helped him correct his French accent when he read Baudelaire to them. Such activities aside, he hung out a lot at the Café du Dôme and the Rotonde, the latter famous for its clientele of Russian and Serbian artists and political conspirators.

Needing to decide what his next course of action was, he considered the alternatives of either volunteering for ambulance duty on the Italian front, as Hemingway and Dos Passos had, or enlisting in the aviation corps. Fliers in the famed Lafayette Escadrille had a life expectancy of about three months. Unfortunately or not, he did not pass the fliers' physical. Finally he opted to return to America and Harvard, where, he said, "I may find the old life again—and the old life a little broadened." He was back in New York by November, dressed in his American Field Service uniform and carrying a bag of souvenirs, with sixty-five cents to his name. Burke and Josephson greeted him at the dock.

From the perspective of 1934 and the publication of *Exile's Return*, Cowley would define his generation's experience of the war as a watershed experience and the culmination of a much longer process of deracination and uprooting. Their education had detached them in spirit from their native land and even their own literary traditions and habits of responsibility. Then as a result of the war, "we were fed, lodged, clothed by strangers, commanded by strangers, infected with the poison of irresponsibility . . . and the poison of danger, excitement, that made our old life seem intolerable." They'd developed, in one of Cowley's signature coinages, "a spectatorial attitude" toward war and peace alike. Some of the cynical judgments that he passes in *Exile's Return* on his generation's experience of the war need to be understood as the product not simply of time and hindsight, but of twin experiences of disillusionment and radicalization. It all too soon became clear after the punitive Treaty of Versailles that Wilsonian idealism had been trumped by old-world cynicism and great power politics, and by 1934 his sharp turn to the left had caused him to see a corrupt capitalism as being at the root of all social ills, especially war and particularly the one he had participated in.

Still, the Lost Generation, like other postwar American generations, would face in real time difficult adjustments to the conditions of peacetime life. Cowley's was unusual only in the extent to which it was able to make genuine literature from its problems. They even managed to turn their disillusion into a kind of victory. As Alfred Kazin observes in *On Native Grounds*, "If it was America that had 'won the war for Europe' as the popular legend had it, it was the new American literature, seizing the vitality that was left in the world, that made the victory its own."

An armistice was a year in the future. As Cowley was voyaging west, tens of thousands of American troops were heading east; eventually two million of them would arrive on Europe's shores, dwarfing all previous foreign military efforts. The universal draft in effect meant that he would have to make some decision as to further military service, a choice made less fraught by the fact that college men had a variety of options regarding officer training to select from. The next three and a half years for Malcolm Cowley would be peripatetic as he tended to the quadruple necessities of finishing his college education, discharging his military obligations, beginning his literary career, and earning enough money to pay for his tuition, food, and lodging.

THREE.

THE LONG FURLOUGH

———

That November of 1917 began the first installment of what Cowley would later call "the Long Furlough," the period between the end of the war and whatever came next. For a bit less than a month he had his first direct experience of New York bohemian life with Josephson and Burke, both still Columbia students, as his guides. They took him to Greenwich Village to the Provincetown Players, famed launching pad for Eugene O'Neill's career as a dramatist, and to the Golden Swan saloon on Sixth Avenue and West Fourth Street, better known as the Hell Hole and to become famous as the setting for O'Neill's pipe-dream epic *The Iceman Cometh*.

After a month's sojourn in Pittsburgh to visit his family, he returned to New York. His place for lodgings and base of operations, then and later, was an apartment building at 86 Greenwich Avenue in the West Village. Cowley's friends from Peabody High, James Light and Susan Jenkins, now married, had moved from Ohio State and rented a rambling seven-room apartment in the building, three or four rooms of which they would sublet to friends. Light acted in and directed plays at the Provincetown Players, while Jenkins worked as a magazine editor of light fiction. Their warren became the gravitational center and often residence of a circle of writers and artists soon to make their mark. The poet Djuna Barnes and the art student and later important photographer Berenice Abbott rented rooms, as did the independent-minded Kenneth Burke, who'd dropped out of Columbia under the influence of Flaubert to live on scant rations of milk and oatmeal and devote himself to literature. Often to be found there were such figures as a pre-conversion Dorothy Day, a suffragette and newspaper reporter who more than held her own at the Hell Hole; Floyd Dell, an editor of the Socialist literary review *The Masses* and a noted prophet of free love, Village-style; and a taciturn Eugene O'Neill.

In February 1918, Cowley returned to Cambridge for his delayed junior year. This would be the closest he would come to "find[ing] the old life again" and he signed up for an accelerated program of five courses—two English, one French, one history, and one philosophy—and earning A's in all of them. Perhaps more important, his steadily increasing stature as a campus writer and, perhaps, the residual glamour of his overseas service—and also, to be frank, the wartime shortage of other candidates, as he would later modestly admit—led to his being offered the position of president of the *Advocate* in late April. He relished the power and prestige this job conferred on him. Editorial work suited his temperament, his orderly work habits, and his habit of curiosity about and steady surveillance of what interesting things were shaking in the literary world. One of his first provocative actions was to invite his poetic mentor Amy Lowell to a smoker at the office of the *Advocate*, in whose pages not that long ago her Imagist theories had been ridiculed. Thoughtfully provided her accustomed cigars, she held her own against the heckling of the undergraduate poets. He had struck a blow for the Moderns in a once retrograde venue.

That semester he began one important new friendship with an older poet and cemented one with another; both associations would continue for their lifetimes. The first was with Conrad Aiken, who is remembered, if at all, for his much anthologized story of psychological horror "Silent Snow, Secret Snow." By the time he died in 1973 he had published some fifty books, including novels, stories, criticism, a play, an autobiography, and many collections of poetry.

That spring Cowley had read and been "impressed and a little frightened" by Aiken's long poem *The Jig of Forslin*, and he tracked him down and suggested they meet at a local hotel for drinks. A graduate of Harvard's class of 1912, Aiken was nine years older than Cowley and already married and the father of two, with his career fully launched. They met in the lobby of Boston's Hotel Touraine, where Cowley recognized Aiken by his orange necktie, "brighter than his Valencia-orange hair." They ended up talking well into the evening. Cowley recalled, "We both liked Boston in decay, we admired the French Symbolists poets, we wanted to accomplish architectonical and musical effects in our poems (I in theory, Conrad in practice), and we were fascinated by the political maneuvers of the poetry world, without wanting to take part in them." Their connection was swift and strong, an unusual occurrence for Aiken, who for the most part was shy and remote from literary society. Conrad Aiken was the second important literary figure Malcolm Cowley became intimate with after Amy Lowell, and he was considerably more relatable, an example to emulate.

The other poet was S. Foster Damon, a talented man who would exceed even Aiken in his quixotic strategies to achieve obscurity. Cowley already knew Damon from the Harvard Poetry Society and their visits to Amy Lowell's residence, but that spring they began to see a great deal more of each other. Damon had graduated from Harvard in 1914 and was now an instructor in English and a graduate student working on a thesis on the late prophetic books of William Blake. His profile had been given a boost the year before when his work was included in the volume *Eight Harvard Poets* along with that of Cummings, Dos Passos, and Hillyer, and he gave Cowley a good deal of help in keeping the *Advocate* appearing regularly and up to editorial standards. He also introduced Cowley to the poetry of Stephen Crane and Jules Laforgue and the fiction of Gertrude Stein and Herman Melville, whose revival was in its early stages.

That June, Cowley and Damon rented a shack for three dollars a month in the Finger Lakes town of Candor, New York, feeding themselves on Cowley-caught trout and Damon-gathered wild strawberries. On July 1, Cowley was to report to the barracks of the Harvard Reserve Officers Training Corps for six weeks of instruction and drills, but before that happened he and Damon pulled off a clever literary hoax—or, to be more precise, a counter-hoax.

In 1916, editors and well-known literary figures began receiving review copies of a book titled *Spectra*, containing the work of two Pittsburgh poets, Anne Knish, a putative Hungarian beauty who wrote in *very* free verse ("Her fair and featurous face / Writhed like / An albino boa-constrictor"—from "Opus 195"); and Emmanuel Morgan, a onetime Parisian expatriate artist who wrote in rhymes. ("If I were only dafter / I might be making hymns / To the liquor of your laughter / And the lacquer of your limbs"—from "Opus 6"). Knish's introduction announced the existence of a new Spectric group of poets determined "to push the possibilities of poetic expression into a new region," and a Spectric method that revealed "the overtones, adumbrations, or spectres which for the poet haunt all objects both of the seen and the unseen world." That the book arrived under the imprint of the respected publisher Mitchell Kennerley underscored its importance and authenticity.

Spectra and the group behind it became the objects of intense interest, helped along by reviews such as this in *The New Republic* by another Harvard-educated poet, Witter Bynner: "There is a new school of poets, a new term to reckon with, a new theory to comprehend, a new manner to notice, a new humor to enjoy. . . . It may be that the spectrists are offering us a means toward the creation or understanding of the essential magic of poetry." The joke was that it was in fact Witter Bynner himself who had written the poems of the nonexistent Emmanuel Morgan, and his friend Arthur Davison Ficke who had written the poems of the nonexistent Anne Knish. The two men, friends and poets of conservative and traditional inclinations, had been annoyed by the proliferation of such newfangled poetic schools as Imagism, Vorticism, and Futurism and, with a great deal of adroit strategizing and advance work, sprung *Spectra* on a gullible world keen to be up on the latest poetic thing. With the help of some coconspirators, they'd managed to keep the joke alive for a considerable period in hoax years, until April 26, 1918, when Bynner was busted at a talk he was giving to the Twentieth Century Club in Detroit, by Royall Snow, still a Harvard undergraduate. "Is it not true, Mr. Bynner," Snow asked, "that you are Emmanuel Morgan and that Arthur Davison Ficke is Anne Knish?" Bynner confessed on the spot, and word of the imposture quickly spread through the literary world.

This news was fresh that June in far Candor in the minds of the two poets, who decided to stage a counterattack on behalf of the Moderns. They concocted a "plowboy poet of Tioga County," a country-bumpkin Ossian by the name of Earl Roppel, and each wrote a clutch of poems of distinct rural inanity meant, they thought, to burlesque as well "the false innocence of lyric poets like Bynner." An example: "At night I sit beside the stove, / So tired I cannot see. / But at my plowing all the day / The great thoughts come to me." To the sheaf of poems they appended a cover letter from this "Bard of the Rushing Cata-tonk" to Witter Bynner himself, telling him in part, "I got your book out of the free library at Owego and read it all through the night and I like it very much though I do not understand it all. It gives you such a picture of life. Now, Mr. Bynner, what I want to say is this: I write some and I feel I write different from most." The letter concludes with the news that Roppel has been drafted, but, the writer adds, "Before I go I would like to have the opinion of someone I feel knows what poetry is on my poems which enclosed please find. Please say what you think because I know they are not as elegant as they would be if I put more time on the writing but I feel I should write about what I know."

At this juncture Kenneth Burke showed up with his flatmate Berenice Abbott, whose handwriting, it turned out, "had exactly the unformed, ingenuous look that Earl Roppel's might have had." They press-ganged the reluctant young woman into not only copying the letter and the poems for Bynner on ruled school tablet stationery, but also making copies of both for Amy Lowell and Conrad Aiken. After mailing the packets, they then left word for the postmaster at Candor to forward any mail for Earl Roppel to Kenneth Burke at 86 Greenwich Avenue. Giving Earl Roppel and his work a mock-solemn burial on the bank of the Catatonk, they then scattered, Cowley to his training camp, Damon to volunteer Red Cross work, Burke to a wartime shipyard job, Abbott back to Greenwich Village.

Two of the recipients replied almost immediately, although the letters were some time in reaching the pranksters. Aiken offered Roppel some measured praise and sent him an inscribed copy of Palgrave's *Golden Treasury* for further reading. Lowell responded energetically, offering to submit his work to Harriet Monroe's *Poetry* magazine, and later that year at dinner at Sevenels telling Damon—who must have struggled to refrain from guffawing—"He has the modern spirit. I don't know where he got it, but he has it." But they never heard back from their primary target, Bynner, and they finally concluded that the hoax had misfired. But it hadn't. Two years later, Cowley wrote up the tale of the fictional plowboy poet for the *New York Evening Post* under the heading "The Real Earl Roppel," and Bynner, let in on the joke, good-naturedly filled him in on what actually happened.

Bynner had been teaching at the University of California, Berkeley, when the Roppel poems arrived, and he and the other members of the faculty had read them and made favorable comparisons to Robert Burns. Bynner had written to Roppel offering help and those letters were forwarded to New York, but either the letters were misaddressed or by that time Burke had moved out of 86 Greenwich Avenue. Either way, the letters came back to Bynner stamped "No such person." Bynner then contacted the Owego library but was told that no one by the name of Roppel had ever checked out his *Spectra* book or any other. So Bynner began to suspect that he'd been pranked. Nevertheless he persisted in his search, contacting the War Department and other agencies. Meanwhile a professor of music at Berkeley had latched on to one of Roppel's poems, titled "Sunset," praising it as "the best patriotic song-poem in America," and he set it to music. Imagine the following verses sung to a huge audience by a chorus of three thousand trained voices:

> *Flag of our country, strong and true*
> *The sky is rosy with your bars;*
> *But as they fade it turns to blue*
> *And radiant with your stars.*

> *And as I watch the setting sun*
> *I call to God apart,*
> *"Give me the soul of Washington,*
> *And give me Lincoln's heart!"*

Cowley earned his sole gentleman's C for his military training, and by the time he returned to Cambridge the government had decided that all able-bodied college students were to serve in the military. So instead of resuming his studies, Cowley reported to Harvard's Student Army Training Corps and then applied to the Field Artillery Officers' Training School at Camp Taylor in Kentucky and was accepted. He frolicked for a week in New York with his friends before reporting for duty. En route to Camp Taylor he'd had the encouraging news that Amy Lowell had sold three of his poems to Harriet Monroe at *Poetry*—"Moonrise," "Barn Dance," and "Danny"—for twenty dollars for the bunch. They were all published in the November 1919 issue, the first appearance of Cowley's poetry in an independent, nonstudent literary magazine, a triumph for an undergraduate writer.

Cowley was at Camp Taylor when the armistice ending the war was signed on November 11, 1918. Released from his service, but still awaiting formal demobilization, he would spend the next ten months in New York at the intersection of Grub Street and Bohemia, before returning to Harvard for a final semester. He would have to make his financially pinched way as a beginning writer and would live the sort of freewheeling, artistically adventurous style of life that would disturb his parents and tarnish his profile once back in staid Cambridge.

In calling this period in his life and that of so many people of his age and inclinations "the Long Furlough," Cowley implied that the end of the war had released them from a life of danger and responsibility into one full of leisure but without clear direction. The war had left them "with a vast unconcern for the future and an enormous appetite for pleasure." Naturally, many of them had gravitated to the southern reaches of New York, "the homeland of the uprooted," as he put it. They came to Greenwich Village, he remembered, less for the Bohemian style of life and thought than because the lodgings were cheap and it was a convenient place to launch their careers. He describes his life at the time as a rinse-and-repeat cycle of waking up in soiled sheets in a borrowed apartment and turning the fifty cents borrowed the night before into breakfast for two; borrowing another half buck for a cheap bottle of sherry for that next night's revels; a revolving menu of rides on the Staten Island Ferry, dances at Webster Hall, talkative poker games, boozy times at the Hell Hole, and impromptu parties.

Cowley describes what he calls the doctrine of the Greenwich Villagers as almost a consciously formulated program centered on freedom of thought and expression, unfettered sexual behavior, gender equality, abandonment of middle-class notions of guilt and shame, and the virtue of constantly moving on. He remembers that time as a kind of war between these principles and the bourgeois values espoused by *The Saturday Evening Post*: "Industry, foresight, thrift and personal initiative." The utterance of any one of those words would have gotten you tossed out of the Hell Hole.

In fact the culture war going on in the United States was more widespread and viciously repressive even than Cowley's words suggest. The historian David Brion Davis has written, "The years from 1917 to 1921 are probably unmatched in American history for popular hysteria, xenophobia, and paranoid suspicion." The declaration of war against Germany and the successful Bolshevik revolution had unleashed a flood of jingoism and fear and hatred of the other, which caused ambient waves of hostility toward just about anyone who did not toe the all-American line. The passage of the Espionage Act in 1917 and the Sedition Act of 1918 gave the government almost unlimited powers to pursue, silence, and jail anyone who spoke or wrote against the war or other current policies. The beloved Socialist leader Eugene Debs, who'd received 6 percent of the popular vote in the 1912 presidential election, was arrested and then convicted of sedition in 1918 and sentenced to a ten-year term in prison. The postmaster general had virtual carte blanche to refuse to send publications he deemed offensive through the mails and he used it against magazines nationwide, especially those of a pacifist or leftist persuasion. The Palmer Raids of 1919 rounded up suspected anarchists and Bolshevists nationwide and deported them with scant regard for due process and their civil rights.

A considerable part of this repression and persecution was directed at the freethinking and -living Greenwich Villagers. So when Cowley in *Exile's Return* notes that the Village he'd moved to was rife with "former people"—former anarchists, former Socialists, former Wobblies, former pacifists and conscientious objectors, former editors and writers for political magazines like the fabled and now former *Masses*—now engaged in new, apolitical, more Bohemian activities, he is registering a cultural defeat that reached far outside the borders of the Village. But Greenwich Village, he would note, turned that defeat into a kind of victory when, with the help of the burgeoning mass media, its habits and styles and preoccupations—short hair and smoking for women, gin-fueled cocktail parties, self-conscious Freudian chatter about neuroses and the evils of sexual repression, a loosening of earlier standards of decorum and propriety in favor of an Oh-you-kid naughtiness—infected middle-class America.

Malcolm Cowley's stance that he was never a fully committed citizen of Bohemia but really just visiting is undercut by the fact that he would fall in love, move in with, and then marry one of the most thoroughly liberated spirits inhabiting the Village. The artist Marguerite Frances Baird, known as Peggy, had previously been married to the one-legged poet Orrick Johns. One biographer of Dorothy Day calls Peggy "a real-life version of Christopher Isherwood's Sally Bowles." Attractive and stylish—some say she was the first woman in the Village to bob her hair—she was sexually free-ranging and had had many affairs, including a fling with Eugene O'Neill. Dorothy Day had been introduced to Peggy by her probable lover Mike Gold and they became close friends and would remain so for the rest of their lives.

Peggy, who regarded sex as "a barrier to be broken down" and affairs as "incidents in an erotic education," was bemused by Day's relative sexual reticence.

A committed suffragette in the years leading up to the passing of the Nineteenth Amendment, Peggy spent ten days in a Washington, DC, jail in 1917 for demonstrating on behalf of women's right to vote. Undeterred, she convinced Dorothy Day to accompany her and several other women on the train to DC to picket the White House. On November 10, some forty women walked through Lafayette Park and were greeted by a jeering crowd and the police, who herded them into paddy wagons. Booked and then released with a warning, they came back again the next day to demonstrate, and this time an exasperated judge sentenced them to serve their terms at an infamous prison, the Occoquan Workhouse, just outside the city limits, which lived up to its reputation for brutal treatment. In protest the women went on a hunger strike; some of them were actually force-fed by tube. After ten days the strike was called off and the women were transferred back to a city jail and then freed, the government having realized that the spectacle of "respectable" middle-class women being treated so harshly was a bad look. Peggy Baird was no mere Village artiste; she was someone with the courage to stand up for her convictions.

Not long after this, Peggy Baird met Malcolm Cowley at a Christmas party at the Lights' apartment. The attraction was swift and strong and by January 1919 they had become lovers and were soon, in Cowley's old-fashioned words, living in sin in an apartment at 16 Christopher Street, "a dreadful, dreadful, dark hole." On the surface this instant romance seems a bit unlikely. Baird had eight years on Cowley, was disorderly in her living habits where Cowley was neat and punctilious, artistic rather than intellectual, spontaneous, and always up for a boozy gathering or an all-night poker game while he would be toiling on his writing at his neatly arranged workspace off in a corner.

It is a fair guess that their original connection had a strong erotic component to it; Baird had considerably more sexual experience than Cowley, but as the photos from that time show, he was a handsome young man with a brushed mustache and full head of hair. On top of that, he had the attractive aura of someone with talent and the innate ambition to make the most of it.

Peggy's openhearted Bohemian inclusiveness and acceptance helped to sand down some of the snobberies Cowley had picked up in his time at Harvard. She also helped to launch him on his career as a freelance reviewer. A former lover of hers had been Clarence Britten, the literary editor of *The Dial*, one of the most venerable of the country's little magazines. It had been founded in 1840 as an outlet for the writing of the New England Transcendentalists and had undergone various changes of editorial direction since then. At this time it was largely political in focus. Cowley visited Britten in his office and the editor pushed half a dozen novels across his desk, with the instruction "Try reviewing these, but don't give them more than a hundred words apiece." The pay would be a dollar each if accepted. Cowley carried the books to a bench in Union Square and spent some hours hastily making notes for the reviews he would bang out the next day. He then took the review copies to a secondhand bookstore on Fourth Avenue and sold them for thirty-five cents each; that $2.10 bought some Bull Durham tobacco for hand-rolled cigarettes and bread, butter, and lamb chops for the evening meal.

In this way Malcolm Cowley first climbed onto the hamster wheel of reviewing. Soon he would make his way to other offices in town, a notebook of clippings under his arm. One of those offices was that of Francis Hackett, the literary editor of *The New Republic*, "a big, red-faced Irishman looking like Jupiter in pince-nez glasses." He was sitting at a scarred and book-piled desk that would be Cowley's desk ten years later. "Miss Updike, perhaps you can find a book for this young man," he instructed his assistant. Miss Updike picked out a novel ti-tled *Victorious* by Reginald Wright Kauffman and handed it over "as if she were pouring a saucer of milk for a starved kitten." Cowley would write a five-hundred-word review for the then-lordly sum of ten dol-lars; it was a hastily produced novel of the Great War that, based on his own experiences, he found wanting. This was the first of hundreds of such reviews and essays that he would write for the magazine. He would always remember the vulnerable and strapped young man he was in 1919 when he was in Hackett's position in the thirties and offer many kindnesses to his young successors who would come calling, clip book in hand. In the early thirties Miss Updike would become his own assistant and Cowley would give reviewing work to Francis Hackett.

The wages of book reviewing are paltry and inevitably lead to a life of precarity and greatly reduced caloric intake. He had to pawn his solid gold Phi Beta Kappa key for three dollars, "the price of three good dinners in 1920." He began to produce reviews with great effi-ciency and his turnaround time was impressive. Robert Morss Lovett, who would later share the masthead of *The New Republic* with him, remembers that Cowley would appear at *The Dial* as soon as it opened to pick up three books. By noon those reviews were handed in, his check drawn and cashed, and the review copies sold. One of the ways he would augment his income was to find work as an extra in O'Neill productions at the Provincetown Players: "I was paid ten dollars a week to be a black ghost in *The Emperor Jones* and a white ghost in a revival of *Where the Cross Is Made*; I never aspired to play the part of any living person." When he caught the deadly influenza that was killing millions of people across the globe, he came perilously close to becoming a real ghost himself. Luckily his friend Lionel Moises, a colorful journalist for the *New York Journal* and a lover of Dorothy Day's, dropped by his apartment and found Cowley in a delirious state. "He cradled me in his arms as if I were a rag doll and carried me to the hospital, just like a Pieta," in all probability saving his life. By this point Cowley, a six footer, was down to 130 pounds.

One day, having skipped breakfast, he was crossing Sheridan Square when he lost consciousness for a brief moment and fell onto the sidewalk. Shaken, he picked himself up and went into a nearby lunch counter and spent his last dime on a cup of coffee and a stale bun. Sitting there, the counterman impatiently asking "Anything else?" he realized the unsustainability of this way of life. He unfurled the want ad section of the newspapers and found some salaried work, first as a theater critic for a giveaway weekly and then as a copy editor and proofreader for *Iron Age*, an industrial catalogue. This gig paid a decent salary for the time, $42.50 a week, and had the added benefit of giving him his first immersion in the protocols of typesetting and printing, a great deal more complex and literally hands-on process in those days. His intimate sense of the processes and realities undergirding the production of printed matter would inform his future criticism and the essays he would produce about the book trade.

Cowley and Baird were now living in a run-down tenement at 107 Bedford Street whose boarders constituted a full menage of Village types—artists, writers, leftists. They once had to spring their landlady from jail for passing a bad check, which would have made being late with the rent on occasion less stressful. He wrote in his memoir *Exile's Return*, "Some drizzly morning late in April you woke up to find yourself married (and your wife, perhaps, suffering from a dry cough that threatened consumption)." In fact, Malcolm Cowley, in the parlance of the time, made an honest woman of Peggy Baird on August 12, 1919, and she did suffer, then and later, recurrent bouts of ill health from various ailments.

However, marriage and monogamy were by no means synonymous in those circles. Peggy and Cowley devised a modus vivendi to accommodate her spontaneity and his disciplined neatness and work ethic, but there would be affairs. On one occasion, when they'd been married less than a year, this led to the unfortunate discovery that they both had contracted syphilis. In those days before antibiotics, the disease could eventually lead to madness and death, so they both had to subject themselves to a most unpleasant course of treatment with the new wonder drug Salvarsan over six months. The bitterness this engendered can be easily imagined and it infuses "Free Clinic," a poem Cowley would soon publish that captures the grim atmosphere of the place where he and Peggy would have to report for their weekly injections. The marriage survived this experience and would last a sometimes rocky twelve years, but it was never the same after it.

Cowley delayed telling his parents about his marriage when he visited Belsano shortly thereafter. When he did, they both expressed their vehement disapproval in different ways; his mother "burst into sudden hysteria, collapsed on the floor, tore at her breasts," while his father fumed in his calmer fashion. Peggy Cowley was everything his mother did not want in a daughter-in-law: an older, already divorced "New Woman" of doubtful morals and indifferent domestic habits, and irreligious. This was flagrantly not the reason they were sending their only son to Harvard, and no further financial support would be offered on that front. For the balance of their marriage, Cowley and Peggy would see his parents for only short visits to Belsano.

Cowley probably could have graduated from Harvard right then with a wartime diploma, but he was determined to complete his course of study and earn a full academic degree for reasons of ego and economics. His sense of self-worth was still closely tied to his academic prowess and he wanted Harvard's prestigious stamp of full approval. Peggy stayed back in New York and then lived with Conrad Aiken in Yarmouth on the Cape for two months, where her short hair (a sign of cultural radicalism then) and flexible morality upset the neighbors, while Cowley returned to Cambridge in October to complete his degree in one grueling semester, taking on a load of six courses and putting aside his own writing while he buckled down. Money as ever was a problem, especially with no help from home, but he squeaked by with a scholarship of two hundred dollars from the Harvard Club of Western Pennsylvania and a fifty-dollar loan from the college.

Harvard, however, did not return Cowley's regard in his final semester. His fellow students had gotten wind of his unconventional life among the freethinkers of the Village and his marriage to one of them, and they disapproved. Painfully, his friend S. Foster Damon in particular disliked Peggy, who'd moved in with him by Christmas, and their friendship cooled. In addition, he'd written an editorial in the November 1918 issue of the *Advocate* mocking the wartime hysteria in Congress and elsewhere over the supposed threat of socialism, which came off as suspiciously Bolshevist at Harvard. This would be the first time a political opinion would subject Malcolm Cowley to opprobrium, and not the last.

He would remember the impact of this snobbery and conservative prejudice in 1967 in a letter to Jacob Davis. He'd been a big literary man on campus as a result of his editorship of the *Advocate*, "invited to the *Lampoon* punches and the *Crimson* punches and various other affairs that were actually amusing." But, he said, "When I came back to college in the fall of 1919, I was treated as if I had smallpox." On the strength of his *Advocate* editorship he'd been admitted to the Signet literary society, a staid and prep-school-dominated group. It offered the advantage of an affordable meal plan, but it was there that the snobbery manifested itself most strongly. "When I went to the Signet to eat because I had no money and could sign chits there, ice formed in the fireplace." Cowley concludes, "I had a complete view of the Harvard social system, going up and coming down. But it didn't leave me with a deep love for the class of 1919." (He would avoid class reunions for most of his life.) He summed up his Harvard experience this way: "I went through Harvard on scholarships, and at Harvard I was almost but not completely an outsider; if I *had* been a complete outsider I should have suffered fewer humiliations."

In the classroom, though, things went far more smoothly. He breezed through his final exams, earning four A's and two B's and a Phi Beta Kappa key, and graduated cum laude in February of 1920 with a bachelor of arts degree. His final day in Cambridge was blessed with a grace note. There was a knock on the door of their attic, and a young man handed him an envelope; inside was a ten-dollar bill folded in a note from his beloved English instructor "Copey" that read, "I thought you could use this." The gift paid their train fare back to Grand Central Station and the taxi to the Village.

The next sixteen months would be Cowley's first extended stint on Grub Street. The freelancer's hustle, an anxious life of constant solicitation and the nick-in-time arrival of checks, would be his primary source of income for the next decade, relieved by stints of graduate study on scholarship and occasional periods of salaried employment. He would get very good at it. He got his copy in on time, his reviews were clear and pleasing to read. The going rate was generally a penny a word and much of what Cowley produced was hackwork, but as he recalled, "Always I tried to make it better work than I was paid for doing . . . Editors liked them because they could be sent to the printer without revision."

Freelancers depend on the kindness of editors, and as a result of this professionalism, he found an increasingly warm welcome in editorial offices around town. One of them was *The New Republic*. Another was the office of Henry Seidel Canby, who was just then starting the weekly supplement *The Literary Review of the New York Evening Post*. He and Cowley would chat about trout fishing (Canby deplored the use of worms) before the handover of books for review. Eventually,

Canby put Cowley on retainer for ten dollars a week, for which he was expected to sort through a pile of books and find the one or two worthy of review.

A review of his appeared in the February 1920 issue of *The Dial*, just as he and Peggy were leaving Cambridge, that held promise for his future as a critic. In the summer of 1919, Clarence Britten had assigned him to review two novels by Sheila Kaye-Smith, at the time a well-regarded British novelist. Cowley got the review in just as the magazine was being bought by two Harvard graduates, Scofield Thayer and James Sibley Watson, both moneyed heirs to great fortunes. Their ambition was to transform *The Dial* into the leading magazine of the radical new tendencies now emerging in literature and the arts that would soon be called, uppercase, Modernism. Cowley's review would be the only one of the already accepted manuscripts that the new editors felt met their high standards. The piece held its own in an issue that included work from Bertrand Russell and Paul Rosenfeld.

This review marked the start of Malcolm Cowley's close association with *The Dial* as a regular contributor just as it was beginning its spectacular run as perhaps the finest American magazine of the arts of the past century. Thayer and Watson's timing was perfect. The decade of the twenties was a time when the so-called little magazines served as a kind of collective skunk works for the radical experiments in form and consciousness being conducted by the emerging Modernist masters. *The Dial* met this moment brilliantly, publishing William Butler Yeats ("The Second Coming"), Thayer's friend and classmate T. S. Eliot (the first American publication of "The Waste Land"), Wallace Stevens, Thomas Mann ("Death in Venice," in its first English translation, by Kenneth Burke), Ezra Pound, Marcel Proust, D. H. Lawrence, Marianne Moore (who would become one of its editors), Gertrude Stein, William Carlos Williams, and Edmund Wilson, and reproducing artworks by the greatest artists of the century.

This was the kind of company any poet and critic at the dawn of his career would dream to be in. Over the next several years Cowley's byline would regularly appear in the magazine over pieces on such writers as Romain Rolland, Katherine Mansfield, Siegfried Sassoon, Aldous Huxley, Marcel Proust, Amy Lowell, Conrad Aiken, and Carl Sandburg. It was an important proving ground for his impressive early growth as a critic. One of the reasons that Cowley became so quickly attuned to the revivified magazine was that he intimately understood its editorial roots. Thayer in particular had been closely associated with *The Harvard Monthly*, and he had been, in his literary inclinations and even his foppish personal style, an arch-Aesthete.

Peggy and Cowley resumed their version of *la vie bohème* in a sparsely furnished fifth-floor tenement walk-up apartment overlooking the Sixth Avenue El, Ashcan School lodgings. One of the time-honored strategies of young artists to combat such straitened circumstances is to figure them as picturesque and indulge in self-dramatization. In one of the prose interludes to *Blue Juniata* he would write, "In this setting of dirt and poverty we passed our post-graduate, post-bellum years, scantily clothed, poorly fed, making drafts against our abundant constitutions, and enjoying ourselves almost feverishly. . . . we had come to erect the sordid into a kind of religion. We worshipped the cluttered streets, the overflowing ashcans, the houses full of people and rats." None of this was new to Peggy, a seasoned Villager for whom day to day and hand to mouth was a way of life, but Cowley was at one level still a middle-class, Ivy League boy-man and his situation got him down. The sometimes grim atmosphere of their marriage can be gauged in such poems as "Interment," in which "boredom . . . lurking in the shadows" will "find our love that we had thought so holy / and take him by the throat and choke him slowly / leaving him dead on the floor." Luckily for marital peace, he published this poem only three years later.

This was a time of postcollegiate drift. His ambitions were both real and inchoate, "a special cast of mind." "I wanted to be a writer, but not a celebrated writer appearing in glossy magazines. I wanted to live obscurely, limit my needs, and preserve my freedom to write something new and perfect at some moment in the future; that was the dream of producing a masterpiece that obsessed the young writers of my age group." He was a sad young literary man, groping for a secure handhold on this whole vexing business of producing and judging literature and actually making a living from it.

Yielding to financial necessity, Cowley took a full-time job as a copywriter at forty dollars a week for a publication called *Sweet's Architectural Catalogue*. The work was mental drudgery but not all that demanding, especially in the summer months when he could even write some poems during office hours. He was able to do his reviewing work on evenings and weekends and he stuck it out there for a full year. The extra money allowed him and Peggy to rent a country house in Haverstraw and trade in the sordid for the sublime for a few months as he lived the life of a commuter. This was clearly a holding action, though.

The big change came in March of 1921, when with the help of Clarence Britten and one of his Harvard mentors, John Livingston Lowes, he won an American Field Service scholarship for a year of graduate study at the University of Montpellier in the south of France, with a year's renewal possible. The stipend was for twelve thousand francs, or about a thousand dollars at the then-current rate of exchange. He and Peggy would both receive a 50 percent discount on their cabin-class steamship fares. The next three months were spent settling various accounts: selling a piano for $250, mending fences with S. Foster Damon, visiting his mentor Amy Lowell, who offered to serve as agent for his poetry while he was abroad.

Cowley and Peggy were joining a considerable wave of American expatriation that summer. It was spreading across England and the European continent, but the primary destination was France, and the Left Bank of Paris in particular. This was one of the most literary-minded migrations in history, and France—with its fabled respect for high art and literature, its roster of modern heroes ranging from Baudelaire and Flaubert to Rimbaud, Apollinaire, and a still-active Proust, its well-earned reputation for advanced thinking and practice in all the arts—was the magnet. Cowley was strongly drawn to the French way of literary life, bold in practice yet balanced in theory. He'd liked what he'd been able to see of it in his time as a camion driver and he was eager for a longer, deeper immersion.

Whatever ex post facto theories would be offered for this expatriation (including some of his own) that lean heavily on ideas of disillusion, persecution, and the need to escape from an unbearably philistine America, Malcolm Cowley at this time left no evidence that he was particularly alienated from his native land. He loved America, particularly its rural parts. The difficulties of his life in New York were what depressed him. In his Bohemian bunker, preoccupied with a genuine struggle for existence and his fitful progress toward maturity, he took little notice of the political repression and cultural censorship that the war had unleashed.

As he and Peggy boarded their liner to France on July 8, 1921, Cowley was glad to be leaving the difficulties of Grub Street behind and excited by the prospect of a direct encounter with the makers of the Modernist revolution that was brewing. He could not have known the extent to which he was about to enter a time and place that would not become simply famous but mythic, to join the society of young writers who would change American literature forever.

FOUR.

LOST AND FOUND

———

Even fifty years ago William Styron regarded the task of reviewing a book about the Lost Generation by one of its most prominent members and historians with fatigue. "It is possible to approach a work like this with just a touch of resentment. We have read about the Lost Generation until our heads are water-logged with its self-congratulation, its nostalgia. One broods over the gallons, the tuns, the tank cars of ink spilled out on the lives and work of these men—Hemingway's bibliography alone must be on its way to several volumes requiring sturdy book ends—and one thinks: Enough." The book that put Styron in this initially peckish mood was Malcolm Cowley's *A Second Flowering*. It overcame his resistance: The review is warm and positive. Still, the whole process Styron decries has only accelerated. The adventures and misadventures and achievements and failures of the small company of American writers and artists who made Paris—or rather a small area of it in the café-strewn Montparnasse district—their artistic home in the twenties have become part of our cultural furniture, a received idea like the Wild West, so encrusted with myth that the actual facts of the case are hard to see.

The tag "Lost Generation" was coined, not by Gertrude Stein or Ernest Hemingway, but by a French garage owner. Stein had taken

her automobile to a garage for repair in a small village in the department of Ain during a motoring tour. The young mechanic who ser-
viced the car fixed it quickly, and Stein praised him to the garage
owner and asked how he'd found such a good worker. The owner replied that he'd trained him himself; it was the older mechanics,
twenty-two and above, who had served in the war who were untrain-
able. These men he characterized as *"une génération perdue."* Stein had
an ear for the resonant phrase, and it stuck in her mind.

As told to Matthew Josephson by the French painter André Masson and the American poet Evan Shipman, Hemingway and the two
men had been drinking quite a bit one evening when they decided to
drop in on Stein's nightly salon on the rue de Fleurus. They were boisterous and interrupted her customary holding forth, and, recalling the
garage owner's phrase, she castigated them, exclaiming, *"Vous êtes tous
une génération fichu* [*sic*]!" ("*Fichu*" is a past participle that can be
translated as "damned.") In 1926, Hemingway used the peeved
exclamation—translated as "You are all a lost generation"—as the epigraph to his novel *The Sun Also Rises*, which became an immediate
sensation and impressed the portrait of literary Americans behaving
badly in France and Spain in the twenties on our collective consciousness for all time.

That generational baptism was some years in the future as Malcolm
Cowley and his wife boarded their French Line steamer. Nothing
raises the spirit of a financially strapped young couple like a highly
favorable exchange rate. For their $125 tickets they would enjoy daily
five-course luncheons and six-course dinners with wine, cigars, and
cognac, a stark contrast to the meager fare they'd been subsisting on in
New York. In point of fact, the American exodus to France was in
some ways made possible, if not actually caused, by the strong dollar
and the weak franc enabling these writers and artists to live in relative
luxury (or at least avoid malnutrition and homelessness) on the income

from poems, reviews, "color" pieces, and various commissions (and, for a few, modest remittances and trust fund income).

At the exchange rate prevailing in 1919, 1 dollar would get you 8 francs. By 1923 that rate had doubled to more than 16 francs. It continued that rise: The best rate for the dollar, 36 francs, came in 1926, not coincidentally the year *The Sun Also Rises* was published, and opened the spigot fully on the surge of American cultural tourists and twenty-four-hour party people. The rate settled back to around 25 francs until the end of 1929, when the stock market crash sent almost everyone back to America. Contemporary readers of Lost Generation memoirs are constantly brought up short by the memoirist's account of feeling suddenly flush and prosperous by the timely arrival at the American Express office of a check for as little as 10 dollars for a piece of writing. The dollar would go even further, startlingly so, in defeated and inflation-ravaged Germany and elsewhere in Europe—which would have consequences for the printing location of some important little magazines.

Arriving in Paris, Cowley made a beeline for the Rotonde café, which, along with the Select and especially, to give it its full name, the Café Brasserie du Dôme de Montparnasse, were in his recollection "the heart and nervous system of the American literary colony." The Dome was gossip central, "their living newspaper," the place to send and receive news of comings and goings, rivalries and friendships, liaisons and breakups, successes and failures. It served as an informal loan office, rental agency, staging area for forays into Parisian nightlife, and "an over-the-table market that dealt in literary futures." Little magazine editors in search of contributors found that a visit to the Dome was more efficient than the mail, and it was a required stop for American publishers on scouting trips headhunting for hot new talent. Soon enough the tourists would arrive as well to gawk at the spectacle of the overcultured and underfunded at work and play.

Surveying the cast of characters, Cowley got the distinct impression, not an entirely pleasant one, that the Greenwich Village scene had reconstituted itself on the other side of the Atlantic. Writers and artists like to think of themselves as fearless individualists, but in fact they tend to run in packs. In a letter to Kenneth Burke, Cowley identified as "going abroad" Djuna Barnes, William Slater Brown, John Dos Passos, a pre–Catholic conversion Dorothy Day, the Danish artist Ivan Opffer, and, as "already abroad," E. E. Cummings. At a party in Paris he noticed Robert McAlmon, poet, partner of the poet Bryher, Left Bank long-hauler, and publisher of the Contact Press; the poet Mina Loy; and the just-visiting Sinclair Lewis, whose blockbuster novel *Main Street* would be the bestselling novel of 1921 and a salvo in the culture war between America's urban sophisticates and its small towns.

Two new arrivals in Paris at about the same time as the Cowleys were Matthew Josephson and his wife, Hannah, who had similarly gotten themselves to Montparnasse without delay after debarking from their steam liner. (He had earlier said to his wife, "If Harding is elected, we must leave the country." He was and they did.) Josephson noted the presence there of his fellow tenants Djuna Barnes and Berenice Abbott, working as an assistant to the painter and photographer Man Ray. At the Dome he made the acquaintance of the genial young American novelist Robert Coates, later to become *The New Yorker*'s first art critic. The gang had arrived, with startling swiftness.

It felt like a second, far smaller and hyper-literary American Expeditionary Force had organized itself and landed on the Left Bank of the Seine and the cultural rather than the Western Front. Cowley called it "a great migration eastward into new prairies of the mind." Another self-exile wittily dubbed the expatriates "the 'Lost Battalion' of my generation." Ford Madox Ford compared the Americans storming Montparnasse to "a herd of stampeding Herefords." And everyone involved seemingly wrote a memoir.

What accounted for this exodus of American writers and artists? The strong dollar and the lure of Paris to a certain caste of Americans cannot be underestimated as causative factors. But the early arriving writers were certainly running away from something as well. The reactionary turn in American politics had fouled the atmosphere, and the start of Prohibition signaled that the censorious bluenoses were coming for their freewheeling pleasures. (It was not clear at first that Prohibition actually would be the force to ignite what Fitzgerald termed "the greatest, gaudiest spree in history.") The values of America's business civilization, inimical to artistic freedom and personal license, were in the ascendant and would result in three successive Republican administrations to spread and enforce them. As Alfred Kazin would write, "resignation, attack, escape" were the strategies that many writers chose to implement, finding themselves strangers in their own country. Cowley would explain it this way: "There was one idea that was held in common by the older and the younger inhabitants of the Village—the idea of salvation by exile. 'They do things better in Europe: let's go there.'"

The chief prophet of the baleful point of view that there was nothing for an artist to do about America except to leave it as quickly as possible was a curious figure named Harold Stearns. This country has not lacked for its critics over its long history, but Stearns brought a special vigor to his attacks. A graduate of Harvard College, class of 1913, he was something of a prodigy who earned his tuition by newspaper writing. He later became one of the early contributors to the nascent *New Republic* and then an editor of *The Dial*. In the August 4, 1920, issue of *The Freeman*, he uncorked a blast posing the question "What Can a Young Man Do?" The two-word answer after some four thousand words of sub-Menckenian sarcasm and invective: "Get out!"

The piece deploys a critique of the situation of intellectually and artistically inclined Americans that would be familiar to any sixties survivor, combining assessments of the conformity and sterility of our commercial life and a decrying of "the steady denudation of the United States of its imaginative and adventurous and artistically creative young men." Stearns, in Thoreau mode, proclaims that "in twentieth-century monotonous majority-ruled unimaginative-existence America the chances are getting slimmer and slimmer everyday of leading any kind of life other than the of the great average," and declares that "there must be something wrong with a culture and a civilization when its youth begins to desert it," as was already happening.

Stearns's essay served as the final chapter of his slim 1921 tome *America and the Young Intellectual*, which went on in the same vein at greater length. He was not finished with his assault on postwar America. He quickly assembled a dogpile of thirty of America's most distinguished and judgmental intellectuals to broaden the case that this was no country for sensitive young men, or really for anyone of any age with a brain and soul.

The editorial meetings of the symposium that Stearns was assembling took place in the basement of his building at 31 Jones Street, often with loud and apparently untroubled partying Villagers on the floor above. Their deliberations resulted in *Civilization in the United States*, a comprehensive indictment of every area of human endeavor—politics, law, education, music, scholarship, sex, domestic life, economics, agriculture, urban life, many others—in America.

Stearns's two volumes and the arguments contained in them are conveniently regarded as a causative factor in the rush of American writers to Europe. But in truth he was really providing ex post facto explanations for a phenomenon that already existed. Josephson writes acidulously that "the only trouble with the theory of Harold Stearns as a latter-day Mahomet leading a pilgrimage of Yankees to the Left Bank of the Seine is that most of us who went there had never heard of him." *America and the Young Intellectual* was published in 1921, when that pilgrimage had been well under way, and *Civilization in the United States* arrived in 1922, by which point American beachheads had been fully established.

There is really no one-size-fits-all explanation for the motives that drew Americans to France at the dawn of the twenties. Malcolm Cowley himself stands off to one side from the general run of expatriate thought and action. He never gave himself over to the rote excoriation of America as the unfortunate abode of culture-free, prejudice-beset, small-minded Rotarians that was the default language of too many of his set. He was not really running away from America; he and Peggy were in flight from the literary rat race of New York City, a very different thing.

By the end of 1921, Harold Stearns had taken his own advice and gone east himself, landing like so many others on the Left Bank. As Cowley would write, "His was no ordinary departure: he was Alexander marching into Persia and Byron shaking the dust of England from his feet. Reporters came to the gangplank to jot down his words." He did not thrive, and his descent from a widely heeded pundit who could command a gaggle of America's most censorious intellectuals to a figure of pathos was swift. He became a well-known Montparnasse barfly and racetrack tout, cadging drinks and peddling hot tips in *Guys and Dolls* fashion. Hemingway would lend Stearns a certain small immortality when he used him as the model for the bibulous Harvey Stone, Jake Barnes's friend, in *The Sun Also Rises*.

Malcolm Cowley was one of the earliest out of the gate to ridicule Stearns, less for his drinking than for his overwrought pronouncements on American benightedness. He first lampooned him in "Three Americans in Paris," poetic portraits of Stearns, Ezra Pound, and Sinclair Lewis that ran in *The Literary Review of the New York Evening Post* on January 14, 1922, under the rubric "The New Curiosity Shop." It begins thus: "Do I remember (it was in *The Freeman* / A very brilliant article, begad) / Last March that a very sophisticated demon /

Told us to go to Europe and Be Bad / New York is ruled by preachers. Buy a ticket / for irreligious France and be wicked."

Cowley's second mockery was much longer and fuller. In the December 1922 number of the little magazine *Broom*, he published a broad caricature of Stearns as "Young Mr. Elkins," a scourge of our native repression and vulgarity. Insiders—which by definition meant the readers of *Broom*—would know that Stearns was the satirical target by such details as "It sent him to Harvard as a classmate of Walter Lippmann." Elkins is an early-blooming genius of sorts who "thunder[s] against billboards, Billy Sunday and Methodism, proportional representation, Comstock, elevated railroads," dreams of "an America delivered utterly from the Puritan yoke . . . A broad leisurely America without machines and Methodism. Sunday baseball in Pittsburgh (or better, Sunday cricket), open urinals and racetrack gambling, the works of Freud and Boccaccio and D. H. Lawrence sold at newsstands openly." He dreams especially of Europe and "of an America which has imitated the best of Paris and Berlin and London, an Anglo-Franco-German America ruled by philosophers and economists." Meanwhile, "American civilization howls outside his window."

Cowley is registering his distaste for and impatience with the knee-jerk disdain for American civilization all too common among the literati and calling for a more tolerant and accepting attitude toward this still-young and brawling and sprawling and vital country. In point of fact, for all its flaws—its Methodism and billboards and even its elevated railroads—he deeply loved his country and always would.

———

The Cowleys spent a couple of months in Paris, paying their respects to one of the local literary monuments, Ezra Pound, ever ready to receive homage and dispense advice, taking in the museums and not neglecting to enjoy the lively nightlife of the newly planted American colony. In August they left Paris, heading for the South of France and the University of Montpellier to report for academic duty, as required by Cowley's American Field Service scholarship. They lingered for six weeks in Dijon, the cobblestoned old capital of Burgundy, drenched in history and restful, if a bit dull, after the excitements of Paris. The quiet proved conducive to productivity—"There was nothing to do but work," Cowley informed John Brooks Wheelwright. Cowley wrote "The Journey to Paris" there, which he described as "an amusing satirical voyage on the order of Dean Swift," a proto-surrealist rendering of his emotions in arriving at the capital of art and culture. This little exercise would appear the next year in the short-lived little magazine *Gargoyle*.

By far the most consequential piece of writing Cowley accomplished in Dijon, however, was his landmark and immensely influential anatomy of his literary peers, "This Youngest Generation," which like those little odes would be published by Henry Seidel Canby the following October in the widely read *Literary Review of the New York Evening Post*. The piece is not perfect: Somewhat inchoate, it proceeded more by intuition and personal experience and sheer cheek—at the age of twenty-three, "it was possible to annihilate in a phrase the life work of an internationally famous man of letters, without fear of being in turn annihilated," he would later write—than by much actual evidence. By 1921 the writers in their early twenties born near the turn of the century had produced only a modest volume of work. Of those he mentioned by name—Cummings, Dos Passos, Damon, Burke, and Slater Brown—only Dos Passos had written a book of note, his Great War novel *Three Soldiers* (1921). In fact the lead paragraph admits as much: "As an organized body of opinion, the youngest generation in American letters does not exist." And yet, as Cowley would write in *Exile's Return*, the essay "expressed clearly enough the ideas which the exiles of that year had packed in their baggage and carried duty-free across the Atlantic."

"This Youngest Generation" is less important for the arguments and predictions it makes than for its declaration that a new literary generation was coming into being. It was the debut of Malcolm Cowley's most persuasive insight as a critic and literary historian: that the American writers who were coming of age in the postwar years, particularly those who'd chosen to expatriate themselves to Europe, constituted a literary group distinct from the generations that had come before, and that attention must be paid. It announced his powerful tendency to think collectively about writers and American literature, especially in respect to his generational cohort, but also in the longer sweep of our history.

The essay had an immediate impact. Harriet Monroe, the influential editor of *Poetry*, tut-tutted about it, patting him on the head condescendingly. In language that had already become antique, she admitted that youth must be served: "The passage of the generations—that is the great poem. . . . Through the battering of young minds alone may each generation forget to grow old, therefore let youth be free and strong, let it have room for its race and its shout . . . ," etc. But she criticized the way Cowley so ungracefully casts off "the too-much honored living" in favor of the new Gallic literary gods and argues for the humility and "gratitude" that he had cockily termed "not a literary virtue." Van Wyck Brooks, in a scolding piece in *The Freeman*, while not mentioning Cowley or his essay by name, harrumphed that "it is an incorrigible infantile frivolity that possesses our writers; they digest nothing; they do not even swallow anything." Cowley threatened in a letter to Kenneth Burke to respond, but he did not, and a good thing too, since he would shortly be augmenting his income by writing reviews for Brooks at the magazine. Overall his piece succeeded in doing what all such generational statements are meant to do: Twit the authorities and elders and get their attention.

Cowley's essay was received far more warmly by the younger generation itself, though they had far less access to the newspapers and magazines to register their approbation. Perhaps the most excited (and excitable) of these readers was the curious figure of Gorham Munson, twenty-six years of age and a teacher with large, if as yet unformed, literary ambitions who had come to Paris to write. The piece lit quite a fire under him.

Meanwhile the Cowleys arrived that October in the pleasant Provençal university town of Montpellier, twenty minutes from the Mediterranean, where they found lodgings and Cowley began his studies. According to his biographer Hans Bak, "he attended sixteen to eighteen classes a week, studied French grammar and pronunciation and read such French classical authors as Corneille, Molière, Racine and Boileau." His plan was to finish his courses and sit for an examination in March of the following year, and then complete a doctoral thesis. He applied himself to his academic duties with a will, and this intense encounter with the French language would be put to excellent use later in the decade as Cowley would find work as a highly skilled translator of books from the French.

On a deeper level, his extended engagement with classical French writing, one of the most formal and rule-bound bodies of work in world literature and one that put the virtues of balance and proportion above all others, spoke deeply to Cowley's own emerging literary temperament. At the age of twenty-four, he was very much a work in progress, seeking to find a suitable relation to the literature of the past and the present, as both a practitioner and a critic. His temperament at this time was pointing him more in the direction of classicism than toward Modernism's feverish experimentation with form and subject matter. The writers and the reigning aesthetics of French classicism suited him at a deep level: "I feel at home in the seventeenth century, as if I had just been introduced to a very pleasant company of very kindred minds. The two sides of it: the grand tragedies in which one could only use noble words, and the low comedies in which one could say anything; there are two waterproof compartments in my mind like that, and I have always felt ashamed of their existence."

As he pursued his studies in Montpellier, Cowley also found the time to supplement his income with freelance essays and reviews for American publications. He was in the habit of delivering dyspeptic remarks to his friends on the distasteful networking and truckling necessary to the launching of a literary career, but he knew how the system worked. His growing mastery of it—reflecting as well his increasingly polished skills as a literary journalist—is evident in the list of American newspapers and magazines to which Cowley became a regular contributor during his two years in France: Henry Seidel Canby's *Literary Review of the New York Evening Post*; the *New York Herald Tribune*; the august journal *The Bookman*; *The Freeman*, a magazine of politics and the arts similar to *The New Republic*, with Van Wyck Brooks as its literary editor and chief critic; and especially *The Dial*. Many of these pieces were for-the-check reviews, albeit crisply done, of authors and books now long forgotten, but a number of his articles went deeper, grappling with some essential literary questions. In them, one can trace the beginnings of the paths that he would follow as a critic.

Many people have assumed that, given Cowley's close association with the figures of the Lost Generation and some of the antics he would get up to in Paris, he was a prime specimen of the flaming literary youth of the twenties. In fact, his consistent admiration for traditional literary forms, for the practice of writing as an honest craft and not an arcane and dense congeries of private symbols and emotions, and for literature as a richly human activity ran counter to the ideas that governed the literary avant-garde during the early years of the Modernist explosion.

Take the stinging rebuke of the superficial aspects of the Left Bank counterculture in mid-1922 that he wrote for *The Freeman*, "A Brief History of Bohemia." The occasion for the piece was a low-key ceremony in the Luxembourg Gardens honoring the centenary of Henri Murger, whose *Scènes de la vie de bohème* and its offshoots, especially Puccini's opera *La Bohème*, romanticized and immortalized the hand-to-mouth existence of his artistic circle in the Latin Quarter. Cowley debunked the idea that the authentic *la vie Bohème* was being lived once more on the Left Bank and elsewhere. In his dyspeptic view the Bohemian ideal had degenerated into "an esoteric cult, like Theosophy or New Thought, to which a man may adhere throughout his life." He observes that the Bohemia of his day was already "a vast industry"—an international phenomenon with its own far-flung infrastructure of clubs, restaurants, magazines, resorts, retail outlets, and even financiers. Cowley concludes, "Starting as a revolt against the bourgeoisie, [Bohemia] has become as much the property of the bourgeoisie as any other business-venture." (David Brooks would revive this idea eighty years later in his work of "comic sociology," *Bobos in Paradise*.)

Cowley's dissents were also registered in more oblique fashion in a number of other reviews and essays from the period. *The Bookman* assigned Cowley the task of interviewing and profiling seven literary figures (at twenty dollars per), with Ivan Opffer along to draw their portraits; the pieces would run from October 1922 through January 1925. Six of the profiles were of figures from an older generation of French writers; only one of them, Henri Barbusse, author of a classic novel of the Great War, *Under Fire*, is much remembered today, at least in the Anglosphere. From the Montparnasse point of view they looked like distinct back numbers, representatives of an older French tradition of clarity and craft and literary professionalism. But Cowley found much to admire in these men and became good friends with two of them, Pierre Mac Orlan and André Salmon, whom he described as "the hated enemies of the Dada group." The novelist, poet, and crime reporter Salmon in particular was just what he was looking for, an associate of the figures who had gathered around Apollinaire and Picasso in the latter's Montmarte studio earlier in the century. He became Cowley's valued guide to modern French literature and art.

Cowley places Salmon in that circle of writers and artists who had done battle against the older, well-heeled Symbolists, in the process creating new modes of poetry and prose and ways of writing about art. He concludes that Salmon and his circle incarnate the kind of truly distinct literary generation that the more disordered American situation had yet to produce, and that Salmon himself is "not a critic . . . not a novelist, a reporter, not even a writer of verse. He is a type unfortunately rare in modern times: a man of letters who has taken all literature for his province." These observations echo the way Cowley would come to think about his own literary generation, and his own ambitions.

The seventh profile subject was an Irish expatriate living in Paris: James Joyce. The piece was written in late 1922, following a series of meetings with Joyce over the summer, in cafés and once in Joyce's "sour and moldy" room in his run-down hotel. (Cowley was so taken aback by Joyce's emaciation and pained expression of suffering that he forgot his questions and asked, "Is there anything I can do for you, Mr. Joyce?" There was: Cowley was sent out, with some relief, to buy stamps.) *Ulysses* had been published by Sylvia Beach that February of 1922, and it immediately became, especially in Left Bank circles, the book one had to have an opinion about; some people—including

Malcolm Cowley—even went so far as to read it before forming their opinions. The book was less a novel than a phenomenon, a fast-moving front that changed the literary weather for good.

The portrait of Joyce that emerges is distinctly lacking in warmth. It may have been Joyce's own considerable self-regard that put Cowley off; during the average meeting, "he'll tell you, probably, about his struggle to write 'Ulysses.'" To Cowley, Joyce and his masterwork represent an extreme literary case: "He is the limit not alone of the epic novel but of naturalism and frankness, even in a true sense, of romanticism. Along the path that he has followed no one can go further." The piece concludes: "He promenades his intolerable genius under the palms of Nice, with unseeing eyes which stare ahead like those of another poet whom seven cities claimed." The obvious distaste here would linger, as a decade later he would recall that "there was something about the genius as cold as the touch of his long, smooth, cold, wet-marble fingers."

A lot of literary limits were reached in that miraculous year of Modernism, 1922. On November 18 of that year, Marcel Proust died, only a few days after having essentially completed his exhaustive self-excavation *In Search of Lost Time*. Its effect on English readers was delayed, since at the time only the first of its seven volumes, *Swann's Way*, had been translated. But Cowley was one of a small number of Americans who had read the four published volumes in French, and a year later he would collect his thoughts on the book for *The Dial* in his essay "A Monument to Proust."

It was an acute appreciation, but one also laced with reservations. Cowley praises the book as "a comedy of manners as elegant and artificial as Congreve, and it is a Shakespearian tragedy expanded hugely: embracing all of these categories it is limited by none." He notes the uncanny quality of the work's first volume, *Swann's Way*, which "makes an appeal to the senses which are inarticulate and fundamental; it goes deeper than reason; it has magic." But he also sees the book as not being entirely a work of the still-new century: "His age is the one which produced Symbolist poets, Henry James, Debussy. . . . if any age can claim him it is certainly not ours." And he notes the extreme conditions of bodily fragility, personal isolation, and unnatural refinement under which the book was produced: "Hatred for natural objects; fastidious ill health; attraction for everything artificial: his life was the sort which might have been imagined by Huysmans or in the Yellow Book." The price Proust paid for his masterpiece, Cowley judges as radical: "His own death was only a process of externalization; he had turned himself inside out like an orange and sucked it dry, or inscribed himself on a monument"—that monument being the book itself, the creation of which almost entirely superseded Proust's actual life.

———

In March, Malcolm Cowley sat for his exams at the university and was awarded his diploma in French Studies with a *mention très honorable*. His preoccupation with classicism would continue as he began to work on his doctoral thesis on the tragedies of Jean Racine (1639–99). But the Provençal charms of Montpellier had faded and the excitements north in Paris and points east were calling. In May he was pleased to learn that his American Field Service scholarship has been extended for another year.

The wolf at least temporarily banished from the door, he and Peggy moved to Paris for the next two months. The metabolic acceleration was immediate, Cowley writing to Burke shortly after their arrival that "Paris is like cocaine; either it leaves you tremendously elated or sunk in a brown fit of depression."

During Cowley's year of academic rustication his friend Matthew Josephson had plunged into the literary and artistic milieus of Paris with impressive American energy and entrepreneurial zeal. He'd established secure footholds in two key areas: the Dada movement and the world of little magazines. Josephson was key to luring Malcolm Cowley into both.

Matthew Josephson is known more today as a journalist and biographer than as the ambitious poet he was at the start of the twenties. He would go on to write well-received biographies of Émile Zola, Victor Hugo, Stendhal, and Thomas Edison, and a nonfiction work on the buccaneering figures of the Gilded Age, *The Robber Barons*, still regarded as a classic. By the time of Cowley's return, Josephson had fully insinuated himself into the Parisian circle of Dadaists and was embroiled in their hijinks.

The Romanian poet Tristan Tzara, along with Richard Huelsenbeck and Jean Arp, had conceived the Dada movement in the midst of the war in Zurich in 1916, staging outlandish and nonsensical theatrical pieces at their Cabaret Voltaire. Tom Stoppard's brilliant intellectual burlesque *Travesties* makes sport of the fact that Tzara, James Joyce, and Vladimir Ilyich Lenin were all in that city at the same time. Although there is no evidence that any one of these figures met another, Stoppard imagines an enraged Tzara spitting the words "Dada! *Dada!* Dada!" in James Joyce's face for his retrograde belief in the efficacy of art. Joyce imperiously responds, "You are an overexcited little man, with a need for self-expression far beyond your natural gifts. This is not discreditable. Neither does it make you an artist." In real life, Tzara was spitting "Dada!" in the face of a Western civilization that was at that moment committing mechanized human slaughter on an industrial scale unmatched in human history. Dada's aggressive nihilism was a calculatedly irrational response to that murderous irrationality. In this context its inspired nonsense made perfect sense. Tzara had the energy and charisma of a true cultural prophet.

In 1919, Tzara moved his traveling Dada circus to Paris to join the editorial staff of the magazine *Littérature*, a pioneering Surrealist publication begun by the poets Louis Aragon, André Breton, and Philippe Soupault. These Frenchmen had a far sounder claim to belonging to a Lost Generation than any Americans. Something like 1.4 million soldiers, 8 percent of all French men, had died in the war, and as medical officers both Aragon and Breton had had grim firsthand experience of the carnage of the Western Front. For the next few years in Paris the activities of the Dadaists and the Surrealists were basically indistinguishable, as the groups joined forces to *épater les bourgeois*. Or, more accurately perhaps, *écraser*: One of Tzara's manifestos proclaimed, "There is a great negative work of destruction to be accomplished. We must sweep everything away and sweep clean." They went about their work with tireless energy, putting on a series of anarchically inventive and outré balls, theatrical performances, readings, and unclassifiable art stunts that would be judged a failure if they did not manage to cause at least a modest riot or scandal or some kind of physical altercation. Tzara's very first public Parisian appearance set the tone: reading a newspaper article while the loud sound of an electric bell rendered what he read completely inaudible.

It would be some months before Josephson would usher Cowley into the circle of Parisian Dadaists. First he lured him into the vital and backbiting world of the little magazines, at the center of which sat Gorham Munson.

Gorham Munson, today an obscure minor figure, was born in 1896, the son of a minister. In 1916, his senior year at Weslcyan, he had his first addictive encounter with bohemianism on a visit to Greenwich Village, and in college that fall he was, in his word, "electrified" by his encounters with the magazine *Seven Arts*, the work of

Waldo Frank, Van Wyck Brooks's *America's Coming-of-Age*, and Freud's *The Interpretation of Dreams*. By 1919 he was living in the Village himself, contributing pieces to various magazines and feeling the first stirrings of the American postwar literary revolt. He was a serial enthusiast with a short attention span, having already cycled in short order through liberalism, socialism, Soviet communism, and philosophical anarchism. By July 1921 those stirrings had moved him to book passage to France with his wife.

In his physical appearance Munson presented as a kind of self-caricature, in Cowley's words "a heavy and dignified young man, already wax-mustached and bald above the forehead"; a pale complexion and round spectacles completed his prematurely professorial affect. This, along with an air of mildly clueless self-importance, may have contributed to his being underestimated. He had two default modes: unmodulated enthusiasm and aggrieved indignation. He had a genuine instinct for talent, and this had led to his friendship in New York with Hart Crane, whose genius Munson recognized very early. It was Crane who wrote to Matthew Josephson in Paris and brokered the first meeting between the two men, in November of 1921 at Josephson's lodgings. The meeting went well; they had in common the fact that both of them had contributed pieces to the local magazine *Gargoyle*, one of the first of the new transatlantic reviews springing up. But both men also found it wanting in a number of ways and expressed a vague desire for, as Josephson would write, "something better, a magazine in which new writers of talent, bound together by a common outlook on art and life and who were interested in new literary experiment rather than in repeating old patterns, could exhibit their work."

Cowley's recent piece "This Youngest Generation" had lit up Munson's imagination and provided almost the perfect template for such a publication. Munson had the money saved up—a thousand dollars—

to float this enterprise, and Josephson, who knew all the writers mentioned in the article, could pull in their contributions. When on a trip to Berlin in January 1922 he discovered that the hyperinflation of the German mark meant, among other pleasant things for holders of American currency, that five hundred copies of a small magazine could be printed for a mere twenty dollars, Munson agreed to go ahead.

So, what one might call the Wars of *Secession* began. Munson hit on the title while visiting the famed Secession gallery in Vienna, where the painters, architects, and graphic artists—most famously, Gustav Klimt—of the Vienna Secession group had exhibited their work. He found the word fresh and expressive and appropriated it. The magazine had no connection whatsoever to the Vienna group, but its distinctly Art Nouveau typeface and cover art hinted otherwise. Munson later wrote that "Mars was certainly present at the birth of *Secession*." Like so many other little magazines, its editorial policy and raison d'être were conceived in opposition to other groups and publications. In his announcement circular, Munson aggressively promised, "It will, in its early numbers, expose the private correspondences, hidden sins and secret history of its American contemporaries, *The Dial, The Little Review, Broom, Poetry*, etc. It already notes in current literature very much that demands hilarious comment." He made good on that incautious promise in the first number of *Secession* with a broadside against *The Dial* for its supposed lack of editorial coherence ("It is no wonder a copy of *The Dial* gives the impression of splitting apart in one's hand") and its continued championing of an already declining Sherwood Anderson. He concludes with heavy-handed sarcasm: "The existence of this *Yale-Review*-in-a-Harvard-blazer is one of the bitter necessities calling for *Secession*." *Broom* and *The Little Review* would come in for Munson's contempt in the second number.

Cowley was present at the creation of *Secession*. Munson's announcement quotes his essay "This Youngest Generation" as its editorial policy, and the first issue of the magazine prominently featured one poem of his, "Day Coach," and the second issue two poems, "Play It for Me Again" and "Poem." But he found Munson's use of his essay to be a doubtful compliment, and he was made uneasy by Munson's un-bridled attacks on magazines that he was also being published in—especially *The Dial*. Nor at the time was he entirely sympathetic to *Secession*'s Dada-slanted contents, with contributions by Louis Aragon, Tristan Tzara, and an enthusiastic apologia for Dada's cultural program and its positive implications for American writers by one William Bray. This piece in particular got up Cowley's nose and he wrote a sharply critical letter about it to Matthew Josephson, not knowing that he had written the piece under a pseudonym. A correspondence of escalating antipathy followed, culminating in a final letter from Josephson typed Dadaistically on Italian toilet paper.

By the time the Cowleys arrived in Paris in the summer of 1922, Munson had returned to New York after his year abroad. He had delegated the editorial duties of *Secession* to Josephson, a decision he would come to regret. At around that time, Munson took a long walk with Kenneth Burke, after which Burke became the third member of the editorial triumvirate of the magazine, with the understanding (or so Munson thought) that submissions needed to be endorsed by two of the three principals. Burke would write to Cowley modestly of his "fond hope of making the magazine a nucleus for a self-hypnotizing group of fifteen or so men interested in literature." Munson had far bigger plans.

Josephson and his wife, meanwhile, had departed Paris for Rome, arriving the day before the historic march of Mussolini's Blackshirts into the city. They dropped in on the offices of *Broom* there to pick up some small checks. During their stay they were entertained by the chief editor and bankroller of that magazine, Harold Loeb. Although he was a Guggenheim on his mother's side, he lived in Europe on a modest income she provided, and underwrote *Broom* with nine thousand dollars realized from the sale of his bookstore, the Sunwise Turn in New York. He'd started *Broom* in 1921 with the poet-editor Alfred Kreymborg. Their intention was to build a sort of bridge between the art and literature of America and Europe. The production values of the magazine far outstripped its competition—rag paper, exquisite design, tasteful typography. Kreymborg had just resigned his post over editorial disagreements, and Josephson's point of view found a ready ear. A job opportunity with a salary beckoned.

Matthew Josephson was nothing if not an operator. In conversations with Loeb he urged on him an editorial policy that was altogether more cutting-edge. He more or less colonized Loeb's mind. He got a job offer as an associate editor of *Broom* for his efforts, a post that Gorham Munson himself had been angling for, even though he had attacked the magazine in *Secession* as "a general merchandise store" and a "kind of clearing house."

Josephson took the job. Loeb, facing a thousand-dollar-a-month deficit for his magazine, had decided to move *Broom*'s headquarters to Berlin, where, thanks to hyperinflation, the printing prices were even lower and the quality even higher. After a pleasant summer in the Tyrolean Alps, Josephson and his wife moved to Berlin themselves. He was now on the masthead of two English-language literary magazines, *Secession* and *Broom*, which had considerable overlap in contributors and missions.

Back in Paris that summer, Malcolm Cowley took his first step from being a contributor to *Secession* to a deeper involvement. He and Peggy had a Wanderjahr of their own that summer, through Brussels and Munich and finally Vienna, where he was to deliver the material for the third number of *Secession* to the printer and proofread it and be on press.

Josephson and Cowley had a scornful opinion of Munson and viewed him as little more than a front man for their own machinations. In New York, Munson, blissfully ignorant of that, proceeded as if *Secession* was a good-faith partnership. He drummed up an astonishing amount of publicity for a five-hundred-run literary magazine with a subscription list of fifty, including praise from Waldo Frank, a critical trend-piece on "the secessionists" or "the new patricians" by Louis Untermeyer in *The New Republic*, other articles by Van Wyck Brooks and Edith Sitwell, and editorial comments in *The New York Times*, *The Dial*, *The Criterion*, and similar highbrow publications. With guileless energy and one suggestive semi-manifesto and twenty-five dollars paid to a Viennese printer, he had conjured up a secessionist movement in the wider literary imagination. That no such thing actually existed was almost beside the point.

Delivering the packet of materials for the third number of *Secession* to the printer in Vienna in September, Cowley and Peggy moved on. He'd been pleased by the second issue of *Secession*, but even though he had a poem in the third issue, he would write to Burke that it "stinks of bad writing, Dada, and the ghetto." He particularly disliked Josephson's heavy-handed fictional chronicle of voyeurism, "Peep-Peep-Parrish," which Josephson had insolently included against Munson's wishes, and he declared that "the third number of *Secession* has to be suppressed and that Matty alone cannot edit another number. Otherwise, to save our self-respect we have got to secede from *Secession*." But when the Cowleys next visited the Josephsons for a fortnight in the Tyrolean Alps, Cowley was won over again. The two young literati on the make joined forces for their next target: *Broom*.

Harold Loeb would be all but forgotten today but for Hemingway's cruel and anti-Semitic caricature of him as Robert Cohn, Lady Brett's lover, in *The Sun Also Rises*. Loeb, a graduate of Princeton, where he was a varsity wrestler, was something of a seeker. He and his first wife had lived for a time at Brocken, a utopian community in upstate New

York of people inclined toward a sort of spiritually minded socialism. Later he had managed the famed bookstore in Greenwich Village the Sunwise Turn, a hotspot of advanced anarchistic and artistic ideas. Although Loeb had literary ambitions of his own, *Broom* had been conceived in an altogether more disinterested and idealistic spirit than *Secession*. He was not ginning up a school or movement; he was simply trying to find the most interesting literary and artistic manifestations of his time. This openness was both *Broom*'s weakness and its strength.

Loeb and Kreymborg had cultivated all the right people upon their arrival in Paris in 1921, who looked warmly upon *Broom*, in part because it paid a competitive per-word rate, in dollars. A reliable cast of high-profile contributors and allies, along with a subscription base in the hundreds, newsstand distribution in the low thousands, and a print run as high as four thousand, made *Broom* a far more secure presence than *Secession* in the world of little magazines. The publication that Loeb and his associates put out stood head and shoulders above its competition in circulation and production values, which helped to camouflage the persistent financial challenges that made *Broom*'s continued existence an uncertain proposition.

Cowley arranged to meet with Harold Loeb in Innsbruck in early September. Cowley had already contributed two of his best early poems to *Broom*, "Chateau de Soupir" and "Mountain Farm," and as Loeb would write, "I wanted more from Malcolm Cowley and Matthew Josephson, more from E. E. Cummings," and new material from Burke, Brown, and Crane. He thought that Cowley and Company "possessed a positive attitude which contrasted strongly with the negation and despair that had obsessed so many of the American literati in recent decades." Loeb has left a vivid description of the deliberate, slow-talking Cowley as he saw him at this first meeting: "Looking like a cross between Foxy Grandpa and the darker Katzenjammer

Kid, Malcolm refused to be hurried. When a question was put to him, the lines between his eyes deepened and the quizzical expression froze. Often the silence seemed interminable. But when he finally spoke, his words meant something." Cowley came away with a new job as a sort of roving editor and translator for *Broom*, which he saw, opportunistically, as "a comfortable lever for meeting any one I want to know in Paris." Future issues of the magazine would now carry the unmistakable imprint of the Cowley/Josephson axis.

Whatever reservations Malcolm Cowley may have had about Harold Loeb evaporated when he read Loeb's long essay "The Mysticism of Money," which ran in the September 1922 issue of *Broom*. The piece was an energetic attack on the anti-Americanism of Stearns's *Civilization in the United States* ("the greatest danger to America: the imitation of European art") and a paean to the beauty and practical aesthetics of American business civilization as found in our skyscrapers, apartment buildings, steam shovels and threshing machines, bathroom fixtures, advertising and commercial art, silent comedies and horse operas, and to our vital native language, "vigorous, crude, expressive, alive with metaphors, Rabelaisian." To Loeb these were all admirable manifestations of our quasi-religious moneymaking culture, and they had already attracted the favorable attention of advanced European artists and intellectuals.

As a cultural essay, "The Mysticism of Money" suffers from a tendency toward overstatement. But as a counterpunch against the prevailing knee-jerk snobbism and despair regarding American culture, it was perfectly timed, and as a kind of manifesto for *Broom*'s mission going forward, it snapped its editorial vision into sharp focus immediately. It was an important turning point, and Cowley in particular responded to it with the fervor of a convert, writing to Loeb enthusiastically: "There was a set of clear ideas, ideas which are fresh to American literature and which ought to revitalize it. . . . Here is

Broom's declaration of principles; all that remains is to apply them."
He would begin that application within a week or so of reading Loeb's
piece by producing one of his own, that barbed lampoon of Harold
Stearns.

The Cowleys' final stop on their itinerary was Berlin. With its swol-
len population of crippled war veterans, valuta-chasing profiteers, sex
workers of all persuasions, and soulless predatory businessmen, the city
resembled the moral hellscape of its George Grosz caricatures, soon to
appear in *Broom*. Cowley would remember, "The general atmosphere
was that of a frenzied carnival in an asylum for incurables." He would
transact editorial business with Josephson and Loeb in his time there,
but the most consequential meeting he had would be his first encounter with the immensely impressive Louis Aragon, the pioneering Surrealist poet who "with his proud head and his ingratiating white-toothed
smile . . . looked like the first intruder from the world of living men,
like Orpheus in hell." Cowley would become a lifelong friend and admirer of this brilliant figure, as well as his steadfast critical champion
and frequent translator. But he could not share Aragon's taste for Berlin's garishly electrified urban disorder, and after three weeks he and
Peggy caught a Paris-bound train full of smugglers carrying German
butter in suitcases and baby carriages under the seat for resale.

Thus began the hectic and eventful final phase of Malcolm Cowley's pivotal two years abroad. These were the eight months, from December 1922 to early August 1923, that would lead the literary
historian Daniel Aaron to call him a "Dadaist extraordinaire." This
brief but intense episode of involvement with radical experimentation
and direct action meant that for the rest of his life, he would often be
taken for a wild man and sometimes called to account for it.

That winter the Cowleys found lodgings in three rooms above a
blacksmith's shop, not in Paris, but fifty miles away in the village of
Giverny, made famous by its resident Claude Monet, still painting his

immortal water lily canvases there at age eighty. It had been an art colony with a significant American presence before the war, but those older residents now looked without favor on this new incursion of wild youngsters. The rural atmosphere of the ancient Norman town suited Cowley; he could fish in the Epte River, where he caught his first European trout. It was a perfect place for him to produce his freelance articles and poems and, toward the end of his time in France, make progress on his doctoral thesis on Racine.

Once every week or two, Cowley would get on a train to spend a Wednesday in Paris. He would catch a branch line crowded with peasants for market day and transfer to the Paris express, his mind racing with excitement over the stimulation to come. His writing about these trips in *Exile's Return* yield some of the most ecstatic passages in the book:

> Paris! You leaped into the first empty taxicab outside the station and ordered the driver to hurry. In Paris the subways were impossibly slow, and the taxis never drove fast enough as you raced from one appointment to another, from an art gallery to a bookshop where you had no time to linger, and thence to a concert you could never quite sit through—faster, faster, there was always something waiting that might be forever missed unless you hammered on the glass and told the driver to go faster. Paris was a great machine for stimulating the nerves and sharpening the senses. Paintings and music, street noises, shops, flower markets, modes, fabrics, poems, ideas, everything seemed to lead toward a half-sensual, half-intellectual swoon. Inside the cafés, color, perfume, taste and delirium could be poured from one bottle or many bottles.

On one of those Parisian Wednesdays in December of 1922, Matthew Josephson introduced Cowley to his Dadaist friends André Breton, Louis Aragon, Philippe Soupault, and shortly thereafter, Tristan Tzara. These were serious men who nevertheless knew how to have fun, and to fight to defend their point of view. Cowley put aside his classical tendencies and reservations to plunge into the Dada movement himself. The Dadaists had vast reserves of intelligence, charisma, energy, and intention, and their public manifestations, a species of cultural action paintings, were impossible to resist. Unlike Proust, they would never retreat into a cork-lined room. Unlike Eliot, their emotional timbre held not a trace of melancholy or neurosis or despair, instead displaying a kind of proto–Marx Brothers anarchic humor. Unlike Joyce in his *Ulysses* phase, their literary works were produced in weeks or days or even mere minutes rather than long years, and they did not require equally long years to fully comprehend. They were just what Cowley was looking for, and soon he became one of their company. And on some days they would travel themselves to their new friend Malcolm Cowley's lodgings to disrupt Giverny's verdant peace with some raucously alcoholic parties. Fully won over, he would now declare that the Dadaists were "the most amusing people in Paris."

One evening Louis Aragon took Cowley and the entire staff of the magazine *Littérature* plus wives and mistresses to a performance of Raymond Roussel's play *Locus Solus*, which for one brief week provoked *Rite of Spring*–worthy demonstrations of vocal outrage or support in its audience. Produced by Roussel himself at a cost of six hundred thousand francs, the play was an exercise in absurdism without a shred of narrative sense, featuring pallbearers, a coffin, a professor, several judges murdered in the first act and revived in the second, and similar irrelevancies. As described by Matthew Josephson, "in one climactic scene a sea siren swims about in a big glass tank filled with undersea foliage, while her lover stands outside addressing interminable speeches to her." At the play's end the professor—who has revealed the work's inner logic (and perhaps that of the Dada movement itself) when he declaims, "What I lose in clarity I gain in mystery"—is carried up and away from a high chair by a rope after an invocation of Saturn.

At each performance Aragon and Breton and Company would loudly applaud the play at every instance of the hate-watching audience's disapproval, who would then even more loudly disapprove of the applause, in a spiral of mutually reinforced anger. The police would reliably arrive—it's not really Dada unless the cops have to be called—and encircle Breton and escort him out as he delivered a speech in defense of spectators' rights. Cowley was bemused but also impressed; he would write a brief and vivid account of the whole experience for *Broom* in which he confessed that "the finale . . . swept me off my feet" and "there was something magnificent in the pointlessness of the scene."

Back in Andover, New Jersey, Burke was becoming increasingly alarmed by the effect that association with the European adepts of the higher nonsense was having on his two friends and fellow *Secession* editors. "Stop Making Sense" was not a program he was ever going to sign on for. Another development that disturbed him was Cowley's increasing interest in the particulars of American life and civilization, however raw and unrefined, as the subject and seed bed for art. He would write to Burke that he had "right about faced on the question of the importance of American material. The change is largely psychological. America in the distance begins to loom up as a land of promise, something barbaric and decorative and rich." This undoubtedly reflects the influence of his new Dada friends, who so admired the speed and vitality and unselfconscious vulgarity of American material culture and especially its music and movies.

Burke wrote back to Cowley in an attempt to get his mind right on the matter of America. He argued that Cowley had mistaken the spectacle of sheer quantity in American culture—so many light bulbs on Broadway, so many floors in our skyscraper—for genuine quality. Channeling Harold Stearns and Van Wyck Brooks at their bluntest, he complained, "There is, for instance, not a trace of that really dignified richness, the richness that makes for peasants, household gods, traditions. America has become the wonder of the world simply because America is the purest concentration point for the vices and vulgarities of the world." He wrote dismissively, "The trouble with Dada is that there are no first-rate Dadaists. They are swine lying in a whole pen of pearls. I refuse to hear more of them."

Cowley's retort was scathing: "Shit, Kenneth, since when have you become a furniture salesman." He compares Burke to a rattle-brained American woman he'd met in Giverny who enthused interminably on the superiority of European wallpaper and even flour paste to the American products. His time in Europe had had the happy effect of freeing him from such prejudices. He high-spiritedly proclaims, "American is just as Goddamned good as Europe—worse in some ways, better in others, just as appreciative, fresher material, inclined to stay at peace instead of marching into the Ruhr. I'm not ashamed to take off my coat anywhere and tell these cunt-lapping Europeans that I'm an American citizen. Wave old Glory! Peace! Normalcy!" With tongue only partly in cheek, he giddily goes all caps: "THE ONLY SALVATION FOR AMERICAN LITERATURE IS TO BORROW A LITTLE PUNCH AND CONFIDENCE FROM AMERICAN BUSINESS."

During this time the Wars of *Secession* were rapidly escalating. None of the combatants behaved well. In September of 1922, Munson had submitted an overlong monograph on Waldo Frank to *Broom*; two months later Loeb tardily but politely declined the piece. Munson was already steaming over this delayed rejection when Josephson sent him another letter, a long one, critiquing the piece. This sent Munson into a rage, and a volley of increasingly testy letters between him and Loeb ensued. Munson's pique was amplified when he learned of Cowley's having become an editor of *Broom*, when he had expected that he was in line to become the magazine's American agent.

Late that year, Josephson pulled his most egregious editorial stunt. Munson had entrusted Cowley's Harvard classmate the poet John Brooks Wheelwright with additional material for the fourth and fifth issues of *Secession*. Wheelwright, an eccentric cane-wielding, bowler-hatted Boston Brahmin, was on his way to Italy, and Munson had accepted his offer to oversee the future printings of *Secession* there and to pay for them as well—though in fact Wheelwright knew nothing about the protocols of print, including proofreading.

For the fourth issue, of January 1923, Munson and Burke had included six poems by one Richard Ashton, a pseudonym. One poem in particular, "The Jilted Moon," struck Josephson, Cowley, and Wheelwright as particularly bad, so they jocularly decided to cut all but the last three lines: "O moon, / Thou art naught but Chinese, / Only Chinese." That was how the poem was printed.

Josephson later made light of the jape. "It was irresponsible; it was not editing; it was murder. But it was done, on the impulse of the moment, and perhaps after a good many potations of red wine." The humor of the thing was lost on Gorham Munson, who, when he saw the new issue, proceeded to black out the truncated poem in every issue he could lay his hands on. In a rage he demanded that Wheelwright offer an apology in the next issue. Wheelwright did in fact print Ashton's "The Jilted Moon," in full this time, in the July 1923 issue, but his rambling and archly incoherent statement was far from contrite.

Wheelwright compounded the damage on multiple counts. He botched the typesetting and printing of the magazine; surviving copies of the fourth, fifth, and sixth issues of *Secession* feature dozens of corrections by hand of the many typos and misspellings that got by him. He undertook to revise and "correct" a Munson essay on the work of E. E. Cummings. And his mishandling of Hart Crane's three-part poem "For the Marriage of Faustus and Helen" in the seventh issue of *Secession* would become infamous. *Broom* had already published the second part of the poem; Wheelwright, misconstruing communications from Cowley, Crane, and Munson, published the poem without that second section, simply noting parenthetically, "(*Printed in* Broom, *January 1923 under the title* The Springs of Guilty Song)." Munson and Crane were close friends, so this blunder hit home. Once again he had to take up an instrument of correction, this time a razor blade, and excise the butchered poem from the issue.

Secession, begun with such high literary ambition, had taken on the aspect of a Three Stooges short, and Munson felt like the butt of the jokes. Cowley and Josephson had regarded him from the start with genial contempt as a kind of useful idiot. Josephson tries to underplay their offenses by admitting that "we were young sparks then, often tactless, and even at times a little malicious with each other."

Another incident of youthful impudence would take place in Giverny in June of 1923. A heavily alcoholic dinner had taken place at a restaurant, which included Cowley, John Dos Passos, E. E. Cummings, Louis Aragon, Harold Loeb, and James Butler, Claude Monet's half-American grandson. Everyone subsequently retreated back to Cowley's upstairs study for more drink and talk. A by now quite drunk Cowley, in Loeb's telling, pottering about, looking for material to build a fire, began repeating with excitement, "Too much *merde*, too much junk. Words aren't enough." Aragon and Dos Passos and Cummings responded to this with great enthusiasm. (Cowley remembers it as a speech against book fetishism because his American books could not be sold in France and were too burdensome to ship back to the

States.) Picking up a bunch of books and magazines, Cowley shouted, "Good only for bonfires!" The others vocally agreed. So they all, Loeb included, grabbed handfuls of books and pamphlets and copies of the *Nouvelle revue française* from the shelves and proceeded to tear them up and pile the results onto an asbestos apron before the stove. Cowley put a match to the pile—"a gesture in the Dada manner," he would call it—and soon a roaring blaze took hold. In the accounts of both Cowley and Loeb, it was E. E. Cummings who sprang into action, unzipping his pants and urinating strategically on the fire until it was reduced to a smoldering and malodorous mess. (One version of this event has Cowley pissing on a leather-bound volume of Racine, but he vigorously denied it.) All that accomplished, the revelers went outside, where Loeb challenged Cowley to a wrestling match. But for all the holds he applied from his days on the Princeton varsity, he found Cowley to be utterly immovable. Then everyone went to bed or caught the last train back to Paris.

———

In Ernest Hemingway's story "The Snows of Kilimanjaro"(1936), a famous writer on safari, slowly dying of gangrene, casts his mind back to scenes from his life. One of the places he remembers is Paris in the twenties, and this in particular: "And there in the café as he passed was that American poet with a pile of saucers in front of him and a stupid look on his potato face talking about the Dada movement with a Roumanian who said his name was Tristan Tzara, who always wore a monocle and had a headache." This is the published version; in the first draft the sentence read, "And there in the café as he passed was Malcolm Cowley." The animus here feels fresh and strong even after a decade and a half. Hemingway was one of those people on whom nothing was lost—especially if it concerned the pecking order of prestige and success in whatever literary milieu he found himself. Clearly something about Cowley bugged him, and it's a good guess that that something involved his having become a rising star as a poet and influential editor and critic at a time when Hemingway was struggling to get his work printed anywhere.

Malcolm Cowley would become very good friends with Ernest Hemingway and his most consistent, penetrating, and loyal critic. Even at the very end of his life he would be defending Hemingway against the mounting attacks on his stature and artistry. But the beginning of their association was rocky. They met at the home of Ezra Pound near the Luxembourg Gardens in the summer of 1923. Hemingway was already there when Cowley arrived for a visit, "a big young man with intent eyes and a toothbrush mustache." Pound introduced them and when Cowley said he had heard about him, "Hemingway gave a slow Midwestern grin." Pound served as one of Hemingway's early literary mentors, and word of his unusual early stories and Pound's high opinion of them as something special and new was already circulating on the Left Bank that spring. Hemingway was working at the time as a reporter for the International News Service, and he later took Cowley to their offices for a look around.

Almost as soon as the American expatriate colony had begun to gather in Montparnasse, feature journalists arrived to tell curious readers back home all about their colorful garb and outré notions and mores. Much like what would happen later with the beatniks in Greenwich Village and the hippies of Haight-Ashbury, these exotic people so seemingly remote from the constricting conventions of middle-class existence made for colorful copy. Some of these pieces were admiring if also a bit taken aback, some were arch and faux-anthropological in the familiar look-at-these-crazy-bohemians-at-play mode, and some were harsh and scornfully judgmental. Hemingway produced an especially nasty specimen of the latter for his employer at the time, the *Toronto Star*, on March 25, 1922. His target was the Rotonde and (he implies) the talentless posers and trust-fund wasters and clueless tourists from the States who swarmed the place nightly. The first sentences set the rancid tone immediately: "The scum of Greenwich Village, New York, has been skimmed off and deposited in large ladlesful on that section of Paris adjacent to the Café Rotonde. . . . the oldest scum, the thickest scum and the scummiest scum has come across the ocean somehow, and with its afternoon and evening levees has made the Rotonde the leading Latin Quarter show place for tourists in search of atmosphere." The pile-on continues with mean-spirited and misogynistic caricatures of the women patrons in particular and the unsupported assertion that "the artists of Paris who are turning out creditable work resent and loathe the Rotonde crowd."

What was eating Hemingway? Certainly jealousy and frustration were root causes. At this point he and his new wife, Hadley, had lived in Paris for less than four months and Hemingway, as ambitious an American writer as has ever lived, had great difficulty placing his unusual, stripped-down stories in even the smallest magazines. Under the tutelage of both Gertrude Stein, who was teaching him the value of simple colloquial English, and Ezra Pound, who was focusing his attention on the aesthetic uses of the resonant, precisely rendered image, he was writing stories that would revolutionize the literary language of the twentieth century. But no one was buying; with minor exceptions his literary work would not see print until Robert McAlmon's Contact Press published *Three Stories and Ten Poems* in August 1923. He was a legendarily hard worker, though, and the high proportion of literary layabouts in the Left Bank's café society aroused his contempt. Hemingway's preferred boîte was La Closerie des Lilas, a few blocks down the boulevard Montparnasse from its intersection with boulevard Raspail, the bustling Times Square of Americans on the Left Bank. He would sit for hours in the day largely undisturbed at the tranquil brasserie, hard at work on his fiction.

In truth, Hemingway was not as socially chaste and remote from the scrum of the scum as he pretended. The writer Nathan Asch remembered that on certain evenings he would, with a studied air of distraction, come striding past the Dome and act surprised when some other writer there would stop him and bring him back to the café, "an overwhelming prize." Even at that time Hemingway possessed a powerful charisma and it needed an audience to be properly appreciated. He would also have well known that the Dome was the best place to procure the true gen on who was up and who was down in the American colony.

At the time of the *Toronto Star* piece, Hemingway would not yet have seen Cowley at the Rotonde or the Dome since he was living in Montpellier. But he was aware of him, because Cowley's poems and reviews were appearing regularly in *The Dial*, a magazine that had turned down some of Hemingway's poems that Pound had sent to Scofield Thayer. One Cowley piece that Hemingway paid particular attention to was his essay "A Monument to Proust." We know this because the title of the piece is used in a strange poem Hemingway published in the obscure magazine *Der Querschnitt*, "The Soul of Spain": "The Dial does a monument to Proust. / We have done a monument to Ezra." But by the time the two men first met at Pound's place, Cowley had made himself highly visible with his new Dada friends, raucous cultural anarchists alien to Hemingway's temperament and style.

The fracas in question took place on July 14, 1923—Bastille Day. The haut monde had deserted Paris for the summer, and the hoi polloi were energetically celebrating the national holiday, Cowley remembered, with "a vast plebian carnival, a general madness in which we had eagerly joined." Now about a dozen of Cowley's circle were seated at the Dome. Present at the table were Cowley and his wife, Peggy,

Harold Loeb and Kitty Cannell, the cosmopolitan American painter Laurence Vail and his sister Clotilde and his then-wife Peggy Guggenheim, Jim Butler and Louis Aragon. Various other revelers would join the group from time to time, including Tristan Tzara and Robert McAlmon. They all were well lubricated to the point that the counsels of common sense had disappeared. So when Laurence Vail suddenly suggested, "Let's go over and assault the proprietor of the Rotonde," Cowley instantly responded, "Let's."

The Rotonde attracted a more Continental crowd than the Dome. A certain percentage of those patrons were politically inclined and Cowley claimed that "proletarian revolts were still being planned, over coffee in the evening, by quiet men." The proprietor was suspected of being a paid informer of the police to listen in on these conversations and finger revolutionary plotters. He also stood accused of having treated some American women with the disdain usually reserved for prostitutes. "A thoroughly disagreeable character," in Cowley's view, who needed to be brought to account.

The group of cultural vigilantes on a mission strode across the crowded boulevard and entered the Rotonde single file. Louis Aragon denounced the proprietor in shapely periods as a contemptible *mouchard* (stool pigeon). The waiters, smelling trouble, formed a defensive formation around their boss. Laurence Vail launched his own volley of insults in rapid French. Then Malcolm Cowley, impatient with all this speechifying, decided to take action and do the American thing: He pushed through the phalanx of waiters and socked the proprietor on the jaw. He was quickly hustled out the door and the group of vigilantes reassembled across the street at the Dome and were reluctantly convinced by Cowley to continue the party elsewhere in Paris. The event was quickly forgotten, as stupid drunken events so often are.

That might have been that, except that sometime after midnight, when Cowley and Company returned to the Dome, he caught sight of the proprietor of the Rotonde and, newly enraged, loudly and most unwisely denounced him once more as a *petit mouchard* and a *salaud* ("bastard"). Shortly thereafter, he found himself being hustled off to the station house by two policemen in blue at either elbow, the proprietor walking alongside them. "I knew I was in trouble," Cowley would write. One of the policemen, visibly drunk, amused himself with some verbal and physical sport: "'I won't punch you in the nose like the New York policemen,' said the drunken man, punching me in the nose." Presenting Cowley to the desk sergeant, the cop rolled up his pants to show a small scratch, the result, he claimed, of being kicked in the shins. Cowley was booked, correctly, for assaulting the proprietor of the Rotonde, and, falsely, for resisting arrest and assaulting a police officer, a far more serious affair.

Tristan Tzara, seeing Cowley being frog-marched away, hurried back to the Dome to retrieve his identification papers and sound the alarm. Peggy Cowley, who had to be roused from an attack of rheumatism in Loeb's apartment on the rue Blanche, and Louis Aragon arrived with the papers and some cash at the station, the flic was bribed with 130 francs to drop the charge of assault ("at least four times more than was necessary," Cowley would write—was there a price list posted?), and he was released after a night in jail.

The preliminary hearing was held the next evening; in the interim "nine young ladies in evening gowns," including Kitty Cannell, Clotilde Vail, and Peggy Guggenheim, had been rounded up and persuaded to testify that Cowley had not been present at the affray and the whole thing was a hoax invented by the café proprietor. His new friend André Salmon, who as a highly visible crime reporter had judicial clout, weighed in with the magistrate on Cowley's status as a respected *écrivain*. The trial was postponed from day to day and finally dropped altogether.

Within a few days the whole thing became a literal international incident when an embroidered article about it appeared in the *New York Tribune* on July 19, 1923, under the headline "Prize American Literary 'Eggs' Boil Over in Paris Latin Quarter." The unsigned piece stated that Cowley, John Dos Passos, Gilbert Seldes, and E. E. Cummings were each fined a hundred francs for their misbehavior. No other account even mentions the last three men. The reporter claimed that when Cowley ("who writes delicate poetry and is no giant") had first volunteered for the mission he was told, "This is a job for a ten-minute egg. [Hence the headline.] You stay here and we'll let you write an ode about it"—surely a complete fabrication. Further fictionalization occurred when he asserted that the gendarmes rounded up several other poets and writers.

Another version of events emanated from Robert McAlmon, no admirer of Cowley and vice versa. But he does claim to have been one of the witnesses who showed up at the preliminary hearing to testify to the bad character of a proprietor "noted for his evil disposition and lack of manners," thereby helping to spare Cowley six months of jail time. In his memoir *Being Geniuses Together*, first published in 1934, McAlmon puts the boot in by calling Cowley "duly ponderous, the young intellectual fairly slow on the uptake." Cowley would return the disfavor in 1968 in a review of the book's reissue by writing that McAlmon was "radically unteachable" and "never in his life wrote so much as a memorable sentence."

To his surprise, Malcolm Cowley discovered that his punch heard 'round the world had acted as a career accelerant. His French literary friends were unaccustomed to the (apparently) common American resort to fisticuffs. "I had performed an act to which all their favorite catchwords could be applied." Some of these were "disinterested" (motivated by considerations of public morality, not personal animus); "violence" and "disdain" for the law; and an "arbitrary and significant gesture." "For the first time in my life I became a public character."

What followed were invitations to dinners and cocktail parties, interviews with the press, solicitations of his work from literary reviews across Europe, even translations of his poems about American skyscrapers and movies and machines in Russian magazines. If he experienced anything resembling contrition or remorse, there is no evidence of it.

At the same time that all this pissing and punching was going on, Cowley was hard at work on his elegant essay on Jean Racine and the literary culture of seventeenth-century France. What makes this even more surprising is that, under the influence of Louis Aragon, Cowley's reading had shifted decisively away from classicism, and he was immersing himself, his biographer tells us, in "such English and French romantics as Monk Lewis, Lord Byron, Gérard de Nerval, and Petrus Borel." And yet, as he wrote to Burke, he was "working on the monumental Racine . . . every night I recite verses to put myself to sleep. Racine can be tremendous."

The effort paid off in a piece of critical writing that announced, more clearly than any other essay he did in his years in France, his potential to develop into a major critic. He places Racine firmly within the conventions of the French theater of the seventeenth century, "suggesting," as he told Burke, "that the existence of conventions is more important than their exact nature." But he sees his subject as well in social and historical context, boldly asserting that "Versailles is one of the two perfect expressions of the seventeenth century in France. The other is the tragedies of Jean Racine." He writes that "this society evolved a set of conventions by which the tragedies of Racine are governed," implying that literature of value cannot be separated from the world in which it is produced, an insight that would inform much of his best criticism. At a time of feverish experimentation in literature and the arts, Cowley calmly looks back almost three centuries to consider the virtues of an enforced formalism and extreme refinement. As he declared, in a personal ars poetica:

The elements of literature are not words but emotions and ideas. To be abstract a literature need not be unintelligible; on the contrary. An abstract literature is one in which ideas or emotions, expressed with the greatest possible exactness, are combined into a unity which expresses a formal value and which is something more than a copy of experience. Evidently Racine comes nearer to this ideal than Gertrude Stein, and immensely nearer than those writers of correct verses who invoke his name today.

Cowley projects himself imaginatively into the world that Racine lived and wrote in, making the reader feel how inextricably linked it was to the literary choices he made. In the future he would do the same thing for his contemporaries and those American writers who came before them. He makes no mention of the piece in *Exile's Return*, perhaps because of the incongruity of its appearing in the midst of so much disorder and misbehavior. But he certainly grasped the value of what he had written at the time, since he arranged to have two hundred pamphlet copies of it produced by a French printer. The essay also ran in two consecutive issues of *The Freeman*. His literary circle of friends were much impressed by it.

The Racine essay was the last piece of writing Cowley finished before he and Peggy boarded a French liner in August of 1923 to return to New York. He would underplay to Kenneth Burke the significance of his two-year sojourn in France: "The famous two years is ending with little accomplished and much learned." This is wrong, at least on the accomplishment side of the ledger. He had established himself, as a poet, a critic, and a literary journalist, as someone whom the editors of the most prestigious magazines and newspapers of the time could depend on for first-rate work. In producing "This Youngest Generation" he had had a once-in-a-lifetime bolt of intuition about his generational cohort that he would elaborate and draw upon for the rest of his life. In part from the perspective that time and distance lend and in part from the influence of his Dada friends, he could see America not as a cultural wasteland but as a country and a subject of great vitality and interest, with its flaws and strengths just like any other country. By being so prominently on the scene and in the mix during a time and place that would become more mythic with each passing year, he had shed his provincialism and acquired a glamour that would lend him considerable prestige and authority that would never wane. These were inarguably two of the most important years of Malcolm Cowley's literary life.

FIVE.

HOME AGAIN, HOME AGAIN

———

Malcolm and Peggy Cowley left Paris on August 2, 1923, the day President Harding died. Ten days later they arrived in Calvin Coolidge's America at the French Line pier in New York. They had five dollars to their name and no favorable rate of exchange to make those dollars go further. No one greeted them at the pier, they could not afford a hotel room, and they had no plans for lodging or anywhere to send their trunk. After a few phone calls, these immediate problems were solved: They were put up for the moment by Matthew Josephson in Greenwich Village, as he and Hannah had returned from France some months previously. They shortly found an apartment on the top floor of a building at 16 Dominick Street at the then-remote southern border of Greenwich Village, "almost in the shadow of the Woolworth Building" and today just a few yards from the entrance to the Holland Tunnel. Cowley would remember it as "the most battered and primitive lodging to be found New York."

A spiritual deflation on the part of Americans returning from time in France, especially to New York City, is an almost universal experience. In *Exile's Return*, Cowley wrote, "New York, to one returning from Paris or London, seemed the least human of all babylons." Despite the fact that Cowley was returning after two years to a country and a city now well into a social, cultural, economic, and technological revolution, he found himself confronting the same set of problems his American Field Service fellowship had allowed him to leave behind: money and time.

He certainly took note of all the visible changes taking place and the fevered excitement in the air. The stock market was on a sharply rising curve and factories and office buildings were being built to supply and service the new consumer economy and its thirst for goods and diversions. Prohibition had lent an air of illicit seductiveness to the once perfectly legal act of ordering a drink. A fabled nightlife featuring showgirls, comedians, and bands pumping out jazz, the soundtrack of the age, flourished in the hundreds of speakeasies and nightclubs that had sprung up under the unwatchful eye of the constabulary—almost all of whom were enriching themselves as well. It was universally agreed that the pleasure principle at last had American puritanism on the run.

The literary world also partook of "the excitement and inflation" of the New Economic Era. "New geniuses were being discovered every week in the leading critical reviews" and "old fogies" were being kicked to the curb. Emerging golden ages in the novel, drama, the essay, and lyric poetry were being proclaimed. Some of this amounted to gaseous public relations on the part of publishers and the press, but not all of it. F. Scott Fitzgerald had created a sensation in 1920 with *This Side of Paradise*, a novel of Jazz Age youth in what we would regard today as mild revolt that had timeliness and vitality on its side. Millay, Stevens, O'Neill, Dos Passos, Williams, Cummings, Lewis, and Cather were all producing important, lasting work. The town crier and chief cheerleader of this lively new scene was Burton Rascoe, whose often breathless column in the *New York Herald Tribune*, "A Bookman's Daybook," functioned for the literary world in much the way Walter Winchell's did for Broadway.

But if "the literary business was booming like General Motors," Cowley and his circle stood somewhat aloof from the assembly line said to be producing geniuses at a prodigious rate. He lamented that "in this distinguished vaudeville there wasn't much place for angry young men without parlor tricks, who talked seriously about the problems of their craft and boasted of having no sense of humor." There are distinct notes of self-importance and self-pity here, but also much truth. They'd had significant firsthand encounters with true literary genius in their time abroad and were not overly impressed by the publicity-savvy wits of the Algonquin Round Table and the ninety-day wonders being promoted by the publishing houses. The best hope of Cowley and his squad—Josephson, Burke, Crane, Brown, Cummings, and, a new addition, the transplanted Southerner Allen Tate—in keeping true to what they had learned was to remain united and "[lay] plans for new ventures to entertain themselves and advance the cause of fine letters." It would turn out to be more difficult than they anticipated.

Cowley addressed the most urgent issue of the scarcity of funds by re-upping with his old employer *Sweet's Architectural Catalogue.* This was, if not a defeat, certainly a strategic retreat. He faced the same painful dilemma that has bedeviled freelance writers without an independent income or a generous patron almost since the invention of movable type. If he chose to live on the income of his writing alone, he would still have to compromise by writing at least part of the time to the demands of the literary marketplace. By taking an office job, he freed himself of those demands, but at most one-fifth of his time could be devoted to "writing for its own sake, to the disinterested practice of the art of letters." The problem with the office job solution, as it took him a while to realize, was that writing that "ceases to have a functional relationship to one's life" can become, like a hobby, a kind of compensation for the qualities lacking in one's day job.

Machine Age America had looked fresh and vital from across the ocean, but once back in its maw it felt considerably more challenging. Cowley and Josephson's ambitious but also quixotic and ill-formed plan had been to somehow transplant to New York the attitudes and activities of the Dadaists that had been so energizing in Paris. They had the idea of hiring a theater for "a literary entertainment" of attacks on and burlesques of the leading writers and critics of the day, interspersed with irrelevant activities "that would show our contempt for the audience and the sanctity of American letters." Thankfully, such an event never took place. Central to the plans of Cowley and Josephson in particular was keeping *Broom* alive as "an organ for the good prose, experimental verse and violent polemics" they felt the age required or deserved. They had found the prevailing literary scene in New York dull and conservative and were determined to shake things up with some advanced guerilla tactics of a European sort.

The magazine had a near-death experience early in the year. Loeb had finally run out of funds in putting together the March issue of *Broom* and he'd sadly called it quits, conclusively enough that letters of condolence from Cowley, Kay Boyle, and others arrived in the mail. But Josephson refused to accept *Broom*'s demise, and he and Cowley quickly devised a plan to move its operations to New York with them, downsize it to a quarterly of sixty-four pages an issue with a reduced trim size, and cease paying contributors or staff (really just the two of them, with other unpaid "board members"). In agreeing to this plan, Loeb essentially ceded all editorial and business control of *Broom*, although he had some nominal editorial input, which was usually ignored. It really was no longer his magazine.

Matthew Josephson may have been deficient in tact but certainly not in energy and savvy. He immediately set about the transplanting and reviving of *Broom* as his sole job. Working out of his apartment on King Street in the Village, he dunned bookstores and distributors for moneys owed; secured a line of credit from his "printing tycoon" brother-in-law covering half of the printing costs; set about raising four thousand dollars in new capital from him and other interested parties; solicited advertisements and new subscribers; performed the multifarious and sometimes crushing editorial tasks that putting out even a so-called little magazine entailed; and even, with his wife and two hired boys, shipped out 2,500 copies of the March 1923 issue of *Broom*, which had languished in the former office for weeks.

For most of 1923, Josephson was working on *Broom* for ten to twelve hours a day, with moral support but small practical help from Cowley, who was working similar hours at *Sweet's* with little time to spare. He somehow managed the small miracle of producing *Broom*, Volume 5, Number 1, August 1923, the first issue printed in the States. The masthead lists as "American Editors" Slater Brown, Malcolm Cowley, and Matthew Josephson, and the contents feature a valedictory essay by Loeb that celebrates the fact that "*Broom* is able at last to give up its vagabond career and settle in the country to which it belongs." He identifies *Broom*'s literary circle as a group whose "centre is a nucleus of American writers of the youngest generation," all of whom share "a whole-hearted disapproval of the generation that preceded them." The contents include a crime fiction pastiche by Cowley, "Snapshot of a Young Lady," a typically hectoring essay by Josephson, "Towards a Professional Prose," and part of his translation of Apollinaire's mock-epic "autobiography" *The Poet Assassinated*.

In early October, *Sweet's Architectural Catalogue* was sent to press and Cowley had the time to turn his attention to *Broom* and pick up at least some of the editorial slack. Contrary to the quarterly plan, there were three more issues to come in 1923, September, October, and November, and they contained significant work from William Carlos Williams, Robert Graves, Wallace Stevens, Louis Aragon, and E. E. Cummings. There was even an excerpt from the legendary Village "character" Joe Gould's *History of the Contemporary World*, perhaps the only evidence in print that he had written a small portion of that elusive work. As a publicist, Josephson proved to have a positively Munsonian knack for attracting attention. Louis Untermeyer in *The New Republic* condemned the Broomists as unfortunate examples of "Young Anarchy" in American letters. Burton Rascoe interviewed Josephson for his "Bookman's Daybook," where he got off such lines as "First of all, we are against all the dead lumber which critics like you have been touting" and extolled the virtues of the writing in commercial advertising over the "shopworn" work of Elinor Wylie, Sinclair Lewis, and Anatole France. *The Dial* would dub the Broomists "skyscraper primitives."

It was fun for Cowley and Josephson and Company to create a stir and annoy the right people, but they realized that outside of the hothouse literary world, their provocations "had the effect of a few people firing off peashooters at the unbreakable plate-glass-and-steel façade of our civilization." Freed from his time-sucking office drudgery for a few months, Cowley "had time to think of literary matters" and that crystallized a growing discontent. The October issue of *Broom* had been intended to be a collection of political manifestos, but as the Broomists were by and large bereft of anything resembling political ideas, it was, he felt, "a sad affair." Feeling adrift in the growing complacency of their prosperous country, he and Josephson contrived a sort of last-ditch, Five Families conclave of various parties involved in *Broom* and *Secession* in an Italian restaurant/speakeasy under the shadow of the El on Prince Street, in an attempt to reenergize their diffuse movement and "brew some stronger liquor." One is reminded of the line from *Animal House*: "I think this situation absolutely requires a really futile and stupid gesture."

In a letter summoning Kenneth Burke to the October 19 meeting, Cowley wrote that "Brown, Burke, Coates, Cowley, Crane, Frank,

[Ramon] Guthrie, Josephson, Munson, Sanborn, [Isidor] Schneider, [Jean] Toomer, Wescott, Williams" had all been invited to the "catholic meeting." Frank, Toomer, and Williams did not attend. Neither did Gorham Munson, who was recovering from an illness in Woodstock and still stewing over various insults and editorial cock-ups and the fact that Josephson and Cowley had transferred all their energies to the rescue of *Broom*, at *Secession*'s expense.

In his absence Cowley had asked Munson to send a statement to be read at the meeting. He did, but instead of addressing whatever diffuse issues were at hand, he produced a lengthy and blistering attack on Matthew Josephson's abilities, opinions, and character, calling him "an intellectual faker" and urging the assembled writers not to have any truck with him or his magazine. "Because his feelings were intense, Munson was betrayed into using a pompous style," Cowley relates. Midway through his reading aloud of the letter, his sense of absurdity got the better of him and he began to declaim theatrically in a manner that heightened the pomposity, and "the effect was unfortunate." The group was already liquored up on bootleg whiskey, and Munson's friends, especially Crane, deep in his cups, took vigorous exception to Cowley's disrespectful behavior. What was meant to be "a general discussion of our problems" devolved into a disorderly rout, with arguments breaking out all over and everyone yelling over one another. "How can you people expect to accomplish anything when you can't even preserve ordinary parlor decorum," Glenway Wescott asked. At eleven thirty the meeting dispersed, all parties angry and dispirited. A drunken Josephson took a swing at Crane in the street, but missed, hitting James Light instead.

Josephson took umbrage at Gorham Munson's umbrage, declaring his letter libelous. The war of words continued until Josephson decided to take direct physical action. He traveled the hundred miles north to Woodstock to stay with Slater Brown in his frigid cabin, and from there presented himself at the home of Murrell Fisher, where Munson was still recovering from the flu. The two literati decided to "take it outside" to a muddy meadow nearby, Fisher presiding as time-keeper and referee. After an exchange of feeble and inefficient blows, they fell to the ground and wrestled clumsily in the mud for a few minutes until both of them wheezily called it quits.

Broom was not done in by this ludicrous wrestling match but by the inability of its editors to rally their circle into the sort of coherent collective action that would have given it shape and momentum. The issues of the magazine they were able to eke out still had some excellent things in them, but the larger point of the exercise was becoming increasingly vague and uncertain. After the Prince Street disaster, the two editors suffered even more demoralization. It fell to the U.S. Postal Service to deliver the final coup de grâce.

In those days a man known to history only as "Mr. Smith" was employed both by the postal service as a censor and by the publishers of some pulp sex magazines of large circulation to read their stuff before printing, to be sure they had not crossed the line in explicitness. The rule was that only one woman's breast could be mentioned per story; two or more would trigger the wrath of the postal authorities. The November 1923 issue of *Broom* contained a story snatched from the slush pile, titled "An Awful Storming Fire" by a Chicago paper-hanger named Charles L. Durboraw. It renders with a kind of primitive and naive surrealism, but also great clarity, the details of a street corner pickup of a woman by a working man. Mr. Smith read it too late to stop any issues of *Broom* from being mailed, but, upset by the story, he sent a warning letter to *Broom* citing Section 480, Postal Laws on Printing and Mailing of Lewd Filthy Matter, telling them that a repeat offense would mean their second-class mail privileges would be revoked.

Unfortunately the January 1924 issue of *Broom* was on press when the letter arrived. It included a story by Kenneth Burke titled "Prince Llan" that is, by most standards, virtually unreadable. However, the first page contains the following sentences: "Their breasts were tight up beneath their shoulders. Their breasts, they stood out firm like pegs. When they walked, one could note their sitters, how they undulated." Breasts, plural, two of them. That much Mr. Smith could read and understand. On January 14 the postal department informed the editors that the new issue was "unmailable." Fifteen hundred copies of the magazine would be returned to them upon a pledge not to mail any copies.

Josephson, alert to any opportunity for publicity, fired off a telegram to a meeting being held that night at Madison Square Garden to protest something called the Clean Books Bill making its way through the New York State legislature. (The bill would be defeated by the opposition of the Senate majority leader, Jimmy Walker, future good-time mayor of New York City, who told his colleagues, "No woman was ever ruined by a book.") He managed to get *The New York Times* to report at some length on the banning in an article in which he was quoted as claiming that he and his fellow editors had been surprised and had no idea what might have upset the postal inspectors.

This was a disaster from which *Broom* could not recover. The much-needed moneys from subscribers and out-of-town bookstores and distributors were forfeit. Six heavy bags containing the copies were delivered to Dominick Street and hauled to the cellar. The best Cowley and Josephson could do with them was to deliver a few hundred copies to New York bookshops, who sold them out quickly once word of the trouble got out. The rest of the copies were disposed of as scrap. The American Civil Liberties Union offered to contest the ruling in court, but the editors were too broke and too broken to pursue legal action. Cowley confessed in a disconsolate letter to Loeb that for "the first time I found myself absolutely impotent, absolutely unmeasured to the work in front of me." *Broom* had reached the end of the road.

Malcolm Cowley and Matthew Josephson took this as a larger defeat than just the demise of a magazine. It represented for them their wider inability, in Cowley's words, "to re-create the atmosphere of intellectual excitement and moral indignation that had stimulated us in Paris among the Dadaists." This project had always been impractical. They'd tried with *Broom* to extol some of the virtues of our business civilization, only to discover that our business civilization did not particularly care about being extolled by a group of avant-garde writers with fancy European ideas.

Josephson, finally tired of getting by on a pittance, devised a radical solution: He borrowed the money to buy a respectable suit of clothes and took a job in a booming Wall Street firm as a stock analyst and writer of market letters for clients and, eventually, as a stock broker himself. "Can anything have been more fantastic?" he asks in his memoir. Well, no. He turned out to be a quick learner and reasonably good at it for the two or so years he pursued this career, until the stress of his clients' losses from his second bear market and a spell of ill health drove him from Wall Street and back into the arms of literature.

Cowley had one more battle left to fight on the fields of literature. Tellingly, the final issue of *Broom*, in January of 1924, coincided with the inaugural issue of H. L. Mencken and George Jean Nathan's new magazine *The American Mercury*. Put out by Mencken's brilliant publisher Alfred A. Knopf, it had secure financial backing and a circulation multiple times that of *Broom*. By 1924, Mencken had so weaponized his signature mockery that he was as feared as he was famous. *The American Mercury* fully reflected his inability to take anyone or anything seriously except his own aggressively proclaimed set of prejudices. The voice of his magazine, satirical, taking relentless and withering aim at anything it deemed to be fair game or a sacred cow, was in many ways to be the sound of the twenties, or at least of its emergent audience of aspiring sophisticates. Mencken in his introductory editorial would characterize the *Mercury*'s intended readers as "the normal, educated, well-disposed, unfrenzied, enlightened citizen of the middle minority." Cowley would put all this more bitterly: "The *American Mercury*, with its easy incredulity, its middle-agedness, its belligerent philistinism, was the expression of a prevailing mood."

The attitudes and antics of the younger avant-garde writers offered the magazine a ripe target, and Mencken took advantage of it. "Aesthete: Model 1924" by the Irish literary journalist Ernest Boyd is a composite portrait and broad burlesque of "This Youngest Generation," a kind of cartoon rendering of Cowley's seminal essay, with a nasty edge. Boyd's semi-fictional Aesthete is a writer still on the near side of thirty who has gone through the familiar stages of his generation's literary development: an Ivy League education that bestowed a light smattering of actual literary knowledge and a heavier coating of de haut en bas attitude; a few temporary radical ideas on loan from the pages of *The Masses*; just enough experience of war to make his posture of worldly disillusionment faintly plausible; travel to Paris and critical time spent in the Left Bank cafés where the taste for advanced French literature and Dadaist cultural combat takes hold; and repatriation to Greenwich Village, where he edits "the luxurious pages of [a] magazine that makes no compromise with corrupt popular taste or, indeed, ordinary intelligibility." The Aesthete stands accused of facile provocations: "What could be easier than to caper in front of the outraged mandarins waving volumes of eccentrically printed French poetry and conspuing the gods of the bourgeoisie?" Also intellectual incoherence in regard to the technological progress he extols: "Thus it becomes possible simultaneously to compare Gertrude Stein with Milton and to chant the glories of the machine age in America."

"Aesthete: Model 1924" is often snide and overdone, but it landed with an audience already cued to dislike those French- and poetry-spouting phonies. Henry Luce's new weekly newsmagazine *Time*, having already perfected its editorial contempt for anything it didn't like or understand, snickered that it "gave Mr. Boyd the intense satisfaction of stirring to obscene and frenzied anger a whole Greenwich Village nestful of half-baked literati whose baseless pretentions to significance it is Mr. Boyd's spirited but impersonal mission in life to deny."

The Broomists and their allies were annoyed at what felt like a cheap shot. Cowley himself would later assert that the piece was "based on the early careers of Gilbert Seldes, Kenneth Burke, Edmund Wilson, and Matthew Josephson, with touches borrowed, I should say, from John Dos Passos, E. E. Cummings, myself, Gorham B. Munson and John Farrar"—the editor of *The Bookman*. Maybe so, but the figure whose résumé checks off the most boxes in Boyd's satirical scheme is quite clearly Malcolm Cowley himself. In *Exile's Return* an agitated Cowley claims, also unconvincingly, "a noble disinterestedness in my anger"—nothing to do with me!—an assertion belied by his public declaration concerning Boyd that "he ought to be punched in the jaw." This threat got around, and when Cowley telephoned Boyd in his Gramercy Park residence to request an in-person meeting to lodge his objections, Boyd refused. This triggered a quick rage in Cowley, who "delivered three round oaths before hanging up." A supposedly apologetic note from Cowley the next day did nothing to disperse the tension in the air, probably because it contained the sentences "I only meant to say that you were a sneak, a coward and a liar. In this description of your character, fortunately, the two of us seem to agree."

So the War of Secession was followed by the Battle of the Aesthetes. Ernest Boyd became a middlebrow culture hero as a result of his broadside and several other semi-imaginary portraits in a similar satirical vein. He would claim that Cowley had threatened to beat him up over the phone. Much sympathy would come his way after some prankish sallies by those thuggish Aesthetes: a series of threatening phone calls from Cowley, Josephson, Burke, and Hart Crane (who "excelled us all in invective," Josephson reported) and a barrage of facetious anonymous telegrams. Burton Rascoe, a friend of Boyd's, wrote of him hyperbolically in his *Bookman* column as "barricaded behind his books, subsisting on depleted rations and grown wan and weary under the assaults and harassments."

The feud between the Cowley circle and Boyd and Mencken's conservative literary crowd smoldered for most of 1924, until it was reignited at the end of the year by the publication of Boyd's collection *Portraits: Real and Imaginary*. The book included the piece that had started the whole squabble, along with the full text of Burton Rascoe's tongue-in-cheek account of Boyd under siege. The literary press once again had an excuse to moralize about this episode. Some counterblast by the Aesthetes seemed to be required, and so the one-off magazine *Aesthete: 1925* was conceived.

In the fall of 1924 the Cowley/Josephson circle had begun hosting weekly literary dinners in the basement of an Italian restaurant, Squarcialupi's, on Perry Street in the Village. When the *New York Evening Post* sent Boyd's book to Josephson for review and quickly withdrew it, the Aesthetes were prodded into action. The dinners shifted into brainstorming sessions for the production of a burlesque of Boyd's burlesque of them and attacks on everyone else worth annoying, in the form of a thirty-six-page magazine titled *Aesthete: 1925*. By December, after an all-day-and-night editorial session in a hotel room and a payment of seventy-five dollars to a printer, six hundred copies of the pamphlet were printed and three hundred of them distributed to bookstores, where they quickly sold out.

Aesthete: 1925 had been undertaken in a mood of lighthearted malice, a spirit of good mean fun. It was a kind of *MAD* magazine written for literary eggheads. The epigraph on the contents page was from Blake—"The road of excess leads to the palace of wisdom"—and a "GUARANTEE" promised that "every article contained in this issue of *A. 1925* is guaranteed to be in bad taste." An editorial commentator named Walter S. Hankel had been invented; his caricature, by Peggy Cowley, conjured up a Gorham Munson with a bit less hair and a lot more mustache wax. Hankel's mock-solemn pronouncements pop up throughout the magazine, along with some bad poems in the modern mode. Wheelwright took aim at critical adversaries from Mencken on down in "Little Moments with Great Critics." Cowley's "To Whom It May Concern" notice assures readers that "Mr. Ernest Boyd is not employed by me as a personal press agent." Boyd is further twitted by Matthew Josephson in his rehashing of his spiked review of his book, and in a mock ad headlined "Be a Critic!" ("In his 'Success Without Talent' booklets, Ernest Boyd tells you the entire secret of how he surmounted such difficulties and more.")

The exercise was a success on its own modest terms, amusing and refreshingly bile-free. The worst you can say is that at times the writers seem to be having more fun than the readers ever would. It got noticed and admired enough so that in subsequent years the Aesthetes were recruited to assemble similar satirical issues of *The Little Review* by Jane Heap and later of *transition* by Eugene Jolas. There were plans to issue a future number of *Aesthete: 1925*, but they fell through from lack of funds and of real commitment on everybody's part. The publication marked the end of something, not the beginning.

Aesthete: 1925 may have been an enjoyable jape, but Cowley: Model 1924 was feeling confused and demoralized. "But five months after my return from Europe I was dispirited, exhausted, licked—by Mr. Smith and Mr. Boyd and the quarrels among my friends, but most of all by myself, by my efforts to apply in one country the standards I had brought from another." Later in the decade, he would write balefully to Edmund Wilson of "this city where every one is so blandly engaged in cutting every one else's throat."

Cowley would clock in joylessly at his office job and grind out copy on items from "accelerators, cement" to "shingles, zinc." He wrote long and self-pitying letters to Kenneth Burke describing his mental inconstancy: "Every day the topic changes, my interests change, I am more or less downhearted. I plan different futures. To read Plato. To construct an aesthetic. To write a novel. To be independent. One aim conflicts with another." Feeling lonely, he even paid a visit to Gorham Munson, who had now become an enthusiastic follower of the fashionable mystic Gurdjieff and his Institute for the Harmonious Development of Man. Cowley got bored and then drunk and went home.

It is hard to escape the sense that the sectarian literary battles that Cowley and his circle had expended all their energy on had missed the real point of the twenties. As the brilliant cultural historian Ann Douglas put it: "New York in the 1920s was a magnet attracting and concentrating the talents of a nation. Modern American culture was in good part the work of a group of people displaced in a metropolitan setting; they realized there talents often fostered and sometimes fulfilled or outlived elsewhere. . . . For a few giddy and glorious moments in the 1920s New York held out to its new inhabitants an extraordinary promise of freedom and creative self-expression."

This new culture came into being at a time of unprecedented technological advances in the means of transmission. By the end of the twenties, one in three Americans owned a radio; three out of four went to the movies at least once a week; new mass-circulation magazines like *Time* and *The New Yorker* clued their audiences into the sophisticated doings of the urban cultural elite; and the advertising made possible through the new mass media fueled a boom in consumption of a wide array of goods and services. There was a racial component to this transformation, in that the new form of music named jazz, so central to the twenties that it gave the age its very name, was the product of an African American culture itself emerging at last from rural and Southern oppression, if painfully slowly. The American popular culture that sprang from these sources was something new in the world, vibrant, irreverent, polyglot, and mongrel in the best sense, almost unstoppable. In the way it erased the last vestiges of Victorian propriety and dissolved many previous distinctions between high and low, it managed to transform American literature as well.

When some years later in 1941 Henry Luce proclaimed the twentieth century "the American Century" and the label stuck, it did so based on two factors: the country's overwhelming industrial, technological, and (eventual) military superiority and the globe-conquering vitality of its popular culture. American writers on all points of the spectrum from the literary to the commercial contributed greatly to that transnational tide and were swept along by it.

That vitality went on spectacular display with the publication of *The Great Gatsby* in 1925 and *The Sun Also Rises* in 1926, an extended big boom moment in American literature. *The Great Gatsby* was a near-perfect moral fable of the Jazz Age that encapsulated, in Cowley's phrase, "the Romance of Money" that Fitzgerald, more than any of his contemporaries, was in thrall to. Hemingway's *The Sun Also Rises*, a tale of expatriated Americans behaving viciously to one another, can be read as a cynical and hard-boiled counterpoint to *Gatsby*'s soft-centered romanticism. It purveys the Lost Generation mystique, wounded, stoic, wised up, and in the know, in its most distilled and potent form. The effect of the novel on American culture was as much behavioral as literary: Cowley would note that soon "the Smith College girls in New York were modeling themselves after Lady

Brett," and "hundreds of bright young men from the Middle West were trying to be Hemingway heroes, talking in tough understatements from the sides of their mouths." With the publication of these books, American literature had finally reached escape velocity.

America was now the place to be rather than flee. This was a sea change so novel and widespread that the distant enthusiasms of a European artistic vanguard and French-style literary politics that the Aesthetes brought back with them from Paris were in the end largely irrelevant. As Cowley would put it, "The Dada movement can't learn to talk United States."

Cowley poured out his bitterness about the literary scene into his notebooks—"I utterly hate and despise the trade and the tradesmen of letters"—and in letters—"the disgusting feature of New York is its professional writers, who are venial to the last degree. Out of business, into literature, there is nobody to respect," he wrote to Harold Loeb. Yet he continued, steadily if not merrily, to toil at the writer's trade.

The year 1924 was in many ways the model for Cowley's 1920s, a period of unremitting freelance reviewing that served to hone his critical skills, if not swell his bank account. Book review editors soon learned that he had a knowledgeable line in French literature, so the next years saw him assigned to review such books as René Lalou's *Contemporary French Literature*; Jean Cocteau's *The Grand Écart*, his first novel; the *Memoirs of Léon Daudet*; and André Gide's *The Vatican Swindle*. He would go on in the balance of the decade to review books by other contemporary French writers such as Roger Martin du Gard, Blaise Cendrars, Julien Green, Henri Alain-Fournier, and François Mauriac and consider older work by Stendhal, Villon, and Baudelaire.

Because it was a cosmopolitan age when Americans still looked to Europe for at least some of their cultural nourishment, and because a number of new publishing houses of taste and ambition had sprung up, Cowley also found regular work as a translator of books from the French. He translated *On Board the Morning Star* by his Parisian friend Pierre Mac Orlan, a cycle of pirate stories; *Joan of Arc*, a high-spirited and highly embroidered biography by Joseph Delteil, who would go on to collaborate on the screenplay for Carl Theodor Dreyer's film *The Passion of Joan of Arc*; and *Jesus* by Henri Barbusse. "There is no one in this country who I think can handle French as you can," Harrison Smith, a prominent book editor at Harcourt, Brace, complimented him.

By far Cowley's most ambitious and important translation was that of Paul Valéry's *Variety*, a collection of his essays. Cowley had met the formidable Valéry during his time in France, and he regarded him as the terminal case of Symbolism-cum-Modernism—of writing as a purely subjective and intellectual exercise. He was also perhaps the supreme example of the writer as imperial self, having stepped away for twenty years from writing for publication to devote himself solely to reading and thinking about what he read. His return to publication had been a triumph, so much so that Valéry was elected to the French Academy, replacing Anatole France.

Paul Valéry was no easy writer to translate—the *New York Times* review of *Variety* called him "a philosopher and a lyric singer, a classicist who suggests Racine and a symbolist who suggests Mallarmé"—nor an easy one to comprehend and explain. On both counts, Cowley succeeded. His introduction, which brings the reader by careful steps into Valéry's sometimes forbidding "defense of the intellect, of the conscious mind," was one of his best early essays. Cowley's encounters with the French literary elite had borne fruit.

The essay in itself would have long-term consequences for Cowley. Edmund Wilson had started a new job in 1926 as an associate editor of *The New Republic* and he accepted the piece for publication. Up to that point Wilson had been ambivalent about Cowley as both a writer and a personality. He had solicited his poems for *Vanity Fair*, but nothing came of that; later, in the wake of the Ernest Boyd affair, which he found "all very funny," he wrote to John Peale Bishop, "I can't handle the *Broom* crowd very much: Cowley, I think, has some ability, but is sort of an ass." The Valéry essay, though, was a first-rate piece of work. Wilson was already thinking hard about the Symbolist movement in literature, the subject of his immensely influential critical work *Axel's Castle*, which has a full chapter on Valéry. The piece's serialization in *The New Republic* was the real beginning of Cowley's lifelong association with that magazine, and also of his working relationship and sort-of-friendship with Wilson, a compound of mutual respect, buried competitiveness, and eventually bitter political disagreement.

When, two years later, Wilson ascended to the position of literary editor, he invited Cowley to become a regular reviewer, an offer that he accepted after some grumbling over past slights from the publication. In smoothing matters over, Wilson called him "one of the best writers in the country." Cowley would become one of Wilson's steadiest go-to writers, in the next two years contributing more than fifteen essays and reviews of a wide variety of books, including Sinclair Lewis's *The Man Who Knew Coolidge*, *The Letters of Charles Baudelaire*, edited by Arthur Symons, and Herbert Asbury's *The Gangs of New York*. He deftly fielded everything he got thrown at him, and Wilson was appreciative: "I think that your little 'Style and Fashion' review is more or less a masterpiece in its way. Your capacity for doing these trivial things well is astonishing."

Cowley found an even more welcoming editor for his reviews and essays in Irita Van Doren, who in the summer of 1925 became the editor of *New York Herald Tribune Books*; formerly employed by *The Nation*, she was part of a literary power trio, the wife of the historian Carl Van Doren and the sister-in-law of the critic Mark Van Doren. Cowley would remember her fondly: "Among the kind-hearted editors I have known, she was by far the kindest." He asserts that it was the dependable income that her assignments brought in that made his eventual escape to the countryside possible. Not only did he translate for her, uncredited, four more of Paul Valéry's essays, he would go on to publish more than forty essays and reviews of his own there over the next five years. Moreover, she rarely tinkered with his copy and ran his pieces in a timely fashion. His work for her continued his expert engagement with classic and contemporary French literature and ranged widely over a variety of other areas. With first the *Tribune* and then *The New Republic* now providing a steady flow of high-end assignments, at, moreover, a higher rate of pay than the smaller magazines he'd been writing for, Cowley's income stabilized and his profile, not as an enfant terrible but rather as a maturing critic to whom attention must be paid, rose considerably.

One little magazine that he fell out with, though, was *The Dial*. His particular beef was with Marianne Moore, whose style as an editor tended toward overactive blue penciling and dilatoriness. She was in the habit of accepting poems and then insisting on changes and deletions; because *The Dial* was a prestigious publication where even major poets strongly desired to have their work appear, they would accede to her edits, but with the sort of discreet grumbling that was becoming more widely known. Hart Crane's memorable private nickname for her was "the Right Rev. Miss Mountjoy." Moore, for her part, had written to a friend in early 1925, "There is no one writing whom I value less than Malcolm Cowley"—this despite the fact that she regularly assigned him reviews and accepted his poems. Her prim, precise style and that of the *Secession/Broom* crowd were oil and water.

Cowley's real troubles with Moore began with her delay in running his review of *Israfel: The Life and Times of Edgar Allan Poe* by Hervey Allen. By the mid-twenties, Poe was well into a period of rediscovery and reevaluation, with important critical and biographical commentary by the likes of D. H. Lawrence in *Studies in Classic American Literature*, William Carlos Williams in *In the American Grain*, and Paul Valéry in an essay in *Variety*. Cowley had followed their lead in estimating his place as a pioneer in the development of modern literature very highly. On one memorable June afternoon in 1924 with Allen Tate and Hart Crane in the latter's Brooklyn Heights apartment, Cowley had spontaneously read aloud Poe's picturesque and rhetorically perfervid "The City and the Sea" ("While from a proud tower in the town / Death looks gigantically down," etc.). It had a galvanizing effect, and later the men strolled the Brooklyn waterfront talking excitedly and viewing the proud towers of Manhattan across the East River. Cowley would warmly remember the bond that evening formed: "Suddenly I felt—I think we all felt—that we were secretly comrades in the same endeavor: to present this new scene in poems that would reveal not only its astonishing face, but the lasting realities behind it."

Two years later, after an evening's discussion with the three cultists about the rash of new Poe biographies then appearing, Edmund Wilson jumped the gun with a long essay on Poe in *The New Republic* taking sharp issue with the overall "tendency to regard him [Poe, that is] as a freak, having his existence somehow apart both from literature and from life" and asserting rather that "Poe was the bridge over the middle nineteenth century from romanticism to symbolism." These were ideas that had been very much on the table that evening and, possibly, fresh news to Wilson.

Cowley was stung by Wilson's unseemly haste—"I hope I haven't stolen your thunder," Wilson wrote to him, unconvincingly. But he had. Cowley had already had a review of Hervey Allen's Poe biography in at *The Dial* when Wilson's piece appeared and turned up the heat on the subject of Poe. Cowley's review overlapped considerably with Wilson's essay in decrying the way biographers had reduced Poe to a caricature and clinical "case," seeking an answer to the putative "Poe mystery" of his fall from brilliance into dissipation and madness in his mother fixation, his sexual impotence, his paranoia, his alcoholism, other flaws of character or psychology. Cowley urged Moore not to hold on to the review lest it become outdated, but that is exactly what she did, asking for minor revisions and eventually running it a year later in the August 1927 issue.

Cowley was justly irritated, and that irritation was reprised in 1928 when his review of a biography of Shelley was delayed for more than half a year, which exacerbated other irritations of longer standing over Moore's habit of picky alterations of his copy—he called it being "Marianne Moore'd"—and a less than diplomatic rejection of his Pennsylvania poems. The Shelley review was his last piece for the magazine, which would fold in 1929. Marianne Moore, for her part, felt that Cowley had been prickly and unappreciative of the editorial hospitality she and the magazine had extended to him over the years. This falling-out would have a painful sequel decades later, when Cowley, by then a Viking editor, locked horns with Moore over her translation of the fables of La Fontaine.

In July 1928, Cowley would publish a long essay, "The Edgar Allan Poe Tradition," in a magazine called *The Outlook*, one of the best pieces from his early career. He was able to elaborate at greater length on the notions about Poe that he could only glancingly touch on in his *Dial* review. It is a thorough appreciation of Poe that combines biographical consideration, literary and cultural history, sharp critical insight, judicious correction of misguided received ideas, deep fellow feeling, and eloquence: "He succeeded . . . in combining old elements so as to form a new world stamped with his own personality, a region out of space and out of time, where the House of Usher crumbles eternally behind a stagnant moat, where Arthur Gordon Pym drifts southward to the Pole, where ravens tap in the night against a lattice, and where Eleonora gathers the everlasting flowers that carpet the Valley of the Many-colored Grass." Here is the true start of Malcolm Cowley's career as a great Americanist.

SIX.

ROARING BOY

———

Malcolm Cowley's cohort had returned not simply to America, but to New York City, knowing full well that the real opportunity to make an impact was there. New York is a city that amplifies the highs of success, but also the lows of failure. Cowley's circle had gone on the offensive with limited effect beyond a few small literary brush fires, so it is no surprise that they once again collectively decided to take their stand elsewhere—to the north and a bit east, in the Connecticut Valley.

In explaining this literary retreat and "Connecticut migration" Cowley indulges in a bit of sociology. In his telling, the literati had begun to merge with the professional class of advertising copywriters, publicists, art directors, photographers, stylists, and lifestyle journalists busily engaged in stoking the acquisitive desires of the new mass-consumerist economy. The writers and artists had fungible skills suited to such tasks and many of them began to sell out for a more comfortable life. Others began to actually succeed in their chosen careers and waxed, if not fat, at least mildly prosperous on publishers' advances and gallery sales and magazine assignments. Soon enough the siren song of the suburbs and exurbs beckoned, but the promise of a way of living more stately and gracious failed to assuage an inner itch. This situation would eventually provide the raw material for a whole literature of suburban discontent.

The larger picture Cowley presents is certainly true, but it doesn't really fit the facts of his particular circle, all of whom would remain fully committed to their literary ideals for their whole lives. He speaks more directly to their actual situation when he writes, "Their real exile was from society itself, from any society to which they could honestly contribute and from which they could draw the strength that lies in shared convictions." In such a mood American writers inevitably begin to hear the voices of Emerson and, especially, Thoreau in their heads, offering the counsels of self-reliance and purposeful removal and isolation.

Kenneth Burke had pioneered this literary mode of rural retreat in 1922 when he bought his farm in Andover, New Jersey; so determined was he to live cheap and rough without modern conveniences that he scorned flush toilets for an outhouse and waited until 1949 to get his farmhouse electrified. But it was the independent-minded Slater Brown who first colonized the area of the New York–Connecticut border for his friends. In 1925 with his new wife, Susan Jenkins, he used a small inheritance to purchase an eighteenth-century cottage with eighty acres of land in a remote and decaying section of Pawling, New York, called Tory Hill, as some Tories had made a last desperate stand there during the American Revolution. "This was the beginning of a new era for all of us," Cowley would recall.

Hart Crane volunteered to move in and help paint the cottage. That Fourth of July inaugurated a long tradition of rural saturnalias, city people arriving in large numbers to drink gin and the local hard cider, go swimming at midnight, watch Crane perform his "cannibal dance" on an ancient stone fence, and in general "gratify every caprice for three days." He served as a combination Puck, Bacchus, and Orpheus at these events. Soon, Allen Tate and his wife, the novelist Caroline Gordon, and their newborn daughter moved to Tory Hill themselves, renting eight rooms in a barnlike house owned by the widow Mrs. Addie Turner and also occupied by her and her aunt. In a moment of generosity the Tates invited the financially beset Crane to come live with them in their half of the house; Crane's oversize personality and poetical working habits made the big house considerably smaller, though, especially in a rugged rural winter. So after a year the Tates moved back to the Village (where Allen Tate "paid" the rent by serving as the most literate superintendent in apartment building history), and Crane would remain for some years, off and on, at Addie Turner's. Matthew Josephson, for his part, bought with his remaining stock market funds a country cottage in Katonah, New York, a short drive from Tory Hill.

The Cowleys were regular guests at the Tory Hill bacchanals and would eventually find their way to Connecticut as well, but their first stop in what would be a two-step rustication began on Staten Island, at that time still a rural and remote borough accessible only by ferry. Their friend Dorothy Day had received what for the time was a windfall of $2,500 from a film option for her novel *The Eleventh Virgin*, otherwise a commercial failure. Day had roomed for a time with the Cowleys in one of their apartments and it was Peggy Cowley who persuaded her friend to buy a bungalow, a tin-roofed fisherman's shack, on the southeastern shore of Staten Island on Raritan Bay. It had no heat or hot water but still, winters aside, offered a pleasant seaside retreat from Manhattan life, and she took up residence there with Forster Batterham, a biology instructor of anarchist persuasion who would become her common-law husband and father of her daughter. By April 1925 they had company in Staten Island when the Cowleys rented a "shacky" five-room house two miles away, with heat and electricity and a bath that Peggy kindly made available to Day. This was the first move in Cowley's plan to eventually resign from *Sweet's*, which he shortly did, and live on the income from freelance writing.

In May of 1926 the Cowleys finally made their transition to the real country when they rented a farmhouse "with exterior nonplumbing that rented for ten dollars a month" in Sherman, Connecticut, just across the state border with New York. They loaded their furniture and books into a wheezing Model T truck that broke down half a mile from the house; their possessions traveled the rest of the way in a farm wagon. In a buoyant letter to Harriet Monroe—*Poetry* had accepted the suite of seven of his poems, to be collectively titled "Blue Juniata," that the *Dial* had turned down—Cowley waxed rhapsodic about his new surroundings: "This is a magnificent country, full of deer, trout, granite and poison ivy." He extols to her the "acres of oak, elm, hemlock, black, white and yellow birch surrounding the bed of a stream where trout sleep in pools below the falls." It is doubtful that Peggy liked their new circumstances anywhere near as much.

The move inaugurated a new rhythm in the Cowleys' lives, the warmer half of the year spent in rural semi-splendor, the winters in a downtown apartment. It was put on more permanent footing when in October 1927 he received the Levinson Prize from *Poetry* magazine for the exceptional quality of his "Blue Juniata" poems. The award came with a hundred-dollar stipend, and he first learned of it from phone calls from Connecticut reporters eager for hometown hero copy. Twenty-five dollars went to buy groceries; the balance was used as part of a down payment on "sixty acres of abandoned farmland and a hungry-looking house half a mile from Mrs. Turner's." Three years later he would take a loan of $732 to complete the purchase, leaving him "completely, beautifully and prodigiously broke."

Cowley's feeling for the country in and around Sherman was deep and abiding. It stirred the mystic chords of memory of his boyhood Belsano summers. One of his color pieces, "Connecticut Valley," offers a vivid portrait of the local scene—some legacy farmers still hanging on and others just giving up after the local farm economy had all but vanished, the new city people like him who bought those old farms and fixed up the houses and grounds and inhabited them on weekends and summers and gave boozy cocktail parties, the melancholy autumn spectacle of apple orchards and grapevines heavy with unpicked fruit.

Whether through literary inspiration or financial desperation—his local bank account was so depleted that he could not cash his checks, instead having to resort to an intricate procedure requiring hairbreadth calculations of bank clearances—his country retreats accelerated Malcolm Cowley's productivity considerably. This is reflected particularly in the excellence and volume of his poetic output during this time. He would publish sixteen poems in calendar year 1926, including the prizewinning suite of seven in *Poetry*.

Judging by these poems, Cowley's muse was calling him back to the Pennsylvania landscape of his youth. They are not time-stamped by the twenties in either subject matter or poetic technique. They have more in common with the melancholy small-town visions of Sherwood Anderson or Edgar Lee Masters—aging farmhouses, swaybacked barns, neglected fields, a landscape thinly inhabited by mute, inglorious Miltons thwarted by life and nearly broken by endless labor. These poems are plainspoken, emotionally direct, haunted by the past and the inexorability of time. Harriet Monroe said of them, "There is nothing facile about Mr. Cowley—he beats his poems out of iron, or sometimes bronze, and hammers them into a sturdily beautiful shape, a shape that bears his own impress. . . . These are man-size poems."

While he would continue to write poems throughout his life, Cowley did his most lasting work in the twenties. And, with the possible exception of his other close poet friend Allen Tate, no one was more involved with this output, as a friend, an editor, and an inspiration through his own poetry, than Hart Crane. Cowley's intimate friendship with the magnetic, prodigiously talented, self-destructive, and finally tragic Crane was, one suspects, the deepest and most complicated of his life.

Hart Cane was a year younger than Cowley, of his generation, and, like him, an only child, but with a different background and a radically different temperament. He was the son of Grace Crane and Clarence Crane, a prosperous Ohioan who ran the Crane Chocolate Company and who invented Life Savers, the rights to which he sold. The marriage was an unhappy one. Grace Crane was a needy neurotic and borderline hysteric, and she and Hart alternately clung to each other emotionally and then quarreled bitterly. Crane recognized and acted upon his poetic gifts early, dropping out of high school without graduating, and leaving home for New York, ostensibly to find paying work and then enroll at Columbia, but in truth to immerse himself in the literary life of the city.

Crane's whole existence was financially fraught. He subsisted on the income from intermittent spells of employment as an advertising copywriter, irregular support from his father and mother and a couple of patrons, and loans and temporary lodgings from sympathetic friends. ("I ricochet-ed 'from roof to roof' without interruption," he once recalled.) His life, inside his family and without, was disorderly to an exceptional degree: countless changes of address, emotional and familial crises, feuds with friends and reconciliations, and a number of suicide attempts, on his part and on his mother's as well. Even by the demanding standard of poets, Crane's was a stormy life.

Crane's real problems, though, were the twin issues of his alcoholism and his reckless sexual appetites. His poetic practice relied to a striking degree on his achievement of a state of visionary ecstasy reached by way of extreme drunkenness, often followed by sexual excess. He was a poète maudit, the American Rimbaud: Like him, Crane consciously sought to derange his senses through drink to reach an extreme state of mind that gave him access to an imagined world more vivid than dull consensus reality, and a wellspring of linguistic inspiration and originality to convey it. These lines from "The Wine Menagerie" offer a compact statement of his poetic practice: "Invariably when wine redeems the sight, / Narrowing the mustard scansions of the eyes, / A leopard ranging always in the brow / Asserts a vision in the slumbering gaze." Plenty of modern American writers were alcoholics, but very few wrote well while drunk. Crane was the exception. But the costs to his health and his dignity were painfully high.

Generations of readers on encountering Crane's poetry have found themselves captivated by his virtuosity, figurative richness, prophetic tone, and insistent iambic rhythms. (He would often write to the sound of rhumba records or Ravel's "Boléro," played on a victrola at maximum volume.) The downside is the cognitive elusiveness of its lyric intensity and associative method, with meanings often buried deep under layers of symbolism, compacted metaphors, and obscure etymology. Sound often outstrips sense. But when it worked, it was glorious and unlike anything else. He was the anti-Eliot, seeking to convey joy and expanded spiritual vistas (much like Whitman) instead of cultural despair.

Malcolm Cowley lived an orderly life, hardly bourgeois, but he met deadlines and wrote to editorial order and always had a fixed address and at least a few dollars in the bank. In every respect Cowley was a methodical man. He was fascinated by Crane as a representative of the literary spectrum far removed from his own—in conventional ways a failure in life but in a literary sense an undeniable success. Cowley and his other friends recognized that they had an unruly genius in their midst, someone from whom much could be expected and much would need to be forgiven.

Malcolm Cowley's first contact with Hart Crane began with a letter. In the March–April 1923 issue of the little magazine *S4N*, Crane reviewed *Eight More Harvard Poets*, which included Cowley's poems.

He found that much of the work suffered from warmed-over Georgian tendencies, but he did call out Cowley's work for particular attention and praise, writing, "A faculty for fresh record, city and road panorama, and ironic nuance, all make Cowley's experiments quite valuable."

Cowley, still then in France, was pleased and wrote Crane to say so, calling it "the most intelligent criticism our book received." He had already been aware of Crane's work and returned the compliment, telling him, "You write with a bombast which is not Elizabethan but contemporary, and you are one of the two or three people who can write a 20th Century blank verse, about other subjects than love, death and nightingales and in other patterns than ti tum ti tum ti tum ti tums." Looking ahead generationally, as was his habit, Cowley wrote that "I hope you don't rush to print a volume. If we all wait three or four years, till our public is formed, we can have a great deal more fun by publishing." Crane would meet Malcolm and Peggy Cowley sometime after their return to New York and a fast three-sided friendship was formed.

Soon Crane and the Cowleys would be making a memorable trip together to Eugene O'Neill's Brook Farm estate in Ridgefield, Connecticut. Newly prosperous from the royalties of the commercially successful *Anna Christie*, O'Neill had bought the large 1890s house and forty acres of land and supplied himself with a full-time European chauffeur and a huge and intimidating Irish wolfhound. Cowley believed that O'Neill had extended his hospitality to assess how he was being regarded by the younger writers beginning to make a stir.

Hart Crane would describe the weekend as "a roisterous time! Cider, belly dances and cakewalks over Sunday at O'Neills." Its climax came when O'Neill took the two men down to the cellar, where barrels of robust hard cider were brewing. "Let's broach a cask," Crane suggested, and Cowley, with a maul and spigot and his "country knowledge," obliged. The hard-drinking O'Neill had been abstinent for some time, but he partook of the first pitcher of the cider. And then another, until Cowley left the two men for the night, Crane loudly declaiming some freshly minted poetry. O'Neill continued to drain the casks the next day and then took a cab to the train station—and disappeared. He was discovered by his wife, Agnes Boulton, a week later, in a room above the Hell Hole, where the owner had stashed him after he'd drunk himself into a coma. She had him driven back to Ridgefield, where after a few days of recovery he began to write *Desire Under the Elms*.

Crane's friends usually enjoyed the roisterous times, but on many occasions he pushed past the limits of decorum and their store of affectionate patience. Cowley's preferred epithet for him was "the Roaring Boy." His energy for work and play, both fueled by alcohol, was unflagging and the barriers between the two permeable. At certain points Crane would absent himself from revels to retreat to a room with a typewriter. Loud Cuban music would boom from behind the door, accompanied by the rhythmic clacking of the keys. Cowley vividly described what would happen next:

> An hour later . . . he would appear in the kitchen or on the croquet court, his face flushed, his eyes burning, his already iron-gray hair bristling straight up from his skull. He would be carrying two sheets of manuscript, with words crossed out and new lines scrawled in. "Read that," he would say. "Isn't that the *greatest* poem ever written?"

Everyone would have no choice but to agree with him, for not to do so would be to provoke rage and tears. Cowley's verdict on the results of Crane's ecstatic methods was positive but also mixed: "At their worst, his poems are ineffective unless read in the mood in which they were written. . . . At their best, however, the poems do their work unaided except by their proper glitter and violence. At their very best . . . they have an emotional force that has not been equaled by any other American poet of our century."

If Crane's revels took place in the city, the evening would usually conclude with an alcohol-fueled crawl along the Brooklyn or Manhattan waterfronts in search of male companionship and sex. These episodes would often end, predictably, in a beating or a robbery or a night in jail, sometimes all three. He found this humiliating, but he could no more curb his quest for sex than he could stop writing poetry—and the drives were not unrelated. Crane's bluff demeanor did not read as stereotypically gay; he usually had a dead or smoldering cigar stuck in the corner of his mouth. "I could never stand much falsetto" is how he explained it. Nor was he a denizen of the gay artistic demimonde; his literary circle consisted almost entirely of married heterosexual couples. But Crane was about as "out," at least to some of his friends, as it was possible for a gay man in the twenties to be. His letters are full of offhand and startlingly frank references to his trawling the docks: One to Cowley enthuses over "the passionate pulchritude of the usual recent maritime houreths" and to "a night with a bluejacket from the *Arkansas.*"

What did Malcolm Cowley really think about this? Although he was not above using words like "pansy" and "effete" in his reviews and essays in a dismissive fashion, he never demonstrated any overt homophobia in his actual behavior, toward Crane or anyone else. Nor did the other members of their circle—they were not sexually judgmental nor in any position to be so—but their persistent worries about Crane's reckless way of life contained a strong component of dismay over his homosexuality, or at least his reckless way of satisfying his sexual urges. Cowley may have privately shared some of these opinions, but he was closer to Crane than the others and he is not known to have offered any judgments on the subject aside from generalized regrets over the disorder that Crane's compulsiveness across the behavioral spectrum brought to his life.

The one lasting romantic relationship with a man that Hart Crane formed in his life was with a Danish American journalist and ship's purser three years his senior by the name of Emil Opffer, brother of the artist Ivan Opffer. Susan Jenkins Brown, who knew both Emil and his parents, made the introduction in April of 1924; their mutual attraction was instant and powerful. Soon he and Crane were experiencing, as Crane giddily wrote to Waldo Frank, "the ecstasy of walking hand in hand across the most beautiful bridge in the world, the cables enclosing us and pulling us upward in such a dance as I have never walked and never can walk with another." That was the Brooklyn Bridge, of course. This almost miraculous confluence of romantic infatuation and poetic epiphany was worthy of a Hollywood romance, and the miracle continued when Crane, with the salary from his new job as a copywriter for *Sweet's* that Cowley had helped him secure, was able to move into a room at 110 Columbia Heights, which had a glorious view of the bridge and much else—"the ships, the harbor, and the skyline of Manhattan, midnight, morning or evening." Here he found the inspiration for much of his greatest work: his long poem *The Bridge* and the lovestruck suite of poems "Voyages," which had Emil Opffer as their muse. Crane would discover that Washington Roebling, the builder of the Brooklyn Bridge, had owned 110 Columbia Heights and overseen its progress from there. He would live at that address, now a rooming house, for some years off and on, by far his most consistent place of lodging. He would send Roebling's son John a signed copy of *The Bridge*.

True to the suggestion of Cowley's first letter to him, Crane waited those three or four years before the flamboyant American publisher of advanced literature Horace Liveright put out his first collection, *White Buildings*, at the end of 1926. Liveright had been on the verge of rejecting the book until Eugene O'Neill promised to write an introduction. But when that proved too difficult for him to accomplish, O'Neill throttled back to a woolly, hard-to-parse blurb, and Allen Tate stepped in to provide the introduction instead. By this time, Crane was well into the composition of *The Bridge*, his ambitious attempt to take on Whitman and Melville and synthesize our history and folklore into his own mythic vision.

Now it was Cowley's turn. But a problem that would dog him throughout his career was the completion of book-length projects. His notebook from the fall of 1926 contains a list of six books that he felt he might be able to publish. Five of them—a history of the Atlantic slave trade, a biography of Charles Baudelaire, two essay collections, and a novel—were never completed.

The one book of the six that did finally make its way into print was "3. A volume of Poems—Blue Juniata." Hart Crane was selflessly, even heroically central to the assembling of that collection, which after *Exile's Return* is the most enduring of Malcolm Cowley's books. None of the plaints he indulged in in his notebooks and letters about the difficulties and fruitlessness of the writing life touched on his poetry, which he regarded as a higher calling.

The push toward the assembling of Cowley's collection began in the summer of 1928 at Tory Hill. Crane had returned from a fairly disastrous sojourn in California with his mother and grandmother earlier that year and now was lodging at Addie Turner's, and Cowley had moved into the nearby farmhouse he'd made the down payment on. Like the rest of his circle he took note of the physical changes, the graying hair and red, puffy face, that Crane's constant drinking was causing. But Crane's energy was unabated, and in July of that summer his pet project was, as he wrote to a mutual friend, to "get [Malcolm's] poems accepted by some publisher or another before twelvemonth.

He'll never do much about it himself, as you know, and his collection is really needed on the shelves these days."

Crane was right about Cowley's lassitude or reluctance. He'd published more than sixty poems in a decade, more than enough to fill a collection, but he was in no hurry to turn them into a book, writing, "I rather preferred to be unknown for the moment—except to magazine readers—and therefore unclassified and free to move in any direction." There is a distinct undercurrent of nervousness in these words. But he gave in to Crane's prodding and in early July they assembled a sheaf of poems and began the joint process of editing them into a book, putting some aside, arranging the rest in some order that made sense. In Crane's view, that meant a structure that produced a coherent sequence of emotions rather than chronologically or narratively arranged. For the most part he refrained from any direct editing of the poems themselves, and when he did, his unusual syntactical sense clashed with what Crane termed Cowley's "genial pedestrianism" and his suggestions were declined. By the end of the summer the manuscript for a book was ready for submission to a publisher, but its author still refrained from doing so. Crane took matters into his own hands that fall. He extracted the manuscript from Cowley, did some minor fiddles with the sequence of poems, and, well pleased with the results, retyped two copies of the book now titled *Blue Juniata*.

One copy Crane planned to take with him on a trip to Europe that December. The other he submitted to a publisher's editor he referred to mysteriously as a "secret arbiter." The reason for this became clear a few weeks later when Cowley heard from none other than his adversary in the little magazine wars, Gorham Munson, now working for the George H. Doran Company. Munson generously put aside their earlier quarrels and made an offer to publish and a modest advance. In his account of these events, Cowley claims that his stiff-necked

Pennsylvania Dutch side kicked in because he did not wish to be "'beholden' to anyone for the structure and publication of my first book." We can surmise, though, that he did not care to have Munson as his editor as well. So he submitted the book himself to his friend and admirer Harrison Smith, who had left Harcourt Brace and started his own publishing imprint in association with the British publisher Jonathan Cape, and it was quickly accepted, with a slightly larger advance. Cowley also liked the fact, as he wrote to Harriet Monroe, that Smith planned to publish poetry with some commercial oomph, "in such a form and with such advertising that it wins back its popularity and economic self-sufficiency."

Then Cowley took the manuscript back with him to his cramped apartment on Avenue B in the East Village and set about reediting his collection. He gave the book an entirely new framework, autobiographical this time rather than the emotional sequence that was Crane's preference, which allowed some poems—fifty-four in toto rather than the previous thirty-five—which he admitted were callow, back in for their narrative value. He divided the book into five sections and wrote introductory, obliquely biographical prose notes to three of them, and gave his poems one final round of edits and revisions. In January 1929 he wrote to Crane in Paris of these developments; Crane, in the midst of, in Cowley's words, the "high life in and out of Paris—absinthe, champagne, chateaux, countesses and counts, cocktail parties, dinner parties, midnight and morning parties," had somehow found the time to almost persuade the playboy poet and sybarite Harry Crosby to publish the book at his Black Sun Press. In June, Cowley sent a set of galleys to Crane, nervous that he would be wounded by the failure to accept his suggestions, but he need not have been. Crane was delighted by his friend's handwork and admired *Blue Juniata*'s new form, writing warmly that "I'm certain that the book is even better . . . a much more solidified unit than it was before. . . .

Really, Malcolm—if you will excuse me for the egoism—I'm just a little proud at the outcome of my agitations last summer."

For the rest of his life Malcolm Cowley would feel profound gratitude to Hart Crane for his "agitations." He would note the stark difference between the widespread caricature of Crane as a drunken rioter with a certain gift and the hard, scrupulous work of the many weeks and generosity of spirit it took to edit and type and peddle the manuscript of a friend, with no thought of recompense. Nor was Crane afflicted with that almost universal occupational hazard of writers: professional jealousy. "The little victories gained by his friends delighted him more than his own victories," Cowley would write. There is ample evidence in Crane's correspondence that this was true. Crane would be the first person to whom Malcolm Cowley would inscribe a finished copy of *Blue Juniata*, writing on the flyleaf "If it's bad, the sin be on your head."

Blue Juniata is a durable work of considerable interest. Its five sections trace a history of the poet and his literary cohort. It proceeds from memories of Cowley's rural childhood summers—Juniata is a river that flows through central Pennsylvania and "Blue Juniata" is a nineteenth-century ballad—his bohemian Village period, the self-chosen literary "exile" to Europe, the unsettling return to New York, and a concluding section of poems with more universal themes—time, love, death, home—on their mind. Such unity as the book has is one of sensibility and personal experience rather than style; Cowley had lived through a period of considerable upheaval in American poetry, and reviewers found evidence of influences as diverse as Masters, Cummings, Eliot, Jules Laforgue, and Vachel Lindsay.

The reviews of *Blue Juniata* were pretty much all that a fledgling author could hope for. Louis Untermeyer, one of the chief arbiters at the time of poetic reputations, in *The Saturday Review of Literature* called it "an auspicious debut" and wrote, "Here we have the material for a searching work, and the author does not fumble his chance; even in the most experimental pages, there is nothing superficial about Cowley." We've already encountered Harriet Monroe's flowery praise of Cowley's work in *Poetry*, and Horace Gregory in the New York *Sun* ("Not even Hart Crane can surpass Mr. Cowley's verbal excellence"), John Chamberlain in *The New York Times*, and Morton Dauwen Zabel in *The Nation* all had complimentary things to say.

By far the best and most perceptive review was by Cowley's close friend Allen Tate in *The New Republic*. The skids had been well greased for this one: "Wilson will see to it that your review is run in NR," Cowley had informed Tate chummily, and Tate had earlier offered some editorial suggestions about the book. This sort of cozy backscratching was a widespread practice in those days. In any case it opens with the kind of quotable quote authors dream of: "Like all of his writing, [*Blue Juniata*] is beautifully finished, and as poetry is of an order very rare in the American scene."

This was a review an author and publisher could take to the bank. *Blue Juniata* was a heartening success in terms of its critical reception and even, in the modest sense of volumes of poetry, commercially, selling out its first printing of a thousand copies. Its publication in many ways was a culmination and consolidation of everything Cowley had looked to accomplish in the twenties, not just with respect to his poetry but also to his gradual ascent to a position of stature in a literary world. With this first book Malcolm Cowley had in a real sense arrived. And his chief cheerleader, as ever, was Hart Crane, who watched the publication unfold with delight, writing to him from Paris, "You're a lucky boy! I've been reading some beautiful reviews of *Juniata* . . . I'm very glad about it all."

Nothing is harder to explain or predict than the workings of literary inspiration and productivity. Despite the satisfaction that Malcolm Cowley experienced in having his first collection well published and warmly received, he would not publish another poem until six years after *Blue Juniata* was published. He would publish three times as many poems in his first fourteen years as a published poet than he would in the next six decades of his life.

In fairness, as 1929 began, Cowley was busier than ever on multiple fronts. For one thing, his marriage was in its final stage of dissolution. And the stance of cultural disaffiliation that Cowley and his fellow writers had adopted was shifting into something different, an internal repatriation to match the physical return of so many exiles to America. Society and the wider world were reasserting their claim on the literary imagination over inner landscapes of visions and emotions. Fastidious distance and aestheticized disdain were proving to be unsustainable attitudes for American writers. On top of this, Cowley was to be offered a full-time job later that year that would change his life.

It bears reemphasizing that the segment of the literary class that Cowley and others of his particular interests and temperament composed stood more than a bit to one side of the attitudes and behaviors we think of when we "remember" the Roaring Twenties. The two great figures of the Lost Generation, Fitzgerald and Hemingway, both possessed a genius for publicity to complement their genius for composition. They got famous and they got rich and they set American literature on a new course, but they were each a unique case, impossible to usefully generalize from. They lived at a higher altitude and breathed different air. Nevertheless, when Cowley would look back on this period four years later in *Exile's Return*, he would cite Fitzgerald as the writer "whose novels and stories are in some ways the best record of this whole period." He quotes the passage from "Echoes of the Jazz Age" where Fitzgerald totes up the casualty list of "contemporaries of mine [who] had begun to disappear into the dark maw of violence"—from suicides who jumped from skyscraper windows to victims brutally murdered in speakeasies and insane asylums. This "wide-spread neurosis" appeared well before the Crash, and it was not, in Cowley's view, solely the fate of a self-selecting, well-heeled cosmopolitan elite badly overdrawn spiritually and psychically.

Much later, Cowley would give a fuller description of the arc of his literary generation's progress. In his view they had been content, even proud, to live simply and frugally in their tenement apartments or rural cabins and stick to their lasts as the gaudy parade passed by. But as the decade progressed and some of the easy money sloshed in their direction and they were taken up by rich dilettantes, "the simple contagion of bad examples" had its corrupting effect. "The recklessness of the 1920s, which had once seemed youthful and appealing, was dying away into nervous tears and drunken exasperation." While he was never a true "roaring boy" in the Crane or Fitzgerald mode, this still would have been informed by personal experience. His vivid description of a feverish round of parties that would greet the new year in this terminal period—the "caravans of taxicabs," the "laughing and screeching together: the friends and enemies, the cuckolds and the cuckolders, the wives and mistresses and the wives' girl," the drunken "quarrels of principles and declarations of eternal faith"—feel firsthand.

But Cowley: Model 1929 was altogether sleeker than preceding versions, demonstrating impressive literary development and many attractive new features. Like many writers he was emerging from the rarefied realm of literary aesthetics to take in the actual world around him. The year 1929 was the pivotal year of his life. The larger world was coming into focus for him. His critical thinking had sharpened and matured and he had found the clear, commonsense prose voice that would serve him so well. These developments were on full display in six reviews and essays he would write for Irita Van Doren in the *New York Herald Tribune* that year.

The first two appeared on successive Sundays in the book supplement. They were a kind of tour d'horizon and stock-taking as he and his generation reached their thirties. The first piece, titled "Our Own Generation," was a fuller development of his seminal essay "This Youngest Generation." Eight years on, Cowley had a great deal more actual evidence and a more impressive body of literary achievement to generalize from. To Cummings and Dos Passos he was able to add such figures as Glenway Wescott, Thornton Wilder, Hart Crane, F. Scott Fitzgerald, and, centrally, Ernest Hemingway. The essay summarizes the generational history of his literary cohort, its education, its influences, its experiences at home and abroad (especially the effects of the war), its preoccupations and ambitions, with a cogency impressive in a still-young critic. Cowley makes the statement, conventional wisdom to us now but far-seeing and even audacious in 1929, that "this wartime generation will be rather important in the history of American letters."

In the next Sunday's follow-up piece, "The New Primitives," Cowley addressed the ambient mood of cultural pessimism that had taken hold in the intellectual class in spite of all the abundant prosperity and hedonism. The book of that particular moment was the drama critic and professor of English Joseph Wood Krutch's *The Modern Temper*, which had defined "the progress of modern civilization as a series of lost illusions." Fitzgerald had famously proclaimed the rise of "a new generation . . . grown up to find all Gods dead, all wars fought, all faiths in man shaken" at the dawn of the decade. More somber figures like T. S. Eliot and Oswald Spengler in his *The Decline of the West* had elaborated on this theme and darkened it considerably. Krutch's turgid little tome packaged all this feel-bad thinking into a potent payload of gloom, and much like such later books as *The Culture of Narcissism* and *The Closing of the American Mind*, it found an unexpectedly large audience and became the subject of much punditry and chatter.

Cowley gestures at these ideas but he is less interested in their truth or falsity than in the way the mood they cast had affected the writers he dubs "the New Primitives." Citing Cummings, Dos Passos, Josephine Herbst, and especially Hemingway, he defines their emerging style as stripped down, deliberately unintellectual, and centering on "simple expressions (especially love and the fear of death) and in judgments of a very simple sort."

The piece made clear that Cowley had been paying Hemingway the closest possible attention. That was even more evident next October when he produced his review of *A Farewell to Arms*, possibly his best and most affecting work. The piece is much more than a book review. It begins by examining Hemingway's stature, achieved with startling speed in a mere six years, as not simply an admired writer, but a literary celebrity who has "expressed, better than any other writer, the limited viewpoint of his contemporaries, of the generation which was formed by the war and which is still incompletely demobilized." The review becomes a vehicle for Cowley not just to consider and praise the novel—which he does, calling it "his first love story" and "undoubtedly the most important book he has written"—but also to rehearse his own particular cohort's experience of the Great War in the ambulance services. In doing so, he puts forth for the first time in print the idea of the "*spectatorial* attitude toward the war" that was so central to his decade's long analysis of the Lost Generation's sensibility. This high-visibility review of a major novel in a prestigious book supplement inaugurated Malcolm Cowley's lifelong critical engagement with Hemingway.

Later that fall Cowley tied a handsome ribbon on his critical efforts for the year with a suite of three review-essays, prominently placed on the front page of the *Herald Tribune*. They consider, as he put it, "the soul of man under American capitalism." In "Machine-Made America" and "The Escape from America" he reviewed books by three social critics, each of whom was decrying the effects on American life of mass production, including the standardization of the artifacts of culture. The news was not good, especially for the middle and the thinking classes: "All of them picture educated Americans as being the slaves of machinery instead of its masters." Cowley largely accepts their critiques, if not their solutions to the problems raised, but instead of raging against the machines, he comes to a surprisingly optimistic conclusion. If American life was being engineered to produce styles of dress and thought and literature and art on almost an assembly-line basis, as it apparently was, then what we now call the creative class had a fairly bright future in providing those things.

The third essay, a review of an encyclopedic history of American poetry by Alfred Kreymborg, formerly an editor of *Broom*, uses the occasion to unpack the realities of "The Business of Being a Poet"—a subject Cowley knew plenty about, much of it dispiriting. By virtue of its tiny financial rewards, as opposed to, at least potentially, novels and plays, poetry "might be the last branch of literature to remain substantially free from commercialization." You can't sell out if nobody's buying. In his view, even America's finest poets had to devote too much of their time and effort not to writing poetry, but to the soul-consuming struggle to stay housed and fed and clothed. In retrospect, given the quite spectacular and permanent achievements of American poets in the last century, Cowley's pessimism was off base. But he was thinking hard about the material conditions under which American writers might possibly thrive and new American literature might be produced.

These six pieces for the *Herald Tribune* gave off a sense of new mastery and maturity. Almost as if in recognition, a job offer landed that would both solve his nagging financial problems and set him on a path of real and lasting power and influence on the literary scene. In early October, Malcolm Cowley went on staff at *The New Republic* as an associate editor.

Cowley tells two versions of how the job came about. In *The Dream of the Golden Mountains*, he states that he was hired by Bruce Bliven, the managing editor and a newspaperman with no particular literary passions. But in a 1972 appreciation of Edmund Wilson's time at and contributions to the magazine, he states, "He [Wilson] had persuaded the other editors to take me on. . . . I must have been one of his enthusiasms." At this time Wilson was recovering from a nervous breakdown that had sent him to a sanatorium, and he was also sensing the winds of change in the country and within himself. He might well have been putting Cowley in a convenient position to replace himself. Either way, the new job represented a great turning point in his career. At the most basic level his steady paycheck of a hundred dollars a week ($1,800 in 2024 dollars) was life-changing. His new job also put him at the center of the national conversation about not just literature, but politics, economics, culture, and international affairs, with the ability to add his own voice to it.

There is a certain irony in the timing. Malcolm Cowley managed to extricate himself from economic precarity at the moment when tens of millions of Americans were about to enter it. The Wall Street crash on Black Tuesday, October 29, 1929, served as the starting bell on a grim new chapter of the American experience that would leave no one untouched and would change the literary weather almost beyond recognition.

As the twenties came to an end, Cowley suffered from "the uneasy feeling of having perhaps belonged to a literary period that was mistaken in its general aims." The sense of an ending, of radical individualism having exhausted its possibilities, was unquestionably strong. He would write that "two or three of one's friends committed suicide for reasons that were artistic rather than financial. It was as if they had wished to write in their blood that an era was ending, and their deaths were so interpreted." We know who two of those "friends" were.

One of them was the high-living, sun-worshipping Harry Crosby, whose double suicide by gunshot with a young woman not his wife on the afternoon of December 10, 1929, in the Hotel des Artistes generated front-page headlines. He left no note or explanation for this shocking act, but Cowley would view it as a cautionary tale of his generation. There is no question that Crosby's life and death made for good copy of the lurid tabloid variety. Bankrolled by his family money, Crosby embarked on a life devoted to excess on every front—drugs, sex, alcohol, gaudy and riotous parties and orgies and entertainments. Pursuing Euro-style decadence with an impressive all-American energy, he was like a Fitzgerald without the essential innocence (and talent) or a Gerald Murphy without the inherent grace (and talent). Essentially, he was a well-funded wastrel, but one with certain literary pretensions, a poet of very modest gifts, and a publisher of genuine taste. Like the Crash, there is something overdetermined about Harry Crosby as the poster boy for Lost Generation recklessness and its consequences.

Cowley actually had a far better and more distinguished candidate for that role, but his end was far too fresh and raw and painful for him to be able to deal with. The second suicide he alluded to was that of his close friend Hart Crane, who killed himself on April 27, 1932. Cowley was intimately involved with the events that led up to that tragic event and its aftermath; emotionally, his twenties really came to a shattering end on that date. It would haunt him for the rest of his life. Three weeks after the event, he would express his reluctance to write about it: "There's a lot of it that doesn't bear setting down on paper: it would seem like the mere retelling of a scandal when, as a matter of fact, it's poignant and tragic."

In 1929, as the manuscript of *Blue Juniata* was making its way to publishers and then to publication, Hart Crane was finishing the manuscript of *The Bridge*. He'd conceived of this "mystical synthesis of

'America'" with the Brooklyn Bridge as the climactic "symbol of our constructive future, our unique identity" as early as February 1923. He had written much of it in 1926 at his family's property on the Isle of Pines in Cuba over a six-month burst of inspiration, and he'd continued to work on it fitfully for the next two years. In January he'd moved abroad to Paris on a modest inheritance from his grandmother, essentially in flight from his mother, who'd done all she could to prevent any money from being paid out from the trust. In the midst of "a social whirl—all sorts of amusing people, scandalous scenes, café encounters, etc."—he'd met and been taken up by Harry and Caresse Crosby, who'd introduced Crane to the nosebleed strata of French society, given him some financial support, and laid plans to publish the still-unfinished *The Bridge* in a limited edition. Despite his accelerating drinking and some unfortunate incidents, including a dispute at Le Select that landed him in a French jail for six days, he was able to make the final additions and revisions to his poem, in France and then back in the U.S., by the end of the year. Although Crosby was by this point dead, Black Sun Press brought out its limited edition of *The Bridge*, with a frontispiece of the famous painting of the Brooklyn Bridge by Joseph Stella, in Paris and New York in early 1930. Boni & Liveright published the American trade edition in April of that year.

The Bridge is today an acknowledged masterpiece, flawed and imperfect but still a masterpiece. As a reading experience it presents many difficulties of understanding, but it consistently rewards the diligent reader with a sense of exaltation and transcendence. It was his heroic attempt to transform the materials of American history and mythology into a symphonically constructed national epic. However, Crane would learn that, much as his hero Herman Melville had experienced with *Moby-Dick*, the production of a masterpiece can be hazardous to one's career and psychic well-being. Shortly after Crane had finished the poem, he and Cowley were walking along a country road, and Cowley, worried for his friend, ventured to offer some advice. He said that Crane had been "devoting himself to the literature of ecstasy" and that the psychological strain of such a pursuit might prove too much for him to bear. Perhaps, Cowley ventured, he might table poetry for a while and try his hand at some "unambitious prose." Crane cut him short. "Oh, you mean I oughtn't to drink so much." "That night I woke up feeling that he was already doomed, already dead," Cowley would write.

Even, or maybe especially, a masterpiece can be misunderstood. Although *The Bridge* received generally good reviews and sold out, like *Blue Juniata*, its first printing of a thousand copies, two negative reviews from men Crane confidently thought of as his firm supporters arrived as painful betrayals. The worst was by his waspish and mercurial friend Yvor Winters in the June 1930 issue of *Poetry*, an unrelenting thirteen-page evisceration that judged the poem to have decisively failed in its epic ambitions by the absence of any narrative structure. In *The Hound & Horn*, Allen Tate saw *The Bridge* as a terminal instance of the romantic impulse in poetry, one that lacked an adequate symbolic or narrative structure. The negative opinion of both men cut Crane to the quick.

At least his friend Malcolm Cowley came through for him. In his review in *The New Republic* of *The Bridge* he did Crane two favors. The first was to duck the by now tiresome critical exercise of taxing him with his shortcomings by bluntly declaring, "The faults of 'The Bridge' I shall leave to other reviewers." The second was to make the focus of his review the section of the poem titled "The River," which even Tate and Winters granted was superb. A visionary imagined journey by the poet, first on a train westward from Manhattan and then down the Mississippi with three hoboes, "The River" succeeds as a kind of *Odyssey* on American waters that concludes, not with a return to Ithaca, but with the grand solemnity of "a slow hymn to the river" (Cowley's words) as it empties into the Gulf of Mexico. Crane blends the registers of the native lingo of his drifters and the resonant sound of American places with his own elevated poetic diction, and Cowley warmly appreciated his accomplishment.

Another problem with the production of a masterpiece is the frequent resulting depletion of financial and spiritual resources. Crane had spent seven years struggling with the long and difficult creation of *The Bridge*, and now that it was in the world he felt emptied of inspiration and purpose. Crane was anything but a careful steward of his talent and he was utterly unable to ride out such a fallow period. He was once again out of money and feared that his poetic gift had departed for good. "Constant anxiety is wearing me out. It has already corroded my mind to the point where I can write neither poetry *nor* the most obvious hack work," he would tell a friend. Meanwhile the intoxication that used to lead to poetic inspiration was now leading only to even more intoxication and even more dismaying outcomes.

The last two years of Hart Crane's life rival the demise of Edgar Allan Poe for their grimness. He was able to secure a Guggenheim Fellowship in March of 1931 meant to bankroll his travel to France, but at the last minute, influenced by some advice from friends (including Cowley) and a reading of D. H. Lawrence's *The Plumed Serpent*, he switched his destination to Mexico City, where he planned to work on another North American epic, on Cortés and the conquest of the Aztecs. He stayed with Katherine Anne Porter, also on a Guggenheim, until a string of drunken episodes caused him to have to remove himself to a residence in the Mixcoac quarter of the city. By now every encounter with a taxi driver held the potential for a tequila-fueled dispute over price, arrest, and a night in jail.

Crane's father died on July 6, and just about the time that Crane left for Cleveland to settle affairs, his old friend Peggy Cowley arrived in Mexico City to seek a divorce from Malcolm Cowley, from whom she'd been separated since the spring. When Crane returned, her presence was a welcome relief from and balm for his many troubles, and the feeling was mutual. "We were 'home' to each other, and both of us needed 'home,'" she would write after his death. Two vulnerable people, together in a foreign country, each at a moment of great sadness in their lives—it is easy, at least on an emotional level, to understand what happened next. Peggy, always fragile in health, had to move from the chilly high altitude of Mexico City to a rented house in the small town of Taxco, a hundred miles or so south. Two days before Christmas Day, 1931, Crane arrived by bus at Peggy's house for a Christmas party. That night, after the revels and the departure of the guests and more drinking and dancing in the town plaza, Hart and Peggy fell into bed to the pealing sound of the cathedral bells and became lovers.

This was a genuine affair of the heart on both sides. Peggy Cowley was the first and last woman Hart Crane ever had sex with, and even during the short span of their affair he would continue to have sex with men as well. ("The old beauty still claims me, however, and my eyes roam as much as ever.") Nevertheless as the affair progressed the couple even began to speak of marriage after Peggy's divorce became final. "I'll make you a good husband yet," Crane declared. They went public with all this in February and Peggy moved in with Crane in Mixcoac. Their relationship was anything but peaceful, punctuated by many drunken breakups and reconciliations.

Word of the affair could only have been unsettling to Malcolm Cowley, an enormously challenging piece of news. We don't know exactly when or from whom Cowley would have learned of it, probably from Peggy, but Crane's letters to him shift slowly from disingenuousness ("Peggy and I had the pleasantest Christmas and New Years together that I remember for ages"—January 6, 1932) to a kind of coy, oblique cheerfulness ("Peggy and I think and talk a great deal about you. . . . We're very happy together—and send you lots of love!"—March 27, 1932). Leave it to Hart Crane to append a chipper exclamation point to a marital situation straight out of an Edward Albee play.

That letter, his final one to Cowley, was sent on Easter along with the text of Crane's last poem, "The Broken Tower," which he began writing almost simultaneously with the beginning of his affair. The arrival of love had accomplished what intoxication could not: It revived his muse. He sent a copy at the same time to Morton Dauwen Zabel at *Poetry*. Crane was riven with worry to know whether his gift, which he'd feared he'd lost, had really returned. But the letter to Zabel never made it to him, and three weeks later Crane wrote him a nervous follow-up, one of his last letters. Cowley had written to Crane with a letter of praise for the poem, but it may have been delayed a bit, what with his new workload at *The New Republic*, and so it would not reach him. The missed connection would haunt him.

The advent of romance and the return of poetry did little to stop Crane's descent into an anxiety-fueled mania. His father's will had left him the equivalent of an annual Guggenheim for some time, an enormous relief once he'd learned of it. But it slowly became clear that the business conditions of the Depression had badly depleted the assets of the estate and little or no money would be forthcoming. His actual Guggenheim Fellowship had ended and Crane was reduced to writing frantic requests to his friends for loans. He was losing faith in his vocation, complaining, "What place is there for poets in this world? What good are poets today? The world needs men of action." He began drinking even more heavily and got into baroque and violent disputes with his houseman. One terrible day he took a straight razor to the canvas of his portrait painted by the artist David Siqueiros. After this he attempted suicide by drinking a bottle of iodine, but Peggy knocked it from his hand. A doctor was called and a sedative was administered. Crane feverishly rewrote his will, leaving everything to a sailor-lover, and then attempted suicide again, this time with a bottle of harmless Mercurochrome. Another doctor's visit, and now morphine and sleeping pills were given to settle him down.

Although late in her life Peggy Cowley would claim that Crane's suicide attempts were not entirely serious, she realized that her lover was beyond her control and they needed to return to the States, where help from his friends and family would be possible. They booked passage on the *Orizaba*—the same ship Crane had come to Mexico on. And after some typically frenzied attempts on his part to procure the necessary funds for passage, he and Peggy sailed from Veracruz to New York with what worldly goods they had. On a stopover in Havana, bad luck struck when a box of matches exploded in Peggy's hand and burned her so badly she almost lost a finger. Bandaged up by a doctor and heavily sedated for her acute pain and told to rest, she was unable to keep tabs on the agitated Crane, who started drinking and went on an all-night tear. What exactly happened was unclear, but he may have propositioned a cabin boy or some sailors in their quarters and he turned up badly beaten and without his wallet or ring. Then he almost succeeded in climbing over the ship's railing before someone tackled him and he was locked up in his cabin.

The next morning, after having her wound freshly dressed, Peggy returned to her cabin to find a contrite Crane there in his pajamas. He had only faint memories of what had transpired the night before, but he knew it had been humiliating. "I'm not going to make it, dear. I'm utterly disgraced," he declared. Peggy told him he'd feel better after he'd gone back to his cabin and dressed and freshened up. "All right, dear. Good-bye," he replied.

Shortly thereafter, Hart Crane walked up to the stern railing of the promenade deck in a coat and pajamas. He folded his coat over the railing and then vaulted over it into the sea. The cries of "Man overboard" went up, and Crane was seen briefly swimming, "strongly," an eyewitness said. Had he decided at the last moment to try to save himself? Life preservers were thrown into the water and lifeboats lowered, but by then he was lost sight of, and for two hours the *Orizaba* slowly circled in a fruitless search before giving up and resuming its northward course. And so Hart Crane suffered an early death by water, like the Romantic poet Shelley, to whom he'd often been compared. "Poet Lost at Sea" the newspaper headlines would blare. Peggy Cowley wired a radiogram to her husband that day at *The New Republic*: "Hart committed suicide meet me." He was at the pier as the *Orizaba* docked in New York.

Hart Crane's suicide was neither a mystery nor a surprise. There are no real unanswered questions about it. But it arrived as shattering news nonetheless. No one was more shattered than Malcolm Cowley. As radically different as they were from each other in temperament and sexual preferences and literary taste, they'd been true brothers in the poetic arts. One of the few books that Crane had managed to carry along with him on his last voyage was his signed copy of *Blue Juniata*. Of all of Crane's critics, Malcolm Cowley was the most sympathetic to his achievements and the least inclined to take him to task for his shortfalls. Those achievements were on poignant display in "The Broken Tower," a permanent contribution to American poetry. How painful it was for Cowley not to be able to tell his friend what he'd achieved, that a man who had written such a great poem had every reason to hope for his future, not despair of it. "It's a love poem and it is really tremendous," he would conclude a heartsick letter to Allen Tate five days after word of Crane's death reached him. He was one of the few people who knew who had inspired the poem, the person to whom such lines as "And so it was I entered the broken world / To trace the visionary company of love" were addressed. Malcolm and Peggy would be united in their own private mixture of grief and unreasonable guilt. And the imagery of the tower would have immediately cast his mind to that evening in Brooklyn Heights when he and Crane and Allen Tate formed their poetic bond on the waterfront.

Cowley did what he could under the circumstances. He wrote to Morton Dauwen Zabel at *Poetry* to explain the botched submission of the poem and got his permission to print "The Broken Tower" in *The New Republic* instead. It ran on June 8, 1932, on the same page as an elegy, "To Hart Crane," by John Brooks Wheelwright. The month before, he wrote an unsigned tribute to Crane in the front of the book, "Death of a Poet." Part obituary, part diagnosis of the conditions that led to his demise, part appreciation of his work, it ended by framing his suicide as "a poem of action which the world could interpret in its own fashion." If Cowley's own poetic impulse had been operative at the time, he might have written his own elegy to his dead doomed friend, something in the vein of Milton's "Lycidas" or Tennyson's "In Memoriam." Instead he turned to prose, memorializing his friend in essays and reviews and memoirs for the rest of his life, pieces full of love and regret and fondness and dismay and appreciation and the kind of unresolved, unending sorrow that a suicide leaves in its wake.

And so the twenties truly ended for Malcolm Cowley two years and five months after the calendar said they had. The failing economy would accomplish what he and his fellow literary insurgents had been unable to. Earlier in the decade the Aesthetes had been firing their peashooters at the unbreakable steel and plate-glass facade of American industrial civilization, to little effect. Now "the Depression was like a crash of breaking glass that let in the cold night air." He would recall, "In the literary world as in the country at large, 1930 was the strangest year of the century," as seemingly everybody did their best to ignore the disaster taking hold. At its end America would be broken and literature could no longer be thought of as a private affair. It was about to go public and political, almost overnight.

SEVEN.

TO THE BARRICADES

Somewhere on the bookshelves or in the attics of aging history and English majors can be found copies of a comprehensive anthology of American writings from the 1930s titled *Years of Protest*. It dates from 1967, when the decade of the thirties was just beginning to acquire its antique patina and serve as fodder for the classes that the book was intended to serve. Most people today would consider the book's cover image all too much "on the nose," but it suits our purpose. The illustrator has rendered a figure of a white male in a suit, standing astride a manual typewriter in a stance of impassioned oratory, left hand clenched in a fist, the index finger of the right hand pointing out forcefully in either accusation or exhortation. The message is clear. Where once the writer was thought to be a figure in an ivory tower, spinning the dross of isolation and inner contemplation into works of exquisite, if hermetic, beauty, he now had burst forth with urgent energy into a world in crisis, and in need of him.

Malcolm Cowley fits the role of that writer perfectly. With startling speed he would transform himself from the beau ideal of the aestheticized twenties into a literary action figure, a man in ceaseless motion riding a wave of cultural and political revolution. He was to be found at the bloody crossroads where literature and politics met, an intersection more ubiquitous in the thirties than in any other decade of American history. Cowley would throw himself headlong into every activist arena and forum, countless panels, picket lines, conferences, congresses, strikes, parades, in city squares and packed auditoriums and church basements and the back rooms of low bars, wherever the new literary language of class revolution was spoken.

Everywhere he went, Cowley carried with him the prestige of his close association with the luminaries of a literary generation that would come to be seen as equal in achievement to that of the American Renaissance of Thoreau, Hawthorne, and Melville. He would be a key figure in the fashioning of that critical assessment. His perch as the chief literary editor and spokesperson for *The New Republic* gave him power and sway among the influential classes of the left. That power, and a certain naivete in political matters, would cause him to make many bitter enemies both on the right and in some sectors of the radical left, leading him to be labeled, with some justice, a Stalinist fellow traveler. It would be a label he would seek to shake for the rest of his life, but it stuck—not least because it was true. The dramatic, strife-torn, and idealistic thirties were Malcolm Cowley's great decade. They were also nearly his undoing.

———

Malcolm Cowley was elected to the editorial board of *The New Republic* on March 26, 1930, less than six months after first being hired, and made his first appearance on the masthead in the November 19, 1930, issue. He was joining distinguished company: the managing editor, Bruce Bliven; the business and economics thinker George Soule; the professor of literature Robert Morss Lovett; the drama critic Stark Young; and Edmund Wilson. Among the powerfully influential contributing editors could be found Jane Addams of Hull House fame; the pragmatist John Dewey, by far the most famous philosopher in the country; the visionary urbanist and social thinker Lewis Mumford; the famed critic of the popular arts Gilbert Seldes; and Rexford Tugwell, at the time a professor of economics who in two years would join FDR's "Brains Trust" and become a key architect of the New Deal. Cowley had arrived at the very center of American intellectual life, a prominent perch that he would soon turn into his bully pulpit.

By 1930 *The New Republic* had established itself as the most important journal of politics and ideas in the country. Its circulation was small, no more than twelve thousand readers at the time, but they were the right twelve thousand people. People who took ideas seriously, people in a position to spread and amplify those ideas and, in many cases, put them into concrete action. The magazine had been founded in 1914; one of its first editors was Herbert Croly, the social philosopher whose influential 1907 book *The Promise of American Life* had attracted the attention of a number of those right people. Chief among them was Theodore Roosevelt, who adopted a phrase that appeared in it precisely once, "the new nationalism," as the slogan of his insurgent Bull Moose Party run for the presidency in 1912. Croly's book became a bible for the progressive movement.

Progressivism is often taken to be identical to liberalism, but it was not. The two philosophies did overlap in their opposition to the vast power of the corporate monopolies of the day. An activist and increasingly centralized federal government would be the only entity able to bring such combines to heel and break them up into manageable entities. Government would also take on the responsibility for ministering to the health and education and safety of Americans through expansive programs and for increasing their prosperity by means of large-scale economic planning, including the nationalization of key industries. The direct election of U.S. senators, the introduction of a graduated income tax, and suffrage for women were other elements of the progressive platform.

But progressivism was a top-down movement, one where elites made the big decisions and which was deeply hostile to class division and social disorder. It was more than comfortable with such noxious ideas as eugenics and restricting immigration to the so-called Aryan races of northern Europe. And it was the "progressive" Southerner Woodrow Wilson who segregated the federal government and praised D. W. Griffith's racist paean to the Ku Klux Klan, *The Birth of a Nation*.

The New Republic was the brainchild of Croly and two other men, the economist turned journalist Walter Weyl and the young Walter Lippmann, who had shed the socialism of his Harvard years to make a glittering reputation with two impressive big-statement books, *A Preface to Morals* (1912) and later *Drift and Mastery* (1914). They found the ideal backers to bankroll their ambitious plans in the persons of cultivated banker and businessman Willard Straight, who had worked for both Teddy Roosevelt and J. P. Morgan, and his wife, Dorothy Whitney, of the New York Whitneys, heir to her father's vast fortune made in streetcar lines and investments in Standard Oil. If these high-minded individuals ever contemplated that much of what would appear in *TNR* was inimical to their class interest, it never interfered with their generous and constant financial support of the enterprise. Nor did the couple ever interfere editorially. Willard Straight died in 1918 of influenza at the Paris Peace Conference; his widow met the brilliant English agricultural economist Leonard Elmhirst two years later and they married in 1925. The couple's hands-off support continued unabated, and their disinterested generosity meant that for much of its long life *The New Republic* operated blissfully and even uniquely free of financial strain.

The editors of *The New Republic* were far more inclined to tinker with the economic and governmental arrangements of the American people than with their editorial template, which never varied from one weekly issue to the next. The layout and type design were austere and lacking in visual interest; photographs and line drawings rarely if ever appeared. It was printed on cheap, fingertip-lacerating butcher paper. Advertising was sparse. In Cowley's words, "Advertisers were tolerated, but there was no attempt to please them," with ads for books, lecture series, and culturally enriching junkets squeezed into the last two or three pages. The front of the book began with unsigned leaders and editorials on political and cultural topics of the day, followed by longer signed articles, mostly on weighty matters of politics or economics or international relations.

The so-called back of the book, the domain that Cowley was to inherit, was for reviews of books for the most part, but also of plays, films, and musical performances, and wide-ranging essays on culture. From the distance of almost a century, the content of the front of the book can seem time-bound, sometimes mind-numbingly granular and technical (foreign bond issues, long-forgotten treaties, banking regulations). The back of the book in issues from those years, in contrast, still gives off a feeling of lively engagement, wit, and erudition.

The twenties were not good years generally for the front of the book. The confidence and élan vital of liberal progressivism had been sapped by the bitter disappointment of the punitive Treaty of Versailles and the assaults on civil liberties perpetrated by the Wilson administration, which at one time had actually heeded the counsels of *TNR*. Wilson was succeeded by three successive business-minded Republican presidents disinclined to fiddle in any way with an economy delivering widespread prosperity and a soaring stock market. The American people had little taste for the kinds of high-minded reform and scolding lectures that were the progressives' stock in trade; they were content to cash in, let the good times roll, and make the kind of whoopee that Prohibition, newfound mobility, and loosening morals made possible. Politically, *TNR* and progressivism were stalled, to the point that Herbert Croly was reduced in 1924 to wanly defining the magazine's goal as "less to inform and entertain its readers than to start little insurrections in the realm of their convictions." This was a far cry from proclaiming the promise of American life.

But the twenties ushered in a literary renaissance as well, and that was very good for the back of the book. The brilliant Edmund Wilson joined *TNR* as an associate editor and chief book reviewer in 1926 and quickly gave it a strong jolt of intellectual energy, setting the agenda for the range of duties the magazine's future literary editors would undertake. He regularly contributed articles and reviews himself on subjects as varied as Harry Houdini, the radical cartoonist Art Young, *Lady Chatterley's Lover*, his literary contemporaries Ernest Hemingway, Thornton Wilder, and John Dos Passos, and the deficiencies of American literary criticism, which he would do much to repair. He would later testify that the task of writing regularly on a wide range of subjects for the educated but not specialized audience of *TNR* helped create him as the writer he became. The same would be true of Malcolm Cowley.

At this time Malcolm Cowley took another crucial step in establishing his domestic stability and long-term happiness when he met and moved in with the fashion writer Muriel Maurer, shortly after he and Peggy began their divorce proceedings. Maurer had grown up in Yorkville, the German section of Manhattan, and attended public schools there. But she dropped out of high school at age sixteen to begin work. Her first job was working for Henry Miller in the personnel department of Western Union as his secretary; someone had spied her reading *Crime and Punishment* in the file room and told Miller she was just the person for the job. She eventually would become the fashion editor for a newspaper called the *Dry Goods Economist* and then a buyer for Saks Fifth Avenue and other stores. She and Cowley made a fast and strong connection, and they would be married once Cowley's divorce was final. He and Muriel would remain married for the rest of their lives; her love and support made his successes and, at times, recoveries, possible.

Cowley had been hired to replace associate editor T. S. Matthews, who was moving on to *Time* magazine, where he would become one its most powerful editors. His duties were the mundane but crucial ones of copyediting and proofreading, as the standards of the magazine in those departments were felt to have fallen badly. One of the first tests of Cowley's blue-penciling skills was to edit a series of articles by John Dewey; "I was appalled by reading his prose in the raw," he remembered. Dewey saw proofs of the heavily worked-over pieces and returned them without comment. Apparently, editing Dewey's tangled copy was a trial by fire all junior editors had to undergo.

Another job of Cowley's was to go to the printers on Tuesday to put the magazine to bed, along with the assistant he had inherited, a young Martha Gellhorn, whom he would describe as "a Bryn Mawr girl with literary ambitions and a lot of yellow hair." Perhaps dreaming of a glamorous future that would include a globetrotting career as a journalist and a stormy marriage to Ernest Hemingway, the details of typesetting and printing did not much engage her, so he eventually took to sending her home earlier and doing the job himself. Gellhorn was heading out the door in any case, and when her replacement, the highly competent Betty Huling, proved more than up to the tasks assigned her, he left those Tuesday chores to her and began to attend the editorial meetings that also took place on those days.

At thirty-two years of age, Cowley was the youngest person at the table, and, tellingly, he later wrote that "like most writers of my own generation I had rather prided myself as being ignorant of economics and contemptuous of politicians." He kept silent on matters like bond issues and banking regulations, but spoke out forthrightly on the things that did engage him, broadly issues concerned with good writing. He began to be regarded by his fellow editors as a literary asset.

Meanwhile, Wilson was becoming scarcer around the office. His groundbreaking study of the roots of Modernist literature in the Symbolist movement, *Axel's Castle*, was in the process of being serialized in the magazine and would appear in 1931 to widespread praise. A study of the life-renouncing tendency of such writers as Joyce, Stein, Valéry, Eliot, and, in the book's most crucial chapter, Proust, to retreat to the ivory tower, it remains one of the great works of criticism of the past century. Wilson's critics and biographers have interpreted the book as a reflection of his nervous breakdown and a pivotal turn against literature for literature's sake in favor of political engagement. One can sense the emerging zeitgeist of the thirties in Wilson's valediction of Proust as "the last great historian of the loves, the society, the intelligence, the diplomacy, the literature and art of the Heartbreak House of capitalist culture." It is even more striking that a critical study of some of the most hermetic and interior works ever produced would express the following sentiments in its final chapter: "Americans and Europeans are both becoming more and more conscious of Russia, a country where central social-political idealism has been able to inspire the artist as well as the engineer. The question begins to press us again as to whether it is possible to make a practical success of human society." Wilson in no way was writing off his Symbolist masters, but he does suggest that the art of the future will harness their breakthroughs in imaginative techniques to broader, more collective, less individual ends.

Wilson would have written those words within a year or less after Black Tuesday, 1929. It is a telling index of just how quickly a sense of possibly terminal crisis had gripped the minds of American intellectuals. In the fall of 1930, he announced that he was resigning his post as literary editor to take to the road and report on the conditions in an

America in accelerating economic free fall. A less likely roving reporter than the shy, portly, and sedentary Wilson can hardly be imagined. Cowley surmised that Wilson had never even been anywhere
west of Pittsburgh. But Wilson's dispatches from the coal mines, car
factories, picket lines, Communist rallies, Los Angeles churches, and
the Hoover Dam in the first year of the Great Depression, collected in
The American Jitters (1932), remain among the indispensable accounts
of that time. So off on the road went Wilson, and into the plum and
powerful job of the literary editor of *The New Republic* moved the
bright young(ish) man who had so distinguished himself by his intelligence in the editorial meetings. The back of the book was Cowley's
to shape. He had arrived.

The speed with which Americans of all classes lost confidence in
the entire free-market system was stunning. On October 28, 1929, the
day before the Black Tuesday stock market crash, the front page of *The
New York Times* portrayed a world that, while hardly placid, showed
little sign of the crack-up to come. A year later, on November 19,
1930, the same day Cowley appeared on the *TNR* masthead, the
Times front page featured this headline above the fold, upper left:
"$1,400,000 Raised in Drive to Provide Jobs for Idle . . . 4,500 Now
Put to Work—Rapid Progress Reported Toward $6,000,000 Goal to
Employ 20,000." The article goes on to report on a campaign by the
leaders of American business, finance, and industry to provide "relief
on a large and constructive scale in the form of employment rather
than charity," complete with the reassurance that "it would not be long
before the country would return to a normal state of prosperity."

The New Republic was well ahead of the *Times* in grasping the severity of the emerging economic crisis. In Cowley's masthead debut
issue, a long unsigned editorial laces into the country's "Bankrupt
Business Leadership" for its "poverty-stricken" lack of ideas "in the
midst of one of the worst depressions the world has ever known." In

"No Money, No Work," Bruce Bliven visited in Chicago the kind of encampment of homeless men that would soon be dubbed "Hoovervilles" and reported on the desperate unemployment situation in Boston, Cleveland, Detroit, Philadelphia, and a half dozen other American cities, in a time when the United States had no unemployment insurance whatsoever.

As Cowley was taking control of the literary pages of *The New Republic*, he had to navigate the backwash from one of the most savage critical hit jobs of the century, by Mike Gold, "Wilder: Prophet of the Genteel Christ" in the October 22 issue. While he was not directly involved in assigning and editing the piece, it set the tone for a great deal of the literary and critical skirmishes just up ahead and must have influenced his editorial thinking. He was not pleased by it. To quote a historian who interviewed Cowley directly about the incident, "While Malcolm Cowley was away for a brief period in 1930, [Edmund Wilson] dipped mischievously into the magazine's barrel of manuscripts and plucked out an attack on Thornton Wilder by Marxist polemicist Mike Gold. Much to Cowley's dismay the offensive review of the popular novelist's *The Bridge of San Luis Rey* (which the other editor printed in its rawest form) touched off what soon become known as 'the literary class war.'"

Mike Gold, born Irwin Granich, the product of the immigrant slums of the Lower East Side, a world he captured vividly in his classic *Jews Without Money*, was a known quantity as a rabble-rouser. He had come up through the radical-Bohemian-anarchist milieu of *The Liberator* and the Provincetown Players and Greenwich Village and was a strident proponent of social revolution and the artist's imperative to help bring it about. In *The Masses* in 1929, ten months before the Crash, he'd written the prescient exhortation "Go Left, Young Writers!," in which he'd predicted, "The American orgy has been pitched on the crater of the historic social volcano," insulted Scott and Zelda

Fitzgerald as "a hard, successful, ignorant jazzy bourgeois of about thirty-five, and his leech-like young wife," and all but ordered America's working class to produce a new proletarian literature. As a critic, he wielded a Marxist sledgehammer and almost everything to him looked like a nail. Gold had already taken a vicious and homophobic swipe at Thornton Wilder in *The New Masses*, calling him "a beautifully rouged, combed, well-dressed corpse, lying among the sacred candles and lilies of the past." This new attack was even worse in every way.

The whole incident is curious. Wilson the critic had reviewed Wilder's work favorably in *The New Republic* earlier and would have known that Mike Gold's crude style would not do, and Wilson the editor should have filed down the piece's sharper edges and expunged the uglier aspersions. But not only did he run the piece as written, but he wrote an unsigned editorial that ran a month later, after the magazine had been deluged by letters, most of them in protest. Everybody seemed to feel the urge to weigh in; the flood abated only two months later with a puckish note declaring, "The Gold-Wilder controversy is hereby called on account of darkness."

Wilson had seized on Gold's piece as the vehicle or mouthpiece for his own mounting disgust with an American civilization in decline, and Wilder was simply collateral damage. As both publicity and prophecy the piece was a rip-roaring success. Mike Gold would go on to practice his literary pugilism as an influential columnist in *The New Masses* and then *The Daily Worker*. Wilson would commence his immensely productive travels across an America in ever-mounting crisis and take an even more radical turn in his political pronouncements. And Malcolm Cowley, whatever his discomfort about this public flagellation of Wilder, whom he admired, inherited a review section that now had just acquired greatly increased visibility and influence and been strongly shifted leftward. Wilson would later write, "The Gold-Wilder case marks definitely the eruption of the Marxist issues out of the literary circles of the radicals into the field of general criticism. It has now become plain that the economic crisis is to be accompanied by a literary one."

There was still a weekly magazine to put out. Bruce Bliven points out with some pride in a memoir that at *TNR*, "five editors, or sometimes only four [Bliven himself, Soule, Lovett, Young, and Cowley generally] got out a paper with about 30,000 words a week of editorial matter, while *Time* was producing about the same quantity with, at that time, something like eighty people." The work was strenuous and the deadlines never-ending, but the conditions were about as pleasant as it gets in the field of high-end opinion production. The magazine was located in three brownstones on West Twenty-First Street in a placid corner of Chelsea, and Cowley took over Wilson's desk in the book department upstairs. Cowley would remember it as an aerie: "There, in a big room under the roof, with its windows looking over a double rank of backyards, I could lead a sheltered life in the midst of the hurricane, almost as if I had been given a post at the General Theological Seminary across the street."

The shabby-genteel atmosphere extended into the offices themselves, which were furnished with a mixture of threadbare carpets, heirloom antiques, secondhand desks, and filing cabinets. Two or three times a week the editors would gather around the large dining room table for excellent lunches and the occasional dinner prepared by a cook named Lucie, who lived in the basement with her husband, Etienne, the butler. At these meetings the magazine's posture toward issues of the day would be hammered out. On Wednesday afternoons the editors would compete in deck tennis in the backyard. Add in the financial security provided by the magazine's benefactors, and a more congenial place to contemplate the accelerating economic disaster can hardly be imagined.

Congenial as well was the sense of camaraderie and high purpose among the editors. Cowley would remember many decades later that "the moral atmosphere, too, was that of a family rather than of a business office." The workplace he recalls was largely free of the poisonous internal politics that so often can infect an enterprise staffed by high-strung brainworkers. Bruce Bliven exercised direction with a very light touch. The chief economic thinker on the staff was George Soule, whose dream of an efficient and well-planned society carried forward *TNR*'s progressive program. The drama editor, Stark Young, tended to his corner of the performing arts, while Cowley had the literary field almost entirely to himself.

Following Wilson's lead and his own growing inclinations, Cowley would pull the back of the book sharply to the left in the months and years to come, creating a disjunction with the generally liberal/progressive slant of the front of the book. A great deal of controversy would result. Many years later, in 1970, Bliven would state with equanimity that Cowley "was always able to defend the reviewers and what they had said, in terms that then seemed adequate in light of all the circumstances." He also claimed never to have regretted allowing Cowley to write a lead review himself without any of the other editors having inspected it.

In those early years of the Great Depression, the editors of *The New Republic* began to feel that the magazine was "curiously close to the center of what was happening in America." The mainstream press was in deep denial about the crisis gripping the country, blowing on any scrap of good economic news like the embers of a dying fire. In contrast the magazine's editors, free of any need to keep advertisers happy, could report the grim truth as they saw it. Letters began to arrive not from the typical *TNR* readers (academics and other professional liberals), but from people like a Chicago brakeman out of work, a small-business man forced to lay off half of his workforce, a bank clerk with a fractured skull from a cop's nightstick wielded against a demonstration of the unemployed, a Midwestern farm mother feeding her children with some form of mush without milk, the cows having gone dry. Visitors from around the globe arrived at the office to tell tales of international woe over Lucie's French cooking: correspondents testifying to famine and repression in Russia; a German émigré professor in flight from crowds chanting "Grease the Guillotine"; political exiles of all stripes from Democrat to Socialist to Communist from India, Hungary, Italy, China; witnesses to violence being visited upon strikers in Appalachian mining towns, California factory farms, Southern textile mills. Also showing up were a fair number of shining-eyed cranks with harebrained schemes, along with some truly visionary if impractical forward-thinkers with elaborate plans for everything from currency reform to top-to-bottom reorganization of society. Any one of these people might have had an important part in a larger and necessary truth. Cowley would write, "We listened to all our visitors if we had the time: stamped-scrip enthusiasts, self-help and barter enthusiasts, silver enthusiasts, single taxers, Townsendites, Social Crediters, primitive Christians, primitive communists, and more and more disciples of Marx and Lenin."

Wilson channeled his own mounting anger and disgust in his famous manifesto and cri de coeur on the social, moral, and economic bankruptcy of the American way of life, "An Appeal to Progressives," in the January 14, 1931, issue of the magazine. It was a fiery and comprehensive indictment of, among other matters, the failures of capitalism-accommodating liberalism to offer any real solution for the human miseries of the deepening economic abyss and the complete emptiness of an American business civilization focused solely on "the momentum of money-making." He stated that "the present depression may be nothing less than one of the turning points in our history, our first real crisis since the Civil War."

Predictably, Marx and the Soviet Union show up midway through the piece. Wilson stopped short of suggesting mass registration in the Communist Party, but he did deliver this exhortation: "I believe that if the American radicals and progressives who repudiate Marxian dogma and the strategy of the Communist Party hope to accomplish anything valuable, they must take Communism away from the Communists, and take it without ambiguities or reservations."

Wilson's slogan struck a nerve instantly, particularly because it was proclaimed in *The New Republic*. Matthew Josephson, who would soon go on staff at the magazine himself, called it a bombshell. Cowley was somewhat flippant initially, writing to Katherine Anne Porter that "Edmund Wilson came out with a sort of Communist Manifesto which has set litry New York to worrying about its political philosophy. Everybody is planning to write his own answer to it, everybody but me, that is." Forty years later he would say, of the many thousands of young people who were brought into the Communist Party or within its orbit in part by Wilson's stirring rhetoric, "I sometimes felt that he had been the old ram who led the flock into the fold and left them to be sheared, while he jumped over the fence." One senses a certain envy in both statements. But Wilson had sounded the tocsin of social revolution for American writers, and soon enough Cowley would be developing his own fluency in the language of revolutionary exhortation.

Cowley would quickly prove his mettle as a literary editor. The list of reviewers and essayists he either retained or attracted, or in some cases discovered, includes many of the most important critical voices of the coming decades. They include Allen Tate (a regular contributor since 1925), Robert Penn Warren (first appearance in 1928), R. P. Blackmur (1929), F. O. Matthiessen (1929), Newton Arvin (1930), Lionel Trilling (1930), Granville Hicks (1930, with one earlier review in 1925), Sidney Hook (1930), and James T. Farrell (1933). More than a couple of people he gave early boosts to would end up becoming his political adversaries later in the thirties and in succeeding decades. One single-time reviewer Cowley commissioned would end up receiving a Nobel Prize in Literature, with his help: William Faulkner. His review of the novel *The Road Back* by Erich Maria Remarque in the May 20, 1931, issue is nothing if not Faulknerian. First paragraph: "There is a victory beyond defeat which the victorious know nothing of. A bourne, a shore of refuge beyond the lost battles, the bronze names and the lead tombs, guarded and indicated not by the triumphant and man-limbed goddess with palm and sword, but by some musing and motionless handmaiden of despair itself." His gifts lay elsewhere.

Wednesday afternoon at *The New Republic* was the time when Cowley, in his words, "received callers" and would become famous among a certain set of struggling scribblers, many of them young, all of them impecunious, as a weekly opportunity for some reviewing work or other forms of succor. He set up what he called "the Indigent Book Reviewers Fund" from the sale of unused review copies to bookstores and would hand over a couple of much appreciated dollars to criticism's neediest cases when reviewing jobs were scarce.

All sorts of supplicants would make their way to the parlor reception area to anxiously await their summons to Doctor Cowley's office up the stairs, nervously sizing up their competitors. One such visitor in December 1931 was the rangy and laconic Erskine Caldwell, already a published author, who had hitchhiked to New York from Maine to wrest an advance on his next book from his publisher. He had slept the night before in the easy chair of a hotel lobby and had ten cents in his pocket. Cowley and Matthew Josephson gave him some cash from the fund and took him out to lunch.

Soon some brilliant graduates of the Vassar classes of 1933 and '34 arrived: Muriel Rukeyser, Mary McCarthy, Eleanor Clark, and her sister Eunice Clark, all of whom got work. Eleanor Clark would become one of Cowley's mainstays, with more than twenty reviews written in the decade, Eunice placed some poems, and Rukeyser would contribute reviews and several of her revolutionary poems to the magazine.

McCarthy was a more complicated proposition. Her late-in-life account of her dealings with Cowley still seethes with the resentments a very bright young woman just concluding a brilliant college career experienced in a situation where all the power resided with an older man. Layered over that were the political antagonisms to come later in the thirties.

"I had my own class-war problems with *The New Republic*," she writes in *Intellectual Memoirs* (1992), published posthumously. On her first Wednesday-afternoon visit there in the summer of 1933 she had come armed with a copy of *Con Spirito*, the Vassar literary magazine she'd edited and written for. She'd been given a book to review, Glenway Wescott's *A Calendar of Saints for Unbelievers*. Her review sounded the essential McCarthy mean-girl note early and forcefully, e.g., "his shortsightedness has made his little collection incoherent and futile" and "the saints are tossed together like the ingredients of a thick and casual pudding."

After this, her sessions in Cowley's office became more strained. He'd smoke his pipe and wiggle his eyebrows and sometimes send her down to Robert Cantwell's office ("unlike Cowley, he was nice") to break the tension. The assignments mostly dried up until May of 1934, when McCarthy was given Lauren Gilfillan's *I Went to Pit College* for review, the memoir of a Smith College graduate who moved, semi-incognito, to a Pennsylvania mining town to live, work in a coal mine, and gather material for a book. McCarthy intuited from the extra space allotted that Cowley wanted a positive notice, "with the result, of course, that I wrote a listless review, full of simulated praise. In short, a cowardly review."

The review ran as McCarthy wrote it, but it was followed by a blistering dissent, signed with the initials O.C.F. That would be staff critic and Navy veteran Otis Ferguson, who donned his overalls and worker's cap to protest the idea of a Seven Sisters reviewer praising the literary stunt of a Seven Sisters poseur. It was a low thing for Cowley to have done, especially to a professionally vulnerable young writer. It is all too easy to imagine her humiliation when she encountered, with no advance warning, the negative paragraphs in the magazine. Not only did he lose the services of one of the best American critics of the past century as McCarthy moved her talents over to *The Nation*, he'd also made a dangerous enemy for years to come.

It was Ferguson who in the summer of 1934 greeted a nineteen-year-old City College junior who had "a heavy Brownsville voice with an engaging note of eagerness" named Alfred Kazin in that parlor, clutching a handwritten introduction from John Chamberlain of the *Times*. ("Here's an intelligent radical.") Passing muster with the gruff Ferguson (they would become close friends), he was eventually sent upstairs to Cowley's office and shortly became a reviewer whose copy, Cowley noted approvingly, didn't have to be edited and a summer regular in doubles of deck tennis, Tom Collinses at the ready. The future author of such classics as *On Native Grounds* and *A Walker in the City* was the most important critical voice to have been launched by Cowley in his tenure at *The New Republic*.

Kazin has left, in his memoir *Starting Out in the Thirties*, a vivid word portrait of Malcolm Cowley at the height of his power as a literary editor. "Each Wednesday afternoon, when I waited with other hopeful reviewers for Cowley to sail in after lunch with a tolerant smile on his face which so startlingly duplicated Hemingway's handsomeness, the sight of Cowley in the vivid stripes of his seersucker suit seemed to unite, through his love of good writing and his faith in revolution, the brilliant Twenties and the militant Thirties. . . . Cowley's face had kept the faint smile of defiance, the swashbuckling look and military mustache of intellectual officers in the First World War, the look of gallantry and sophistication that one connected with the heroes of Hemingway." He cites Cowley's "kindliness" in the way he dealt with the needy would-be reviewers on those afternoons and expresses heartfelt admiration for him as a critic: "Cowley was an expressive poet, and he had such a gift of clear style, he had such distinguished literary standards and associations, he had translated so many books from the French, he had known so many writers and had worked on so many magazines, that I felt in reading him that I had been led up to the immense spread of literary tidbits."

Clearly the young Alfred Kazin was in awe of all that Cowley had done and represented. But some other, contradictory feelings were stirring inside him, social insecurity and its close relation, resentment. It may be hard to credit now, but the route to real literary prestige and advancement once ran through the practice of book reviewing, and Malcolm Cowley was at the time perhaps its most conspicuous gatekeeper. Kazin made his way swiftly into the inner sanctum that was the *TNR* circle, but he was always painfully aware that he was also a working-class young man from a poor Brooklyn Jewish background, with the accent and, no doubt, wardrobe to prove it. (As Norman Podhoretz, another Brownsville boy in a hurry, wrote in *Making It*, "One of the longest journeys in the world is the journey from Brooklyn to Manhattan.") He had the sense of being watched—and indeed Cowley would remember being amused by this talented young man "so strenuously on the make" and would judge him not to be "a sharp or sympathetic observer of the sorrows of others." Considering himself to be an awkward wallflower from remote Brownsville, Kazin found those back-deck gin parties to be painful ordeals, during which he sharply felt his lack of social skills and watched others—John Cheever in particular—make small talk with the grace of those who had been taught the secret handshake early. These feelings would resolve into a strong dislike of Cowley, whom he would claim had been "unfailingly snotty" to him when he was "young and unknown" and "unfailingly surly and worse" later on. "Snotty" and "surly" do not occur anywhere else in the list of adjectives ever applied to Malcolm Cowley.

Kazin titled the section of *Starting Out in the Thirties* that first appeared in the May 1962 issue of *The Atlantic Monthly* "The Bitter Thirties." In that piece his antagonism toward Cowley is on display as he describes him making certain that the young writers never forgot "that he had been at Harvard with Dos Passos, had drunk in Paris with Hemingway."

Kazin's frequent companion in the parlor on those Wednesday afternoons was the notorious (in his words) "professional Village bum" Joe Gould, the toothless and bearded terminal eccentric eventually made famous by Joseph Mitchell, one paw perpetually extended for a handout or a free drink, the other clutching a manila envelope supposedly containing some manuscript pages of his mythical "Oral History of the World." He'd bounce around the parlor floor in a manic fashion, making a pest of himself until summoned by his fellow Harvard alum Cowley, who would give him either a buck from the reviewers' fund to augment his diet of Automat ketchup sandwiches or occasionally a book to review that would often within the hour be sold to a bookstore for ready cash. Cowley would write in his memoirs, "Once or twice I tried giving him a book for review, but that was a failed experiment." Let the record show that in fact Joe Gould actually published six perfectly coherent reviews, heavily edited no doubt, in the magazine, and some political doggerel.

Malcolm Cowley's most significant literary discovery, John Cheever, came to his attention not in one of those Wednesday scrums, but with an unsolicited manuscript sent in the mail. In March of 1930 the seventeen-year-old Cheever had been shown the exit from his Braintree prep school, Thayer Academy, for his generalized academic recalcitrance and, perhaps even worse, smoking behind the tennis court. Already strikingly precocious in his reading, he studied *The New Republic* and decided that a newish editor there, Malcolm Cowley, might be receptive to the vengeful account he was writing of the school's intellectual and moral deficiencies. So off went a copy of "Expelled" by Jon [*sic*] Cheever, with a cover letter stating that his reading of the editor's poetry collection *Blue Juniata* suggested that he'd be a sympathetic reader of the piece. Cowley read the story and experienced the shock of recognition that every true editor lives for. "I had felt that I was hearing for the first time the voice of a new generation," he would write decades later.

Cheever's piece took the form of a work of thinly veiled autobiographical fiction, and *The New Republic* hardly ever published short stories, especially by young unknowns. Undaunted, Cowley took up the cause despite the other editors' resistance and, for the first time but certainly not the last, he persuaded a reluctant employer to do what was good for it. Cut down somewhat in response to Bruce Bliven's observation that "it's awfully long," "Expelled" appeared in the October 1, 1930, issue, with an editor's note mentioning Cheever's age and saying that "he reproduces the atmosphere of an institution where education is served out dry in cakes, like pemmican." The story has never appeared anywhere but in the pages of *The New Republic*; it is a simply astonishing debut, in the grace and unshowy elegance of its style and the quietly lethal irony with which it nails the school for its jingoism, its smugness, and its true raison d'être, to get as many students into Harvard as possible.

On the strength of that publication, the now eighteen-year-old Cheever came to New York and presented himself to Cowley at *The New Republic* in person. Invited to a cocktail party at Cowley's apartment nearby, he promptly began downing bathtub Manhattans "lest anyone think I came from a small town like Quincy, Massachusetts," and ended up vomiting all over the wallpaper in the hallway. Despite this disastrous start, Cowley took the young writer under his wing. It was actually a couple of years later that he moved to New York to "make my fortune" and rented a squalid room on Hudson Street for three dollars a week. He became a "Holy Wednesday" (Cheever's words) regular, the review copies and occasional writing assignments helping to pay for the stale bread and buttermilk he claimed to have lived on for a winter. He soon became practiced enough at literary cocktail parties to ignite the keen and lasting envy of Alfred Kazin and published a number of reviews and three short stories in the magazine in the next few years.

At this beginning of what would become a lifelong friendship, Malcolm Cowley did John Cheever two more life-altering favors. The first was to write a letter of recommendation for Cheever in 1934 to Elizabeth Ames, the executive director, strict housemother, and benevolent presiding spirit of Yaddo, the writers' and artists' colony in Saratoga, New York. After his magical debut, Cheever's writing and his career had stalled badly and his morale suffered accordingly. As Cowley wrote to Ames, "During the last year he hasn't appeared so frequently in print, but he hasn't ceased to develop, and I feel sure now that he will fulfill the remarkable promise that was held out by his first sketches." Cheever shortly was awarded the first of many residencies at Yaddo, where he and the place took to each other. On the practical side, it provided him with solid meals and pleasant housing when he was in need of both. He would do some writing there, while also getting up to mischief of a sexual and alcoholic nature, a phenomenon known as "the Yaddo effect."

The second favor was to offer crucial advice that would set Cheever on the path of becoming perhaps the quintessential *New Yorker* story writer. Cheever's first attempt at writing a novel had failed, and in Cowley's view his talents were more suited to the short-story form.

But by 1935 he was facing a dispiriting string of rejections from magazine editors and he complained about it at the Cowley dinner table one night. The diagnostician in Cowley realized that the lengths of the stories Cheever had been producing—six to seven thousand words—were just too long for the editors to accept. So he devised an inspired assignment for Cheever: Knock out four stories of a thousand words each in the next four days and he would "see if I can't get you some money for them." This Cheever dutifully did. One, "The Teaser" (as in strip-), could be gotten past Bliven as a color piece and was published in *The New Republic*. By Cowley's account, "the other three ministories, plainly fictions, I sent along to Katharine White, then fiction editor of *The New Yorker*, and she accepted two of them." Blake Bailey, Cheever's biographer, tells a slightly more complicated version of this breakthrough, but the fact was that, within a month, two of his stories, "Buffalo" and "Brooklyn Rooming House," deft if slight slices of Depression life, would appear in the magazine, to be followed by 119 more over the course of Cheever's career, one of the most storied of the century.

———

By the beginning of 1932, the third year of the Depression, a sense of bewildered hopelessness had gripped the American people, as well as a smoldering anger against their political leaders for the smug and groundless reassurances that "prosperity was just around the corner." The chief target of these feelings was the Republican president, Herbert Hoover, who continued to preach individualism, self-reliance, fiscal rectitude, and voluntary charity as solutions to the country's ills, the causes of which baffled him as much as everyone else.

As Cowley later wrote, "Revolution was in the air." That thought, so alien to the American democratic ethos, was being widely contemplated or feared or even planned, and not just in the pages of *The New Masses* and *The Daily Worker*. The widespread incidence of civil unrest in the country, much of it accompanied by violence, lent credence to the idea that some sort of revolution was brewing. In Iowa, dairy farmers, normally the most conservative of citizens, blockaded all shipments of milk into Sioux City and emptied them into a ditch as a protest against the two cents a quart they were being paid. A nation-wide farmers' revolt against foreclosures also took hold, with lawyers and judges being threatened with nooses and in one case murdered. On everyone's mind was the example of the successful Bolshevik revolution of 1917 and the apparent ongoing success of the Soviets in bringing a backward feudal economy into the industrial age with startling speed.

Much of the violence in the early years of the Depression was occasioned by strikes and other forms of strife between labor and management, and the worst of it took place in the coal mining regions of the East and especially in Harlan and Bell Counties in eastern Kentucky. In the annals of the battles between American capital and labor, the brutal and protracted strikes in "Bloody Harlan" have become something like an American version of the Trojan War. Much of the longevity of these events in historical memory can be attributed to the famous American writers who made it a cause célèbre. Some of them, Malcolm Cowley included, traveled there to report on conditions as eyewitnesses against fierce local opposition, courting physical danger.

The radicalization of Malcolm Cowley, by his own account, began in earnest at a meeting in Theodore Dreiser's New York studio in an ornate duplex apartment in the famed Ansonia building in April of 1931, crowded with novelists, critics, editors, and journalists of note—"almost everyone in the literary world . . . who had expressed an interest in the fate of American society." Dreiser spoke that evening as a concerned social reformer, citing the miseries of the new depression, the vast unemployment and economic and nutritional precarity, the cluelessness of the politicians and financiers, the horrible situation of the coal miners of Kentucky facing violent repression and starvation. And what, the pink-faced, triple-chinned Dreiser asked, pulling a large white linen handkerchief back and forth through his hands, were the assembled writers and editors going to do about it all? "The time is ripe for American intellectuals to render some service to the American worker," Dreiser demanded. "There had been nothing like it since the hopeful days before the Great War," Cowley recalled. Dreiser floated the vague idea of forming a committee to collaborate with the International Labor Defense (ILD), the activist legal arm of the American Communist Party, to support various labor causes and combat political persecution.

There shortly was formed an organization called the National Committee for the Defense of Political Prisoners (NCDPP), with Dreiser as its chairman, Lincoln Steffens as treasurer, and a long alphabetical list of writers, artists, and academics as members. The NCDPP was essentially the writers' auxiliary to the ILD and one of the first of the many front organizations the Communists would establish in the thirties to attract the support of middle-class intellectuals without requiring the more fraught decision to join the Party officially. It was the first formal organization, editorial employment aside, that Cowley had joined since college.

Theodore Dreiser was as good as his word. He first lent his name and that of the new committee to a fundraising drive for the Scottsboro Boys, nine young Black men being tried in Alabama for the trumped-up charge of raping two white women. The ILD had, to its credit, taken up their defense in vigorous fashion. He then turned his attention to the plight of the sore-beset coal miners in Appalachia. The price of bituminous coal had plummeted, and the mine operators felt they could squeeze a profit margin from their activities in only one way: by cutting the wages of their workers. By 1931 the miners of eastern Kentucky were making less than thirty-five dollars a month, considerably less than they had been earning the previous decade. The work was notoriously dirty and dangerous and they were paid by the ton—and even then, they were being short-weighted by crooked scales. On top of that, the miners were paid not in cash but in scrip, redeemable only at company stores at about fifty cents on the dollar.

The ever-opportunistic Communists and their National Miners' Union took the workers out on strike with expert militancy. In response the mine operators imported cadres of armed thugs, and with the complete cooperation of the local constabulary and political establishment instituted a reign of terror and surveillance, including the dynamiting of soup kitchens and the murder of prominent striking miners, crying "Reds" all the while. The result of two bitterly opposed and heavily armed camps in the close quarters of small towns and constricted valleys and hollows were many shoot-outs and a number of fatalities on both sides.

Directly into this volatile situation a fact-finding commission organized by Dreiser traveled to Kentucky. Accompanying him were Dos Passos and six other writers of note. Arriving in Pineville, Kentucky, on November 5, 1931, they proceeded to take public testimony from miners and their families, union organizers, and even local officials. In terms of both documentation and publicity the Dreiser Committee's mission was a great success, widely covered in the national press and even internationally. Eventually, members of the committee would testify as to their findings before a Senate subcommittee. In April 1932 they would publish *Harlan Miners Speak: Report on Terror-ism in the Kentucky Coal Fields*, an essential primary document on the brutal realities of Bloody Harlan that still makes for heartrending reading.

Dreiser and Company had blazed a trail to the mountain towns of eastern Kentucky and, much like the civil rights volunteers of the Freedom Summer of 1963 did for the Deep South, identified them as a key battleground in the struggle for justice. In January 1932 one of the Dreiser Committee members, the historian and novelist Charles Rumford Walker, visited Malcolm Cowley at *The New Republic* with a proposition. The positive attention had encouraged the miners to go on strike and they intended to stay out, as they said, just as long as their families had "maybe not enough to eat, but just enough to breathe." But even that modest goal was in danger because relief trucks were being ambushed by deputies, and relief kitchens destroyed. His idea was for another mission of prominent writers to visit, not Harlan this time but the putatively safer town of Pineville in Bell County, and "open up the situation"—that is, aid fundraising efforts for relief and pressure the authorities to ease back their campaign of terror. Walker found a receptive audience in Cowley, as *The New Republic* was already editorially focused on the coal miners' plight.

In short order another visiting committee was formed. Its members assembled on February 9 in Knoxville, Tennessee, where the strike activities were being directed. It included Cowley, Edmund Wilson, the editor Quincy Howe, the experienced labor reporter and novelist Mary Heaton Vorse, the journalists Liston Oak and John Henry Hammond Jr. (later to become famous simply as John Hammond, civil rights pioneer and the genius A&R man for Columbia who discovered Bob Dylan), Dr. Elsie Reed Mitchell, the writers Polly Boyden and A. M. Max, and the novelist Waldo Frank, who was selected as chairman of the group. Also with them was Allan Taub, a lawyer for the ILD who had spent more than a little time in Kentucky courts and jails, as well as reporters for *The New York Times*, UPI, and the AP and a newsreel cameraman from Paramount. They were determined not to provoke the authorities in any way and to follow scrupulously whatever rules they laid down, to stay out of jail, and also to be able to distribute the food in an orderly fashion and do some fact-finding of their own. "We were all as peaceful as little babes," Cowley would testify in Congress.

The next morning they were greeted with the ominous news that eighteen-year-old Harry Simms, a union organizer, had been shot and was dying in a Knox County hospital. Nevertheless the group piled into cars hired for the occasion and headed north to Kentucky through the Cumberland Gap, accompanied by trucks carrying $1,500 worth of milk, canned goods, and other staples purchased the day before with their own funds. Their plan had been to stay several days in Pineville to distribute food and clothing, organize future relief efforts, and test whether the miners' rights as Americans were being violated. In fact the writers' group would spend less than ten tense, nerve-racking hours in Pineville.

On his way north, Cowley saw a crowd of some thirty men with rifles and shotguns at a crossroads leading to Harlan. "They're fixing to keep you out of Harlan County," the driver informed him. More armed deputies were awaiting them at the Pineville city line, and then in the courthouse square, mingling with a sizable crowd of miners. Machine guns bristled from the third-story windows of the courthouse. The National Miners' Union had led the group into something like a trap. For six weeks the miners had been forbidden to hold a meeting, and now the union had summoned them into town for food distribution and "free-speech speaking." The town authorities, alarmed by the sudden influx of striking miners and what were surely revolutionary Bolsheviks from New York, arranged for a show of armed force to greet them. Cowley hadn't seen so many guns since his time on the Western Front.

A series of tense and bizarre discussions and confrontations between the writers and the authorities ensued. At a meeting at the Pineville

Hotel with Mayor Brooks, a dentist, and the local gentry and the mine operators, Waldo Frank demanded the right to distribute food and meet with the miners in town to hear their grievances and difficulties. This was met with a list of blanket prohibitions: "We must not talk with the miners or we would be arrested. We must not print or distribute any handbills or we would be arrested. We must not invite any miners to our rooms in the hotel or we would be arrested for holding a meeting. If we wished to distribute our food outside of town, we must first get the permission of the county attorney."

The Pineville county attorney granted permission for the food to be distributed on a county road outside the town, if no public speaking took place. This the writers did, despite harassment from thirty or so armed deputies. The milk was spilled onto the ground, two hundred pounds of salt pork were stolen by one of the sheriff's men at gunpoint, and a truckload of clothes coming from Cincinnati was diverted some miles down a dirt road by the blockade and the driver was shot. Two members of the mission, the playwright Harold Hickerson and the relief worker Doris Parks, were arrested for giving speeches, not having heard of the blanket prohibition. They were to spend some days in the Pineville jail.

Cowley showed great coolness and physical courage. John Hammond would write in his memoir, forty-five years later, "Malcolm Cowley, particularly, defied the deputies and their guns and was slugged for his efforts." When the thugs were trying to open the tailgate of the truck to confiscate the relief supplies, Edmund Wilson recalled, "Malcolm . . . held it against them with a gun poked in his back." And Allan Taub, in the course of talking to Hammond in order to quash a rumor that Edmund Wilson had turned tail and fled—he absolutely did not, a fact that Cowley himself confirmed with Wilson's biographer—said, "Of course, Malcolm Cowley was the most courageous of us all."

The Paramount cameraman had been filming some of these events, a crucial piece of documentary evidence. Worried that the deputies would soon seize the negatives, Cowley got Hammond, who had arrived in his own car, to drive the man out of state right away. They made it to Knoxville safely, the film intact, and the footage was eventually shown in newsreels across the country, although probably not in Kentucky.

Back in Pineville that evening their luggage was unsuccessfully searched for evidence of criminal syndicalism—an all-purpose charge that basically meant causing the kind of trouble we don't want around here. They made a brief visit to some miners who were languishing in jail, returned to the hotel, made plans to visit some mining camps in Bell County and bring more relief supplies to Harlan County the next day, and then went to bed. But they were rousted out at ten thirty p.m., told to pack their bags, and were hustled over to a locked police court, where after half an hour the judge told them they were being dismissed "for lack of prosecution." They were escorted back to the hotel and greeted by deputies, coal operators, and merchants, all armed, calling themselves "night riders and citizens." They were told that they were going to be driven out of state.

What happened next played out like a scene from a film noir. Two by two they were placed in the backs of automobiles. Allan Taub and Waldo Frank were quite consciously put into one car as the two most prominent troublemakers as far as the authorities were concerned (and Jewish to boot). Cowley and Quincy Howe were in another. In their car were two men and a girl up front, and in the back to guard them was a deputy named John Wilson, who was reputed to have killed a number of miners for "resisting arrest" and who was himself later found dead with a bullet in his back, likely in retribution. (Edmund Wilson gives a vivid description of him as "a sinister old buzzard in a black slouch hat and a long black coat.") As the car drove along the dark mountain roads, Cowley experienced the helpless feeling of be-ing "like a patient being wheeled into the operating room" and thought that his only recourse in the event of violence would be to scream at the top of his lungs. The grim byplay in the car added considerably to the sense of menace and foreboding. The driver, a coal operator, ex-pressed his regret that Deputy Wilson was unable to stop the miner who'd escaped earlier in the day. "I'll fix him," he replied laconically; "next time I see him I'll take him to jail or I'll kill him." After a stop for some Cokes the driver applauded the shooting of Harry Simms in Knox County: "The deputy knew his business. He didn't give the red neck a chance to talk, he just plugged him in the stomach. We need some shooting like that down here in Pineville."

Finally the motorcade of some twelve cars halted at a paved semi-circle at the Cumberland Gap, on the state line. Howe and Cowley were told to get out of the car, as were the others. "This is the operat-ing room," he thought at that moment. Then the headlights were all turned off, and a loud scream—"low, piercing, continued"—shattered the darkness. The scream came from Allan Taub, who was hit on the head eight or more times with an automobile jack or tire iron and who sustained a broken nose and bad bruises on his head and shoulders. Waldo Frank was also bludgeoned and fell to the ground, stunned and bloodied with deep head wounds. The headlights came on and a voice was heard to declare, "The two Jews got into a fight."

Then Herndon Evans, the editor of the *Pineville Sun*, walked up to the bloodied lawyer and taunted him, "Taub, now you can give us a speech on the Constitution and all of the amendments. This will be your last chance in Kentucky. Later you can give it to that committee." Evans wore a number of hats in Pineville; one of them was as the co-ordinator of relief for the Red Cross, in which capacity he blocked much-needed food and medical supplies from reaching the striking miners. Another was as a stringer for the Associated Press, and he quickly busied himself spreading the libelous disinformation that, as he told a UPI reporter and wrote himself, "Frank and Taub began fighting each other to give the appearance of being attacked," so they could later make trumped-up charges as to their mistreatment at the hands of Pineville's kindly citizens.

After one final search of the luggage to confiscate a blank reel of motion picture film, the night riders drove away and the stranded writers made their way down into the town of Cumberland Gap. From there they managed to get cab rides back to Knoxville, arriving just before dawn for a few hours' sleep.

The next day the writers bent to their real tasks, publicity and fundraising, at which they proved highly effective. The evening edition of the *Knoxville News-Sentinel* of February 11 featured a four-column headline: "Novelist Beaten; Writers Ejected," with a widely printed photo of Waldo Frank with his head wrapped in bandages, and, in spite of his having his skull fractured the night before, a long and detailed account by Frank himself of the previous day's events. The wire services were also quick off the mark, helped apparently by the early escapee John Hammond, and the story ran that very day and the next in papers nationwide, including *The New York Times*.

Cowley and most of his companions then took a night train to Washington, DC, where they managed to have a meeting with the sympathetic progressive Republican senator Bronson Cutting of New Mexico. He promised to arrange a formal Senate hearing on the conditions of the Kentucky miners, and he made good on that promise. A Senate subcommittee with Cutting as chairman heard testimony over several days in May from Cowley himself, Allan Taub, a couple of Kentucky miners, and the prominent theologian and social activist Reinhold Niebuhr. In the course of the hearing a considerable amount of the testimony gathered by the Dreiser Committee was entered into the congressional record. Cowley delivered a compact account of the events of February 10 in Pineville, and Taub gave more extended and lawyerly testimony about the state of due process and constitutional rights in Harlan and Bell Counties and his own brutal beating.

Cowley's version of these events, "Kentucky Coal Town," was published in the March 2 edition of *The New Republic.* In his analysis he deploys a vocabulary of class struggle new to his writing: "We learned first of all—and this was our most lasting impression—that class warfare is raging nakedly in southwestern Kentucky . . . in Bell County today there are only two classes, and a state of armed warfare exists between them." He poses the familiar which-side-are-you-on challenge: "It is a battle in which everyone must take his stand; there is no compromise. Whatever is black to one class is white to the other; whoever brings relief to the miners is an enemy of the operators—and they run him out of town." He ends the piece with an ironic and bitter evocation of some primal American freedoms clearly no longer operative. On the road above the Cumberland Gap he had seen in the headlights a tablet recording how the Wilderness Trail through the Gap had been the path through which Daniel Boone and thousands of settlers after him had streamed into Kentucky, "hoping to find freedom and free land." But for their descendants, the miners, such mobility was no longer possible. "If they want freedom they have to stay in one place and fight for it."

Malcolm Cowley's dramatic ten-hour sojourn in Pineville, Kentucky, was the moment when his transformation into that literary action figure on the cover of *Years of Protest* began. Soon after returning to New York he and Wilson held a press conference announcing that they were to take part the next day in a picketing on Wall Street of the offices of the Morgan, Mellon, and Rockefeller interests, all of whom had financial investments in Kentucky mines. At a fundraising rally shortly after, Cowley made his first foray into public speaking since dropping out of the Harvard debating team, proclaiming all the sentiments proper to the occasion in an increasingly loud voice to per-haps 1,500 people. Some of the newsreel footage smuggled out of Bell County was also screened, and this event, like many others to follow, featured movingly direct testimony from miners imported for the oc-casion and "bleak homespun music the hall had never heard before, hill tunes and barn-dance numbers, the whining twang of steel guitar strings," hauntingly played and sung by other miners.

Cowley made the speech again in Philadelphia, and it was followed by many, many similar speeches, increasingly practiced and effective, to conclaves large and small throughout the thirties.

Edmund Wilson and John Dos Passos would in time come to the conclusion that they had been used by the Communists in their Ken-tucky missions and gradually began to withdraw from radical activi-ties. Cowley and hundreds of other writers both famous and obscure headed in the opposite direction. Wherever the class struggle erupted, they would heed the siren song of the Communist Party and organize a writers' committee. As in Pineville, they never actually won strikes, but they did raise awareness and money for relief funds, and in time their actions led to a political commitment to a new way of living and thinking. As he writes at the end of his account of these events in *The Dream of the Golden Mountains*, "I found myself committed to 'the movement' by working and speaking for it (and in some measure, I suppose, by the sense of importance that comes from working and speaking). I was also committed by the hungry, ragged, but clear-eyed look of the miners' wives, by the talk of shooting men in cold blood, and by the machine guns pointing at me from the Pineville court-house. This was another war, as the steel-mouthed coal operator had said, and I knew which side I was on."

Experiences like this, and the rousting of the Bonus Marchers by the U.S. Army from their encampment on the Anacostia Flats in Washington, DC, served to accelerate the already steady movement of many writers to the left and into the orbit of the Communist Party. Cowley was a witness to the sorry conclusion of this seismic event as the marchers scattered north and west in broken-down vehicles, and he would write angrily about it in *The New Republic*.

As was usual in these years, the chief pied piper and diagnostician of this shift was Edmund Wilson. Readers who only know the political Wilson of the thirties from the pieces collected in *The Shores of Light* (1952) or the superb reportage assembled in *The American Earthquake* (1958) have not been exposed to the full force of his radicalism and disillusionment. He assembled those collections with the clear intent of hiding the extent to which he fully accepted the Communist point of view concerning the collapse of capitalism and the moral bankruptcy of bourgeois American society. As Cowley himself noted after Wilson died, the version of "An Appeal to Progressives" he reprinted was toned down from the original text that appeared in *The New Republic* on January 14, 1931. This was his fervent manifesto on the social, moral, and economic bankruptcy of the American way of life, with its instantly famous exhortation that American radicals "must take Communism away from the Communists." Two more such fiery pieces appeared in that magazine in early 1932 that were never reprinted. The first, "What Do the Liberals Hope For?" in the February 10 issue, attacks such centrist figures as the economist Stuart Chase, the historian Charles Beard, and the pundit Walter Lippmann for their tempered belief in the ability of American democracy and the capitalist system to pull the country out of its tailspin. He heaps scorn on liberals because "they are still sold like other middle-class Americans on the values of the middle-class world which they criticize." Statements identical to these hostile sentiments could have been found in abundance in *The New Masses* or *The Daily Worker*.

Three months later in the same magazine, Wilson published a famous two-part article titled "The Literary Class War." The first installment shows Wilson at his critical best, a survey that addresses the question "What does a revolutionary literature mean in America?" with the acuity that made him our greatest critic. Only the first third of this installment was reprinted in *The Shores of Light*, though. In the second installment a week later, Wilson takes virtually all other American writers to the woodshed with such smug and offensive salvos as this: "So far as I can see, nine-tenths of our writers would be much better off writing propaganda for communism than doing what they are at present: that is, writing propaganda for capitalism under the impression that they are liberals or disinterested minds." "Communism has . . . for the first time brought humanity into the great world of creative thought and work," Wilson concludes with a ringing flourish.

What is so telling about the political climate of opinion among the literary class at this juncture is that essays so violently contra liberalism should have appeared in the country's leading liberal journal.

Later that summer a piece in *The New Republic*, "Leftbound Local," unsigned but almost certainly by Cowley, took a cooler and more empirical look at the perceived "mass literary movement towards communism" since 1929. The evidence adduced came from a survey of fifteen critics and writers, none of them Party members, conducted by the independent left journal *The Modern Quarterly*. It found that by and large they were in agreement on such propositions as "the inevitable failure and collapse" of American capitalism, the necessity for writers to engage in some fashion with the social crisis, and that becoming a Communist philosophically (but not formally) "deepens an artist's work." Much scorn was heaped by the respondents on what for the time was the middle way of socialism as an inadequate and futile response to conditions, summed up by John Dos Passos's quip that "becoming a socialist right now would have just about the same effect on anybody as drinking a bottle of near-beer." Cowley concluded that the leftward swing by American writers was real, albeit less a "Red

Express" than a "leftbound local," and that "American literature is about to assume a different character."

Franklin Roosevelt goes entirely unmentioned, let alone endorsed, in the survey. Given the epochal transformation his administration effected on American life, it is hard for us today to remember how little excitement or even interest FDR generated among the chattering classes. The only people who seemed to actually like and trust him were ordinary voters. The onetime Socialist Walter Lippmann, now opinion-slinging for the solidly Republican *New York Herald Tribune*, famously dismissed FDR as "a pleasant man who, without any important qualifications for the office, would very much like to be president."

In the pages of *The New Republic* that election season, one can discern at best lukewarm approval for Roosevelt, his main strength or attraction being that he wasn't Herbert Hoover. The real heat in those months among *TNR* liberals was really being generated on behalf of Norman Thomas, the Socialist candidate. The left literati were even more scornful of FDR, Dos Passos writing in the hard-boiled manner he affected in those years, "Roosevelt or Hoover? It'll be the same cops." In that time of human suffering and passionate confusion about both its possible causes and cures, third (and fourth and fifth and sixth, etc.) parties sprang up in numbers never before seen, each with a distinct political point of view and a plan for what ailed the country. Cowley remembers that twenty-three minor-party names remained on the ballots of various states, including Prohibition, Labor, Socialist-Labor, Farmer-Labor, Progressive, Liberty, Populist, National, and Security. The background of this confusing welter of splinter parties helps makes comprehensible the attraction of the Communist Party to so many intellectuals; its program was politically coherent and, by comparison to most others, it looked like a robust and going concern.

In his lively memoir of the thirties, *Infidel in the Temple*, Matthew

Josephson recalls that in the summer of 1932 an ad hoc committee of writers and intellectuals took shape to support the Communist ticket, William Z. Foster for president and James W. Ford, the first African American to run for high office, for vice president. (Their platform may be inferred from the title of Foster's campaign book, *Toward Soviet America*.) An "Independent Committee" was formed of what by now must be called the usual suspects, including Malcolm Cowley, Sidney Hook, Lincoln Steffens, Newton Arvin, Meyer Schapiro, Wilson, and Josephson, and on September 12, newspapers nationwide reported on the call for "intellectuals" (the scare quotes used in the piece are telling) to mobilize behind the Communist Party and vote for its candidates as "the only effective way to protest against the chaos, the appalling wastefulness, and the indescribable misery inherent in the present economic system."

The next step for what would formally be called the League of Professional Groups for Foster and Ford was to do what intellectuals do best: write a pamphlet, *Culture and the Crisis*, addressed "to the writers, artists, teachers, physicians, engineers, scientists, and other professional workers of America," setting forth the reasons for supporting the Communist candidates in the forthcoming election. In Cowley's telling, most of the pamphlet was written by a man named Lewis Corey, an ex–Party member who under his original name of Louis Fraina had helped to found the American Communist Party before being excommunicated. In his view Corey-Fraina deployed language with all the flair of algebraic equations, and the product was made even more arid by the section on the Party platform written by an in-house pundit, "a collection, gritty as crushed limestone, of all the party slogans." Cowley and Josephson and the other literary men had to go to the mat with their new political allies to preserve at least some of the pamphlet's appeal to the highly educated and intellectually independent class of readers they hoped to persuade, and Cowley was eventually allowed to contribute a preamble closer to the common tongue than the Marx- and Veblen-inflected prose of the rest of the pamphlet. He was particularly proud of this extended metaphor: "The United States under capitalism is like a house that is rotting away; the roof leaks, the sills and rafters are crumbling. The Democrats want to paint it pink. The Republicans don't want to paint it; instead they want to raise the rent."

Fifty-thousand copies of *Culture and the Crisis* were printed in early October and quickly distributed through the network of Workers' Bookshops and sold for a nickel a copy. Whatever its literary deficiencies, the pamphlet remains one of the essential evidentiary texts of the hard left turn of American writers in the thirties. Fifty-two luminaries signed the piece, including, in addition to the names mentioned above, Langston Hughes, Erskine Caldwell, Robert Cantwell, Countee Cullen, Granville Hicks, and Sidney Howard. It is doubtful whether most of these people would have read the text before endorsing it, and of that group only Sidney Hook, Corey, and perhaps Hicks would have had anything more than passing competence in Marxist theory. But most of these writers had spent the aesthetic twenties cultivating an attitude of scorn toward the philistinism of America's business civilization, and the adjective "bourgeois" was a highly fungible insult, easily transmissible into the political realm they were entering.

After the pamphlet, the rallies. The League held a crowded meeting that month in the Great Hall of Cooper Union, the same auditorium where Lincoln delivered his famous campaign speech against the expansion of slavery. Two thousand attendees, many of them Communists come to inspect their new intellectual allies, heard the writers deliver the innocent and fervid words of fresh converts to a new faith. James Rorty, the father of famed pragmatist philosopher Richard Rorty, even testified that his revolutionary commitment had started him up to writing poems again, and read two of them to a likely puzzled crowd. The writers left the meeting elated at their reception and with nine hundred dollars in box office receipts to fund the cause.

This event was followed by two election dinners held simultaneously at Webster Hall and the Manhattan Lyceum, attended, if the breathless report in *The Daily Worker* is to be believed, by "two thousand professional workers, including writers, artists and scientists," with thousands more putatively having been turned away. The speakers included Matthew Josephson, Scott Nearing, Mike Gold, and, most prominently mentioned, Malcolm Cowley. His recorded words offer a clear picture of his thinking at that moment, unclouded by hindsight and selective memory: "It wasn't the depression that got me, it was the boom. I saw all my friends writing the tripe demanded by the present order, stultified and corrupted and unable to make real use of their talents. After that, I began to discover the reason for this state of affairs, which comes from the nature of the ruling class, which lives by exploiting everyone else."

The two main speakers at the dinners were Earl Browder, head of the Communist Central Committee, and William Patterson, the Communist candidate for mayor of New York. The presence of these big guns indicated that the Communists knew they had scored a publicity coup. But Browder's remarks contained a note of ideological caution for these new comrades and fellow travelers that "the movement among the intellectuals cannot occur independently, it can only occur on the basis of the most profound mass movement taking place below among the millions of workers and farmers in this country." Browder was telling these American intellectuals that they must set aside their impulses toward independent thought in favor of collective action and Party discipline.

The issue was touchy and complex. In 1928 the Comintern decided that capitalism had entered a so-called Third Period of imminent collapse that was ripe for proletarian revolution. Under such urgent circumstances, militant discipline had to be maintained and anything that smelled in the least of reaction and/or deviationism expunged. But in 1929 an international literary congress held in Kharkhov, Russia, attended by a delegation of American writers, issued a series of directives aimed at attracting more writers and intellectuals to the Communist cause while making sure they would toe the Party line. Writers like the ones who joined the League of Professional Groups and signed *Culture and the Crisis* were regarded as assets by the Communists, but they also harbored the dangerous tendency to think and act for themselves. Over time their fears about the latter tendency would be realized, as several of the signers of the pamphlet would become ideological apostates and avowed enemies of communism.

The League of Professional Groups for Foster and Ford may have generated a lot of excitement among the elites, but their effect at the polls was negligible at best. Roosevelt won over Hoover by a landslide, with a plurality of 7 million votes. A surge for Norman Thomas predicted by pollsters dissipated in the last week of the campaign, as the Socialist vote was 885,458, half the number predicted. The Communist candidate garnered 103,152 votes, the largest it would ever poll in a national election but only slightly ahead of the Prohibitionist Party.

The League of Professional Groups, meanwhile, would shortly succumb to that malady endemic to most radical movements: factionalism, accompanied by an overweening focus on correct theory over political pragmatism. The most combative of these factions were the Trotskyists; Cowley would watch them at meetings, with their "outbursts of contempt and hatred out of all proportion with their ostensible causes," and think of the conspirators in *Julius Caesar*. At one of these meetings he gave "a hot speech" pleading that such useless and bitter hairsplitting be put aside for discussion and actual activities of a practical nature. It was well received but fruitless; soon enough no more meetings would take place. But, writes Cowley, "the Trotsky faction didn't like it at all, and from that moment many of them regarded me as a dangerous misleader to be exposed and annihilated."

Nothing like euphoria greeted Roosevelt's election. He remained a largely unknown quantity, his program for action against the vast suffering in the nation was vague and unformed, and he was still four long months away from taking office. In the meantime, history offered one more grim tutorial for Malcolm Cowley in the form of another march on Washington, by the Communist-organized Hunger Marchers.

There had been previous Hunger Marches, on Washington and all throughout the country, many of them sizable. It was said that the largely Communist-controlled Unemployment Councils that flocked to these events were to be found in 340 towns and numbered 300,000 members. In December 1931 the Communists had sent more than 1,500 "delegates" from such councils in an efficiently organized first National Hunger March to Washington to parade and demand measures like unemployment insurance, emergency relief, and old-age pensions. The march was met by a police presence that outnumbered them by three to one. Hoover refused to see them when they arrived at the White House.

Cowley and his coworker Robert Cantwell learned that delegates from Unemployment Councils nationwide were converging on Washington on December 4 for a second National Hunger March. The Bonus Army debacle was still fresh in everyone's mind and Major Ernest Brown, the new DC police chief, was threatening to take a tough line on protesters. Cowley and Cantwell drove to DC to report on the event for *The New Republic*.

The march itself was a genuine logistical feat. Thousands of delegates from across the United States had to manage to arrive in the city at the same time, despite the necessity of staging fund- and morale-raising rallies at stops all along their routes. Food, clothing, gasoline, oil, lodging, and repair parts for the trucks had to be procured with the severely limited funds available. Another obstacle was the considerable police interference along the way. Despite such difficulties, the marchers all contrived to arrive in Washington on the same day and most of them at the appointed hour.

On December 4, Cowley and Cantwell drove along with a western column of the march, "a convoy of wheezing old trucks with banners tacked to their sides," thirty miles southwest in Virginia. As the column approached Washington it merged with the traffic of Sunday drivers on rural outings heading back into the city. At the Key Bridge, respectable-looking vehicles were shunted to the left and allowed to enter the city unhindered, while the shabbier cars and trucks were first directed to the right, then halted, and eventually escorted by motorcycle police to a desolate and remote area of New York Avenue in the northeast quadrant of the city along a carefully concealed route. The two reporters, decently dressed and driving a well-maintained automobile, had some difficulty convincing the police that they wanted to turn to the right with the jalopies rather than to the left.

The designated area had been chosen for a topography that offered a narrow and natural stockade or cul-de-sac, a deep ravine of twenty feet with railroad tracks at the bottom on one side and a steep clay bank rising another twenty feet on the other. All sides of this improvised laager were heavily guarded by police armed with rifles and machine guns and gas bombs, both tear gas and the newly developed DM or "vomit" gas. Plainclothesmen, some pretending to be marchers themselves, circulated among the crowd to gather intelligence; three military planes buzzed overhead; and four thousand Army Regulars at Fort Myer across the Potomac remained on high alert. So paranoid and fearful was the national government, so unable to empathize with the plight of 2,500 threadbare, unemployed, hungry, unarmed, and by now thoroughly exhausted men and women arriving in the capital with the peaceful aim of marching down an avenue, that it brought the crushing weight of the state to bear upon them.

Cowley and Cantwell may have traveled to Washington as reporters, but they were far from journalistically neutral. The next day, as reported in *The New York Times*, the two of them, along with Mike Gold, John Herrmann, Charles Walker, and Felix Morrow, issued a statement protesting the conditions in the ad hoc concentration camp and the armed force being marshaled against the marchers in violation of their constitutional rights. At the same time, members of the League of Professional Groups in Washington announced that they were seeking an injunction against the actions of the superintendent of police.

The marchers had to exert considerable discipline and restraint in the face of extreme and repeated verbal and physical provocations on the part of the police. In the early hours of Tuesday, December 6, they finally secured their parade permit. That morning their representatives simultaneously presented petitions to the vice president and the Speaker of the House, and three thousand Hunger Marchers paraded along Pennsylvania Avenue, watched by an estimated seventy-five thousand onlookers. On the Capitol steps, women and children would taunt members of Congress returning for their lame-duck session: "Feed the hungry! Tax the rich!" The demonstrators were again heavily outnumbered by the police.

Cowley ends his *TNR* piece on the march with the kind of image that might easily have concluded one of the proletarian novels just coming into favor: the Red Front Band still playing the "Internationale" amid an engulfing sea of cop blue on a broad Washington avenue—as upbeat a note as could be wrung from a thoroughly dispiriting experience. He took a more critical stance in his memoir almost half a century later, when he wondered why the Communists had kept putting themselves in situations where their discipline earned them the kind of moral victory the Hunger Marchers had won over the police, but little or nothing of a real political nature. He admitted that he did entertain doubts about the alliance he and his literary class had formed with the Communists, but "in those days, however, doubts like that were always adjourned for want of leisure to consider them."

The period from the stock market crash and his joining *The New Republic* in late 1929 to the end of 1932 was transformative for Malcolm Cowley's career as a man of letters. He left his scuffling bohemian past behind him to ascend to a position of editorial power and influence at the most prestigious journal of opinion in the country. The essays and reviews he wrote, the books he selected for review and the writers he assigned to review them, and his voice on the great issues of the day in *TNR* editorial conclaves shaped literary taste and intellectual discourse. He had become an eyewitness to capitalist and governmental repression and drawn the conclusion that class warfare and even a revolution of some form, however ill-defined, were inevitable. He was drawn into the sphere of Communist activities, and his pronouncements on literary matters sometimes became ideologically tinged, and not to their benefit. In his essay "Inside the Whale," George Orwell wrote that "on the whole the literary history of the thirties seems to justify the opinion that a writer does well to keep out of politics." The example of Orwell himself contradicts this stricture, but it is hard to read these words and not think of Malcolm Cowley.

EIGHT.

LITERARY POLITICS

———

Meanwhile, there was still literature and its critical assessment, by Cowley himself and the reviewers he assigned, week after week, in *The New Republic*, as well as in the book he was writing, an account of the forces that shaped its makers of his generation, *Exile's Return*.

The world of literature was increasingly consumed by urgent debates about its purpose, especially in relation to politics. No figure more tirelessly personified this era than Malcolm Cowley. A survey of his extracurricular activities in the political realm in the thirties is astonishing.

Malcolm Cowley signed and often helped to write manifestos, statements of support, and letters of protest. He signed a letter protesting the Fish–Dies Bill calling for the expulsion of noncitizens who could be shown to believe in the abolition of private property and a system based on common ownership (i.e., Communists). As a member of the Writers and Artists Organizing Committee in Support of the International Labor Defense of the Scottsboro Boys he signed a letter to the governor of Alabama protesting their outrageous conviction for rape and sentences to death by electrocution. He was one of ninety-eight writers urging American citizens to express their moral outrage at the indiscriminate bombing of civilian targets by the Fascist rebels against the democratically elected Spanish Republic. As part of the executive committee of the League of American Writers, he signed a letter addressed to President Roosevelt in support of the Federal Writers' Project, which was then (in 1937) under political attack. Along with 180 other writers, artists, actors, and professors, he signed "A Statement" by American Progressives on the Moscow Trials" supporting the guilty verdicts against Nikolai Bukharin and other figures as just and necessary actions taken "in the international fight of democracy against fascism."

As the chairman of the American Committee for the Struggle Against War, Cowley was one of the leaders of a parade through the Financial District to South Street, where he addressed a rally against Japanese aggression. ("We have shown these capitalists that we are not going to fight their wars for them.") He addressed an anti-Hitler rally of fifteen thousand Communists and sympathizers in Madison Square Garden on the suppression of opponents to Hitler's government and assailed Nazi terrorism as "a picture of the best capitalism has to offer in the present stage of the crisis." Along with such prominent publishing figures as Alfred A. Knopf and Warder Norton he attended a reception at the New School to celebrate the tenth anniversary of the Communist publishing house International Publishers. He was one of the "Committee of Sponsors" of the Twentieth Soviet Anniversary Ceremonies held at Carnegie Hall of all places, at which the Soviet ambassador Alexander Troyanovsky was awarded the Golden Book of American Friendship with the Soviet Union. He joined five congressmen, Earl Browder, William Z. Foster, A. Philip Randolph, and a familiar roster of writers on the Mother Bloor Celebration Committee to organize festivities for the seventy-fifth birthday of the legendary Communist activist and labor organizer.

Along with Sidney Hook and Joseph Freeman, editor of *The New Masses*, Cowley spoke on "Culture in a Communist Society" at a symposium sponsored by the League of Professional Groups. With Freeman and Granville Hicks he served on a panel discussing "The American Literary Scene" from the liberal and the revolutionary point of view at Webster Manor, Mike Gold moderating. At "A Frank and Open Discussion Which Concerns Every Honest Supporter of Peace and Freedom!" at the Mecca Temple, he addressed the question "Where Do the Liberals Stand?" with Mauritz Hallgren, author of *Why I Resigned from the Trotsky Defense Committee*, and three other pro-Soviet writers. In early 1937 he chaired a panel at the Mecca Temple titled "Spain in Defense of Freedom" of three writers—Ralph Bates, Anna Louise Strong, and Robert Minor—who were eyewitnesses to the war. He chaired a panel of four "progressive cultural leaders" on "Lenin's Contribution to Modern Thought" on the occasion of the fourteenth anniversary of his death, arranged by the American Friends of the Soviet Union.

This is far from a complete list of the whirl of such activities that Malcolm Cowley threw himself into for almost an entire decade. There was something reflexive and indiscriminate about his near-automatic participation in whatever he was solicited for. When he was questioned by a government agent a few years later about specific front organizations he had been associated with, his memory consistently failed him. These may in some cases have been convenient lapses, but it is likely the associations had been made in a rote and absent-minded fashion.

It is no accident, as Marxists like to say, that the majority of these actions and events have been gleaned from the pages of the Party's newspaper, *The Daily Worker*, in advertisements, listings, and news items. Few of these failed to include the identifying line "literary editor of *The New Republic*," signaling that these front organizations had captured the support of a powerful influencer in a high temple of liberalism. As a result of his tireless and enthusiastic activities, Cowley came to be seen as the very model of the "fellow traveler"—a term generally understood to apply to those people who were sympathetic to the Communist cause and the Soviet Union even though they were not formal members of the Communist Party, like Cowley and most of his cohort. In his book *Literature and Revolution* (1923), when Leon Trotsky used the term to describe a type of doubt-beset literary supporter of communism, he sniffed suspiciously, "As regards a 'fellow traveler,' the question always comes up—how far will he go?"

In the American context, the term at first had friendlier connotations. When Mike Gold, no ideological softie, returned from the Kharkov Plenum on revolutionary literature in Russia in November 1930, he declared with uncharacteristic latitude that it was of vital importance to enlist all friendly intellectuals into the ranks of the revolution. The doors should be opened wide to fellow travelers. As the thirties progressed, especially as the hostility to ideological wayfarers and dissenters gave way to the inclusive we-the-people stance of the People's Front, fellow travelers were not just cultivated and welcomed by the Party, they were seen as key to a strategy of attracting broad support in a country generally indifferent or deeply hostile to Marxism. Later, in the forties and fifties, as the atrocities of Stalinism were revealed and a Red Scare gripped the country, "fellow traveler" became a term of distaste and opprobrium and would dog Cowley for the rest of his life.

It is not a term he ever attempted to avoid. As he would write decades later, "I would never be more than a fellow traveler, and yet I was an ardent one at the time, full of humility, the desire to serve, and immense hopes for the future." The disasters of the early years of the thirties had paradoxically expanded the range of historical possibilities in a kind of sudden great awakening, where the close-at-hand things like intimate relationships fell away to reveal glorious vistas of social potential that evoked an uncharacteristic rapture in Cowley's prose: "There were mountains rising into the golden sunlight. We could not reach the mountains alone, but by joining forces with the working class we might help to build a bridge for ourselves and for all of humanity."

Why, then, did Malcolm Cowley never formally become a member of the Communist Party? Because, as he later explained, he had what he called "reservations." One was that the Party itself, with its strict discipline and austere task-orientation not unlike a religious order, was not all that welcoming to writers and intellectuals because "they had ideas of their own" and were never likely to behave like the Party's hardworking loyal foot soldiers. "They wouldn't have me . . . except in return for a greater sacrifice of freedom than I was prepared to make." The "sacrifice" was not of time or effort but of his need, his right, to think matters through for himself. But his strongest reservation had to do with his bedrock loyalty to literary standards. While he felt— and publicly stated on many occasions—that the revolutionary move- ment could be helpful to writers by ending their isolation and enlarging their perspectives, he was put off by the mostly hack writers who car- ried CP cards and the clichéd language of the Party press. "Nobody actually a Communist seemed to write good English prose."

Cowley would continue to produce book reviews and literary com- mentary of a high order throughout the decade, but a certain amount of cant and special pleading began to creep into his work as his revolu- tionary fervor took hold. One example is a piece entitled "How the Russian Revolution Influenced Me as a Writer," which appeared in *The Daily Worker* on September 23, 1934. It contains the following sentences: "The Russian Revolution means more to me now than any other event in history. . . . The revolution is still the most important event not only in history but in current affairs. The battle for the lib- eration of the working class in other countries is being fought today chiefly in Russia. When it has been won there so thoroughly that the cotton mill hands in North Carolina and the tenant farmers in Alabama all know the success of it and cannot any longer be filled up with lies about famine and collapse in Russia—then will come a new stage of the revolution in the rest of the world." He contrasts the putatively vast audience enjoyed by contemporary Russian writers with that of the Americans who "address their work to a small audience of snobs."

A second example is a poem that appeared under the title "A Poem for May Day" in *The Daily Worker* on April 30, 1936, seven days before it also ran in *The New Republic* under the title "The Last International." Cowley labors to evoke an apocalyptic and Goyaesque battle between the resurrected legions of the proletariat dead, "betrayed and bastinadoed, burned at the stake / slow-starved in prison or exile, buried alive," and the forces of oppression and reaction personified by "barons . . . and bankers and archbishops / driven before the whirlwind of the dead." Here the Social Muse speaks in the secondhand language of revolutionary exhortation.

For most of the thirties, Malcolm Cowley lived in a state of paradox and contradiction. His social conscience, awakened by firsthand experience, ignited in him an urgency and a genuine passion for political change and economic justice. The times in America seemed to demand some kind of revolution in the affairs of men, and to so many on the literary left, the Communists had the most convincing and compelling program for getting there. So he joined those literary intellectuals he called "the men of good will" and made himself as useful as he could, in any way he could. But his literary conscience ran deep, and he understood that even his fellow-traveling loyalties to Communist causes entailed a surrender of intellectual independence. Cowley's most profound and lasting loyalty was, first, last, and always, to language, and the ways that Communists deployed that precious resource seemed to him to debase its currency. The tension between these two realms would escalate year after year for him in ways that were exceedingly painful.

———

Somehow, during these years of professional advancement and personal transformation and hectic and at times near-daily political activity, while performing a full-time job editing a book review section for a weekly periodical and writing reviews and occasional commentary and essays himself, Malcolm Cowley managed to write a 308-page book, *Exile's Return*. A near-century after its 1934 publication, it remains in print in an edition revised in 1951, and has stood the test of time. It is the foundational text of that flourishing academic and pop cultural industry, Lost Generation Studies.

The timing for Cowley's composition of his first prose work was fortunate. The memories of his literary generation's experiences were still fresh. But the advent of the Depression had created a decisive historical chasm between a fraught now and a suddenly distant then. And the field was clear for Cowley's pioneering effort; no real consensus about the Lost Generation's achievements existed.

The germ of the idea for the book traced back to his first tentative generational statement, "This Youngest Generation," for the *New York Evening Post* in 1921. By the fall of 1929, Cowley had begun discussions with the firm of W. W. Norton for a collection of some twelve essays on aspects of the Lost Generation's experience by various contributors for the sum of one hundred dollars per, with the unpromising title *Whither and How*.

Matters began to take more definite form in the early spring of 1931 when Cowley wrote to Elizabeth Ames at Yaddo, telling her that

"Mr. Matthew Josephson came forward with an exciting idea, that of writing a cooperative volume of literary memoirs in order to illuminate the intellectual and social background of the present generation of writers," and suggesting that Yaddo might serve as the locus of a conference for five or six of the contributors. Ames assented, and so the week before the mansion opened for its regular guests, Cowley, Josephson, Kenneth Burke, Robert Coates, John Wheelwright, and Evan Shipman, a horse-playing drinking buddy of Hemingway's, arrived for their conference. Decades later he would recall, "At Yaddo we had a high old time. Evan Shipman found a horse room and a bootlegger. We talked, we explored the countryside, and I wrote. Some of the others pretended to write, but they didn't get anything done. I was launched on my book." What had begun as a collective consideration of the American literary situation was now to be the work of one man.

Like any sensible memoirist, Cowley began at Yaddo with his most surefire material: the fisticuff-enhanced contretemps at the Rotonde in Paris, which had already taken on a legendary cast. By the end of that summer he had made enough progress to fill five substantial serializations in *The New Republic* over the autumn of 1931: "Exile's Return," an overview of his attitudes and those of his writerly cohort as they made their way to Paris and eventually back to the States; "Significant Gestures," exciting Left Bank adventures among the Dadaists; "Coffee and Pistols for Two," the little magazine wars and the painful demise of *Broom*; "Women Have One Breast," censorship battles with the U.S. Postal Service and the Ernest Boyd feud; and "Manhattan Melody," about the peculiar miseries and indignities of literary life in New York.

The pieces were fresh, thoughtful, and candid, with a tone of disillusion without bitterness. They portrayed the ambitions and achievements and failures of the Lost Generation with an insider's intimacy that attracted attention, most of it positive.

Three days after the final installment of November 18 of the work in progress in *The New Republic* this brief item appeared in *The Saturday Review of Literature*: "Recently, we mentioned Malcolm Cowley's articles in *The New Republic*, and we are now able to state that they will appear in a book to be called 'The Lost Generation,' which W. W. Norton & Company will publish in the Spring of 1932." The announced pub date was wildly overoptimistic. Progress was frustratingly slow for author and publisher alike through that dark and hectic year, as Cowley's increased responsibilities at *The New Republic* and his newfound political commitments ate up all his time; only two installments of the book saw print in the magazine that fall, about his generation's educational experiences and his ambulance service in the Great War. So he resorted to taking limited leaves of absence to work on the book, leaving the book section in the capable hands of Otis Ferguson and Robert Cantwell.

His first ten-week book sabbatical, in the spring of 1933, arrived courtesy of his friends Allen Tate and his wife, Caroline Gordon, who arranged for pleasant (and free) lodging on a farm called Cloverlands, owned by one of Gordon's Tennessee cousins, on a tract of land called the Meriwether Connection. Cowley left New York for the nine-hundred-mile drive in his Ford roadster the morning after a large and peaceful May Day parade and rally at Union Square. On his second day on the road he stopped in Towson, Maryland, for a one-day stay with Scott and Zelda Fitzgerald and their daughter, Scottie, who were renting a large house on a parklike estate called La Paix.

Scott was in the final stages of finishing the novel he'd been struggling with for eight years, titled at that time *The Drunkard's Holiday*, the book that would become *Tender Is the Night*. Zelda was in a fragile state after a mental breakdown that had resulted in a stay at a sanitarium. Her stabs at writing and then ballet dancing having failed, she was now trying her hand, no more successfully, at drawing. Cowley was dismayed by her appearance. Where once she had been the very incarnation of magnetic vivacity, "now there was hardly a trace of beauty or silkiness. Her face was emaciated and twitched as she talked." After she went to bed that evening, Cowley and Fitzgerald settled down in the underfurnished and uncarpeted living room—Cowley seated in a creaky armchair with a bottle of bootleg whiskey on the side table, Fitzgerald standing and declaiming, with a glass of what he said was water that he paused several times to refill—for a conversation that stretched into the early morning hours.

Fitzgerald did most of the talking. He recalled Zelda's salad days as "the belle of Montgomery" whom he met at the Governor's Ball, musing that "sometimes I don't know whether Zelda isn't a character that I created myself." He humble-bragged about his peasant roots and "a streak of pure vulgarity that I like to cultivate," and said that Edmund Wilson had him reading Marx. He sandbagged Cowley by slyly asking, "What did you think of *The Great Gatsby*?" Shockingly, Cowley had not read the book and was eventually forced to confess that. His confession unleashed an aggression in Fitzgerald: He dragged Cowley to his study to point out a foot-high pile of manuscript pages for his novel ("It's good, good, good," he boasted) and later brought his face right up to Cowley's like a prosecutor and asked accusingly, "What do you know about writing? Did you ever write a book half as good as *The Great Gatsby*?" Then suddenly the aggression stopped and Fitzgerald sheepishly confessed that the glass of "water" he'd refilled multiple times was in fact 50 percent grain alcohol. With that, his natural courtesy returned and a tired Cowley was shown his room for the night.

When Cowley awoke the next morning Fitzgerald was already at work with his secretary in his study. After a brisk horseback ride with Zelda and then a visit with John Dos Passos, who was recovering from rheumatic fever at Johns Hopkins Hospital, he drove away from La

Paix on the next leg of his journey, Scott, Zelda, and Scottie waving goodbye from the porch. At a tourist home in Virginia that evening he made a long entry in his notebook about the haunting visit. The memory of that brief visit gave Cowley plenty of food for thought as he drove west to Tennessee to finish his account of the glories and failures of the literary twenties.

Cowley was headed into far different Southern terrain than the mountainous Appalachian armed camp of the year before. Cloverlands would be an idyllic reprieve from the storms battering the country. On his first morning in the brick antebellum house he'd been given, built in the style of older eighteenth-century Virginia mansions, he was awakened by the sound of a woodpecker pecking away at a pecan tree outside his window. The rolling landscape was lovely, "a gentle and cultivated land, *un pays doux* that made me think of the Ile de France." Meals were provided by Gordon's cousins Henry and Clyde, breakfast served at his house by a servant, dinners and suppers at theirs, a groaning board of produce picked from the farm that day and fresh-slaughtered lambs and chickens and country hams, and bass caught from the pond. There was no radio in the house, and the local paper eschewed national news, so the talk at the supper table and later on the porch revolved around the vagaries of raising tobacco and the kind of local and familial storytelling Cowley recognized as one of the bedrocks of Southern writing. As a guest and as a Northerner suspected of holding unconventional opinions, he politely avoided political topics that were likely to ruffle feathers in a state where Robert E. Lee, Stonewall Jackson, and Nathan Bedford Forrest were still regarded as recently departed heroes.

After Cowley had finished his morning writing, Tate and Gordon graciously squired their guest about the countryside—"Don't be afraid of him, we've taken out the fangs," they told their grocer—and filled in their curious visitor on its history. Gordon's cousin Gus came over to the car to discuss crops and suddenly started quoting from Virgil's deep-dyed agricultural poem the *Georgics* in Latin. Cowley scored a point for his hometown when, after the three of them sang along on "Swanee River" and "My Old Kentucky Home," he informed his hosts that Stephen Foster, the composer of these tunes and many other Confederate favorites, was in fact a Pittsburgh boy.

The talk become even more high-toned when he was driven to Nashville to attend a reunion of the Fugitive group, named after the little magazine that had launched a Southern literary renaissance in 1922. In attendance were Tate, John Crowe Ransom, Donald Davidson, Robert Penn Warren, Andrew Lytle, John Gould Fletcher, and other contributors to the group's famous 1930 manifesto-cum-essay collection, *I'll Take My Stand.* The culturally conservative Fugitives (also referred to as the Agrarians) assiduously defended the communal, tradition-minded Southern way of life against the putatively anomic and exploitative Northern industrial system. In some ways their ideas anticipated the later back-to-the-land movement, and the contrasts they drew made their Jeffersonian Southern yeoman farmer way of life seem attractively humane. But the Agrarian program had nothing to say about the gross inequities of the sharecropping and tenant farming system that still widely prevailed, and resolutely refused to face up to the racial atrocities of slavery and the tyrannical Jim Crow system that had taken its place.

As Tate's friend and guest and as an editor of the influential *New Republic* Cowley was respectfully received. A number of the guests certainly regarded the Depression now underway as justification for their hatred of the Northern industrial system (and even payback for the Civil War, perhaps). Listening to the Agrarians talk, Cowley decided that a number of them harbored an unspoken sympathy for John C. Calhoun's vision of "an Athenian democracy in the South, supported and given leisure by a subject race," and all were blind to the ugly economic and racial realities of their beloved territory, clinging to an idealized portrait of life in the Southern states.

By mid-July the heat and his yearning for Muriel's company led him to pack his books and papers into the rumble seat and begin the long trip back east. Driving through bluegrass country in Kentucky, he noticed dozens of newly fashioned yellow log cabins with sap still running from the freshly cut logs dotting the steep hillsides. He learned that the cabins had been built by hill people returning from futile searches for work in the north or in Harlan County. This was Agrarianism Depression-style—desperate families clearing trees from hillsides never meant to be cleared, completing the destructive cycle of two centuries of despoiling the land, tilling thin and rocky soil that would be exhausted by the second crop and washed away to shale. The idyll was over. Cowley's sharp-eyed observations on this trip formed the core of a piece he would publish in *The New Republic* on August 9, 1933, on this last-ditch return to the land, "Mountain Slum." As a hitchhiker Cowley picked up mordantly remarked, "If the Indians have any sense, they won't ever take this country back."

By mid-fall he had delivered a nearly complete manuscript of his book to Norton. In a letter of November 6 his editor enthused that "it seems to me that you have improved the book 98% since the last time I saw it" and "the first half . . . is the best thing of its kind that I have ever read, both from the standpoint of ideas (especially the whole conception of the uprootedness of this literary generation) and from the standpoint of literary criticism (where your stuff on Joyce seems to me superb)." But he expressed serious reservations about Cowley's concluding chapter, "The Story of a Suicide," about the Brahmin poet and publisher Harry Crosby, whose double suicide with his mistress in a room in Manhattan's Hotel des Artistes on December 10, 1929, made sensational headlines and served, perhaps too conveniently, as an emblem of the disastrous end to an era of excess. The editor had two related criticisms. The first concerned the chapter's length; in writing so extensively about him, "you give more space to Crosby than anyone else including yourself." The second was a distinct distaste for Crosby himself: "The reader may conclude that Harry Crosby was morally a lunatic and nothing else, and why all this pother about a wealthy young man who has gone nuts?" The firm suggestion was for Cowley to considerably cut that chapter and thus Crosby's presence in the book.

A reader of *Exile's Return* who knows Malcolm Cowley's personal history will be pained by his choice of Harry Crosby as its capstone subject rather than Hart Crane. But at the time, his sorrow over Crane's suicide made it impossible for him to go there. "I couldn't yet bear to write about the death of a close friend." In any case he'd been given his marching orders by his publishers, along with the pressure of an unrealistic on-press date of late December, one month away, and a pub date of February the following year.

That pub date, like others before, soon came and went, and by March, Cowley had to take another leave of absence for a writing retreat, this one at a rustic inn in the remote and sleepy town of Riverton in north-central Connecticut for sixteen lonely days. He had borrowed Harry Crosby's diaries from his wife, Caresse Crosby, to take with him to Riverton, and as he later told her in a letter of apology for not having secured her permission for quoting, in her words, "big chunks" of the diary in his book, "I was trying to pick out, not the personal passages, but just the ones that helped to interpret Harry's character." Cowley returned to *The New Republic* with the sense that his book was just about ready for publication.

The book he gave to his publisher was in galley proofs and corrected by the last week of April when Warder Norton, the firm's founder and a man "who bore himself like a retired British major," intervened. He thought that ending the book with a suicide was too abrupt, and prevailed upon Cowley to quickly produce an epilogue for a more conclusive ending. The deadline: May 1, new text to be returned with the page proofs. He missed the May Day parade and rally in Union Square that year in order to stay home and write the last pages of his book, but he compensated for his absence by channeling its political spirit and message. As he later put it, "I hoped I was doing my part in solitude to institute the new order of the ages" and "wrote with more vehemence than I might have felt at another time."

Of the fourteen book pages of epilogue that Cowley produced on that May Day morning, most offered a lyrical final evocation of the period and events and figures he'd covered, followed by a discussion of the crucial role art and artists play in human culture and society. But then on the eleventh page comes this: "And now you turn to the political questions that have been playing an always greater part in literary discussions. *Should artists, you ask, take part in the class struggle?*" The answer Cowley provided was an emphatic "Yes!" "It can offer," he wrote, "an end to the desperate feeling of solitude and uniqueness that has been oppressing artists for the last two centuries, the feeling that has reduced some of the best of them to silence or futility and the weaker ones to insanity or suicide." In other words, a cure for the literary alienation and malaise of the twenties. Participation on the workers' side of the class struggle by artists would restore color and significance and tragic dignity to a world that capitalism and science had almost leached of meaning. "The subjects are everywhere. There are great days ahead for artists," Cowley concluded. He wrote "New York, May 1, 1934" on the last page of the manuscript and then crossed out the "1" as being ostentatious.

Cowley remembered May Day of 1934 "as the high summit of my revolutionary enthusiasm." There is more than a trace of regret in that statement. The highly politicized conclusion to his conclusion that he wrote on that day placed an unfortunate time stamp on a work that otherwise sought to see his literary generation in a far broader and even timeless perspective. Its agitprop style was jarringly at odds with the nuanced approach of the rest of the book, and Cowley would eventually regret his surrender to the zeitgeist of the early thirties. Nevertheless, that afternoon he handed over his page proofs and epilogue to Warder Norton, "who showed less than a proper enthusiasm, it seemed to me, for what I had written," and *Exile's Return* was at last ready to go to press.

Malcolm Cowley's book was the first to take the Lost Generation as its subject matter, and it partakes of none of the burnished nostalgia of the we'll-always-have-Paris memoirs that would follow. In fact, Cowley dismisses the words "Lost Generation" as "a pretentious phrase" and asserts that "the exiles invented the international myth of the Lost Generation" as a way of coming to grips with the effects of its encounters with European art and culture.

Exile's Return is a serious attempt to make the case for the coherence of the shared experiences of his literary generation, which he declares, boldly, to be "the first true generation in our literature." The book eludes easy classification. The subtitle he chose, "A Narrative of Ideas," while somewhat vague, has the virtue of emphasizing that *Exile's Return* has a number of arguments to make and not simply experiences to relate. In the late sixties, when Truman Capote's claims for *In Cold Blood* had made the term au courant, Cowley ventured that "I might even point to *Exile's Return* as a non-fictional novel . . . done rather deliberately in that form." There are many extended passages that partake of the freedom of fiction to adopt and inhabit differing points of view. But no one genre quite captures all the ways Cowley went about his task of fashioning this generational biography.

Much of the book is written in straightforward memoir form, with the "I" firmly identified with Cowley himself. But very often that "I" will suddenly shift to the "you" of second-person address—as in, "You woke at ten o'clock between soiled sheets in a borrowed apartment." The "you" here is Cowley, but the shift in pronoun implies that a lot of other people were waking late in similar circumstances. He freely avails himself of the pronoun "we" just as often, asserting a collective unity to the experiences being related. And sometimes, in taking an aerial view of some prospect before him, Cowley will adopt the omniscient third-person "they" of standard nonfiction.

There are also extended passages of literary criticism, letters, and texts by and from figures in the book, social commentary, newsreelish lists, and even some poetry. The somewhat experimental form and shifting styles of *Exile's Return* mirror the quest of its generational protagonists to devise new literary approaches to capture unprecedented experiences and emotions. The influence of John Dos Passos's novels, particularly his epic *U.S.A.* trilogy, two volumes of which had been published and which Cowley would hail upon its completion as the first true collective novel, can be felt in the book's formal elusiveness, its collagist approach, and its frequent tone of hard-boiled disillusionment.

One way of reading *Exile's Return* is as a cautionary tale of cultural and spiritual defeat. The "exile" of Cowley's literary generation was self-chosen. Comprehensively alienated from their native country and the Babbittry of its business civilization, they sought to distance themselves from it internally and geographically. Their sojourns in France were "almost pilgrimage[s] to the Holy Land" where artistic values prevailed. Paris may have been a movable feast, but it could not be transported. Once back in the States, they huddled together in urban bohemias or scattered to nearby rural enclaves, coping as best they could with the material and economic requirements of life. In trying to accomplish their creative tasks these writers and artists labored, Cowley wrote, "under a feeling of real discomfort. Something oppressed them, some force was preventing them from doing their best work."

So they employed various strategies of escape from that oppression. There was the retreat into pure art—but as Cowley illustrates in his acute considerations of those modern hero-saints of literature, Eliot, Joyce, and Valéry, that religion of literature had become a dead end. (*Axel's Castle*, a book *Exile's Return* is in intimate conversation with, makes something of the same point.) There was the resort to primitivism—back to the land, nature and body worship, sexual disinhibition, thrill-seeking adventurism. But as the cautionary tale of Harry Crosby illustrated, the road to excess usually leads to even more excess and eventual madness. A final strategy was simply movement for movement's sake, a frenzied hegira to the South of France, the Greek islands, the Dalmatian coast, any place affordable and picturesque enough to serve the purpose of a Getting Away From It All. But somehow civilization and its discontents always kept being packed with the baggage.

Every book of value reflects the prevailing temper of the time during which it was written, and *Exile's Return* was written in an atmosphere of crisis and despair, when the old assumptions no longer sufficed. Cowley's diagnosis of the futility that gripped the creators of American literature was so grim and encompassing that it required some sort of remedy, and a sizable group of American writers had by 1934 decided that the cure for what ailed them was solidarity with the working class, the overthrow of the capitalist system, and some kind of revolution, however ill-defined. The perfervid May Day epilogue that Malcolm Cowley appended to his book was not the product of some momentary enthusiasm, but the logical, even foreordained conclusion to the "narrative of ideas" he had fashioned. Politics had become the answer to the big questions about the nature and purpose of literature.

Someone joked that the anxiety-filled period between the delivery of a book to a publisher and its actual publication was "the calm before the calm." Alongside Cowley's anxiety about a thundering silence greeting *Exile's Return*'s publication was the fear of critical knives being out. A man in his position made enemies, known and unknown. Hovering over those practical worries was a more personal concern: "I had taken the risk of speaking candidly about my own life. I had my share of that almost universal but also specifically American weakness, the craving to be liked—not loved, not followed but simply accepted as one of the right guys. Any judgment of the book would have been a judgment of my private self."

On the first score he had nothing to worry about. The time between his return of the pages of his book and its pub date was blessedly short: *Exile's Return* was published on May 28, 1934, a Monday. On the preceding Sunday evening he was able to go to the newsstand to buy the next day's edition of *The New York Times*, with a complimentary notice by their influential literary columnist John Chamberlain. The next morning he was able to buy six other New York morning papers, all of which carried notices. Far from being greeted with near-silence, Cowley's book uncorked a flood of reviews and smart-set chatter, to the point that a mere week after publication, Chamberlain called it "the most-argued-about book of the Spring."

On the second and third scores Cowley's worries were realized. Not that *Exile's Return* lacked for positive reviews. Chamberlain's piece was warm and thoughtful, beginning "When future Parringtons are looking for a key to American literature of the post-war period, they will find it in Malcolm Cowley's 'Exile's Return.'"

The out-of-town papers ran plenty of positive and timely notices as well. John K. Sherman declared in *The Minneapolis Star*: "Mr. Cowley has written the Odyssey of the 'Lost Generation.' . . . It is a fascinating story, made the more so by grace and wit in writing." A widely syndicated review by Alfred McEwen, a professor of English at the University of Virginia, declared it "a stimulating book. Its greatest value is that it records ideas and influences upon American and world literature that would otherwise never have found expression." Cowley's fellow fellow traveler Bernard Smith, a Marxist-inclined critic and Knopf editor, gave the book a predictably warm review in *The New Masses*.

But it is a truth universally acknowledged that one nasty review can erase the good feelings engendered by any number of positive ones. In this case, there was more than a sufficiency of dissenting reviews to accomplish that. Moreover, many of the negative notices were laced with sarcasm, a personal hostility often bordering on venom, and a kind of bogus incredulity that someone would take the journey of the Lost Generation writers seriously. In a follow-up column in the *Times* on June 7, John Chamberlain wrote that "a curious thing about the reviews of this book is that no one under 35 attacked it and that no one over 35 praised it. Is this an example of the age war in criticism?" It was.

William Soskin in the *New York American*, a conservative Hearst paper, finds virtues in Cowley's generational tale, but takes sharp exception to Cowley's political conclusion and teases him and his cohort for their "futilitarian" tendencies. "Nothing stopped Cowley or Josephson or any of his colleagues from writing great masterpieces then—nothing except their own limitations." He then asserts, "Nobody wrote great books in the past decade. Mr. Hemingway is growing dim. So are his colleagues." Oops.

Ludwig Lewisohn, then fifty-two, took the stern, disappointed-father approach in his review in *The Nation*. "Arrested emotional development creates a perpetual dissatisfaction with reality in any of its phases . . . There is not a detail in Mr. Cowley's book that does not echo and reecho this powerlessness to do anything with reality." As for Cowley's leftward turn, a cod-Freudian diagnosis is offered: "He seeks the mother womb, the dark, undifferentiated sea at the beginning of things. He wants to drown in the mass."

Lewis Gannett, forty-three, in the *New York Herald Tribune* scoffed at the exiles as a "little group of serious thinking drunkards . . . They felt there was something superb in starving for three days while waiting for papa's next check." He expands on this financial libel—of Cowley's dramatis personae, only Harry Crosby and sometimes Hart Crane had independent incomes—by inquiring how the Lost Generation figures managed to afford their rural retreats in New Jersey and Connecticut.

One long review of *Exile's Return* raised broader literary and social issues. Bernard DeVoto's piece "Exiles from Reality" in the influential *Saturday Review of Literature* was "the worst review of all," as Cowley termed it, the most comprehensive and vicious attack mounted against his book and his literary generation.

DeVoto was a culturally conservative and temperamentally combative critic, academic, historian, editor, and all-round man of letters and a significant figure on the American scene for decades, chiefly for his long-running and widely read column in *Harper's Magazine*, "The Easy Chair." A "belligerent westerner" by birth and lifelong allegiance, as his biographer called him, he arrived at Harvard in 1915, the same year as Cowley, but as a late-arriving transfer from the University of Utah he was shut out from many of the college's social and literary activities. This probably was the root of the considerable chip on his shoulder that DeVoto carried for life against the effete and parochial (in his view) Eastern literary culture. As a critic, DeVoto presents the figure of a literary man who expended considerable energy arguing for the marginality and even complete irrelevance of much of what is considered literature to the wider culture.

This point of view is on florid display in "Exiles from Reality." DeVoto begins with a tortured Freudian analysis of the author and his Lost Generation figures as uprooted and hence emasculated and suffering from a "castration complex" that is at the root of a "free-floating anxiety." Cowley would write a bit self-pityingly that "he made me feel like a friendless man accused of being Jack the Ripper."

DeVoto moves on to his real theme: that *Exile's Return* is not "a history of a generation" but rather "the apologia of a coterie." In the larger scheme of things Cowley's subjects were fatally seduced by "the religion of art, includ[ing] a necessity to be great artists," a species of "megalomania" that the vast majority of writers are in DeVoto's view blessedly free of; unburdened by the castration complex, they simply get on with their work, writing "books to which the canons of eternity need not apply." The Lost Generation writers were too ambitious, unwilling to toil at good, honest middling work.

DeVoto went on to declare that Cowley "continually mistakes the emotions of his friends for the structure of society" and that "it is a fact, however painful to writers, that the literary have only slight importance." To some Americans they are "moderately important, but in ambiguous ways—at best as a form of diversion, at worst as an accessory aid to peristalsis"—i.e., bathroom reading. DeVoto's ideal republic of letters would appear to be that of an army of typewriter-equipped worker bees untroubled by ego, ambition, neurosis, and inner conflict, let alone anything resembling genius or madness, industriously producing ersatz literature for an undemanding public. This philistine point of view allows him to dismiss *Exile's Return* as "altogether subjective" and the works and experiences of writers like Fitzgerald and Hemingway as irrelevant to American culture. DeVoto's attack initiated a simmering feud with Malcolm Cowley that would flare up repeatedly in years to come.

All in all, the critical gauntlet was a bruising experience for Cowley. To F. Scott Fitzgerald he complained that "I'm getting a swell run-around from the critics. I wish some of them had read it." To John Brooks Wheelwright he moaned, "What a ton of brickbats my own book has been receiving this week. Often books are more severely reviewed, but never in my experience have they been severely reviewed at such great length." He was clearly still smarting about it almost a half a century later, after the furor over *Exile's Return* had long since abated and the book itself was solidly in print, fully accepted as a classic, and widely studied in colleges. Cowley would write, "It all seems amusing in retrospect, but the impression it gave me of being exposed and helpless, a criminal chained and taunted in the marketplace, was a shattering experience while it lasted." In his own reviewing he would demonstrate "rather more kindness than I had shown in the beginning." It would be two decades before he would finish another full-length book.

As for *Exile's Return* being "the most argued-about book of the Spring," having an opinion about a book doesn't always require one's having read it, let alone bought it. When all the shouting was over, *Exile's Return*'s first-year sales were a mere 983 copies. It was hardly the first or last important book to have been a commercial flop on its first publication.

In late December 1932, Malcolm Cowley had been imperiously summoned to the national headquarters of the John Reed Clubs on the second story of a loft building in Greenwich Village, to receive a critique of his article on the Hunger March in DC and a dose of ideological correction. That an organization of young, mostly penniless and unpublished Communist writers felt justified to "summon" the most influential literary editor in the country for instruction says volumes about their cocksure convictions. In a corner office Cowley was made to listen to an extended line-by-line picking-apart of his piece, which, among other deficiencies, did not adequately emphasize the leadership of the Communist Party or the growing militancy of the masses; did not mention the participation of Negroes and other minority groups; failed to explain the role of the Washington police in the capitalist conspiracy; and "revealed my petit-bourgeois illusions and my insufficient grounding in the Marxian dialectic."

Cowley's response was amused but polite. He said that the article they seemed to demand could have been produced by simply reading *The Daily Worker*, thereby saving him the trouble of traveling to Washington, but it would never have been printed in *The New Republic*. Leaving the office, Cowley took in the atmosphere of "excitement and clutter" in the dusty, cigarette-butt-strewn larger clubhouse: flannel-shirted and worker-capped young men arguing volubly in groups, playing chess, studiously reading *The New Masses* for the latest ideological news. He was getting his first close-up look at the restive and far from happy group of writers that would succeed his own.

The John Reed Club, named after the swashbuckling American journalist who covered the 1917 Russian Revolution and wrote about it in *Ten Days That Shook the World*, was founded by members of the editorial staff of *The New Masses*, including Mike Gold and several others, in the same month as the 1929 Wall Street crash. The next month's issue announced, "The radical artists and writers of New York have organized the John Reed Club. The group includes all creative workers in art, literature, sculpture, music, theater and the movies. . . . The purpose of the club is to bring closer all creative workers; to maintain contact with the American revolutionary labor movement." Although their slogan was "Art is a weapon in the class struggle," the club was initially independent of the Communist Party. That changed a year later after delegates of the club attended the Kharkov Congress of Revolutionary Writers and returned with detailed instructions from the Party for a program of action "intended to guide every phase of our work," including a directive to open new chapters nationwide. By the time of Cowley's dressing-down, more than two dozen local outposts of the club had been opened in cities across the country and had become havens for young writers and artists.

The resentment felt by the younger writers and artists over their radically diminished opportunities and prospects was palpable. Cowley wrote that "perhaps they were the least fortunate of all the 'generations' that had begun to succeed each other every five or ten years." They still had to live with their parents. A strapped publishing business no longer offered advances, even in the unlikely event a house was interested in publishing work by an unknown writer. There were little magazines about, but almost none of them paid for poems and stories and their circulation was minuscule. Work of any kind, let alone brain work, was nearly impossible to find. A sojourn in Paris was unthinkable. Bohemian glamour was unavailable.

As Alfred Kazin points out, "The Thirties in literature were the age of the plebes—of writers from the working class, the lower class, the immigrant class, the non-literate class, from Western farms and mills—those whose struggle was to survive." Figures such as James T. Farrell, Robert Cantwell, Edward Dahlberg, Henry Roth, John Steinbeck, Erskine Caldwell, Nelson Algren, and Richard Wright had each in his own way matriculated in a school of hard knocks, and they flourished those experiences in their personal affect and in their work. None of them exactly wrote so-called proletarian novels, a very precise and delimited genre just coming into favor, but they clearly had seen the insides of assembly lines, lumber mills, fish canneries, tobacco barns, gin mills, flophouses, and tenement slums. They were marked, and hardened, by scarcity and strife.

The New York chapter of the John Reed Club put out the first issue in February of its new literary magazine, *Partisan Review*, a publication destined to play an important part in the country's intellectual culture in the decades to come. Each branch of the club had its own magazine: *Leftward* in Boston, *Left Review* and *Red Pen* and *Kosmos* in Philadelphia, *New Forces* in Detroit, *Left Front* in Chicago (Richard Wright and Nelson Algren both wrote for it), *Partisan* in Hollywood, others in Oklahoma City and Davenport, Iowa. The magazines gave the working-class members editorial experience and a place to see their work in print, and the clubhouses provided a genuine social life, a forum to express and receive opinions on art and revolution, and a network to share news about jobs, parties, places to live.

So it was shocking for Alexander Trachtenberg, the head of International Publishers, the Party's imprint, a man referred to as its cultural commissar by Cowley and others, to announce at a national meeting of 1,200 members of the John Reed Clubs in Chicago in September 1934 that the clubs were to be dissolved and a congress of far more established writers of leftist tendencies convened in their place. Richard Wright, in attendance, wrote a vivid account of his reaction in his essay of political disillusion in *The God That Failed*:

> I was stunned. . . . Why? I asked. Because the clubs do not serve the new People's Front Policy, I was told. That can be remedied; the clubs can be made healthy and broad, I said. No; a bigger and better organization must be launched, one in which the leading writers of the nation could be included, they said. I was informed that the People's Front policy was now the correct vision of life and that the clubs could no longer exist. I asked what was to become of the young writers whom the Communists had implored to join the clubs and who were ineligible for the new group, and there was no answer. "This thing is cold!" I exclaimed to myself.

The Party had decided that the John Reed Clubs and their young true believers had to be sacrificed given the changed world situation.

The prescribed hostility of the so-called Third Period of international communism toward its natural and potential allies on the left had been disastrous. It had handed Germany over to the Nazi Party when a more united front might have held Hitler at bay. That victory had invigorated Fascist movements in Spain, France, Italy, and many other countries.

So the Comintern decided to shift direction and construct a big ideological tent, the People's Front, welcoming enough to encompass almost anyone of left-of-center tendencies. Earl Browder, the head of the American CP, coined a contradictory phrase that served as the Party's slogan for the last half of the thirties: "Communism is twentieth-century Americanism." Gone at once were the aggressive salvos against competing Socialist parties and the liberal programs of the New Deal. As Cowley put it, "After recklessly finding enemies, the movement would soon be looking everywhere for friends." Social fascism was out. We the People was in.

The John Reed Clubs had been part of the Party's long game—a literary and artistic farm team to develop the stars of tomorrow's bright and shining future. But the changed geopolitical situation had injected a new urgency into its strategic decisions. It was time to bring the major leaguers onto the field. One of the most conspicuous of them was Malcolm Cowley, who had already demonstrated his goodwill toward the Party and his energetic and pliable nature. As a member of the smallish five-man organizing committee, he attended a number of informal meetings in the Village in early 1935 where an initial draft of an announcement of a proposed congress and its intentions written by Granville Hicks was hashed over. He found himself in the familiar position of trying to keep the turgid Party boilerplate to a minimum in favor of clear syntax and the common tongue. He had little success.

The "Call for an American Writers' Congress" appeared in the

January 22, 1935, issue of *The New Masses*. The piece invites to "a Congress of American revolutionary writers to be held in New York on May 1, 1935 . . . all writers who have achieved some standing in their respective fields who do not need to be convinced of the decay of capitalism, of the inevitability of revolution." One of the actions the Congress was expected to take would be the establishment of the League of American Writers, an American branch of the vanguard and already well-established International Union of Revolutionary Writers.

Some participants in the Congress, including Cowley himself on occasion, tried to frame it as a many-sided and spontaneous proto–People's Front celebration, but the language of this announcement made its hard-shell Communist intentions unmistakable. The document was signed by sixty-four boldface literary names of the day, including Cowley, Dreiser, Caldwell, Cantwell, Hicks, Farrell, Algren, Lincoln Steffens, Nathanael West, Langston Hughes, and even Richard Wright. Conspicuous by their absence were Edmund Wilson and John Dos Passos, already well along in their retreat from the Party orbit.

The next task facing the organizers was to determine just who would get to attend the conference and speak at it and who would not. The ideological tent being erected was bigger than in years past, but some sort of admissions policy was still felt to be necessary. The man in the driver's seat on this issue as on so many others was Trachtenberg, who was felt to be the owner of superior knowledge direct from the fabled "Ninth Floor" of the Party headquarters at 50 West Thirteenth Street and thus from Moscow. He exercised tight control in restricting participation to what were felt to be reliable writers, declaring a bit gnomically, "It is time to count noses." Cowley interpreted this to mean that "the congress should apply political standards . . . Waverers might be invited—that was something new—but not declared enemies of the party leadership such as Max Eastman, Sidney

Hook or V. F. Calverton"—all by this point independent radicals who had publicly broken with orthodox Communist positions.

The other literary figures to be excluded were those who were felt not to measure up to the stated yardstick of having "achieved some standing in their respective fields." This meant the vast majority of young writers belonging to the John Reed Clubs. It pushed many of them away from the left altogether or into the growing camp of Trotskyists. Three decades later, Cowley would state that "in my mind, it was one of the origins of the great schism in the literary movement later on."

The first American Writers' Congress had its opening session, not on May Day, but on Friday, April 26, 1935, at the Mecca Temple on West Fifty-Fifth Street, a Moorish-style auditorium built in 1923 for the Shriners. The attendance was impressive; nothing remotely like the Congress had ever taken place before. Two hundred sixteen carefully curated delegates to the conference were arrayed on the stage. In the audience were, according to one report, "four thousand people [who] bulged the doors at Mecca Temple, stood in the aisles, hung over balconies, sat on the stage of the covered seats, and cheered themselves hoarse as a parade of distinguished writers and critics sounded the death knell of 'art for art's sake.'" *The Daily Worker* put its head count at closer to five thousand. The atmosphere was electric with anticipation.

Statements were delivered by the novelist Waldo Frank, the non–Party member who had been nominated as the chairman of the nascent League, and Earl Browder. While hailing the movement of "the overwhelming number of writers who are producing living literature" to the side of the class struggle and "escap[ing] from the corruption that is debasing bourgeois intellectual life," Browder was careful to offer some reassurances to his literary-minded and perhaps wary listeners. He stated that the Party well understood that the fact of his speaking to the Congress "does not constitute a commitment of the participants to the Communist Party." Furthermore, the Party had no interest in imposing political conformity on its members' work: "The first demand of the Party upon its writer-members is that they shall be good writers, constantly better writers, for only so can they really serve the Party. We do not want to take good writers and make bad strike leaders of them."

After a number of congratulatory cables and telegrams from notable writers across the globe were read, it was Malcolm Cowley's turn to speak. He gave his fellow fellow travelers crowd the red meat they craved. He began with a rather labored joke about Hitler being "the most discriminating critic in the world" for driving all the good writers out of Germany and keeping all the bad ones. He then launched on a tirade: "The brutality of our society, with the increasing indifference and heartlessness of the upper classes to human suffering, is a sure sign of its decay. Art and culture cannot live in such a world." As he warmed to his theme he conflated the state of affairs in the already Fascist states of Europe and the still functioning Western democracy. He finished with a bald appeal to his listeners' self-interest, claiming that a novel in the Soviet Union the year before had had a first printing of five million copies and that the first printings of volumes of poetry were always at least five thousand.

There followed more speeches, and then the proceedings of the Congress moved downtown to the New School, where for two days that weekend more than twenty longer papers were read and numerous discussions on the craft and philosophy of proletarian and revolutionary literature took place. These speeches and papers were later collected into a volume titled *American Writers' Congress.*

Malcolm Cowley's contribution, "What the Revolutionary Movement Can Do for the Writer," is notable for what it reveals about his critical thinking at this point in the thirties. He tried to square his fevered rhetoric of the evening before with what he as a critic and editor and poet himself knew about the realities of literary production in America. The paper begins with some strictures as to what the revolutionary movement *cannot* do for our almost universally middle-class writers. It cannot transform "bourgeois novelists" into "proletarian novelists" instantly or at all. Examples of great fiction written by middle-class writers about working-class lives are rare because they lack the "inwardness" we demand of fiction. He cautions that "writers who join the revolutionary movement in the expectation of being saved or being endowed with leadership or being reborn to genius" are chasing a delusion.

That caution delivered, he goes on to list the "practical inducements" that are on offer. The first is that of "an audience—the most eager and alive and responsive audience that now exists." Then there is the vast new range of real-world subject matter on offer, freeing the writer from the played-out dead end of the inner-directed bildungsroman or novel of sensibility. In grappling with the social world, the writer gains perspective on himself, learning the lesson "that art is not an individual but a social product." Cowley then moves on to the questionable assertion that poets as diverse as William Wordsworth, William Blake, Baudelaire, and Arthur Rimbaud did their finest, most lasting work inspired by the revolutions of their youth, and what followed from them later was either silence or of negligible value. Many critics and biographers would vigorously disagree. Summing up, Cowley asserts that adopting the revolutionary perspective will give writers "the sense of human life not as a medley of accidents, but as a connected and continuing process . . . it gives the values, the unified interpretation, without which one can write neither good history nor good tragedy."

Cowley is treading a careful line. His literary conscience is keeping him from the full, vulgar Mike Gold/brawny proletarian scorn being heaped on bourgeois literature in other sessions. Yet he wants his audience to feel that the revolutionary perspective will help them, not magically but still transformatively, write better, deeper, more lasting novels, plays, and poems.

One outlier at the Congress was Cowley's oldest friend, Kenneth Burke. The sometimes politically naive Burke addressed the subject of "Revolutionary Symbolism in America." He tried to focus his audience's attention not on the inevitability of proletarian revolution, but on the central function of myths and symbols in getting the revolution accepted by the masses. His message was simple: The revolutionary cause in America would be far better served, *"purely from the standpoint of propaganda"* [italics his], if it were to substitute the phrase "the people" for "workers" in its appeals to the country. His argument was that the word "worker" did not engage the aspirational values of the largely middle-class American population, whereas "the people" gestured in the direction of a larger unity and offered "the advantages of nationalistic conditioning."

Burke might as well have suggested an alternative to the cross as a symbol of Christ's suffering at a Church synod. When the discussion period commenced he immediately found himself the target of an angry crowd of offended Marxists. Joseph Freeman, editor of *The New Masses*, got up, "throbbing like a locomotive," Burke recalled decades later, and shouted, "We have a snob among us!" Mike Gold followed and "put the steamroller on me." Friedrich Wolf pointed out the ominous similarity between "the people" and the use Hitler made of the phrase "*das Volk.*" Other speakers noted that such American proto-Fascists as Huey Long and Father Coughlin frequently employed "the people" in their appeals to our darker political side. At the end of the session, Burke felt "slain, slaughtered."

Timing is everything in political life. The decade before, disaffected anarchists returning from the Soviet Union were called "premature anti-Communists." A decade later, members of the Abraham Lincoln Battalion became known as "premature anti-Fascists." Cowley would conclude that Burke had simply had the bad timing to reveal himself as a premature People's Frontist. Three months later, on August 2, Georgi Dimitrov, general secretary of the Comintern, delivered an hours-long speech to a huge international crowd of delegates, laying out in great detail the new People's Front party line, with specific reference to the American situation. Unlike Burke, he was greeted at its close by a rousing ovation and cries of "Hurrah! Long live Comrade Dimitrov!" This speech would have a seismic effect on left politics across the globe and in this country, and soon enough "the people" would replace "workers" in the vocabulary of leftist writers and speakers, precisely as Burke had recommended.

Another outlier that weekend was the prickly novelist and critic James T. Farrell. He would become so "embittered" (Cowley's word) by the way the event played out that he would write a Festivus-like novel, *Yet Other Waters* (1952), largely to air his grievances. The Congress coincided with what would have been the absolute peak of his literary prestige, the publication of *Judgment Day*, the concluding volume of the Studs Lonigan trilogy. That very Sunday *The New York Times Book Review* ran a rave by Harold Strauss, and the next day John Chamberlain devoted his influential Books of the Times column entirely to the book, calling it "one of the powerful works of modern fiction" and "a work of art." Roping in Farrell was a coup for the Congress.

But Farrell was nursing increasing doubts about the Party's controlling nature. He had been educated at the University of Chicago and, unlike most members of the literary left who had acquired their Marxism less by reading and study than by osmosis, Farrell was extremely well read in Marxist literature and let people know it. It seems likely that Trachtenberg and his string pullers were wary of what the unpredictable Farrell might say or do, so they scheduled his paper to be delivered at nine a.m. at the New School, when attendance would be at its thinnest. No more than thirty people showed up in the large auditorium for his session. He never forgave this perceived slight.

Farrell delivered a survey of the short-story form in the hands of modern left writers that was a first-rate piece of literary criticism, probably the best speech of the conference. He offered an acute analysis of the ways a revolutionary viewpoint needed to emerge organically from a story's details, not glued on at the end as pedagogy.

It was not this paper that got Farrell into trouble. At the very end of the fifth and last session that evening, Farrell rose to his feet and quixotically, "without knowing why he did it," called out, "I move that the Congress close by singing *The Internationale*." Applause followed and the hundreds of people in the room arose to belt out the anthem of international communism. Gold and Trachtenberg were furious at Farrell and said so. "They'll say the writers were run by Communists," the Trachtenberg figure in Farrell's novel complains. Cowley speculates that, by then, clear instructions to soft-pedal the Party control of the proceedings had been delivered to the Ninth Floor.

Cowley would become one of the targets of Farrell's score settling in *Yet Other Waters*. He is easily recognizable in the book as "Sherman Scott," the somewhat pompous and slippery editor of the "liberal rag" *The New Freedom*. Scott is given to self-serving reminiscences of the twenties and little sermons on the salutary effects of country life. More seriously, he adheres to the positions of the comrades even when they are clearly in the wrong, and he is not above using his powerful position to manipulate writers like Farrell and even punish them. It is a portrait of Cowley painted from the most critical position possible, and while some of it had a basis in fact, it is laced with the enmity of many battles to follow.

After the stirring speeches came the far less exciting administrative slog of establishing the League of American Writers as a going con-cern. A national council of fifty writers had been named, and from that a group of seventeen were elected "to the executive committee, who will guide the central work of the body in New York." Malcolm Cowley was elected. There was no office to meet in, no letterhead sta-tionery, no secretary, no money in the till, and the president, Waldo Frank, was headed off to Paris for the Writers' International Congress for the Defense of Culture, which attracted a glittering list of literary luminaries. At this conclave the new political language of the People's Front would be even more obviously in evidence. The much-covered event lent an impetus to such committee meetings that managed to be held over the next few months.

That summer the Cowley family, which now included Muriel, Malcolm, and their new son, Robert, born on December 16, 1934, moved into a rented quarryman's cottage in Millstone Point between New London and Niantic on the still idyllic Connecticut shore. There he could spend four "magical" days a week fishing, swimming off the rocks, feasting on lobster, and literary woolgathering before heading back to New York City for three days of concentrated work at *The New Republic* and the usual welter of extracurricular political activities. The magic was diminished in midsummer when Cowley attempted to cast from the shoreline rocks and slipped and fell, breaking his left arm above the elbow. Another fisherman had to help him back to the cottage, and Muriel drove him to the hospital in New London. He was put in a splint, an elaborately cantilevered contraption of steel rods and heavy rubber bands that required him to sleep in an armchair for two months and type his next ten weekly pieces for the magazine with one hand.

After six weeks it was time for Cowley to resume his weekly com-mute. Making his way back and forth from Connecticut to New York and to various meetings and functions in the city was challenging. On his first train trip back, on September 10, he recognized a local man whom he knew to be an official of the railwaymen's union and, in Wobbly terms, "a labor skate"—a union official who really functioned as a henchman of the owners. But it was this class enemy who kindly directed Cowley to an aisle seat to allow room for his elaborate cast, who carried his suitcase for him along the concourse of Grand Central, and who offered to hail him a cab. That evening, after putting in his workday at *The New Republic*, he attended a contentious meeting of the League of American Writers in a loft building on West Twenty-Third Street. The subject was the eternal one in literary circles: money, perpetual shortage of. In the company of writers now officially pledged to aid suffering humanity in any way they could, the one-armed Cowley had to carry his heavy suitcase up the stairs and then back down again by himself. No one offered to help, and the group in front of him let a door swing shut in his face. Sweat fogged his spectacles as he had to open the door with one hand and then hold it open with his foot as he swung his heavy suitcase out. Then the same thing happened with the second door. Finally on the street, he then had to fruitlessly wave his good arm to try to flag down a cab, all the while thinking dark thoughts about the new society to come. "I still had my dream of comrades marching shoulder to shoulder, but it was retreating into the deeps of my mind," he would later write in remembering that dispiriting day.

A cascade of further mishaps and health issues made Millstone Point feel less an enchanted kingdom than a cursed land. A couple of weeks after the cantilevered cast came off, Cowley managed to trip over a tree root and break the same arm in the same place. At least the cast that the same startled doctor devised—"Hello, I didn't expect to see you again today," he remarked—was less elaborate and more comfortable. That cast was removed after six weeks, but then Cowley came down with appendicitis, which required a two-week stay at the same

New London hospital. Finally a persistent ringing in his left ear was diagnosed as tinnitus, the first symptom of a deafness to come, which would be as striking an aspect of his personal presentation (prominent hearing aid earpiece, booming voice) as his mustache, tweed jackets, and pipe. So the Cowley family gratefully retreated back to New York City, where Muriel found a new apartment for them in the Village.

The task of filling the empty coffers of the League of American Writers fell in good part on Cowley's shoulders. The first effort was a dollar-a-head benefit dinner and discussion at John's Restaurant in the Village in honor of Sinclair Lewis and his alternative history novel, *It Can't Happen Here.* His biographer Mark Schorer calls it "one of the comic episodes of that lugubrious decade." Cowley had some reservations about the book's literary quality, but its anti-Fascist message fit in perfectly with the League's stated objectives. There may have been some hope as well of luring Lewis, America's first winner of the Nobel Prize in Literature, as a member.

The invitation letter was signed by Cowley, Henry Hart, and Genevieve Taggard and guaranteed "no publicity, no uninvited persons, real talk for mutual benefit." Lewis attended with his wife, the powerful columnist Dorothy Thompson, and drank a great deal, "his face . . . like a rubber mask drawn tight over his skull," while he listened to half a dozen speeches in praise of his book and its anti-Fascist message. At that point he decided to let the hot air out of the balloon, standing up to declare, "Boys, I love you all, and a writer loves to have his latest book praised. But let me tell you, it isn't a very good book—I've done better books—and furthermore I don't believe any of you have *read* the book; if you had, you would have seen I was telling you all to go to hell." (The novel really is also harsh on communism.) He concluded with an absurdist flourish: "Now, boys, join arms; let's all of us stand up and sing 'Stand Up, Stand Up, for Jesus.'" Cowley and the poet

Horace Gregory chose this moment to make their exit from the travesty while the guests indeed joined arms as commanded and belted out the old hymn.

Malcolm Cowley would remember the period of about eighteen months from the summer of 1935 to the end of 1936 as a brief moment of good feeling he terms "the High Thirties." The mood of the country had lightened since the grim crisis years of the early Depression. The country had drawn back from the abyss. Talk of revolution had largely disappeared everywhere except on the rabid Coughlinite right, replaced by the rhetoric of we're-in-this-together, not just of the People's Front, but in the wider American culture. The Dow Jones Industrial Average was up 80 percent from its post-Crash low. Six million more Americans were employed than at the worst period of unemployment, and the blizzard of New Deal programs had removed the raw fear of destitution and even of starvation from the country's psyche. The widespread public works projects—new roads, bridges, parks, schools, hydroelectric dams, municipal buildings of all purpose and description—had made America's cities better places to live and work. As a result, FDR's popularity with the voters exceeded that of any American president since 1820: In his 1936 campaign for reelection he defeated the hapless Republican candidate from Kansas, Alf Landon, in a historic landslide. Furthermore the Democrats took unshakable control of both houses of Congress: 334 seats in the House of Representatives and 78 in the Senate.

There was still plenty to worry about. "The High Thirties" completely passed by millions of Americans, including the farm families immiserated and dispossessed by the Dust Bowl. The travails of the Okies and Arkies and Texicanos fleeing their denuded land in caravans of spavined and overloaded trucks and flivvers would become a permanent part of our cultural memory largely as a result of John Steinbeck's indelible 1939 novel, *The Grapes of Wrath*. Cowley would review the book favorably under the headline "American Tragedy," concluding, "It belongs very high in the category of great angry books like 'Uncle Tom's Cabin' that have aroused a people to fight against intolerable wrongs." But this mass dispossession, as well as the "Great Migration" of African Americans from the Southern states to Northern cities, took place largely out of sight of observers in the Northeast.

It was a high season in the professional, political, and personal life of Malcolm Cowley. The move of *The New Republic* in January 1935 from its old brownstone home to an ordinary Midtown office building on Forty-Ninth Street was the occasion for nostalgia; gone were the now retired butler Etienne and cook Lucie (replaced by "a merely passable cook" for irregular dinners) and the alcohol-lubricated games of deck tennis. Gone as well were the old-shoe comfort and atmosphere of the Chelsea quarters and environs, replaced by the high modernist designs of the architect William Lescaze, enamel and leather and mahogany furnishings that made the office look, to Cowley's eye, "like the tourist-class lounge of an ocean liner." Far fewer penniless reviewers and "proletarian poets" were now making the trek uptown to this high-rent neighborhood, and Cowley "felt like a spy in enemy country, unsafe in my disguise as a junior executive."

The setting may have changed, but no one reading *The New Republic* would have noticed any difference in the editorial product they put out. It remained the most visible and influential magazine of opinion and the arts in the country. The bigger and permanent changes were in Cowley's private life. His marriage to Muriel had ripened into a loving partnership that would last for the rest of their days. As noted, he became a father to their first son and only child on the morning of Sunday, December 16, 1935. Cowley wrote a glowing letter to his seven-month-old son the rainy afternoon before his disastrous fishing excursion: "You were lucky in your parents, and for this reason, that both of them love life and laughter and people, animals, children, landscapes, swimming, eating, working, making love. . . . Your parents love each other and begot you so that their love would have an enduring sign . . . your father thinks of [your mother] and loves everything from her curly blue-black hair and moist long laughing eyes and freckled eaglebeaked nose down to the belly where you slept for nine months."

In the spring of 1936, Cowley began negotiating to purchase an old tobacco barn to remodel into a house and seven acres of land in the rural village of Sherman, Connecticut, seventy miles northeast of Manhattan, well suited to his plan to spend three days a week in the city attending to *New Republic* business and his many political commitments. He'd been alerted to the property for sale by his painter friend Peter Blume, who lived right across the road with his wife, Ebie, in a cottage he rented for ten dollars a month. Living within walking distance were Matthew and Hannah Josephson and Robert Coates, so literary society would be close at hand. With plentiful woods for hunting, a stream for fishing, and ample room for vegetable gardens, the property perfectly suited his countryman's ways. Sherman would become his and his family's beloved home for the rest of his life—fifty-four years, until his death in 1989.

The price on the property was $1,300; Cowley had a bank balance of $300, but the remaining $1,000 was provided by his kind secretary, who insisted on lending him the money. So the property was his, but what followed was a complicated morass of leveraged loans (including a federally guaranteed mortgage of $6,500; thank you, New Deal) and contractor disputes, at the end of which "I was to find myself possessed of, or by, a seven-room house, a cornfield, a brier patch, a trout brook, and a crazy edifice of debts to be razed, stone by stone." Mr. Cowley was building his dream house, not a suburban mansion but a rural retreat with, for some time, few of the modern conveniences.

On the evening of Thursday, June 18, the Cowleys threw a party at their Village apartment to take proper leave of New York. Tout le monde, literary division, was invited—"Communists, anti-Communists, New Dealers fresh from Washington, diehard liberals, all-for-artists, and dissenters of various types, including a brace of Technocrats and a said-to-be fascist." (That was the wealthy Seward Collins, owner of *The Bookman*, where he expressed his Mussolini-esque ideas.) It was a contentious and opinionated crowd, but on this occasion weapons were, figuratively speaking, checked at the door. Even James T. Farrell left at home the shillelagh he'd lately been pummeling Cowley with. Popular topics of conversation and general agreement included the geriatric Supreme Court that had been knocking down New Deal programs and the mounting civil war in Spain. Young Rob slept through the din in his crib.

The next day Malcolm and Muriel drove up to Sherman to find that the well driller they hired had yet to hit water. She had lived all her life in the city, and the many complications of moving from city to country and building a new house more or less from scratch put new strains on the marriage. Country life was hard on an urbanized former fashion editor; she mistook a patch of poison ivy for grass, with dismal results, and when she saw what she thought was a rat as big as a dog, she told her husband, "I can't stand it any more." (It was actually a possum.) But gradually she adjusted, or maybe surrendered.

The move to Sherman entailed far more than the mere mechanics of geographical change and professional routine. For the next few decades the rhythm of his days and weeks would be dictated by the need to stay in the city as his regular salaried employment and many side gigs, paid and unpaid, required, followed by the return to his rural fastness. The U.S. mail would of necessity become his main means of communication, as the more than twenty-five thousand letters in his papers at the Newberry Library demonstrate. Despite his political disagreement with the Agrarians, in moving to Sherman he, like they had, was stating, "I'll take my stand." In "The Dry Season," the most rural clutch of poems in the 1968 edition of *Blue Juniata*, he expresses an impatience with and ambivalence about the hectic form of literary life he and his friends have chosen: "Hurry, the printer is waiting, the letter must go out, the important visitor is coming at four o'clock. Hurry or you will miss the Washington train." It was a recurrence in midlife dress of the disgust he'd felt in the twenties at the endless hustle and shrewd calculation and unflagging careerism of the New York literary racket. His new home was a retreat, a fortress, a life elsewhere.

Malcolm Cowley was already marked, and sometimes mocked, as a country boy in his circle of literary city slickers. Life in Sherman would only accentuate his differences. The dry reserve and unhurried manner of speech of his New England neighbors would in time slow his own even more. Only a small percentage of his confreres would have been able or inclined to catch a brook trout, let along clean and filet it. Even fewer would have kept a loaded rifle at the ready in the bathroom to take potshots out the window at passing deer or unwelcome varmints like groundhogs. Plenty of the editors and contributors at *The New Republic* could deliver at will a sharp line of patter about land use, population density, and enlightened agricultural policy, but it was Malcolm Cowley who served for four decades on the Sherman zoning board, wrestling with the nitty-gritty details of traffic flow and business districting and, quite successfully, helping to ward off the threat of suburban sprawl, as an aerial view of still verdant and largely un-subdivided Sherman can reveal. His life there cemented his status as the least "New York" of that brilliant and combative tribe, the New York intellectuals. He both was and was not one of them.

When Malcolm Cowley came to Sherman, he came to stay. One of his best poems, "The Long Voyage," begins with this stanza: "Not that the pines were darker there, / nor mid-May dogwood brighter there, / nor swifts more swift in summer air; / it was my own country."

This was written in 1938, two years after his move. One of the earliest landscaping projects he undertook was to plant a line of small pine saplings, all procured gratis from the Civilian Conservation Corps, on a rise a hundred yards or so from his house. They prospered, and eight decades later a visitor can look out from the house on Church Road and admire Cowley's arboreal handiwork: a majestic stand of tall pine trees in the near distance. He began at once to transform his patch of Sherman into his own country.

NINE.

THE BITTEREST THIRTIES

"The High Thirties" would fade away as FDR's second term commenced. FDR's overwhelming plurality in electoral and popular votes and in both houses of Congress and his anger at having key New Deal laws struck down led him to concoct his infamous scheme to "pack the Court," a legislative push to appoint a new Supreme Court justice for every sitting justice over seventy years of age. It backfired disastrously. His bill went down to defeat in the Senate, 70 to 20, and the congressional insurrection would shortly defeat or table other FDR measures. The social innovations of the New Deal were effectively stalled.

In 1937 a period of relative labor peace came to an end with an epidemic of nationwide strikes, many of them violent and in some cases fatal. A sit-down strike at a General Motors plant in Flint and a brutal, bloody clash between the police and strikers at a Republic Steel plant in South Chicago that left ten dead and ninety wounded were two of the many incidents that led Secretary of Labor Frances Perkins to call that year the most savage in the history of twentieth-century labor up to that point.

Roosevelt followed his political miscalculation with an economic one that had equally unfortunate consequences. He had always been a foul-weather Keynesian, allowing himself only reluctantly to be talked by his Brains Trust into deficit spending to offer relief and create jobs for sore-beset Americans. All the encouraging economic news as he began his second term in 1937 led him to believe it was now the time to make good on his campaign pledge to balance the federal budget. But the actions necessary to do so spiraled the fragile recovery into a new recession. A rush of panic selling caused a second "Black Tuesday" stock market crash on October 19, 1937, and by the spring of 1938, five million formerly employed Americans were out of work and 14 percent of the population was on some form of relief.

These and other failures of judgment reinvigorated a virulent opposition on the right to Roosevelt and the New Deal reborn from the ashes of the 1936 election. As detailed by Marquis Childs in *The New Republic*, FDR, in "challeng[ing] the rights and privileges of the ruling clique in America," ended up being "feared and hated by the rich and a large section of the middle class." Where during his first term such criticisms were kept largely private, FDR-haters felt free now to give public voice to accusations that he aspired to a dictatorship like Mussolini or even Caesar, that he and his New Dealers were either Communist dupes or outright Reds (often accompanied by anti-Semitic sneers against "radical Jews"), that his administration was owned by John L. Lewis and the CIO and the army of the unemployed. FDR famously declared of plutocrats, "I welcome their hatred." He got more of it than he may have bargained for.

The international situation was even more ominous. The Fascist countries of Europe were on the march. Italy under Mussolini had invaded Ethiopia in 1935, a brutal conflict and occupation that lasted until 1939. Hitler's Germany continued to accelerate its programs of rearmament and anti-Semitism, culminating in the Anschluss, the forcible annexation of Austria into Nazi Germany in March of 1938, and Kristallnacht in November, the mob-fueled nationwide pogrom against Jewish businesses and synagogues. Far worse lay ahead.

Most consequentially, perhaps, for the American cultural left, in 1936 the far-right Nationalists led by Francisco Franco launched a civil war against the democratically elected Popular Front Spanish Republic. The Western democracies, chiefly Great Britain, France, and the United States, maintained a steadfast neutrality in the conflict, while Germany and Italy both provided support to the Nationalists in the form of armaments and troops. Into this terrible vacuum stepped Stalin and the Soviet Union, who gave considerable financial and military support to the Loyalists. The Spanish Republic became a passionate rallying point for the People's Front movement in those years.

Disagreements over the best ways to confront reaction at home and fascism abroad would gradually dissolve the unity of the People's Front. Many of the bitterest disagreements centered on the question of just what Stalin's intentions were and to what extent his Soviet Union was either a progressive but as yet imperfect workers' paradise in mid-construction or a tyrannical and unprecedented totalitarian state. It was impossible for someone to be a supporter of both the People's Front *and* Leon Trotsky, the hero of the Russian Revolution, now in exile in Mexico and under relentless and vicious attack from Communists and fellow travelers around the globe. These controversies would splinter the cultural left into warring sects and provide the seemingly inexhaustible fuel for cultural disputes and elephant's-memory paybacks that stretched almost to the end of the twentieth century.

Against this background, Malcolm Cowley continued to pursue his activities as a critic, editor, poet, and political activist. He was even more productive as a critic and reviewer in these years, which is saying something. In order to begin paying off the debts incurred by the purchase and remodeling of his Sherman retreat, he had signed a contract with *The New Republic* that required him to write a weekly review or essay every issue. He didn't quite meet his quota, but from 1936 to

1938 he produced ninety essays and reviews for the magazine, or one every week and a half, an impressive record.

Most of Cowley's reviews hold up well, a testament to the hard work he performed to reconcile some complex and even contradictory aims. Few book reviews survive their moment. Cowley's don't quite have the almost implacable intellectual authority of Edmund Wilson's; the high mandarin seriousness of Lionel Trilling's; or the sleek and impressive efficiency of Robert Cantwell's, who had a reputation as the best pure book reviewer of the thirties. What you get in a Cowley review is something clear and searching, never didactic, written by someone widely read and committed to literary values, and always personal in tone. The conclusions he reaches feel arrived at after hard thought and internal questioning, not delivered ex cathedra. "In effect," he writes, "I was speaking for myself, on my own responsibility, to what had become my own circle of readers."

Let Alfred Kazin's verdict stand as testimony to the success of Cowley's approach to reviewing: "The lead review in *The New Republic*, a single page usually written by Cowley himself, brought the week to focus for people to whom this page, breathing intellectual fight in its sharp black title and solid double-columned lines of argument, represented the most dramatically satisfying confrontation of a new book by a gifted, uncompromising critical intelligence. . . . Cowley made his points with unassailable clarté and concreteness; he *made* an article each week that one had to read and could remember." Cowley stood in relation to books in the thirties much the way Pauline Kael did to films in *The New Yorker* in the seventies: It was a requirement in intellectual circles that you have an opinion about his opinion.

How Marxian (to use the adjective he favored) was Malcolm Cowley's critical practice in the thirties? The question was clearly on his mind in 1967 when he wrote an essay on reviewing; he devotes a full page to the matter. He points out that Marxism provided a coherent method of judgment and interpretation to critics in the thirties, a chaotic time when they "were looking for a scheme of values, a direction, a skeleton key that would unlock almost any sort of political or literary situation (and help them write a cogent page)." This echoes something he wrote to Kenneth Burke as early as 1931: "In running a book department, I've noticed that even unintelligent reviewers can write firm reviews, hard, organized, effective reviews, if they have a Marxian slant. There must be something to it." He quotes his own statement on the issue in the 1934 epilogue to *Exile's Return,* to the effect that the smallest matters from the price of groceries and a broken love affair to the great world events in Russia, China, and Spain can be viewed as part of a vast "historical pattern" that the lens of class struggle can provide moral clarity to.

Certainly in the heat of the revolutionary moment, Cowley could substitute wishful thinking for rigorous logic in trying to have it both ways: literary aestheticism and social function seamlessly fused. But with some conspicuous exceptions, his literary reviewing skewed fairly consistently toward the cultural center. He far more often was Emersonian—the sage who advised in "Self-Reliance" "to believe your own thought, to believe that what is true for you in your private heart is true for all men"—rather than Marxian. Rarely was Cowley systematic, in the thirties or later, let alone a purveyor of Marxian rigidity.

In 1939 Cowley stated baldly, "I am not and never was a Marxist critic, in the sense of wanting to judge all literature by its direct bearing on the class war and the proletarian revolution." With qualifications and certain exceptions, this is true. For one thing, in the thirties he functioned as a free-range critic and reviewer: Of the hundreds of books that came under his scrutiny, the majority of them had little or no political content. Here is a representative sampling of some notable books he reviewed: Thomas Mann's *Joseph in Egypt*; Margaret Mitchell's *Gone with the Wind*; Van Wyck Brooks's *The Flowering of New*

England; Carl Van Doren's *Benjamin Franklin*; William Faulkner's *Pylon* and *The Hamlet*; F. Scott Fitzgerald's *Tender Is the Night*; Thomas Wolfe's *Of Time and the River* and *The Web and the Rock*; T. S. Eliot's *Collected Poems: 1909–1935*; Evelyn Waugh's *Decline and Fall*, *Black Mischief*, and *Vile Bodies*; Ernest Hemingway's *Death in the Afternoon*; and E. E. Cummings's *ViVa*. These reviews are free of ideological bias or judgment.

Many of the novels that Cowley reviewed did have explicit political content, and in such cases he would make his sympathies clear. His review of the Socialist and ex-Communist Ignazio Silone's *Fontamara*, an allegorical narrative about the Fascist depredations of the peasants of an Abruzzi hill town, is warmly appreciative, seeing Fontamara as "a concave mirror in which the whole of Fascist Italy is reflected in miniature." His review of the literary action hero André Malraux's novel of the Chinese revolution, *Man's Fate*, is even more enthusiastic, a dithyramb to the heroism and fellowship of its doomed protagonists that "ends by casting more light on our own bourgeois society than on the Chinese Communists who died to change it." Sometimes you can sense his political sympathies tipping the literary scales, as in a 1933 group review in which he concludes that an utterly forgotten Russian novel about the Five-Year Plan and the attempt of a Soviet brigade of workers "to beat the world's record for pouring concrete" is "somehow more human than the three from Central Europe"—including Joseph Roth's classic of the last days of the Austrian Empire, *Radetzky March*.

However, Cowley privately expressed disdain for much of what was known as proletarian literature. He takes issue with the proletarian writers for their crudeness and their "eagerness . . . to renounce the art of making patterns out of words for the easier task of writing caution-ary tales and artless sermons." The conversion experience to commu-nism and the class struggle that was so powerful for so many rarely if ever resulted in works of true literature: "I cannot think of one truly distinguished work of art that any of them produced while still regarding himself as an all-the-way Party member." As for the so-called proletarian novel, it was as formulaic and unvarying as a drugstore paperback western. Late in life Cowley offered this sarcastic précis of such books: "In effect most of the proletarian novels were about an unsuccessful strike. It had a stock plot. There is a brave worker, brave but untrained. There is an older man who comes into the factory and organizes the workers with the help of the younger man. There is a strike, and in the violence that follows the strike, the older man is killed. But the younger man, having found a sturdy young proletarian woman, walks off into the dawn, determined to spread the message."

So Malcolm Cowley kept a careful distance between himself and orthodox Marxist thinking in literary matters. He was, however, a supporter of a literary phenomenon of the thirties termed the "collective novel," which had strong connections to leftist politics, and of one practitioner of the form in particular, John Dos Passos, and his massive three-volume chronicle of American greed, futility, and spiritual decadence, *U.S.A.* Cowley defines the collective novel "simply as a novel without an individual hero, a novel in which the real protagonist is a social group." In his reviews of the second volume of the trilogy, *1919* (1932), and the third, *The Big Money* (1936), he discerns in Dos Passos's work two tendencies: what he calls "the Art Novel," the chronicle of a creative individual's struggle to assert his or her individuality and independence in a venal and heartless world (usually defeated); and the social novel, a panoramic, multicharactered saga of the huge, impersonal forces that shape and warp individual destinies. Cowley saw that Dos Passos had, in his use of such innovative literary devices as the Camera Eye, the Newsreel, and the pocket biographies of representative Americans, managed to employ the techniques of Modernist literature (aka the Art Novel) to lend depth and sophistication to his epic tale of individual and social decay in a capitalist world. In doing so, Cowley declared, Dos Passos had written "a landmark in American fiction," which he most certainly had. He'd also written a work that satisfied Cowley's dual and sometimes contradictory tendencies as a critic more fully than any other work of the thirties.

On the evening of June 4, 1937, a capacity crowd of 3,500 people in Carnegie Hall was in a state of excited anticipation. It was the opening session of the second American Writers' Congress organized by the League of American Writers, and a very special speaker was awaited. For the time being, however, the crowd had to settle for the opening remarks of the chairman for the evening, Archibald MacLeish; statements cabled from afar from various writers of note; and the lesser excitements of such speakers as Walter Duranty, the former Moscow bureau chief of *The New York Times* and an apologist for Joseph Stalin. Backstage the organizers were experiencing high anxiety because no one knew where the star of the evening was or when he might show up.

Finally, at around 10:30, Ernest Hemingway arrived, obviously drunk, accompanied by his glamorous new mistress, Martha Gellhorn, "who had been through hell in Spain and who came shivering on in a silver fox cape chin-up," in the acerbic words of Dawn Powell. "Why the hell am I making a speech?" Hemingway could be overheard muttering backstage. He had been in Spain for two months earlier in the year, holed up in high war correspondent style with Gellhorn in the Hotel Florida in besieged Madrid, filing dispatches on the civil war for the North American Newspaper Alliance and working on a documentary titled *The Spanish Earth*, footage from which would be shown that evening. He had identified himself with the cause of the Spanish Republic and had become its highest-profile literary propagandist.

Hemingway's speech was well received. He told the crowd that "there is only one form of government that cannot produce good writers, and that system is fascism . . . because fascism is a lie, it is condemned to literary sterility." He hailed the bravery of the Republican troops in combat and gave a rosier picture of their successes on the battlefield than the facts would support. A theme of his remarks was the challenge that "the difficulty of trying to write well and truly" about war presents: He exhorted his comrades to eschew doctrinal hairsplitting to become eyewitnesses to "war for any writer to go to who wants to study it." Having survived his first and by and large last bout of speechmaking, Hemingway and his entourage then retreated to the Stork Club. In her letter to John Dos Passos, Dawn Powell described the speech: "His sum total was that war was pretty nice and a lot better than sitting around a hot hall and writers ought to all go to war and get killed and if they didn't they were a big sissy."

The League of American Writers and its Communist influencers had scored a publicity coup in luring Hemingway into the fold. Malcolm Cowley does not appear to have had any personal role in bringing him to Carnegie Hall, but he was active behind the scenes in organizing the Congress. He was one of the nine repeat signers of the announcement of "A National Congress of American Writers" in May, out of the more than seventy signers of the one for the previous Congress. The roster was considerably more centrist this time, in that it excluded such clearly identifiable Communists as Earl Browder, Alexander Trachtenberg, Joseph Freeman, and Mike Gold; in their place were such establishment figures as MacLeish, the playwright Marc Connelly, the critic and historian Carl Van Doren, and Paul de Kruif, author of the medical classic *Microbe Hunters*. This was in accord with the People's Front strategy. The announcement this time was largely free of revolutionary jargon and put the urgency of supporting the Spanish Republic and the international struggle against fascism front and center.

As before, the opening Friday-night gala was followed by two days of papers and workshops at the New School. Cowley did not speak at the opening session, but he did present a somewhat slapdash talk about the literary trends of the thirties in which he slagged the *New York Herald Tribune* and *The New York Times* as the two "most radical newspapers in the country" because the volume of their reporting gave too broad an opportunity for readers to draw unsound conclusions. This was an eyebrow-raising charge for the literary editor of a prestigious liberal publication to lodge. Earl Browder again put forth the Communist line at the opening session that writers had to engage in the struggles "now rending the world" or they would remove themselves from "the life of the people, which is to say, from the source of all strength in art." He also took the opportunity to denounce "the Trotskyite wreckers" who were rejecting the verdicts of the Moscow show trials that had been emerging in the past year and, he claimed, serving as treacherous fifth columnists in Spain. Other speakers took similar positions, and the bitter Communist/Trotskyist schism would emerge into the open in the session on criticism, which was commandeered by six renegade attendees, including the combative recent Yale graduate Dwight Macdonald.

Of greatest significance for Cowley was his appointment to be the League's representative at the Second International Congress for the Defense of Culture to be held in Madrid the next month. This would be his first trip outside the country, a short sojourn to Mexico aside, since the twenties. The opportunity to see at first hand the heroic struggles of a Socialist government under Fascist attack and to communicate in person the support of the American literary community was an honor for him. It would also be a test of his ability to see beyond the surface of events.

Holding the Congress in the midst of a brutal civil war in the city that was on the front line of the conflict was a huge logistical challenge for the organizers, and it would expose the delegates to artillery and aerial bombardment by Franco's forces. The Congress had been scheduled for Madrid as far back as June 1935, well before the civil war started, and the invitation from the Spanish writers had been accepted again twice the next year. As Cowley would write in his report in *The New Masses*, the organizers of the Congress were "simply fulfilling [their] obligations" and "showing the sympathy of writers all over the world for the men who are fighting fascism in Spain."

Cowley arrived in Paris in early June, and after spending nearly a month getting the necessary papers from embassies and consulates and police headquarters, he drove to the Pyrenees with Dick Mowrer, a reporter for the *Chicago Daily News* who was making his second trip to the front and traveling in his own car. As they neared the border town of Le Perthus on July 1, they were stopped and subjected to rigorous and unfriendly examination. The welcoming Republican soldiers on the other side of the border barely glanced at their passports and waved them on with a Red Front salute. On the way to Barcelona they saw grim evidence of a campaign of indiscriminate aerial bombardment of civilian targets by the Nationalists, "a new kind of warfare, without reason, without honor," Cowley described it. (The carpet-bombing of the northern Basque town of Guernica by German aircraft, immortalized by Picasso's painting, had taken place on April 26.)

Arriving at a hotel in Barcelona at dusk, they were forced to unload all their luggage, spare tires, tools, and twenty tin liters of gasoline for safekeeping before garaging the car. Sitting in a café, they noted that "on account of unusual circumstances" they had to pay for their drinks upon receipt—the air raids meant that many customers would flee before paying their tab.

Catalonia, away from the front, was an industrial powerhouse, "a great source of soldiers and supplies for republican Spain," but its political situation, a blizzard of acronyms representing an unruly and byzantine weave of warring left ideologies, constituted a huge headache for the central government. It was a genuine laboratory for social equality as well as political revolution, with experiments in villages such as abolishing money and the division of all possessions equally. The UGT, the Socialist party, and the syndicalist labor unions, the CNT, were in a bitter power struggle, and even further to the left were the Anarchists, who, true to their name, fought the disciplinary attempts of the Republic sometimes as hard as they fought Franco. Finally, way, *way* to the left were the legendarily fractious POUM or Marxist Workers Unity Party ("more or less allied with the Trotskyists," Cowley would note disapprovingly), who had been the force behind a bloody uprising in May, soon put down. One historian estimates that as many as 1,500 lives were lost in the conflict. Cowley's judgment on Catalonian politics was that "they could not settle their internal struggles without dragging machine guns into the streets," and these internecine struggles were fatally counterproductive to the all-important war effort. He smelled "an almost sinister type of revolutionary dilettantism" in the air, especially among the journalists, and he noted approvingly, "Almost all the Anarchist posters had disappeared from the walls" and that the vacant POUM headquarters were in shambles and guarded by government Assault Guards.

As it happened, just the week before, an English volunteer by the name of Eric Blair, who had fought with the POUM militia for almost five months on the Aragon front, had managed to board a train from Barcelona to cross the border into France with his wife, Eileen Blair, and two English comrades, thereby escaping what would have been almost certain assassination by the Communists. Blair—who under his pen name, George Orwell, would become arguably the most famous and influential writer of the twentieth century—was a member of the English Independent Labour Party (ILP) and a fiercely independent radical himself with an unshakable commitment to social equality. He had come to Spain in late December of 1936 with some vague journalistic ambitions, but he quickly found himself attracted by the uncompromising revolutionary program of the POUM forces.

The lanky Orwell was considerably taller than his Catalonian comrades and presented an inviting target for Nationalist snipers. On May 20, he took a bullet through the neck that missed his carotid artery by a millimeter. He was evacuated to a series of divisional hospitals behind the front lines and finally, once declared out of danger, moved to a POUM convalescent hospital in a suburb. But the flood of poisonous Communist propaganda against the Anarchists and anyone associated with POUM had begun in earnest, and Orwell came to understand that he and his wife and friends were in danger. Some of his ILP associates had already been arrested, and, as he would later learn, Andrés Nin, the head of POUM, had been seized by the Communists and tortured and killed by NKVD agents. A murderous putsch was underway. So Orwell applied for his discharge from the militia on medical grounds and joined his wife in the foyer of the Hotel Continental. Because POUM had been declared illegal and the hotels were being carefully watched, Orwell and his two friends John McNair and Stafford Cottman had to spend the next few tense days in hiding, walking the boulevards and sleeping in abandoned churches, until they could manage to cross the frontier safely.

The murderous Communist purge of the Catalonian revolutionaries represented the first eruption outside the Soviet Union of the Stalinist terror that would become a defining feature of twentieth-century totalitarianism. The grim world of Arthur Koestler's *Darkness at Noon* and, embryonically, Orwell's own masterpiece, *1984*, had arrived. A month after his escape, Orwell would report in *The New English Weekly* that "there is no doubt whatever about the thoroughness with which [the Spanish government] is crushing its own revolution-aries. For some time past a reign of terror—forcible suppression of political parties, a stifling censorship of the press, ceaseless espionage and mass imprisonment without trial—has been in progress." He goes on to declare, "The real struggle is between revolution and counter-revolution; between the workers who are vainly trying to hold on to a little of what they won in 1936, and the Liberal-Communist bloc who are so successfully taking it away from them. . . . Communism is now a counter-revolutionary force." Time and history have validated Or-well's firsthand view of Stalinist treachery in Spain.

None of this is hinted at in the long multipart account of Cowley's trip to Spain that would run, soon after his return, in *The New Republic*. It is unfair to compare the insights to be derived from a sixteen-day tour with Orwell's intimate five months' experience of Spanish war and politics on the front lines. But what is striking is Cowley's rote and unquestioning acceptance of the Communist-dictated Popular Front version of events, his clear hostility to the Catalonian revolu-tionaries, and his inability to perceive how the Soviets had taken con-trol of the politics of the civil war.

On July 3, Cowley and Mowrer drove two hundred miles south to Valencia, the capital of the Spanish Republic and the location of the first session of the Writers' Congress. Cowley's mood lightened con-siderably once they arrived. Valencia, although closer to the actual war than Barcelona, had an uplifting air of confidence and commitment. The next day he wrote a speech, had it translated, and delivered it at an afternoon session at the town hall.

Toward dawn at his hotel, Cowley underwent his first air raid. Mowrer, who had experienced many bombing raids in Madrid, had them both crouch at the head of their beds to protect against frag-ments if the bombs landed in the square. "We sat there in the absolute darkness arguing without warmth, and feeling—at least I felt—like a rabbit going down a hole," Cowley recalled, as they listened to the throb of trimotor bombers and the dull thud of anti-aircraft fire and bombs exploding at a distance.

At ten o'clock the next morning Cowley and the other delegates were driven in a long motorcade the two hundred miles inland to Madrid. He noted thousands of troops bivouacked by the roads, Republican planes flying low back from the front, fields with barbed-wire entanglements, and—with his countryman's eye—a landscape exhausted and eroded by centuries of overgrazing and careless feudal stewardship.

Entering Madrid at twilight, Cowley saw a bustling European city with crowded cafés and sidewalks full of pedestrians, with few visible signs of it having been under siege for eight months. Only in the light of morning did the destruction of the war become clear: an old church destroyed by bombing, its roof caved in; apartment houses with entire walls sheared off to reveal the rooms within; children playing in the heaps of rubble left from shelled houses. In his report, Cowley strove to accentuate the positive, praising the fortitude of the Madrileños in going about their work and play as if the front of a desperate war were not a couple of miles to the west, easily within Fascist artillery range.

One evening Cowley climbed to the roof of his hotel to take in the spectacle of "the sky cut into a checkerboard by powerful searchlights," the thunder of guns from the west, the fires burning behind Fascist lines. "I should have been full of pity for the sleeping city," he wrote, "but instead I felt what was almost a frenzy of admiration."

The sessions of the Writers' Congress that began on the morning of July 6 coincided with a major Loyalist offensive on the Sierra Front. Cowley awoke that morning to the rumble of artillery fire that reminded him of the Western Front in 1917. The noise of bombs exploding kept interrupting the speeches, and at one point two soldiers rushed the platform to display Fascist banners captured at Brunette, where the bulk of the fighting was. They announced that the offensive had advanced an impressive sixteen kilometers.

Cowley estimated that about eighty delegates from twenty-eight countries as far away as Chile and China made it to Madrid, an impressive showing in light of the many obstacles that had to be overcome. Attendees included Stephen Spender, Sylvia Townsend Warner, and John Strachey from Great Britain; Aleksey Tolstoy and Ilya Ehrenburg from the Soviet Union; André Malraux, Tristan Tzara, and Julien Benda from France; many Spanish literary figures of note; and a considerable contingent of writers from Latin and Central America, including the poets César Vallejo from Peru and Pablo Neruda from Chile. The American delegation consisted of Cowley and the journalists Louis Fischer, the first American to enlist in the International Brigade and a future contributor to *The God That Failed*; and Anna Louise Strong, a prolific journalist-historian and passionate lifelong supporter of the Soviet Union and Chinese communism.

Like every such conference, this one largely involved writers taking their turn before a microphone. It also had soldiers standing guard alongside the speakers' platform and a military band that kept breaking into the "Internationale" unpredictably, requiring the attendees to stand at attention with raised fists each time. Purely literary subjects took a back seat to the politics of the moment. One after another a Cuban, a Pole, a German, a Bulgarian, a Frenchman, "a whole parade of nations" stepped forward to proclaim their support for the Spaniards' struggle.

These sentiments were shared by the vast majority of American literati. In the spring of 1938 the League of American Writers published a thick pamphlet titled *Writers Take Sides*, summarizing the results of a poll of 418 authors on their opposition to Franco and support of Republican Spain. Only 7 writers, including the poets E. E. Cummings and Robinson Jeffers, declared themselves neutral, and just one brave soul,

Gertrude Atherton, offered support for Franco and fascism over what, she argued, was de facto communism. All the rest echoed the sentiments of Ernest Hemingway—"Just like any honest man I am against Franco and fascism"—though few emulated his terseness.

Late that evening at dinner the writer-delegates from the International Brigade were singing marching songs when the hotel began to shake from a new Fascist bombardment. A hundred writers were herded in darkness to the lowest floors to wait it out. Their reactions varied from near-hysteria to stoic calm. When the explosions let up, Cowley, Strong, and the English delegation left the hotel to witness a conflagration two blocks away. The apocalyptic spectacle put him in a somber mood: "The end of the world, I think, will be like this— not a sudden immense catastrophe but a slow attrition, as in Madrid . . . not a great disaster but an accumulation of small disasters, while people carry on their business and try to repair the damage, never quite fast enough to keep up with the attacks of the enemy."

Cowley would spend ten more days in Spain, including two more sessions of the Congress, one in Valencia on July 10 and a concluding one in Barcelona on July 12. Air raids aside, he did not see much of the war. The closest he came to the front lines was a tour with twenty other writers to Guadalajara to the northeast, where the war had ground down to a stalemate: impregnable Fascist and Loyalist trenches two thousand yards apart, too distant for either side to inflict much damage. Moving on to Brihuega, a ravaged town that four months earlier had been the site of a fierce battle, he and Anna Louise Strong stopped by a fountain, where she proceeded to take pictures of a little Spanish boy "against a background of utter ruin and desolation." Looking at his face, Cowley thought of the far luckier children of Sherman, Connecticut. He had already on more than one occasion found himself enchanted by the children of Spain and moved by their plight. He suddenly made a startling decision.

"Listen, Anna Louise," he declared. "Why couldn't I adopt some Spanish children and take them back to the States—four or five of them, perhaps, or three? I think they are the finest kids in the world." Strong, who had spent a good deal of time in Spain and knew its bureaucratic ins and outs well, said there was no reason this could not be arranged. So Cowley shortly found himself being interviewed in Madrid by the woman in charge of war orphans, of whom there were quite a few, the result in part of the indiscriminate Fascist bombardment of civilians. In under an hour the arrangements were concluded: The authorities would pick out two girls and a boy between three and five years of age—"the children of workers, not rich people or intellectuals," she was careful to explain—for adoption. Meanwhile, Cowley traveled to Valencia to arrange passage for his charges on the airliner that flew to France. All that was left to do was to arrange for the children's passports at the American consulate there. However, the vice-consul informed him that adopting a child did not exempt that child from the immigration quotas set for Spain, and only 252 Spanish immigrants a year were being allowed into the country. So he really couldn't be of any help in this case, but in a clumsy attempt to be reassuring, the vice-consul said, "If the children stay in Madrid, I'm sure they'll be taken care of."

"Yes, Franco's bombers will take care of them," Cowley replied bitterly. He was so ashamed of this outcome that he asked Strong to go in his stead to the children's bureau to explain the result. The American official may have done Cowley a favor. The desire to adopt, while sincere, was not at all thought out. He had not asked his wife, Muriel, how she might feel about taking in three Spanish war orphans, when the burden of raising them would have fallen on her.

The other players in the drama of the civil war who most attracted his sympathies were the American volunteers of the International Brigade, the members of the Lincoln Battalion. Three thousand–plus soldiers of the Fifteenth International Brigade had been used as cannon fodder in the fighting along the Jarama River earlier that year and taken fearful casualties; the Americans lost almost a third of their men in a half hour's fighting. They had spent seventy-six straight days on the front lines, and then, after a few days' respite, were sent back. Cowley deeply admired their courage, endurance, and unshakable devotion to the cause of the Republic under the most trying circumstances.

He visited several hospitals to speak to the wounded American volunteers. He found most of the hospitals "good by wartime standards," but "[one] of them—Hospital 16—was bad by any standard." It was crowded with cots holding the seriously hurt, and the general conditions were hot and dangerously unsanitary, with unemptied bedpans, blood-spotted sheets, buzzing flies, and few nurses or doctors around. Cowley and Dick Mowrer asked one "wounded boy" if they could do anything for him, but he stubbornly maintained that everything was fine, unwilling probably to register a complaint about conditions in front of two newsmen. For the most part, though, the Americans he spoke to in those hospitals were well cared for and in good spirits. They shared their battlefield experiences frankly, but without bitterness or complaint, despite reasons for both.

Cowley would be haunted by these men of the Abraham Lincoln Battalion and their fate for the rest of his life. One of the last and longest pieces he ever wrote, "Lament for the Abraham Lincoln Battalion," ran in *The Sewanee Review* in the summer of 1984, when he was eighty-six years old. He described their experiences in battle, sad chronicles of incompetent leadership, coldhearted calculation, and human waste. He also evoked how poorly the survivors among these idealists, who gave their all for a doomed cause, were treated once the civil war ended: hounded by the FBI, howled down in Congress and persecuted in the right-wing press, and used by the Communist Party for fundraising purposes but given little in the way of help in gaining employment or medical treatment. Cowley's verdict on them and their fate was bleak and bitter: "The plain facts to remember are that the volunteers offered themselves unselfishly, that all of them suffered, and that half of them died of their wounds. Their zeal and their losses both made them resemble medieval crusaders; Spain was their Holy Land. Like earlier crusaders they were massacred by their enemies and used without compunction by their allies. The part they played in the Spanish war now seems a long record of heroism and victimage."

Cowley never spoke or wrote about how much of the Soviet control of the Republic's conduct of the civil war he knew about. It is telling, though, that Cowley would steadfastly avoid reading George Orwell's classic memoir *Homage to Catalonia* until 1978. And it would take him until 1982 to publish an essay bluntly titled "No Homage to Catalonia." He offers due praise for Orwell's vivid account of the misery of life on the Aragon front, the accuracy of his firsthand reports from Barcelona, and his "poet's intuition of the future"—of the prospect of a repressive social order built on a foundation of lies. But he dissents against Orwell's case for the Catalonian "revolution-firsters," whose blind passion for, in his view, their own social revolution led them to fight harder against the "victory-firsters"—the Republican government and their Communist supporters—than against the Fascists. His view in 1982 was very much the same view as he had in 1937: "The Communists advocated a policy for Spain"—victory first, social revolution to come later—"that was in many ways inescapably logical, and right." The difference in 1982 was that Cowley was also forced to acknowledge the "terrible flaws" in the pursuit of that policy: the ruthless tracking down of dissidents, the confessions extorted by torture, the secret executions, the systematic deployment of falsehoods against opponents. He ends the piece with a hedged mea culpa: "Totally engrossed by the war, I didn't look hard for flaws in that stern but necessary program. . . . It wasn't my business to examine closely into [the Russians'] manner of being helpful." Well, why wasn't it?

John Dos Passos did, and Cowley's time in Spain and the convictions he formed there would lead to an unfortunate conflict with him. In early March of 1937, Dos Passos sailed to Europe, chiefly to write and produce the documentary movie *The Spanish Earth*, along with Dutch documentary filmmaker Joris Ivens and Hemingway.

Dos Passos's first stop in Spain was Valencia, the capital, to get his correspondent's credentials in order and to look up an old friend and translator of his, José Robles. Robles was the scion of an aristocratic Spanish family who had returned to Spain to work on the Republic's side, first as a cultural attaché and later as an interpreter for the ranking Soviet general Goriev. Others in his family were working on the side of the Nationalists; his brother was an officer in Franco's army. Locating Robles proved impossible because, as his distraught wife would tearfully inform Dos Passos, he had been arrested several weeks earlier and was being held under conditions of total secrecy. Dos Passos recalled something that the Italian anarchist Carlo Tresca had warned him of at dinner before he boarded his ship: "If the Communists don't like a man in Spain, right away they shoot him."

In fact, José Robles had already been shot and killed by the Communists, for reasons that remain unclear. This was already known to two Americans, the writer Josephine Herbst, who had been told of it in strict confidence in Valencia, and Liston Oak, who worked in the Propaganda Department of the Republic. But no one dared to inform Dos Passos of this in the atmosphere of supercharged paranoia, so he was reduced to frantically canvassing the government offices in Valencia and then in Madrid for news of his friend's fate, only to be given the runaround with empty reassurances that Robles would soon be found. He finally learned the truth of Robles's execution from the head of the Republican counterespionage service.

Family portrait, 1910:
Josephine, Malcolm, and
William Cowley

The farmhouse
in Belsano where
Malcolm Cowley
was born, ca. 1950

Malcolm Cowley and Kenneth Burke,
Peabody High School yearbook photos

A munitions camion of the kind driven by Cowley
for the American Field Service

Amy Lowell at Sevenels, her family home

The board of *The Harvard Advocate* the year
Cowley joined it

The broad-browed
Gorham Munson
in a portrait by
Ernest Fiene

Matthew Josephson
in 1923, photographed
by Charles Sheeler

Broom cover and logo

Secession cover

Hart Crane and
Peggy Cowley,
unlikely lovers
in Mexico

Hart Crane in
Brooklyn Heights

Malcolm Cowley
in 1929, the year
he went on staff at
The New Republic

Addressing a political gathering, one of hundreds
such in the thirties Cowley attended

Cowley fishing—and therefore happy

Holding his newborn son
Rob in one arm, the other
in a cantilevered cast

The tobacco barn in Sherman that Malcolm and
Muriel converted into their home

A typical gathering chez Cowley in Sherman, this one in 1946.
From left to right: Alexander Calder, Peter Blume, Malcolm Cowley,
Louisa Calder, Ebie Blume, Tanya Stern, Muriel Cowley

COWLEY IN CARICATURE

From the verso of *Exile's Return*

American Writers' Congress,
1936

Line drawing by Alexander Calder: 1946

Abstract portrait painting
by Alexander Calder: ca. 1945

*The New
Masses*, 1939

Ernest Hemingway, shooting a documentary in Spain

Alfred Kazin, City College

John Cheever at Yaddo,
mid-thirties

ID card for
employment at
the Office of
Facts and Figures

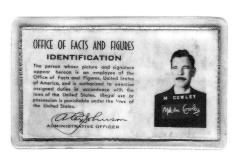

Whittaker Chambers
on his way to testify
at the Alger Hiss trial

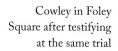

Cowley in Foley
Square after testifying
at the same trial

Neal Cassady and Jack Kerouac, lit bros forever

William Faulkner, Malcolm Cowley,
and John Dos Passos at an awards ceremony
at the American Academy

Ken Kesey's
author photo for
*One Flew Over the
Cuckoo's Nest*

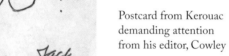

BOO !

Jack

Postcard from Kerouac
demanding attention
from his editor, Cowley

Cowley with his two granddaughters, early seventies

Cowley and Kenneth Burke at Penn State in April
1985, just before Burke's eighty-eighth birthday

At the bar in his Belsano birthplace,
May 11, 1985—his last trip from Sherman

Dos Passos's search made many people deeply nervous or annoyed, no one more than his friend Ernest Hemingway. He complained that Dos Passos's persistent inquiries were stirring up trouble and casting a shadow on all the international correspondents with the Spanish government. Hemingway also accused Dos Passos of being naive about where things really stood politically. Hemingway always felt that he had the inside line, and he had been convinced by his sources that Robles had probably been a traitor and deserved his execution. He callously shared all this with Dos Passos at a ceremonial luncheon for one of the International Brigades.

The resulting rift between the two men would never heal. The disheartened Dos Passo remained in Spain for two weeks, but he distanced himself from the making of the film. He attempted to get a death certificate so his friend's destitute wife could get life insurance money to live on. Far from being naive, he was much better informed than Hemingway on the truth of how it stood in Spain. In his view Hemingway had been played perfectly by the Communists. In late April, Dos Passos left to return to Paris and the States, stopping in Barcelona to interview the soon-to-be murdered Andrés Nin. While he was there he also had a bracing and frank conversation with George Orwell, recently back from the front. On the way back across the border into France, Dos Passos allowed a badly frightened Liston Oak to travel with him in the guise of his assistant, perhaps saving him from the same end as Robles.

Hemingway, for his part, took revenge on Dos Passos by energetically putting about libels, such as that he was a Trotskyite and that he had fled Madrid in cowardly fear for his life after the first night of bombing. He would eventually write a polemical play titled *The Fifth Column* that posits that Madrid was rife with traitors like Robles who deserved exactly the same fate. In a scurrilous 1938 article in a short-lived magazine called *Ken*, Hemingway caricatured Dos Passos as a bald-pated, nearsighted journalist whose dispatch accusing the Republican government of the murder of thousands of their own Loyalists only he, Hemingway, was able to prevent from reaching print—a malignant fabrication in every detail, Dos Passos's pate and eyesight aside.

When Hemingway set his mind to put something about, it really got about. Upon his return to the States, Dos Passos would begin to be shunned and even pilloried by his former friends and admirers on the left for his, to them, inexplicable apostasy in the matter of the noble cause of the Spanish Republic. The affair accelerated his already well-advanced process of disillusionment with communism and its People's Front facade.

At their stormy final meeting in Paris at the end of April, in response to Dos Passos's assertion that he would tell the truth as he had learned it of José Robles's murder, Hemingway predicted, "You do that and the New York reviewers will kill you. They will demolish you forever." Hemingway spoke the truth. The predicted crucifixion would arrive in 1939 with the publication of his first novel since the triumph of *The Big Money*, *Adventures of a Young Man*. Cowley hammered in one of the nails in the pages of *The New Republic*.

Dos Passos's novel is a kind of inverted *Pilgrim's Progress*, in which a thwarted idealist, Glenn Spotswood, travels through many of the familiar episodes of left radical activism to enlist in the International Brigade in Spain—only to arrive not at some political Celestial City but at an engineered battlefield death for his ideological unreliability. It is the product of Dos Passos's comprehensive disillusionment with the ceaseless dissembling and manipulations of the Communists, and his bitterness over the murder of his friend Robles. But while *U.S.A.* was the epic result of a vast and many-peopled argument against the spiritual depredations of American life, *Adventures of a Young Man* narrows Dos Passos's vision down to a thesis-driven and predictable exercise in revenge.

The attacks came from various angles. In the Marxist *New Masses*, the reviewer Samuel Sillen called the novel "a crude piece of Trotskyist agit-prop" and proclaimed that Dos Passos's "literary failure is very definitely related to his reactionary political orientation." Reviewers from publications closer to the political center were more inclined to regret the book's decline in quality from the literary heights of the *U.S.A.* trilogy and blame its deficiencies on its overly explicit and narrow political content. Clifton Fadiman's verdict in *The New Yorker* was typical: "Whatever representative value the story has is marred by the introduction of a special theme—intra-Communist party politics . . . the general reader is hardly apt to get all heated up over it." Mary McCarthy wrote the shrewdest and most honest critique in *Partisan Review*. While praising the novel for "its honesty, its courage, its intellectual clarity," she deemed it an "unsatisfactory book" for its absence of simple human feeling. The intellectuals with whom Glenn Spotswood consorts she found to be "harsh and repulsive caricatures" and he himself was reduced to "the status of a stooge."

Malcolm Cowley's review in *The New Republic*, bluntly titled "Disillusionment," stood out from the others. He took *Adventures of a Young Man* quite personally and as a result wrote an extremely personal and hurtful review. Much like McCarthy's, his negative literary judgment of the book hinges on Spotswood's being "simply not interesting or strong enough to carry the burden of the story." But the real intent of the piece is to deliver a lecture to Dos Passos about his political naivete from his, Cowley's, wised-up perspective as to the real facts in Spain. He rehashes the Robles affair and the painful crack-up with Hemingway with such smug and mistaken asides as "People who ought to know tell me that the evidence against him was absolutely damning." From start to finish, the piece is cocksure and condescending.

If Cowley's intention was to wound John Dos Passos, he succeeded. The implications of the piece forced Dos Passos's hand and he had to write a dignified letter to the magazine in self-defense, outlining what he had discovered before he felt entirely comfortable that he had gleaned all that could be learned about the death of José Robles. It must have been a painful exercise to have to do so prematurely. This sentence captures the tone of the letter: "As the insurance has not yet been paid I am sure that Mr. Cowley will understand that any evidence he may have in his possession as to how Jose Robles met his death will be of great use to his wife and daughter, and I hope he will be good enough to communicate it to me."

American literary history offers few more painful ironies than the contrast between the effect that the Spanish Civil War had on the careers of John Dos Passos and Ernest Hemingway. Dos Passos went to Spain, saw beneath the surface of events, and got almost everything right, and yet the novel that resulted essentially put paid to his stature as one of the reigning giants of American literature. Hemingway went to Spain, was expertly manipulated, and saw only the surface of events through the distorting lens of his giant ego, and got many important things wrong. Yet the novel he quarried from that experience, *For Whom the Bell Tolls* (1940), became one of his bestselling and most highly regarded novels and one that revived his critical reputation, which had been flagging throughout the thirties. Cowley would give it a rave review in *The New Republic*, calling it "certainly the best and richest of his novels."

In 1936, F. Scott Fitzgerald published one of the most famous literary artifacts of the thirties, his essay "The Crack-Up," an intimate account of his spiritual depletion. Malcolm Cowley returned from Spain in 1937 to confront a different kind of crack-up occurring in his world, that of the literary-cultural left. Despite the camouflage afforded by the apparent unanimity of support for Loyalist Spain, the fissures dividing the different groups were already well advanced and now ever-widening. As one of the most highly visible fellow travelers on the scene, he attracted a great deal of attention, much of it unfriendly. He was forced to navigate many tricky and perilous fault lines and, in doing so, made a number of serious mistakes and missteps that would haunt him for the rest of his life. He would place himself in the unenviable position of essentially having few or even no allies. The Communist Party, the Socialists, the Trotskyists, quite a few liberals, and the anti-Communists all had him on their do-down list, sometimes for similar, sometimes for different reasons. In the final years of the thirties, Malcolm Cowley would undergo his own politically charged version of Fitzgerald's crack-up, with bitter and long-standing consequences.

One of the most important fault lines was where one stood on the matter of Stalin's most visible political opponent, Leon Trotsky, the hero of the Russian Revolution, now thrust from power and living in exile in Mexico. Trotsky always managed to rub Cowley the wrong way. He gave voice to that irritation early in his radicalization in 1933, in a long review of his monumental *History of the Russian Revolution*. Much of the review is devoted to applying Trotsky's theories and tactics of proletarian revolution to the American situation, also thought to be at least potentially revolutionary. In this regard its American publication could not have been more timely. But Trotsky was not one to undersell his position; Cowley wrote that he "presented himself with a modesty too ostentatious" and "displays that archdiabolical pride which is both his virtue as an individual and his most dangerous quality as a statesman. Lucifer would have written a book like this about the civil war in heaven." He also takes exception to Trotsky's vindictive fury against Stalin.

Cowley next took aim at Trotsky in 1936 when he decided to "review" his autobiography, *My Life*, in *The New Republic* six years after it was first published. He registers the same complaints as before against Trotsky's vainglory and self-dramatization: "There is too much buttering of his ego, there are too many testimonials quoted . . . He will not admit that he was ever wrong in any important question." There is much more in this vein, all of which may have been accurate—even the most devoted Trotsky follower would have acknowledged his sizable ego—but beside the point. Rather than entertain even the possibility that Trotsky's nemesis Stalin was less a true revolutionary than a power-hungry autocrat, he blames Trotsky's fall on his blind insistence on pursuing a policy of "permanent revolution" and "his persistent failure to recognize Stalin's ability."

That review triggered perhaps the most notable attack Cowley ever suffered: a five-thousand-word screed in the *New Militant* by Felix Morrow, a former CP member turned Socialist Workers Party stalwart and devoted Trotsky supporter. The title and catch line of his piece was "Malcolm Cowley: Portrait of a Stalinist Intellectual: The Saga of the Literary Cop Who Patrols *The New Republic* Beat for Stalin." What followed was an exercise in political vituperation that psychoanalyzes Cowley and his literary cohort as having latched on to Stalinist communism as a quasi-religious substitute for their failed project of literary bohemianism. Morrow's barrage was a symptom of how hostilely Cowley was coming to be regarded by the anti-Stalinist left.

The other fault line that divided the American radical left in these years was the controversy over the Moscow show trials. In four public, carefully stage-managed and internationally publicized trials in Russia from 1936 to 1938, an astonishing number of the most powerful and revered heroes of the Russian Revolution and the creation of the new Soviet state confessed in exhaustive detail to crimes of mind-boggling villainy and complexity. The majority of them were executed.

The ultimate target of the proceedings was the conviction before the bar of history of the one figure not in the dock, Trotsky, who was painted as the Great Satan and arch-conspiratorial enemy of the revolution. The whole affair presented the possibility of, to borrow a phrase, "a conspiracy on a scale so immense as to dwarf any such previous venture in the history of man." The necessity of taking a stand on the truth or falsity of the testimony offered by the defendants constituted a stark political either-or. As James T. Farrell would later put it, "If the official verdict of the trials were true . . . the co-workers of Lenin and the leaders of the Bolshevik revolution must be considered as one of the worst gang of scoundrels in history; if the Trials were a frame-up, then the leaders of Soviet Russia were perpetrating one of the most monstrous frame-ups in all history."

Much of the American left and all of the fellow-traveling sector signed on to the gang-of-scoundrels scenario, including, conspicuously, Malcolm Cowley. In 1936, after the execution of sixteen of the defendants for conspiring to assassinate Soviet leaders, an unsigned editorial in *The New Republic* titled "The Trial of the Trotskyites in Russia" dismissed out of hand the possibility that their confessions might have been coerced or tortured out of them, or that the whole affair might have been an elaborate fabrication to discredit Trotsky. "We see no reason to accept any of these labored hypotheses, or to take the trial at other than face value," it declared. There is no way to tell whether Cowley wrote it, but it sounds like him.

The piece also accords with Cowley's even more vehement endorsement of the truth of the trials in his review the next year of a verbatim transcript, translated into English, of the first batch of confessions, put out by a Soviet publishing house, which he declared, "By all odds the most exciting book I have read this year . . . Judged as literature, *The Case of the Anti-Soviet Trotskyite Center* is an extraordinary combination of true detective story and high Elizabethan tragedy with comic touches." It proceeds at length to undermine the arguments of "many well intentioned liberals" that the executed revolutionists would have been incapable of trying to destroy the nation they had fought to create and that the trials were a meticulously staged fraud. Cowley states that "the major part of the indictment was proved beyond much possibility of doubting it," going on to tick off such perfidies as plotting to assassinate Stalin and his circle, causing railroad accidents in the Urals and Siberia and explosions in chemical and power plants, and handing over strategic chemical secrets to German agents and mobilization plans to Japanese spies. He concludes his long exercise in credulity by arguing that the Soviet Union "is still the most progressive force in the world" and one that required the fullest support in the fight against fascism.

A long private letter from Edmund Wilson to Cowley dissented. He wrote, "I believe you are mistaken about the trials" and "I imagine that not a word of these confessions was true." He goes on to make the larger observation that "there is at the present time a complete double standard of truth in the Soviet Union . . . One has to remember that everything that emanates from the government is pure propaganda intended to lead simple people and cooked up solely to meet immediate ends with hardly even the pretense of consistency or truth to the historical record." Wilson had the benefit of reading and speaking Russian, of having the firsthand experience of living in the Soviet Union for four months in 1935, and of being far more deeply read in the literature of Marxism and socialism. This was the first in a series of increasingly blistering letters Wilson would write to Cowley over the next few years on the subject of his political credulity. Cowley's response to this one was evasive—"I went so dead on the Moscow trials that I can't get around to answering your letter. . . . I have noticed that Trotsky himself walks on eggs when it comes to discussing the guilt of the accused. To the best of my knowledge, he has never said that they were innocent."

By this time the relentless assaults on Trotsky had so roiled the American left that the American Committee for the Defense of Leon Trotsky, an ad hoc group comprising such non-Stalinist intellectuals as Reinhold Niebuhr, Edmund Wilson, John Dos Passos, Sidney Hook, and Norman Thomas, took the extraordinary step of organizing a formal inquiry into the truth or falsity of the charges against Trotsky. They recruited to head it John Dewey, the most respected and incorruptible elder figure on the American left. The proceedings took place in thirteen hearings over eight days in April 1937 in Coyoacán, Mexico, at the villa of Diego Rivera. The star witness was Trotsky himself, who testified at great length and in English (and occasionally German) six hours a day, lucidly, logically, persuasively, bolstered by documentary evidence he had assembled to refute the charges lodged in the show trials. "Imagine Robespierre or Cromwell under such circumstances," an eyewitness observer wrote.

The broad and energetic attack against the Trotsky tribunal included an infamous "Open Letter to American Liberals" that ran in the March 1937 issue of *Soviet Russia Today*. The letter exhorted them to refuse to help the Dewey Commission in any way as an unwarranted intrusion in the legal proceedings of a sovereign state and ally against fascism, and was signed by a glittering list of eighty-eight fellow-traveling literary and intellectual luminaries, including Malcolm Cowley. Less visible but still effective was the aggressive campaign of intimidation, through personal visits, phone calls at all hours, denunciation in the Communist press, and even bribery, against those liberals who became known to favor the commission's work.

The tribunal went about its work scrupulously and honorably, in particular John Dewey, who performed his work as chief judge in a fashion commensurate with his stature. At the close of the trial, Trotsky delivered an impassioned climactic speech on his life experiences and the nature of Stalinism that was so dramatic and effective that the audience broke into spontaneous applause. The verdict of the judges delivered a full exoneration of Trotsky for the trumped-up charges lodged against him in the Moscow trials.

Cowley once again signed an open letter, titled "The Moscow Trials: A Statement by American Progressives" in the May 2, 1938, issue of *The New Masses*, that reaffirmed belief in the guilt of the convicted defendants and urged support of the Soviet Union as an ally against fascism. The signers numbered almost 150 names, not simply those by now-familiar writers and artists, but also such luminaries of the American theater as Harold Clurman, Marc Blitzstein, and Jules (better known to us as John) Garfield. Cowley did admit in private, in a letter to Edmund Wilson, that he actually felt that the letter was only "about three-quarters straight." Doubts had begun to creep in.

John Dewey, influenced by his work on the Trotsky commission, had soured badly on *The New Republic*'s abandonment, as he saw it, of its liberal principles in its move to the Stalinist left. The magazine had criticized the commission's formation, and Dewey was particularly upset by the anti-Trotskyist slant of the literary back of the book section, Cowley's lookout. He also found plenty to complain about in the front of the book, including a piece by Walter Duranty, thick with innuendo and unsupported allegations and empty on proof, that endorsed the convictions and findings of the Moscow show trials.

To Cowley fell the task of responding to a long critical letter that Dewey had sent to Bruce Bliven. He argued that, contrary to Dewey's assertion, the reviewers chosen for books on economics and politics were not in the hands of a clique, and he noted that the majority of his own reviews had nothing at all to do with politics. (Which was true, but it made the politically tinged reviews stand out all the more.) He copped, yet again, to his dislike of Trotsky and his distaste for the abuse he suffered from his supporters, but denied that he was a slave to Stalin and the Comintern. He ended on a sorrowful note, writing, "I feel a deep respect for your own work and for its spirit of inquiry and fair-mindedness and should feel deeply hurt if it ceased to appear in *The New Republic.*"

But it did. Dewey, whose name had been on the masthead of *The New Republic* since 1914, resigned. True to his gentlemanly nature, Dewey did so privately, but his absence was widely noted. It was a serious blow to the prestige of a magazine that had until recently been regarded as the intellectual standard-bearer of American liberalism.

A year later Malcolm Cowley picked a fight that would have lasting implications.

Partisan Review was one of the only little magazines associated with the John Reed Clubs to survive the death sentence imposed on them by the Communist Party. It shed its Communist orientation when it emerged from a fourteen-month hiatus in December 1937 under the dual editorship of Philip Rahv and William Phillips, with Mary McCarthy, Dwight Macdonald, and F. W. Dupee filling out the masthead and James T. Farrell in the wings. *PR*'s transformation initiated its takeover of American intellectual life. Its blend of Modernist fiction, art, poetry, and criticism with blunt and brilliant political commentary set the intellectual tone, in New York and nationwide, for many years to come.

The contents of *Partisan Review*, Volume 4, Number 1, the new incarnation, include Edmund Wilson on Flaubert's politics, Lionel Trilling on contemporary Marxism, Dupee reviewing Kafka's *The Trial*, Macdonald on the limits and virtues of *The New Yorker*, McCarthy on the theater, poems by Wallace Stevens and James Agee, a prose poem and etchings by Pablo Picasso, and Delmore Schwartz's cinematic fantasia of his parents' ill-starred marriage, "In Dreams Begin Responsibilities," a landmark in American fiction.

The two chief editors, Rahv and Phillips, were in later years less than candid as to the political orientation of the early years of *PR*, which is generally viewed as a straightforwardly Trotskyist enterprise, and with good reasons—one of them being that Trotsky himself wrote for them at their invitation. Another is that Macdonald, McCarthy, Farrell, and Dupee were all vocal supporters of Trotsky. Alan Wald, one of the best historians of the New York intellectuals, ascribes this lack of candor to something that he calls the politics of memory. For many such people Trotskyism was a way station or halfway house on their journey to various flavors of anti-communism: liberal anti-communism, right-wing anti-communism, neoconservatism, etc. But Trotskyist anti-Stalinism was *not* anti-communism. Trotsky was as dedicated a Communist revolutionary in 1937 as he was in 1917; he simply felt that Stalin had betrayed the revolution. This uncomfortable fact is something many Trotskyists did their best to blur or hide as they moved in their differing degrees from the political left toward the center and right.

The "Editorial Statement" that opened the December 1937 issue was at pains to declare the magazine's political independence, especially from the Communist Party, but more broadly "from the senseless disciplines of the official Left to shape a new movement." Instead, "our editorial accent falls chiefly on culture and its broader social determinants." The editors hedged this assertion, however, by also stating, "Any magazine . . . that aspires to a place in the vanguard of literature today will be revolutionary in tendency," thereby maintaining their anchor on the left flank.

By Malcolm Cowley's lights, the new *Partisan Review* was entirely too political in its editorial choices, and the politics behind those choices was wrongheaded. He was also no doubt rankled by the attack mounted by Sidney Hook in the December 1937 issue against his friend Kenneth Burke's *Attitudes Toward History*, which memorably begins, "The greatest difficulty that confronts the reader of Burke is finding out what he means." It did not help that the book was published by an imprint called the New Republic Series.

Cowley had previously made fond-uncle noises of encouragement toward the magazine; now they ceased. On October 19, 1938, he gave vent to his irritations in a peevish broadside in *The New Republic*. Admitting again his "confirmed bias against Trotsky and his admirers," Cowley goes on to accuse the magazine of violating its declaration of political disinterestedness and literary independence by its endorsement of André Gide's attack on the Soviet Union and Philip Rahv's "abuse" of the second American Writers' Congress. He decries what he sees as the accelerating "attacks on the Soviet Union, on literature and the arts in the Soviet Union, on politics in the Soviet Union, on American friends of the Soviet Union, a grand anti-Russian campaign under the infra-red banner of the Fourth International [aka the party of Leon Trotsky]." He summons up the shades of literary magazines past such as *The Dial* and *The Hound & Horn* that *PR* should be emulating and concludes with the deliberately provocative line: "Put a green cover on [*Partisan Review*] and today you could hardly tell it from *The American Mercury*." This was a category error: The anti-communism of *The American Mercury* was straightforwardly reactionary and had little to do with *PR*'s complex ideological posture.

From one point of view, Cowley, the literary editor of the most prestigious opinion magazine in the country, was punching down at an upstart challenger with tiny circulation and tenuous finances. From another, however, he had taunted a junkyard dog who soon would be escaping through an open rear gate. The response arrived from Dwight Macdonald, in a long letter excerpted in *The New Republic* and printed in full in *Partisan Review* in its next issue.

Macdonald pegs Cowley's piece as "a malicious and politically motivated attack masquerading as a matter of literary differences." Macdonald focuses on the inconsistencies in Cowley's position, pining for the "pure" literary magazines of the twenties in his critique while preaching the necessity of political engagement for the writer. "Who is this Galahad of Pure Literature who demands that *Partisan Review* emasculate itself politically? . . . Isn't this the same Mr. Cowley we remember exhorting us at Writers' Congresses to climb up on the bandwagon of revolution? Isn't this the Malcolm Cowley who not so long ago wrote an article in defense of political censorship of literature?" (He had, in "There Have to Be Censors" in *The New Republic*, a low point.)

Cowley responds to Macdonald's response in a piece titled "Red Ivory Tower." He argues that Macdonald had deliberately misread his critique, and that politics, as *PR* construed it, was less a matter of concrete action and almost one of metaphysics and religion: "a doctrine of salvation by revolutionary faith alone." He concludes by calling for "a truce while there is still time. Let's forget these quarrels about the international communist movement which are so convenient for the international fascist movement." It's a high-minded suggestion, but neither he nor anyone else did anything to put it into action.

The *Partisan Review* crowd never quite got over their sense of moral superiority in having apprehended the evils of Stalinism relatively early and the pleasures of demonstrating it by denigrating fellow travelers like Malcolm Cowley. They enjoyed the smug sensation of having been on the right side of history, all too publicly. Such attacks also had the collateral virtue of helping to obscure their own Marxist, committed revolutionary pasts.

Malcolm Cowley got many stinging letters about his politics from friends like Allen Tate, Hamilton Basso, and Van Wyck Brooks. His treks to the mailbox in Sherman must have been anxious little trips. The most acutely painful of those letters arrived from Edmund Wilson. One of them was sent on October 20, 1938, in response to the attack on the *Partisan Review*. Wilson decries the comparison of *PR* to *The American Mercury* ("a more serious distortion of the truth in the interests of factionalism than anything I have ever seen in *Partisan Review*") and moves on to a stern talking-to: "What in God's name has happened to you? . . . I don't suppose you are a member of the C.P., and I can't imagine any inducement short of bribery or blackmail—which sometimes appear in rather inobvious forms and to which I hope you haven't fallen a victim—to justify and imitate their practices at this time. You're a great guy to talk about the value of a non-partisan literary review after the way you've been plugging the damned old Stalinist line . . . at the expense of the interests of litera-ture and to the detriment of critical standards in general!" He emits a final plea: "I wish you would purge your head of politics—revolutionary and literary alike—and do the kind of valuable work of which you are capable. I think politics is bad for you because it's not real to you."

Cowley responded to this barrage as best he could in a long reply. He expresses some regret about *The American Mercury* crack on rhe-torical grounds, while pointing out that both it and *PR* "are embarked on an anti-Communist crusade that has become a fixation" and that the styles of both featured "a cold supercilious sneer." He pegs *PR*'s ideological stance at the time as an attempt to have it both ways: The editors thought of themselves as Marxist revolutionists still, but they'd actually lost faith in any prospect of revolution. He restates his own position as "generally Pro-Russian, pro-Communist, but with impor-tant reservations." Those reservations include a distaste for the treat-ment of Soviet writers and artists, and the fact that it was "a country that let two or three million of its own citizens starve to death." But Cowley continues to mount a stubborn if increasingly rearguard de-fense of Stalin and takes the results of the show trials at face value.

These were bleak and unhappy years for Malcolm Cowley. He would remember the winter and spring of 1938 as a time of discour-agement in private life and his hopes for the world at large. His note-book for the year begins with this doleful entry: "Writing as of January 1, 1938, I might register the immense retreat that socialism has taken everywhere . . . from democracy on the march to fascism everywhere on the offensive." Nowhere was this offensive more painfully apparent or successful than in Spain, where the year 1938 saw Franco's Nationalists win steady victories over the beleaguered Republicans. By April 1, 1939, the Nationalists had entered Madrid unopposed and the Republican forces had surrendered, the most dispiriting defeat of the decade for progressives everywhere and a devastating setback for the People's Front.

As the thirties progressed to their disastrous conclusion at home and abroad, Cowley experienced feelings of disjunction between the roles he played and the causes he supported in public and his private, inner life and thoughts. Some falseness had crept into his sense of himself. His job as the literary editor of *The New Republic* had become just that: "I did my job," he would recall. "I ordered and edited the sort of book reviews about which I wouldn't have to argue with my senior colleagues, Bruce Bliven and George Soule." He was grinding it out, playing it safe (except in some of his own reviews, which were not safe enough). The Sisyphean sense of having to fill x columns of empty space with y numbers of words, his own and others, week after week, began to eat at him. What was it adding up to? To Kenneth Burke he lamented, "At forty I wish I could get to work on some enterprise that would advance little by little, maybe only a paragraph or a stanza every day, but would go ahead remorselessly until, at the end of years, I would have piled up a monument. Instead of that I still fiddle around."

The New Republic itself seemed to him to have lost the intellectual freshness and excitement of the pre-1935 period, and Cowley felt that he himself "was becoming not so much a person as a name on letterheads, a presence behind a desk, a possible source of favors—in other words, a bureaucrat." He would come to feel that he had "committed more than a simple error, almost a sin against myself, when I failed to resign from the paper and strike out in some new direction." But he was a man with a family and a mortgage on a country home that had to be paid off.

Malcolm Cowley had prided himself on his Emersonian self-reliance and independence as a reviewer and thinker, trusting his own instincts to deliver the right relation to the book or the issue at hand. But now he was not writing and acting in a fashion fully consonant with his deepest inner feelings. A change had to come.

It did, but slowly. One index of his inner migration away from politics was his relative lack of involvement in the third American Writers' Congress in 1939, which took place from June 2 to 4 in New York City. Cowley was one of the signers of the announcement of the Congress, but he took no part in the proceedings, simply attending some sessions and leaving a day early to weed his overgrown garden in Sherman. The League's membership had expanded to some eight hundred writers, much of that growth from, as Cowley would later sniffily observe, "many writers who had earned their standing through publishing in the cheapest sort of popular magazines"—pulp writers of the romance, detective, and western genres. About a third of the sponsors of the Congress were screenwriters, reflecting the Communist Party's new emphasis on infiltrating the Hollywood dream factory.

The timing of the third Congress was unlucky. By April 1 of that year Nationalist forces had entered Madrid, and Franco had declared victory. There would be no flashbulb-popping, crowd-generating speeches by Ernest Hemingway and other luminaries this time. For the most part the Writers' Congress resembled more a Writers' *Conference* of the pedestrian postwar variety, without much talk of the ominous political situation.

Then, on August 23, 1939, everything changed, with the stunning announcement of the Nazi-Soviet Non-Aggression Pact. Earl Browder, when previously asked whether Stalin might form an alliance with Hitler, had replied, "I could easier imagine myself being president of the U.S. Chamber of Commerce." The announcement effectively was the start of World War II. Hitler and Stalin lost no time in carving up

Poland from the west and east respectively, and the German invasion triggered treaty declarations of war by France and Great Britain. It scrambled the landscape of the left into incoherence.

The Communist press immediately adopted a posture of denials and tortuous rationalizations. *The New Masses* declared, "Since the Soviet Union has never intended or planned violence, or any aggressive action, or any attack upon Germany, these provisions in no way constitute a departure from Soviet foreign policy." For the progressive liberal sector, however, the fact that Stalin would cooperate in any way with the most threatening Fascist dictator and country on earth was a wake-up call as to his capacity for duplicity and naked, principle-free realpolitik quite as bad as any imperialist or Fascist power. The retreat of liberals and former fellow travelers from the orbit of the Communist Party and even qualified support for the Soviet Union as a beacon of hope for a better world became an exodus.

The nonaggression pact finally broke the conspiracy of silence, a sort of high-minded omertà among the men of goodwill, concerning their suspicions about the Soviet Union's antidemocratic policies and programs and Stalin's brutal reign of terror. Even *The New Republic* was shocked out of its *tout comprendre, c'est tout pardonner* posture. Its first editorial on the pact was headlined "Stalin's Munich," a stinging comparison. Then in November it published an extraordinary two-part article by the universally respected foreign correspondent Vincent Sheean titled "Brumaire: The Soviet Union as a Fascist State," a comprehensive indictment of Stalin and the terror state he created and the reactionary tyranny he was now engaged in.

Two aspects of Sheean's piece stand out in particular. One is his statement that "these two articles will constitute the first criticism I have ever made of the Soviet Union, and the first time I have been willing to discuss Stalin (or even, in fact, to mention him) in print." The other is his forthright analysis of the way that the blind faith of

Western liberals and radicals in the Russian Revolution and the post-revolutionary regime "has been strong enough to withstand contemplation of the most horrifying and bloodthirsty terrorism of modern times because, and simply because, the end has seemed good." Sheean follows this up with the observation of the fact that "most of them knew nothing whatever about the Soviet Union did not materially weaken their attachment to it as an idea." At the end of his life, Cowley would confess, "The truth was that I knew nothing about Russia except from printed accounts."

The closest Cowley ever came at that time to denouncing Joseph Stalin in print was at the end of a piece about a sensational book called *In Stalin's Secret Service* by W. G. Krivitsky, the nom de guerre of a self-described Soviet "general" and onetime secret agent and now defector to the United States. Much of the book offers his version of the dark deeds he performed for the OGPU in Germany during its abortive uprising, in Spain during the Civil War, and in Russia during the purges. Cowley's review is skeptical about Krivitsky's account: "[Krivitsky] wants us to believe something that seems highly improbable—namely, that there was never any plot against Stalin and that all the victims of the purge were wantonly executed." But in his last paragraph Cowley writes, "The truth is that [this] book, for all its dubious passages, belongs to a series of writings and events that have caused me to change my judgment of Soviet Russia." He concludes this way: "Krivitsky—and scores of others like him—are the natural products of the attempt to impose state socialism on a nation by means of a secret police. Blame for their careers does not rest with them as individuals. It rests with men like Yagoda and Yezhov, the heads of the OGPU, and ultimately it rests with Stalin himself, who used and sacrificed them all to enforce his own dictatorship."

This would be as far as Malcolm Cowley would go in public in his denunciation of Stalin until decades later. It was by no means far enough for Edmund Wilson. After reading the Krivitsky review, Wilson let loose in a letter to Cowley: "I get more and more puzzled and disturbed by your political position as time goes by. The literary editor of the *N.R.* ought to be in a situation to be independent of entanglements with movements, parties and groups if anybody is in New York, but you seem to have given hostages to the Stalinists in some terrible incomprehensible way. Just at the time when it seems to me that the normal thing would be frankly to discard your illusions, you have been carrying on in a way that matches *The New Masses* at its worst." He recapitulates Cowley's lapses of judgment in the Robles affair and concludes with a parallel to Krivitsky: "You write better than the people in the Stalinist press, but what you are writing is simply Stalinist character assassination of the most reckless and libelous sort."

Edmund Wilson was not quite a friend, but he was most certainly Malcolm Cowley's literary conscience. His criticisms hurt badly, and they resulted in one of the most heartfelt and sorrowful letters Cowley would ever write. In almost three thousand words he fights back against Wilson's charges in respect to Robles and Krivitsky, gives in to an understandable impulse of self-pity concerning the barrage of attacks he'd been under from Felix Morrow and so many others, indulges in some broad speculations on how and why Marxism had had such disastrous results in Russia, and tries to absolve himself of responsibility for *The New Republic*'s Stalinist reputation. Then comes this:

I am left standing pretty much alone, in the air, unsupported, a situation that is much more uncomfortable for me than it would be for you, since my normal instinct is toward cooperation. For the moment I want to get out of every God damned thing. These quarrels leave me with a sense of having touched something unclean. They remind me of a night a dozen years ago when I went on a bat with a lot of noisy and lecherous people I thoroughly despised, while realizing that I was one of them. We stayed a long time in a Harlem speakeasy, down in the cellar. When I came up the stairs at last, I saw the Negro doorman standing in the light of morning with his hands the color of cold ashes, and that is how I felt I was inside. Sometimes I feel like that today. Getting involved in these feuds and vendettas of the intelligentsia is like being an unwilling participant in a Harlem orgy.

This was the letter of a man who was heartily sick of politics, and who was looking for the exit from an arena he was not really suited for.

That exit was conducted in a relatively private manner. Cowley was too proud and perhaps stubborn to shrive his soul and recant in public his mistakes of judgment and his fellow-traveling past. That would have given aid and comfort to his enemies on the Trotskyite left and the Red-hunting right. Since he had never been a member of the Communist Party, he could not, like Granville Hicks had, resign from it with a showy public letter, nor could he write the kind of confessional essays that ex-Communists such as Richard Wright, Arthur Koestler, Ignazio Silone, and Stephen Spender contributed to Richard Crossman's volume *The God That Failed*. The one concrete public action he did take was to write a letter of resignation on July 29, 1940, from the League of American Writers, the organization that he had helped to found and that he'd vigorously supported since 1935.

———

For all his alienation from his job as the literary editor of *The New Republic* and the political attacks that came with it, Cowley continued to produce a back of the book of the highest literary quality. Cowley himself produced important reviews of such novels as Steinbeck's *The Grapes of Wrath* and Richard Wright's *Native Son*. Literature was and would remain his pole star. In 1939, W. H. Auden, who'd been contributing poems to *The New Republic* since 1933, had moved to New York City and become one of Cowley's steadiest and best go-to reviewers, with five reviews that year to his credit. Then in the October 18, 1939, issue the magazine published Auden's most famous poem, "September: 1939." This was an editorial coup: Its ninety-nine lines distill the grim ambience of disaster, despair, and dogged if wistful determination as the hopes of a "low dishonest decade" expired. Auden later tried to disavow his poem, but it remains the locus classicus of the period's mood.

There exists a videotape of a long interview Malcolm Cowley gave in 1982 to the Communist Party oral histories archive of the Tamiment Library at his house in Sherman. The interviewer asks Cowley bluntly, "Did you feel that you were a dupe at all? Did you get a feeling of being duped by Communism in the thirties?" Cowley pauses for a beat. He leans forward and then back, as if the question has taken him aback. He then answers a bit more slowly than he has previously been speaking.

"People who became disillusioned with Communism were always accusing other people of duping them. But didn't they dupe in turn? It was, not to misuse the terms, a conspiracy of dupes and dupers. So that I never felt any animus against the people who preached Communism at me. They were sincere, and if I was converted, that was my own folly. Or ignorance, rather."

He goes on. "I really can't understand, except psychologically, the constant accusation of being duped and fooled by the Party that you hear. . . . The duping went right up to the top in Moscow, it went right up to Stalin himself, who was preaching one thing and practicing another. So that came down to a great deal of falseness and hypocrisy all down the line, because the man at the top was ordaining that. But for the rank and file I had nothing but sympathy and sorrow."

It is a poignant commentary on Malcolm Cowley's experiences in the literary and political wars of the thirties that, four decades later, at eighty-four years of age, he still, probably for the hundredth time, had to answer that question.

TEN.

PASTS, USABLE AND NOT

———

Malcolm Cowley may have wished that he could be done with politics, but politics was by no means done with him. This would become painfully clear very quickly.

Much as when he and Peggy departed for France in 1921, Cowley had a great deal of company when he decided to put some distance between himself and his former faith in the shining example of the Soviet Union and the necessity of class revolution. As the historian Daniel Aaron put it, "The retreat from Moscow by the intellectuals seemed to be motorized." You might even call the return of much of the literary left to its former allegiance to the bedrock principles of liberalism and American democracy a second exiles' return. Like most retreats, though, this one was ragged, disorderly, and tinged with the bitterness of defeat and a feeling of guilt.

Cowley and his kind took a great deal of abuse from their former comrades on the People's Front. Aaron provides a ripe bouquet of vicious epithets hurled in their direction: "pseudo-Marxists," "arrogant slummers," "ideological Fifth Column for capitalism," "fascist mystics," "canting apologists for Big Business and the British Empire," and "half-baked eclectics" for starters. Their most energetic and vituperative critic would be Mike Gold, whose series of articles in *The Daily Worker* on the subject was later collected into a pamphlet titled *The Hollow Men*. In Gold's view the retreat from the support of Communist positions by middle-class liberal intellectuals, climbers, cynics, and mental prostitutes to a man, could be attributed only to their hatred of the working class. Gold mocked Wilson's former climbing on "the proletarian 'bandwagon' with the arrogance of a myopic, high-bosomed Beacon Hill matron entering a common street-car."

In a July 1941 article titled "The Michael Golden Legend," Cowley struck back, claiming that Gold had fabricated a chimerical world in which the thirties represented, after the self-absorption of the literary twenties, a triumph of class-based literature, one betrayed, however, by fair-weather just-visiting bourgeois intellectuals voting their class interests with their feet. This caricature grievously misrepresented the complicated motives of the many writers who moved left and then back again, and ignored the perfidies of Stalin and the craven rationalizations of the party that caused their disillusionment. Cowley gives credit to the Communists for having helped to liberate much of the cultural energies of the decade but in the end concludes that their inflexible demands for political discipline proved all too stifling.

The prodigals like Cowley also took abuse upon their return to the political center. The center-left critic John Chamberlain had pleaded for an olive branch in a letter to *The New Republic*: "Now that a corner has been turned in history, let's call off the dogs on all sides," asking for a kind of united front of all anti-Stalinists. James T. Farrell, the Trotskyist equivalent of Mike Gold, was not in a forgiving mood. In *Partisan Review* he argued that Stalinism was, despite the defectors, still a powerful force in political life, and he cast doubt on the sincerity of their careerist motives. "After all, what does Joseph Stalin care about Malcolm Cowley?" he wrote, sticking the needle in.

In a sense, magazines like *The New Republic* were also political prodigals, edging back to their progressive and liberal democratic origins after extended flirtations or full-on romances with Communist positions. Of the magazine's editors, Malcolm Cowley was by far the most visible figure in its shift leftward, but Bruce Bliven and George Soule, its chief editors and writers for the front-of-the-book pieces on economics and politics, were not immune to the romance of the Soviet Union or to engaging in Stalinist apologetics. After the nonaggression pact such tendencies largely vanished from its pages, but the damage had been done.

The New Republic never issued anything like a formal apology or explicit statement of a change of political direction in this period. But it signaled such a change with the publication in its February 26, 1940, issue of an unsigned editorial titled "Sixteen Propositions." This distinctly chastened piece rehearses the reasons why Soviet Russia commanded such a disproportionate amount of attention and loyalty from liberal progressives and tries to formulate the foundation of a new posture. Several of its propositions would have ignited a fierce response on the left had they been put forward two or three years earlier—that the faith in Russian socialism had not been justified by its performance as an economic or political system, that orthodox Marxism as preached by the Comintern had lost the intellectual verve of Marx and Engels while encouraging "fanaticism and hypocrisy," that the evidence of the Moscow trials revealed a moral breakdown in the Soviet state. The subtext of the editorial was clear: We are done with Stalin and Stalinism as any kind of political inspiration or guide.

The actual author of this piece was Malcolm Cowley. He may have published it unsigned because he wished to avoid the personal abuse from all directions that it would have triggered. It might have been better in the long run if he had signed it, though, as it represents a detailed statement of his political posture that he could have pointed to in the bitter battles to come.

———

All through the terrible year 1940 the subject of the progress of the war in Europe and the question of whether or when the United States would have to enter that war on the side of England and France was the major preoccupation of the writers and editors of *The New Republic*. The magazine was cautious and tentative on the need for American preparation and involvement, vacillating between wishful thinking (perhaps Hitler might somehow be stopped?) and hand-wringing (was it already too late for anything to be done?).

But the owners and backers of *The New Republic*, Dorothy and Leonard Elmhirst, were becoming increasingly impatient with its uncertain call to arms. While still maintaining their strict policy of nonintervention in editorial matters, they had watched the magazine's leftward Stalinist drift through the thirties with mounting alarm. Now, with the fate of Great Britain and the future of liberal democracy around the globe on the line, that policy was about to change.

In early fall of that year, Malcolm Cowley arranged to take a book leave of three months, during which time his duties as literary editor would be taken over by Edmund Wilson. The book he had in mind was a sequel to *Exile's Return*, one that would examine the political journey that his literary generation had undertaken in the decade just concluded. That a book of this sort was wildly premature did not seem to have occurred to him. The truth was that he had yet to do the hard work of reckoning with his own experiences and choices.

This was only one of the reasons why he made no progress on the book. Shortly after his return home, Muriel discovered that she had breast cancer and had to go to New York to have an emergency mastectomy. The operation was successful, although Robert Cowley, five years old at the time, remembers that "she nearly died." It initiated a period of great pain for her and tremendous strain and worry for the Cowley family. While Muriel had her operation and then initial period of recuperation at Lenox Hill, Malcolm took a room nearby on East Seventy-First Street. They left their son in the care of their good friends and neighbors on Church Road in Sherman, Peter and Ebie Blume; not surprisingly, upset to have been separated from his parents, he began to have regular nightmares and for a time refused to eat. By November 20, Muriel was discharged and they returned home, although she had to go back to the city twice a week to have her wound dressed. With his parents back home, Robert soon recovered his equilibrium.

On top of all this, that was the time for the Elmhirsts, in Cowley's words, "to have a great shake-up and shakedown" at *The New Republic*. Edmund Wilson used his temporary position as literary editor to attempt a sort of coup to oust Bruce Bliven, whom he had always despised, and put himself, George Soule, and Malcolm Cowley in charge. But as he would later confess to Alfred Kazin, "I'm a terrible conspirator," and as a result of the "farcical in-office *Putsch*," in Kazin's words, Wilson was fired by Leonard Elmhirst and would no longer contribute to the magazine.

The mood at *The New Republic* was tense. "For a time the atmosphere around the office was like Moscow during the purges," Cowley wrote to Burke with presumably unintended irony. Bruce Bliven emerged on top. He was promoted from managing editor to editor in chief and quickly did some cleaning house. He demoted two of the most important editors, George Soule and Malcolm Cowley, removing both from any frontline editorial responsibilities. Cowley believed that Leonard Elmhirst regarded both of them as too radical. By January 1941 the magazine was urging Congress in its editorial pages to declare war on the Axis powers.

One irony in all this was that Cowley agreed with the shift to interventionism, although he felt the magazine had shifted gears too abruptly. But none of this was his lookout anymore. His job for *The New Republic* now allowed him to stay at home and write a weekly book page, either a review or an essay, with a reduction to his salary of fifty dollars a week. He comforted himself with the thought that it could have been worse, and that the reduced demands would give him time to work on his book about the thirties. But he had been removed from a power seat in American letters.

That same month of December, Cowley would end up accepting a fateful invitation to a lunch at a Manhattan hotel with a formerly radical writer, Whittaker Chambers. Employed as a writer and editor at *Time* magazine, Chambers told Cowley that he wanted to interview him for an essay about the effect that the Hitler–Stalin Pact had had on American writers.

Cowley knew who Chambers was from the literary scene of the thirties. Chambers was a member of the class of 1925 at Columbia, and his classmates and friends had included Lionel Trilling, Meyer Schapiro, and Clifton Fadiman. He joined the Communist Party in 1925, years ahead of so many other writers, and he eked out a living doing writing and editing for party publications and such freelance work as translating Felix Salten's *Bambi* from the German. In 1931 he gained a measure of respect and even celebrity for his story of heartland agricultural devastation in *The New Masses*, "Can You Make Out Their Voices?," which was regarded as one of the few Communist works of genuine literary value. It was adapted into a play by Hallie Flanagan, future director of the Federal Theatre Project, that was produced nationwide.

In 1932, however, Chambers dropped out of sight for six years when he was recruited as a spy for the Communists. He moved to Washington and lived an underground existence as the procurer and courier of documents purloined by agents for the Soviets in the State Department—one of them, Chambers famously would claim, being New Deal golden boy Alger Hiss. However, he became disillusioned with communism after news of Stalin's purges and show trials emerged. He left the spy network and went on the run with his family, fearing for his life. In April 1939 he reemerged and joined the staff of *Time* magazine, where one of his first big pieces was a cover profile of James Joyce on the occasion of the publication of *Finnegans Wake*. He wore his fervent anti-communism and his religiosity as badges of honor, and his influence on Henry Luce's turn rightward was considerable.

Discretion was not Chambers's style. He was a strange man, and that strangeness was on full display during his lunch with Malcolm Cowley. So peculiar and over-the-top were some of his pronouncements, and so outlandish his claims, that Cowley wrote down a detailed account of the unsettling encounter in his notebook on the train back to Connecticut. He had listened with alarmed fascination as Chambers unspooled the tale of his life in the Communist underground and his defection, his seemingly paranoid perception of traitors, spies, and assassins everywhere, and his conviction that the "Christian Democratic counter-revolution" was now at hand. Cowley felt that he was being put on notice. Chambers paid the four dollars for lunch, and Cowley wrote, "It will cost me a great deal more when the article comes out."

The first payment on that bill came due a month later when Chambers's essay "The Revolt of the Intellectuals" appeared in the January 6, 1941, issue of *Time*. Written in the slick and mocking tone that the magazine had perfected, it provides an account of the intellectual journey of such fellow-traveling figures as Lillian Hellman, Waldo

Frank, Newton Arvin, Dorothy Parker, Donald Ogden Stewart, Malcolm Cowley, and even such solidly center-left writers as John Steinbeck and Archibald MacLeish, from their literary alienation in the twenties to their current political disillusionment. None of this was wrong exactly, but it was all delivered with an implied sneer. "Meanwhile the intellectuals, refugees once more in their lonely remodeled farmhouses in Connecticut and the Berkshires, thought it over. . . . Malcolm Cowley, writing a book 'to clarify my mind,' craved only to be left in peace to lick his spiritual wounds."

In his Connecticut retreat Cowley did his best to adjust to his new situation, diligently delivering his weekly copy to *The New Republic*. But his demotion and reduction in salary began a period of real financial difficulty for his family. A lot of the food that ended up on the Cowley dining table had to be either grown in one of their three gardens or caught in a nearby stream or river or shot. As Robert Cowley recalls, "You might say that the taste of woodchuck was, for my family, the essence of 1942."

Readers of *The New Republic* would not have noticed any real difference in the weekly pieces Cowley wrote for the magazine. He reviewed Auden's first book of poetry written in America, *The Double Man*; massive novels by the French masters Jules Romains and Roger Martin du Gard; the final posthumous volume quarried from Thomas Wolfe's packing crate of manuscripts, *The Hills Beyond*; Virginia Woolf's final book, *Between the Acts*, published shortly after her suicide; and, highly favorably, Ernest Hemingway's blockbuster comeback novel, *For Whom the Bell Tolls*.

The darkening situation in Europe and the prospects for a truly global war drew his attention by way of reviews of books on the broader military and geopolitical situation, including *Blood, Sweat and Tears*, a collection of Winston Churchill's recent speeches, and correspondent William Shirer's *Berlin Diary*. His interventionist convictions were clearly on display. His review of Arthur Koestler's *Darkness at Noon*, destined to become a classic on the nature of Stalinist tyranny, brought Cowley face-to-face with the kind of ugly facts that had eluded his attention in Spain. Once again he stubbornly floats the possibility that there had been a nearly successful plot against Stalin, but he credits Koestler with having created in his hero Rubashov a convincing portrait of the sort of Soviet true believer who felt powerless to refute false charges under the weight of psychological and physical torture.

His fullest statement on the nature of communism and its appeal appeared not in *The New Republic* but in an obscure collection of essays titled *Whose Revolution?: A Study of the Future Course of Liberalism in the United States*, whose other contributors included Granville Hicks; Roger Baldwin, a founder of the ACLU; John Chamberlain; James Burnham, ex-Communist and author of *The Managerial Revolution*; and Cowley's Red-hunting tormentor Eugene Lyons. At nine thousand words, one of the longest pieces he ever wrote, "Faith and the Future" outlines all the ways that communism, despite its doctrinal hostility to religion, acts on its true believers and adherents like a secular religion. Far from moving on from politics, Cowley was stewing incessantly about the dynamics of belief that had led him and so many other literary intellectuals astray. He was genuinely bitter about *The New Republic*, sourly writing to Burke, "The NR under Bliven's editorship seems to me to be a pretty sad mess . . . a lowbrow sheet for highbrows."

On top of all this, the bad war news being delivered to him over the radio, as he confessed in a September 28 letter to Archibald MacLeish, gave him "a terrible feeling of not doing enough, of being out of things . . . in these times writing doesn't seem to be enough. I itch to do more work." Soon enough, MacLeish would be in the perfect position to do something about that.

In the first half of the twentieth century Archibald MacLeish occupied an impressive position in American letters. He was a literary statesman, a figure comparable in some respects to France's André Malraux; he has been described as Roosevelt's minister of culture. His glittering résumé featured a stellar four years at Yale, including editorship of *The Yale Review*; combat service in the American army in World War I as the commander of an artillery battery; graduation with highest honors from Harvard Law School and a period lawyering at a prestigious white-shoe law firm in Boston; years in France as a Lost Generation personage in the twenties when the call of poetry proved stronger than the law; a career of decades as one of the most highly regarded American poets and dramatists, which garnered him three Pulitzer Prizes and many other awards; a high-profile position as a writer and editor for seven years for *Fortune* magazine; a five-year term (1939–44) as the librarian of Congress, one of the most effective and influential persons ever to hold that post; and considerable experience writing speeches, including the 1941 inaugural address for FDR, who had nominated him for his job at the library. He moved with equal ease and dexterity in the corridors of power and literary society, and was the only person who could claim to have been an intimate friend of Ernest Hemingway's *and* Franklin Roosevelt's.

MacLeish was a loud and influential literary voice calling for American entry into the war in Europe, a position in total accord with FDR's inclinations. Roosevelt well knew that MacLeish's contacts in the worlds of journalism and literature could prove useful in generating favorable attention for his policies. So it was a natural step for the president to appoint MacLeish on October 24, 1941, the head of a new government agency to be called the Office of Facts and Figures, whose mission was to "formulate programs designed to facilitate a widespread and accurate understanding of the national defense policies of the Government." In plain English the OFF was intended to serve as a propaganda agency for the administration's war programs.

With a modest initial budget of one hundred thousand dollars, the OFF would in time, and especially after the attack on Pearl Harbor and the declaration of war, swell to employ some 350 people, including such writers as McGeorge Bundy, Arthur Schlesinger Jr., Malcolm Cowley, and many other journalists, academics, and editors of note. It would later be renamed the Office of War Information.

The offer of a job at the OFF as something called a chief information analyst came to Cowley in November, and within a week he had settled his affairs and moved to DC. Shortly thereafter in early January, Muriel and Robert packed up the car and drove down to join him. His salary was a "lordly" (and much welcome) eight thousand dollars. He compared the bureaucratic tenor of the OFF to "General Motors being run by the faculty of the University of Chicago, or better of Columbia" and noted that in a government agency with salary caps, the struggle for power replaces the struggle for money. As for his actual job, it basically consisted of various writing assignments. One of them was to write an essay on "Freedom from Want" for a pamphlet explaining at greater length the ideas behind FDR's famous "Four Freedoms" speech; the other writers were E. B. White on freedom of speech, Reinhold Niebuhr on freedom of religion, and Max Lerner on freedom from fear. He would also draft some speeches, not delivered, for the president himself.

In retrospect, one has to ask how someone as politically astute as Archibald MacLeish thought that he could hire someone as politically radioactive as Malcolm Cowley and not run into trouble. As soon as his job was announced, Cowley was being investigated by the FBI, which was fully aware of his numerous associations with radical groups and Communist front organizations. He believed, with good reason, that at least one of his Trotskyist enemies, specifically Sidney Hook, had cooperated with the FBI in fingering him as a dangerous Stalinist. Within a month, Cowley found himself the target of invective and innuendo.

On January 13, two Republican congressmen decried the appointment of such "fellow travelers" as Malcolm Cowley and Joseph Lash, an intimate of Eleanor Roosevelt's, to government posts. The next day the *Chicago Tribune* reported on this with the headline "Congress Hears Communist Gets $8,000 U.S. Job." (Cowley's salary almost never went unmentioned subsequently; "It Pays to Be a Communist" was the way one newspaper put the matter a week later.) That same day, the *Brooklyn Eagle* ran an item headed "Rosy Dawn in Washington," which sneered at "Joe Lash, the pinko who's made a career of youthfulness right up to middle age" and "Malcolm Cowley, another comrade," and asked, "And how do you like them apples, Mr. and Mrs. Taxpayer?"

On January 15, Congressman Martin Dies, the notorious and long-winded chairman of the House Un-American Activities Committee, took to the floor of the House for a full hour to decry the hiring of government workers with a background of connections with and sympathies toward Communist causes as part of a supposed "fifth column on American soil" seeking to subvert American democracy. After warming up, Dies rounded on the day's main target:

> I regret to say that the flow of Communists and Communist sympathizers into Government positions has not entirely ceased. Only last week the Office of Facts and Figures took on its staff as chief information analyst one Malcolm Cowley, at a salary of $8,000 a year. For at least 10 years Cowley was one of the most ardent Communist intellectuals in the country. The files of our committee show 72 connections of this high-salaried Government employee with the Communist Party and its front organizations.

Dies goes on to cite twenty of those connections, which were essentially accurate. (The one falsehood was that Cowley never was, as

Dies claimed, on the staff of *The Daily Worker*.) He ends his attack with a burst of heavy rhetorical sarcasm: "Surely there are thousands of capable newspapermen in this country with records unstained by long service to communism who are far more competent to fill the position of chief news analyst in the Office of Facts and Figures than this energetic campaigner for Communist Party candidates."

The conservative press energetically took up the cry. Westbrook Pegler was an ardent opponent of the New Deal, a rabid anti-Communist, and a self-styled tribune of the little guy whose syndicated newspaper column "Fair Enough" reached millions of readers. On January 31, his column repeated and amplified Dies's attack on Lash and Cowley. Mocking claims that neither of these men were Party members with the overbearing sarcasm that was his stylistic signature, he suggested, "if you want to be a dirty Quisling and a disrupter, go ahead and read false meanings into past expressions of such patriotic men, so devoted to the capitalistic system." Another Pegler column, "Taxpayers Have a Right to Know," took up once again the matter of Cowley's salary and proclaimed that "the angry little guy in the barrel" has a perfect right to demand that "the government show him that his money is being spent for legitimate purposes." Not only was the Roosevelt administration making room for filthy subversives in its bureaucratic warrens, they were paying these Reds a king's ransom.

A more personal angle of attack was taken two weeks later in *Time* by Whittaker Chambers in an unsigned "review" of Cowley's chapbook collection from New Directions, *The Dry Season*. Cowley's exile from *The New Republic*'s office had given him more time to devote to his poetry. He had written seven poems since then, five published in *Poetry* and two in *The New Yorker*. None of them had anything resembling political content. The other poems in the book all dated from 1937 or later, and two of them, "Tomorrow Morning" and "The Last

International," were explicitly left-political. They made the book a target-rich subject for Chambers's attack.

Chambers's review ran not in the Books section in the back, but right up front on the first page of the U.S. at War section. It begins, "Most inopportune book of the month is *The Dry Season*, a slim, sage-green volume of 17 poems by Malcolm Cowley, sometime literary editor of the *New Republic*, now chief information analyst of the Office of Facts and Figures. Congressman Martin Dies recently charged Cowley with having had 'seventy-two connections . . . with the Communist Party and its front organizations.' Two of the poems in *The Dry Season* seem designed to make Dies lift his calculations to 74." He goes on to quote some of the unfortunate agitprop-heavy lines from "Tomorrow Morning" and "The Last International" to pigeonhole Cowley as a flaming Red. The review ends by granting that the other poems "reveal sound, minor poetic talent."

On the one hand, this was an ugly sucker punch. On the other, Chambers was not misquoting Cowley's poems nor, in fact, mischaracterizing them. They *were* revolutionary in their sympathy and general intent. It did no good for Cowley to protest, as he did in a letter to *Time* a month later, that his book had been published late the previous year, or that "The Last International" was a fantasia of revolutions that had taken place across the world after the war, or that his lines had been quoted out of context and had no application to the American political milieu, or that "the country all of us love" was not "in grave danger of being overthrown by a determined rabble of poets and literary editors." The damage was done.

MacLeish wrote to his old boss Henry Luce to protest this ambush. He suggested that if Luce was in search of "serpents," he could find plenty of them at Time Inc. Like, for instance, Whittaker Chambers. *The New Yorker* came to Cowley's defense in its Notes and Comments section, mocking in its tongue-in-cheek fashion the size and specificity of Dies's accusation of "seventy-two connections" to Communist entities. "It was the 'seventy-two' that staggered us. We could understand that a man we might run into any time at a cocktail party might belong to one or two subversive organizations, or even a handful, but hardly seventy-two. Any man who can edit a book department, write poetry and reviews, and keep up with the meetings and various un-American duties of seventy-two subversive organizations is a man whose hand we are glad to have shaken."

Cowley himself was kept busy writing multiple letters in his own defense, protesting his loyalty and proclaiming his fealty to America. "I was born in this country. I love this country, and I will do anything that one man can do to defend it. . . . I want to serve this country by any means within my power." The longest of these letters, and the hardest to read, were two he wrote to one George Gould, a government investigator who had interrogated him. At the end of one letter, a long explanation of and apologia for his career as an editor and literary journalist, Cowley is reduced to pleading for his economic future. "If it were now decided that my record made me unfit to be a government employee . . . it would make it very difficult to for me to sell articles, get lecture dates or find an editorial job. It would mean that I and my family were paying a heavy price indeed for wishing to serve the government during its worst emergency."

In truth, Cowley could do very little to defend himself. The attack on him was but one of many against prominent liberals, part of a wider reaction against the New Deal. The fevered habits of mind that historian Richard Hofstadter would later dub "the paranoid style in American politics," and which would find their fullest and direst expression in McCarthyism, had already infected the body politic. Cowley was saddled with that impossible task: trying to prove a negative, that he would never have acted in any way to harm the security of the country.

It did not help matters that a good many of the facts marshaled against him by Martin Dies and others were true. He had worked actively on behalf of a Communist candidate for president in 1932. No one who has examined Cowley's activities in the thirties can doubt that he had contacts and dealings with seventy-two Communist or Communist-adjacent organizations. He had lent his name to a great many causes.

MacLeish had actually received Cowley's FBI file and, against protocol, showed it to him so he'd know exactly what he was up against. It was considerable, a thirty-page single-spaced document covering his political activities from 1935 to the present. Cowley was upset by the many flatly inaccurate items in his dossier—"secret" Communist Party conferences he'd never attended in cities he'd never visited—and that he'd been informed on by some literary figures whose style he recognized. It was a chilling glimpse of the surveillance state that J. Edgar Hoover had created. Deeply dismayed, he went so far as to plead directly with the FBI, the Justice Department, and even with Attorney General Francis Biddle to at least get the facts straight in his file, but all his efforts were unavailing.

The painful conclusion of this episode was essentially preordained. On March 12, Cowley wrote to MacLeish to submit his resignation from the Office of Facts and Figures. The letter contains a certain amount of self-justification in respect to the campaign of persecution he was subjected to. It also makes the point that he was but one of the hundreds of loyal government employees who had had their private lives opened to harsh scrutiny and their past activities distorted into grounds for distrust.

Cowley's resignation became national news. An AP dispatch on March 19 ran in *The New York Times* and dozens of other papers nationwide. The piece quoted passages from his resignation letter, and MacLeish's response that "I have not always, as you know, agreed with your opinions, but I have never doubted that you were a sincere and loyal believer in government of the people, by the people, and for the people." In an editorial titled "Justice for Federal Workers," *The New Republic* decried the harassment of government employees for, in many cases, having simply supported the New Deal programs, and quoted two more paragraphs from Cowley's letter on the matter. Martin Dies took the occasion to crow, "After my exposure Mr. Cowley resigned his post" at the OFF and also suggested that the American people would welcome the similar resignations of his newly targeted victims. Cowley would be a recurring target of his committee's smears for some time to come.

Seven years later, this episode and particularly his collision with Whittaker Chambers would have a dramatic coda. Chambers had made attempts to alert the Roosevelt administration to the existence of a Soviet spy ring that had penetrated the State Department and other government agencies, but he had been unsuccessful in moving it to action. Part of the problem was that, seeking to avoid his own criminal prosecution, he had been less than candid about the nature of the network he'd worked in, characterizing it as a "study group" rather than an espionage organization.

This changed spectacularly on August 3, 1948, when Chambers testified before the House Un-American Activities Committee to the names of several secret Communist Party members in the New Deal he had been in contact with. The most eye-catching of those names was that of Alger Hiss, Harvard Law graduate, clerk to Oliver Wendell Holmes Jr., figure of note in the Agriculture and State Departments, an architect of the United Nations Charter, president of the Carnegie Endowment for International Peace, and an associate of Secretary of State Edward Stettinius Jr. at the Yalta Conference, where he helped to draw up plans for a postwar liberated Europe. Chambers claimed that Hiss had been his closest friend in his underground group.

Two days later, Alger Hiss testified before the same committee that he had never been a member of the Communist Party, nor had he had any contact whatsoever with Whittaker Chambers. The whole matter might have petered out from there but for the strenuous efforts of a freshman congressman from California, Richard Nixon, who smelled something arrogant and phony in Hiss, and a chance for his own political advancement. Nixon pursued the investigation relentlessly and Chambers eventually produced evidence not just of party membership but of actual espionage on Hiss's part, including the infamous rolls of microfilm hidden in a pumpkin on his Maryland farm. The end result of all this controversy, which riveted the nation for months, was that Alger Hiss sued Whittaker Chambers for libel, and the next year, Hiss was indicted for perjury for testimony he had given to a grand jury as to whether he had ever known Whittaker Chambers or been involved in espionage activities.

Alger Hiss's trial for perjury was not simply a personal matter between him and Whittaker Chambers. In effect, American liberalism and the New Deal itself were on trial for their possible carelessness with American security, and the word "treason" was being thrown about. The entire liberal establishment mobilized to defend and support Alger Hiss in any way it could.

A. J. Liebling, the *New Yorker* journalist, had learned of Cowley's odd lunch with Chambers back in 1941, and he and Hiss's counsel, Lloyd Paul Stryker, persuaded him, somewhat reluctantly, to testify for the defense. He later calculated that his testimony would end up costing him forty thousand dollars in lost income from jobs he might otherwise have had. If Chambers could be shown in other instances to have been a liar prone to wild and unsupported accusations, his testimony against Hiss would be undercut. The opportunity to get back at Chambers for having sandbagged him twice in the pages of *Time* would have been on his mind as well. His bitterness on the subject can be gauged by his assertion that "I wouldn't convict a yellow dog of having the mange on Chambers' word." So on the morning of June 23, 1949, Malcolm Cowley appeared in a packed federal courtroom in Foley Square in New York City to testify for the defense in the perjury trial of Alger Hiss. One paper characterized his surprise appearance as a "bombshell" that "provided the greatest sensation of the trial to date."

Refreshing his memory of that long-ago lunch with Chambers from his notebook, Cowley described "in a booming, ponderous voice" Chambers's disheveled appearance (he "looked as if he had slept on a park bench the night before") and his paranoid affect ("we were surrounded by spies, traitors and conspiracies"). Chambers had feverishly related his own history in the Communist underground and then he began to reveal the names of Communist agents in the government, Cowley said, all minor figures. In his recollection, Hiss's was not one of them. Then Chambers "mentioned another name which I shall not mention here." Under Stryker's stern instructions, though, he did mention it: Francis B. Sayre, Woodrow Wilson's son-in-law, former assistant secretary of state and high commissioner of the Philippines. According to Chambers, Cowley testified, he was "the head of a Communist apparatus in the State Department." This mention of so trusted an establishment figure in this context was so shocking that Stryker quickly rose to declare that "Mr. Sayre was a loyal member of the government at all times." If Chambers could finger so unlikely a figure as a Communist so cavalierly, how could he be trusted on anything?

Malcolm Cowley's testimony that morning was so electrifying, one reporter wrote, that Alger Hiss's court appearance later that day was a bit anticlimactic. Stryker told reporters that Cowley's testimony was "a shattering blow to the prosecution's case" and it proved that Chambers was "a psychiatric rattlesnake, willing to strike in any and all directions." Cowley's courtroom appearance made national headlines and was reported on by Eric Sevareid on the CBS radio network. His son heard that broadcast in Sherman and was impressed by his father's new celebrity. The next day, though, while bicycling home from a friend's house, he became the target of rocks thrown from a culvert by two boys he'd known at the Sherman School. "Commie, Commie, Commie bastard!" they shouted at him.

Effective as Cowley's testimony was, it was not dispositive. Hiss's first trial ended in a hung jury. Cowley reprised his appearance at the retrial later that year, and that time, Alger Hiss was convicted of two counts of perjury and ended up serving forty-four months in Lewisburg federal prison. Thus Malcolm Cowley became a small player in a consequential episode of the Cold War. It turned out to be impossible for him to leave his political past behind him. For decades the innocence of Alger Hiss and the perfidy of Whittaker Chambers would be articles of faith among liberals. Over the years, however, Hiss's claim of his innocence of the charges against him has eroded as more evidence has emerged from various archives here and abroad, and the consensus today is that it was sweaty and evasive Whittaker Chambers and not smooth, unflappable Alger Hiss who was telling the truth.

———

The Cowley family returned to Sherman, Connecticut, in an understandably low mood. Without Cowley's "lordly" government salary, their financial privation returned. It was April, planting season, so he got to work with his hoe and shovel in their three vegetable gardens. His son remembers that this was a time when he first noticed his father's deafness, which would only become more acute as the years passed. Cowley felt his painful isolation from the wider literary world, as he complained to Newton Arvin, in the "Hermit Kingdom" of Sherman. As some of his sorrowful letters from this time show, the political missteps that had brought him to this pass continued to gnaw at him. He dutifully resumed the chores as a weekly reviewer and essayist for *The New Republic*.

The next two years were a period of retreat, retrenchment, and a fundamental rethinking of a new, apolitical way for him to be an actor in the literary arena. As he wrote to MacLeish a year later, "I retired into a state of estivation last summer, something like a bear's hibernation—but then in the fall I got back to work. . . . Literature has to keep retiring into the catacombs to rediscover itself." It was not all that engaging a time for him to be a book reviewer, though. American literature was on something of a hiatus as it adjusted to the profound national emergency and a world in transformation. He discovered a number of worthy and interesting books to offer his measured praise to, but the truth was that, with the exceptions of William Faulkner's *The Hamlet* in 1940 and *Go Down, Moses* in 1942, both of which Cowley reviewed, the first years of the forties seemed to him devoid of any truly important American fiction.

Cowley for the most part avoided in his choice of books and topics any real, direct discussion of political material. As many of the nonfiction books he reviewed concerned the ongoing war and the world it was creating, he could not avoid the subject of politics entirely, but he was generally circumspect on these matters. In only one case did Cowley step outside his zone of self-protection to address a political issue directly, in "The Sorrows of Elmer Davis," a full-throated defense of that distinguished journalist and broadcaster, who at the time was the director of the Office of War Information. Davis found himself under fire from conservatives and had to navigate the backwash of a mass resignation on principle by fifteen of his employees. Cowley could relate.

One week Cowley decided to look around his own postage stamp of rural New England soil and see how the war had affected the home-front community, and it resulted in a sharply observed piece, "Town Report: 1942." In some ways the town of Sherman, which he calls Sheridan, felt remote from the war. He found not all that much war talk, and the radio at the grocery store was more likely to be tuned to a baseball game than news reports from the front. Rationing of food and tires and, especially, gasoline meant that trips were difficult, so the community had drawn in on itself. People would grumble, but the local rationing board was fair and they understood the necessity for the sacrifices. The new requirements and bureaucracies of civil defense had the effect of drawing together the community "by the new tasks it is called upon to perform." The piece ends with an excellent specimen of Americana in wartime, the description of a scrap collection drive in which Cowley participated with the men of the town. They collected twenty-five tons of cast-off relics, a vast archeological dig into Sherman's past, old Fords and trucks and tires and milk cans and farming implements. His conclusion: "It is in most ways a better and friendlier town in wartime than it was in peace."

In respect to the war, Cowley had the sad duty of writing a remembrance of his friend Otis Ferguson, who'd died on a cargo vessel that had been sunk in the North Atlantic. After Pearl Harbor, Ferguson had joined the merchant marine. Cowley had discovered the profane and immensely likable Ferguson, and he'd proved to be an excellent editor, incapable of stomaching cant, and a pioneering reviewer of the popular arts. His death brought the war home.

At the end of this two-year period, Cowley paused to take in a broader view of the prospects for American literature, from the points of view of its present state and future creation and the growth and nature of its audience. In "Books by the Millions," he surveyed the various experiments in the expansion of book production and distribution, especially the invention of the mass-market paperback by Pocket Books in 1939 and the efforts to provide a wide variety of reading material to Americans in uniform. As to the nature and quality of those books, he was far less certain. In "American Literature in Wartime" he complained of the absence of books that engaged at a high level with the worldwide crisis that the war represented. He asked, "Where are the novels about America in emotional confusion and terror? . . . Where are the political treatises by authors who recognize that we are entering a new age? Where shall we turn for a discussion of our real problems at home? And, to ask an older question, where are the war poets?" American writing at this time was in a state of suspension, and so was he.

In early 1944, however, he did complete one of his most influential and lasting pieces of literary journalism, a profile of the great Scribner's editor Maxwell Perkins for *The New Yorker*. While he is justly famous today as perhaps the finest book editor of the past century, as a result of A. Scott Berg's widely read biography, Perkins at the time was "a gray-hatted eminence" little known outside of literary circles. This was so, even though Thomas Wolfe had breached his anonymity by portraying him as George Webber's loyal editor in his autobiographical posthumous novel *You Can't Go Home Again*. A shy, puritanical man of Yankee New England heritage and moral habits, that was the way he wanted it. Perkins had drawn unwanted attention to himself by, as Cowley wrote, "introduc[ing] the bad boys of letters into one of the citadels of Victorian publishing"—the staid Scribner's, home previously to the likes of Henry James and Edith Wharton. Under Perkins's guidance, "the firm took a sudden leap from the age of innocence to the lost generation." The baddest of those boys were F. Scott Fitzgerald, Ernest Hemingway, and Thomas Wolfe, champion attention-getters, and their fame had spilled over in Perkins's direction.

The New Yorker had in fact tried to commission Thomas Wolfe to write a profile of Perkins in the thirties, but Perkins had scotched the idea. So they were receptive when Cowley suggested that he write one. As a master middleman of literature himself, he not only admired his subject, he understood intimately why, as he told his editor William Shawn, Perkins was "the nearest thing to a great man now existing in the literary world. Legends are clustered round him like truffles round an oak tree in Gascony." He did months of preliminary interviews in preparation for bearding Perkins himself. After the expected obstacles of self-effacement and excessive modesty, Perkins agreed to be interviewed. Cowley's stature as an eminence himself and an important critic helped him win Perkins's trust and cooperation. Over the course of a number of meetings, Perkins shed his distrust and loosened up.

So Cowley set to work writing up all he had learned, and he produced a profile so long but also so winning and informative, not simply about Perkins himself and his roster of famous writers but about the mysterious ways of publishers as well, that *The New Yorker* decided to run it in two installments in their April 1 and April 8, 1944, issues. "Unshaken Friend"—the title is taken from Wolfe's dedication of a novel to him—is the source of much of the history and many of the anecdotes about Perkins that have by now entered into literary lore. The wearing of a felt hat "which looks something like an upturned soup kettle" down around his ears in the office. The three racy words in Hemingway's manuscript of *A Farewell to Arms* that Perkins felt he had to run by Charles Scribner II, one of which so embarrassed him that he at first could not even write it down. The epic yearlong editing with his volcanic author Wolfe of the three-thousand-plus-page manuscript of *Of Time and the River*, about which Perkins declared simply, "This book has to be done." Cowley unearthed delightful small details, such as the time in the Scribner's office when a muscular woman tried to persuade Perkins to publish her book on Swedish massage. "If you don't believe me, Mr. Perkins," she shouted at him, "just feel the muscles of my abdomen!" The piece reads speedily and has a wit and a lightness that stand out from most of Cowley's output, the result, no doubt, of his effort to meet *The New Yorker*'s audience more than half-way and also of the magazine's famously stringent and, some have felt, intrusive editing process. Cowley told Shawn he was grateful for the close attention, even though the magazine's constant demand for facts, facts, and more facts from the checking department required months of further research. As he wrote some forty years later, "They were a damned botheration, but they had given me a new respect for small hard facts simply stated, a feeling that I was never to lose."

"Unshaken Friend" gave a large audience an inside look on the literary racket. One segment of that audience paid especially close attention: emotionally needy writers. As Berg writes, "The flow of manuscripts into Scribner's became nearly overwhelming." As Cowley put it, "They dreamed of being adopted by Perkins as his spiritual children and of having him transform their inspired ramblings into deathless masterpieces." Perkins himself groused for a while about Cowley's comment that he dressed "in shabby and inconspicuous grays," but he was in fact pleased by his prose portrait and told some friends that "I wouldn't mind being like that fellow."

Cowley's check from *The New Yorker* for the piece would have been one of the most generous of the year, but he had put considerable time into it and it was only a temporary stay from his financial anxiety. In fact, in October 1943 the Cowley family had moved from Sherman to share a crowded apartment with the Coates family in Manhattan so that he could more easily make the kinds of contacts that would help him find more and better-paying work. But in spring of 1944 an unexpected lifeline appeared, almost miraculously, that would solve Malcolm Cowley's money problems. It would have notable consequences, not only for him and his family, but for American literature.

His good angel was Mary Conover Mellon, who with her husband,

Paul Mellon, the son of former Treasury Secretary Andrew Mellon, had founded the Bollingen Foundation to support and publish the work of Carl Jung and eventually many other writers and scholars. The Bollingen Series would become one of the most intellectually fertile and adventurous publishing enterprises of the postwar years. It was Mary Mellon who conceived of a Five-Year Plan to offer some writers of merit a yearly income sufficient to free them from having to perform any work outside of their creative endeavors. By contract they were required to devote their full time to such work and to assign to the foundation 20 percent of the proceeds from any literary work completed during the five years of the grant. The first four writers—and as it turned out, the only ones—selected for the plan were the novelists Denis de Rougemont and John Hyde Preston, the playwright Stanley Young, who also worked for Bollingen as an editor, and Malcolm Cowley.

It was Stanley Young who informed Cowley that he was going to receive a yearly income of $5,500, or almost $98,000 in current dollars, for the next five years. This windfall arrived without warning, and at first he kept his excitement in check, scarcely able to credit such good fortune. But then, as he wrote back to Young, "I began thinking about projects and possibilities until I couldn't sleep"—particularly books he'd wanted to write but that his chores for *The New Republic* had forced him to postpone. As requested, he listed for Young what those projects were. Harvard University Press wanted to collect his essays on French literature, and W. W. Norton wanted to do the same for his essays on contemporary American writers; these two books never came to pass. He hoped to translate the poems of his friend and mentor Louis Aragon, which he would in fact do. Most important, though, he wanted to write a one-volume history of American literature from its beginnings to the present day, a considerable job of work that he estimated would take him at least three years.

In fact he was already in discussion with a publisher for such a book as of the month before. As he wrote to his editor at Doubleday, Doran & Company, he'd been encouraged in this direction by his scrutiny of the existing competition, books that were either out of date or dusty and academic, or both. The emphasis of his book was intended to be *literary*, which is to say focused on "the importance of the imagination as a literary quality" and the singularity of the creators, and not necessarily historical or representative of broader trends. Readability was also a key aim: "Conceiving the book largely as a *story*, I hope to make use of some fairly dramatic conflicts and contrasts—Franklin in France, Poe against the New England school, Whitman and Emerson, Maxim Gorky's visit, etc."

It is a sadness to relate that Cowley never completed this history, eventually returning his advance. It held the clear potential to be one of the essential books about our literature. But it was not for naught. For the next several years, the history would guide much of his reading and his efforts in other, related directions. The important effect that the Mary Mellon miracle had on Malcolm Cowley was that it gave him all the time he craved to read, and to think. As he wrote to Stanley Young: "I would like to write about the books of today from the standpoint of the classics, and to write about the American classics as if they were books that had just appeared. Nobody else is doing that; hardly anybody can; and yet it is exactly what our literature needs and deserves."

Turning himself into that new sort of critic was a slow and internal journey. Jazz musicians sometimes resort to a ritual they call "woodshedding." It means practicing one's instrument intensely, but with a purpose that is philosophical and even spiritual and not simply technical. A woodshedding musician removes himself from the constant flurry of gigs to retreat and recharge his or her relation to the instrument and to the whole enterprise of creating music. As the virtuoso saxophone player Sonny Rollins, who famously used to woodshed on the Williamsburg Bridge, once said, "You have to be practicing when the spirit comes." Malcolm Cowley was able to woodshed—to read attentively, meditatively, voluminously, constantly, encyclopedically—in his chosen field of American literature for the next few years without the stress and distraction of having to make a living and support his family. Like Whitman, in his own way Cowley was able, book in hand, to loaf (or "loafe," as Whitman spelled it) and invite his soul.

The timing of this transformation was propitious. In becoming one of the finest readers and students of American literature, he met the cultural moment head-on. At just this time, the phrase "a usable past" came into vogue in American literary discourse. It had been coined in 1918 in *The Dial* by Van Wyck Brooks, who decried the sterile nature of the academic study of American literary history at the time. "I suspect that the past experience of our people is not so much without elements that might be made to contribute to some common understanding in the present." The past, if carefully studied and properly understood, might be put to some use in solving the dilemmas that faced writers now. Or as Cowley would write in reviewing Brooks's *The Times of Melville and Whitman*, we might in this fashion discover "a living tradition—a body of experience transmitted from generation to generation of writers; an accumulation of standards that would serve them as unwritten laws; a medium in which they would be supported like swimmers in a sea."

In uncertain times we naturally tend to look to the past for solace and for lessons as to how we handled uncertainties and worse back then. The critic Mark Greif has called the period from roughly the early thirties to the early seventies "the Age of the Crisis of Man." His fascinating study of this period examines the way intellectuals and imaginative writers thought about this time, which swept long-held moral, philosophical, political, and literary values off the board. The rhetoric of crisis had become their lingua franca. In early 1943, Cowley wrote, "I doubt that there was ever a time when so much hope and faith and black despair, so much heroism and cowardice and treachery, were crowded into so short a span of years—from the October Revolution to the Moscow trials, from Munich to Stalingrad, from Pearl Harbor to Stalingrad." A year later he would write of the recent past, "Surely there was never a more anguished time in the history of modern man."

Alongside all this fear and perplexity as to what kind of future awaited us were questions as to what kind of country the United States was going to be in the coming decades. As an Allied victory came into view, the one thing that was clear was that we were going to be the most powerful nation on earth, the only one whose economy remained not simply untouched but transformed and energized by the conflict. All this power and prestige raised large issues about what sort of culture America actually had. If, as had become unmistakably clear, the world really was now living in "the American Century," the nature and contours of American identity would become a matter of urgent inquiry, not simply for us but for our allies and, as it would turn out, our adversaries. Our literature past and present would now be subject to a different kind of scrutiny. To put it bluntly: Could our claims to greatness as a nation be sustained without a parallel greatness in our literature? And if our literature was in fact "great," what were the specific nature and future prospects of that greatness?

This was the subtext of what Cowley and other critics and scholars were writing and thinking about in the postwar years. Some important excavations had already been performed in the quest for a usable past. In 1941 the critic and literary historian F. O. Matthiessen had published his important study *American Renaissance*, which gave a lasting name to the literary achievements of the middle decade of the nineteenth century and established the work of Emerson, Thoreau,

Whitman, Hawthorne, and Melville as permanently canonical. Mark Greif calls it "very likely the most influential book of literary criticism of America, ever." Cowley was impressed enough to write the author that "there is absolutely no American critic who is doing fresher and more valuable work." In 1942, Alfred Kazin published his lyrical masterpiece *On Native Grounds*, which examined American prose fiction from the struggles of the Naturalists to break past the barriers of gentility in the 1890s to the present. And Brooks's multivolume *Makers and Finders* series of histories, which began with *The Flowering of New England* (1936) and *New England: Indian Summer* (1940), cast a nostalgic glow on a literary past he had previously disparaged.

This period was the crucible of a new academic discipline that emerged at this time, called American Studies, which broke through the barriers that had separated American history, literature, folklore studies, political philosophy, popular culture, and other formerly discrete areas of inquiry. "The search for a usable past" could have served as its compact, six-word mission statement. American civilization—which, it now dawned on many scholars and unaffiliated intellectuals, we actually had—was too large a phenomenon to be understood from a single point of view.

In the years after the Mellon grant, Cowley was able to cut down his writing for *The New Republic* considerably and eventually sever his contractual connection to the magazine. Relieved of the burden of a weekly deadline, he was able to devote the necessary time for deep dives into individual writers and subject areas. The result would be the production of far longer and more carefully researched and considered essays than his previous regime of reviewing had allowed.

Some of the results were as impressive as anything Cowley ever produced. The long essay that he wrote as an introduction to the 1947 volume *The Complete Poetry and Prose of Walt Whitman*—so long that he serialized it in four installments in *The New Republic*—was an exceptionally fresh and original assessment of a poet too often reduced to a full-throated booster of the American scene. Cowley conceded that "*Leaves of Grass* is an extraordinary mixture of greatness, false greatness, and mediocrity." He affirms that greatness by penetrating to the heart of the "miracle" that transformed Whitman at age thirty-six from a hack newspaperman and journeyman carpenter to an American prophet who managed to conflate the nature and fate of the country with his own mystical revelations. The essay provides a brilliant biographical-critical assessment of Whitman and his work, one that takes in his genius, his unprecedented originality, his prophesying, his self-promotion, his personae and masks, his fabrications, his humbug, and even his charlatanism, giving us the poet and the man in full. Of note is the forthright manner in which he handles Whitman's homosexuality, speculating convincingly that his episodes of mystical revelations were strongly connected to instances of sexual breakthrough. The essay also inaugurated Cowley's lifelong campaign in support of the view that the best way to encounter Whitman's special genius was to read *Leaves of Grass* in its original, self-published 1855 edition, before it gathered its heavy accretion of lesser poems in the several expanded versions Whitman would publish over the decades.

Cowley at this time had to go to the mat yet again with his and his generation's adversary Bernard DeVoto—"a Studs Lonigan of letters," *Time* would dub him—over his book *The Literary Fallacy*. Picking up where he had left off, DeVoto accused the writers of the twenties of grievously misrepresenting an America that was in truth democratic, cheerful, and dynamic. Their "fallacy" was assuming that "a culture may be understood and judged solely by means of its literature . . . that literature is the measure of life." This of course got under Cowley's skin badly, and he mounted a counterattack in *The New Republic*, asking why, if the work of his cohort was so objectionable and trivial, had it only grown in stature and influence, especially among younger writers. Sinclair Lewis erupted even more volcanically with his response, "Fools, Liars, and Mr. DeVoto," in *The Saturday Review of Literature*.

In the wider world, the final defeat of Japan arrived in a fashion that mixed joy with dread. Japan had been brought to unconditional surrender only by the devastation first of the city of Hiroshima on August 6 and three days later of Nagasaki by atomic weapons whose existence only a small number of people on earth had been aware of. On his forty-seventh birthday, August 24, 1945, Cowley unburdened himself of his worries for the future in light of humanity's new potential for self-destruction in a mournful letter to Kenneth Burke.

It begins: "It's my birthday and a slow cold rain is falling and in general it's a good time to write a letter, except that I haven't anything much to say. The atom bomb. We can't keep it out of our minds. It gets worse as time goes on and we learn about its effects." As those effects slowly became public, "you get a new picture of the way radioactivity will wipe out our world, not in a good healthy smash . . . but rather in slow leukemia, the world simply made uninhabitable." He segues from this vision of an inevitable apocalypse to our coming life: "In the great imperial republic of the twentieth century, we'll be rich, we'll all have three automobiles, we'll have to have them, by law . . . we'll have to have a good time, by God, so we might as well grit our teeth and eat, drink and be expensively merry, for tomorrow we'll be blown sky high."

What disturbs Cowley even more than the soulless triumph of consumer capitalism is "the want of sympathy and the want of imagination that are coming to distinguish this country." The "cold-blooded, abstract, self-righteous cruelty, in the name of freedom and democracy," with which he feels we dealt with Germany and Japan might well be turned against us in the future as an envious world watched us preen "on the top of the heap." The writers of Cowley's generation had watched the Western democracies botch the prospects for peace through arrogance and vindictiveness; his fear of a repeat performance, but this time with the possibility of the end of human life all too likely, is natural.

Mary Conover Mellon died prematurely of a heart attack while riding in Virginia on October 11, 1946, at the age of forty-two. Not only was Malcolm Cowley bottomlessly grateful to her for the gift of the Five-Year Plan, he clearly was fond of her personally. The letters he would write to her occasionally not only kept her up to date on the literary activities he was engaged in, as required by the plan, but contained much detail about his day-to-day life as a country squire in rural Sherman. His relief from the exhausting tyranny of weekly deadlines is captured in this passage: "The sort of work I love now is work day after day, coming to my desk in the morning to find page 110 of a manuscript in the typewriter and finishing a paragraph started the afternoon before; then going on to write three or four pages more while feeling all the time that the work will go a little farther tomorrow and tomorrow." These letters were the opposite of cut-and-dried progress reports; he unbends and brings Mary Mellon into his "psychological study" to share the insights into American literature and particular writers that these happy new working conditions were affording him. It was a considerable shock when he received word of her death.

The Bollingen Foundation quickly moved to inform the four members of Mary Mellon's "stable" that the agreement between them and Mary would in no way be affected by her death. Some years later the foundation closed the books on the Five-Year Plan and forgave any more debt the writers might have owed by contract from their earnings. Malcolm Cowley was by far the most productive of the group. William McGuire, the historian of the Bollingen Foundation, estimates that "he published more than 120 articles and reviews, plus a number of lectures, several translations, and five books" during his five years of support and just after. He would write to the foundation in 1954, when his account was written off, "For the records of your office I would like to add that the contract with Mrs. Mellon was a turning point in my career, that I haven't had any grave trouble in supporting myself since the contract ended, that I hold Mrs. Mellon responsible for any little success I may have achieved, and that, if I were a Catholic, I should keep a candle burning to her memory—but the candle does burn, if only figuratively."

Two of the books that Mary Mellon's generosity made possible were anthologies that would alter the future of American criticism and literature.

ELEVEN.

THE PORTABLE MALCOLM COWLEY

———

The American publishing industry would become one of the chief beneficiaries of the newly booming postwar American economy. Publishing houses, like so many other businesses, had struggled from the diminished purchasing capacity of American readers, so the new markets for books that opened up during the war arrived as a welcome lifeline and even something like a bonanza. At its peak in 1945, more than twelve million American men and woman were serving in active duty in the armed forces. Early on in the conflict the government decided that those people were going to require books to read—to fill up their considerable leisure time between wartime tasks, for technical training purposes, and even for morale building and grasping the core democratic and American principles that they were putatively fighting for. As a government poster of the time put it, "BOOKS ARE WEAPONS IN THE WAR OF IDEAS."

The numbers being thrown about were heroic. In May 1943 the Council on Books in Wartime, a group of librarians, booksellers, and trade book publishers, announced plans to distribute 35 million copies of so-called Armed Forces Editions of fiction and nonfiction titles to Americans in uniform at no cost to them. These lightweight, double-columned paperbound books had full-color covers that anticipated the brashly commercial ones that would adorn mass-market paperbacks after the war, and they were designed to be flat enough to slip into almost any uniform pocket. At first blush the plans to publish 25 to 50 new titles a month in first printings of 50,000 each seemed wildly overambitious, but the Armed Forces Editions vastly exceeded all expectations. By 1947, almost 123 million copies of 1,322 titles had been shipped to Americans in uniform, an eclectic selection of commercial bestsellers, mysteries, westerns, classics like *Tom Sawyer*, and nonfiction titles. Two of the most popular titles were Betty Smith's wholesome and nostalgic *A Tree Grows in Brooklyn* and Kathleen Winsor's banned-in-Boston, racy-for-the-time *Forever Amber*.

America's armed forces took to these books with a passion and carried copies with them everywhere, from the landing craft of the D-Day invasion to the beaches of Saipan to the Aleutian Islands. For millions of men and women these books were their first real exposure to literature of any sort, and the Armed Forces Editions were justly credited as a central factor in the postwar explosion of literacy. Wallace Stegner, whose novel *The Big Rock Candy Mountain* was in an Armed Forces Edition, called it "the first great experiment in the mass production and mass distribution of books."

Producing these books was good business and even better optics for publishers, but they hardly represented a financial windfall. Publishers received a 10 percent premium for overhead above and beyond their costs of production, and publishers and authors each received a royalty of one-half cent per copy. Still, here after a decade-plus of lean years had appeared a vast potential new market for the printed word. So the Viking Press was instantly receptive when its author famed Algonquin wit and drama critic Alexander Woollcott proposed to assemble a collection of writings for Americans in uniform. Inspired by patriotism and by nostalgia for his own service as an unlikely sergeant in World War I as a correspondent for the enlisted men's paper *Stars and Stripes,* Woollcott conceived *As You Were: A Portable Library of American Prose and Poetry Assembled for Members of the Armed Forces and the Merchant Marine* as "an anthology designed (without profit or royalties for anyone) for the pocket of the American soldier. By the use of thin paper we can get in quite a lot." Indeed they did. Part literary sampler, part light reading, part American civics lesson, *As You Were* included stories by Ring Lardner, Ernest Hemingway, Dorothy Parker, and familiar chestnuts from Poe, Twain, O. Henry, and Bret Harte; poems by Emerson, Whitman, Dickinson, Frost, Sandburg, and Millay; and, in a section titled "American Fact," the Declaration of Independence, Lincoln's Second Inaugural, speeches by Oliver Wendell Holmes Jr., and Emma Lazarus's "The New Colossus," the poem inscribed on the Statue of Liberty.

As You Were was published in March 1943, shortly after Woollcott had died of a heart attack. The book sold more than one hundred thousand copies, successful enough that Viking quickly followed it up three months later with *The Portable Steinbeck*, edited by his Viking editor and close friend Pascal Covici. Viking realized that they had hit on a good formula for the collection and presentation of writing by great authors that was suited to readers, in and out of uniform, looking for an introduction to their work. Thus was born one of the most successful, well-loved, and long-lived publishing enterprises of the American postwar period, the Viking Portable Library.

The Viking editors swiftly commissioned five more Portables, including *The Portable Shakespeare* and *The Portable World Bible* and lighter fare such as *The Portable Dorothy Parker* and *Six Novels of the Supernatural*. Like the Armed Forces Editions, the early Viking Portables were well-traveled books, carried around the globe with our armed forces. Marshall Best would relate that, slipped into uniform pockets, "we heard of their stopping a good many German and Japanese bullets." At this point a Portable volume devoted to Ernest

Hemingway became inevitable. His career and literary reputation had been revived by the overwhelming success of *For Whom the Bell Tolls* in 1940 after his uneven work of the thirties. Hemingway was now not simply the most admired and visible novelist in America, he was probably the most famous writer on earth. The logical editor to assemble such a volume was Malcolm Cowley, Hemingway's most consistent and passionate critical champion, who'd reviewed every one of his books since 1928, with the exception of *Green Hills of Africa*. So Viking reached out to Cowley and he agreed to edit the anthology for a flat fee, with no royalties, of five hundred dollars.

Luckily the living grant from Mary Mellon and the Bollingen Foundation had arrived, so Cowley could afford to undertake the work such a project required. It fit loosely into his plans for writing a history of American literature, which he was approaching in an author-by-author fashion. There were risks attached to it as well, as the notoriously prickly Hemingway would certainly take careful note of both selections for the anthology and, especially, whatever biographical facts and critical remarks he would include. One of Cowley's most quoted sentences is "No complete son of a bitch ever wrote a good sentence." Hemingway puts that proposition to a strenuous test.

You could never know what would set off the volcanic and vindictive writer; even the best-intentioned piece might light the fuse, and Cowley well understood that "Hemingway had the bad habit of never forgiving anyone for giving him a hand up." He probably had gotten a whiff of Hemingway's tendency to disparage him in letters, as in this to John Dos Passos in 1932: "Don't let a twirp like Malcolm Cowley shake your confidence in those damn swell Camera Eyes." (In fact, Cowley was at the time one of Dos Passos's most fervent critical supporters.) There does not appear to have been any initial direct communications between Cowley and Hemingway about the anthology, but Scribner's required Hemingway's approval of both the overall project and the licensing of permissions for the various selections.

Cowley began by rereading, notebook at the ready, the body of Hemingway's work to date, which amounted to five novels of varying length, three story collections, one play, two works of nonfiction, and a handful of as yet uncollected stories. The 642-page book he assembled included the complete texts of *The Sun Also Rises* and the astonishing debut collection *In Our Time*; modest excerpts from *A Farewell to Arms*, *To Have and Have Not*, and *For Whom the Bell Tolls*; nine other short stories, including "The Short Happy Life of Francis Macomber" and "The Snows of Kilimanjaro"; and the epilogue to *Death in the Afternoon*, which amounts to something like Hemingway's mission statement on the art of writing. *The Portable Hemingway* provides, in its generous contents, a perfectly fine and economical introduction to his body of work, while leaving three of his novels and one of his works of nonfiction as mostly terra incognita for the reader's further exploration.

Cowley's editorial introductions, and particularly the long critical essay that begins the book, broke new ground in the understanding of Hemingway's subtle and unsettling literary art. At that time, "subtle" was not a word that was much used in relation to Hemingway. By 1944 a consensus had hardened that Hemingway was a writer of meticulously and almost fanatically controlled surfaces, an artist of brute fact over psychological depth. For all the Modernist techniques he'd learned from his early tutors—Pound's precisionist imagery, Stein's fidelity to American speech patterns, Anderson's homely poetic poignancy—what you read was what you got. Cowley knew there was a great deal more to be found in his work than that. As he later recalled, "I was outraged by the critical judgment, then widespread in academic circles, that Hemingway was a Naturalist."

Cowley's introductory essay both sharpens the focus and expands the depth of field in the understanding of Hemingway's work. He begins in a lyrical mode: "Going back to Hemingway's work after several years is like going back to a brook where you had often fished and finding the woods as deep and cool as they used to be." But something has changed, because "this time there are shadows in the pool that you hadn't noticed before, and you have a sense that the woods are haunted." After a swipe at the academic critics who'd carelessly "treated him as if he were a Dreiser of the lost generation," Cowley wrote, in a phrase that would often be quoted, "Going back to his work in 1944, you perceive his kinship with a wholly different group of novelists, let us say with Poe and Hawthorne and Melville: the haunted and nocturnal writers, the men who dealt in images that were symbols of an inner world."

In one stroke, Cowley had transformed the view of Hemingway as the inheritor of an American literary tradition with a much longer lineage than Naturalism. Cowley notes the profusion of human corpses and mutilated animals and morally damaged characters—punch-drunk fighters, battle-fatigued soldiers, traumatized veterans—that abound in his fiction. "Here are visions as terrifying as those of 'The Pit and the Pendulum,' even though most of them are copied from life; here are nightmares at noonday, accurately described, pictured without blur." Hemingway's clean, well-lighted places, upon closer examination, were heavily shadowed.

Attuned to the roiled depths underneath the surface of Hemingway's fiction, Cowley discovers symbolic meaning in many of his details and distinct elements of ritual and myth in the way his situations play out. The many images of walls and similar obstacles that recur in his work become associated with death, as does the constant rain that falls in *A Farewell to Arms* during, for instance, the disastrous retreat from Caporetto and while Catherine Barkley is dying in childbirth in the hospital. And when Frederic Henry dives into a flooded river before his desertion from the Italian army, the action assumes the aspect of a baptismal ritual cleansing him for his entry into a new life. The impotent Jake Barnes in *The Sun Also Rises*, Cowley suggests, might serve as the Lost Generation's stand-in for the wounded Fisher King in Eliot's *The Waste Land*.

Once the reader is alerted to the subterranean, symbolic, and even mythic and sacramental meanings in Hemingway's work, a surface and simpleminded reading of his work is no longer possible. Cowley includes a certain amount of biographical material in his introduction that mentions Hemingway's harrowing experiences in Italy, but he does not press hard on an autobiographical interpretation of his work. He makes this point obliquely through his reading of the work, though, and a host of Hemingway scholars and critics were quick to take the hint. Hemingway's life and his fiction would in the coming years and decades become conflated and, to his dismay, he would be subjected to an accelerating barrage of psychological scrutiny. Like many artists, Hemingway practiced a kind of magical thinking in regard to his creative powers, and he experienced having his psyche dissected in public as a threat to his craft.

At the time, though, Hemingway pronounced himself well pleased by what he jocularly called the potable as well as Portable Hemingway. He wrote Cowley a warm letter from Finca La Vigía in October of 1945 that read in part, "A few days ago I got the book and liked the introduction very much. See what you mean about the nocturnal thing now. Hope will have some luck writing now to get you some good new specimens to get the old scalpel to work on." Cowley was relieved to have pleased rather than offended this most important audience of one. In another letter Hemingway reported that he'd been teased by some GIs while embedded as a war correspondent in his friend Colonel Buck Lanham's regiment in the Hürtgen Forest; they'd read the book and chided him as a haunted nocturnal writer, to which

Hemingway had responded, "Well, I'll be a haunted nocturnal son of a bitch."

The Portable Hemingway was a success. It sold a handsome thirty thousand copies in its first year and forty-five thousand over the five-year duration of its license from Scribner's. Its introduction set Hemingway criticism in a fruitful if sometimes overdetermined new direction by making Hemingway's own experiences and psychological states a focus of attention. Postwar America was about to enter an Age of Psychology, and Cowley had helped to reposition Hemingway and his work for this paradigm shift in the culture. The rigor and care that Cowley brought to his editing of the book raised the Viking Portable Library to a new level of literary sophistication and helped it become the academic staple it would remain.

Perhaps most important, Cowley's introduction rendered Hemingway's work *teachable*. By situating Hemingway's work in the larger sweep of American literary history and discovering symbolic depths there that had previously eluded other critics, he helped make that work congenial to classroom discussion. For the New Critics already in the process of establishing their academic hegemony, he became a fit object for their close readings and painstaking exegeses. Here was a Hemingway retooled, refreshed, and scrubbed clean of a tired set of received ideas and lazy critiques.

The Portable Hemingway even had a significant cameo in a big-budget Hollywood movie. In the 1958 adaptation of James Jones's novel *Some Came Running*, the bitter returned war veteran and failing novelist Dave Hirsh—played by Frank Sinatra no less—settles into a hotel room in his Illinois hometown, pours out a slug of whiskey neat, and pulls five Viking Portables from his duffel bag and arranges them totemically on the desk: "his five major influences," the Portable Hemingway, Fitzgerald, Steinbeck, Faulkner, and Wolfe. In the novel we are told that Hirsh's girlfriend had sent all five of them to him overseas as they were published, and "he had dragged them halfway across Europe," including at the Battle of the Bulge. Here on display was a certain kind of mid-century American literary ambition. It demonstrates the considerable reach and prestige the Portable series enjoyed.

———

Cowley did Hemingway a great service with his superb work on the Portable volume, but he was at the very height of his fame and prestige and was in no way in need of a boost at the time. The situation could not have been more starkly different for the writer he would next select for the Portable treatment, William Faulkner. In this case he was mounting one of the most important rescue missions in American literary history, comparable perhaps only to the rediscovery of Herman Melville's work in the early twentieth century after decades of obscurity and neglect. And happily, Faulkner was alive and able to enjoy the fruits of rediscovery.

Malcolm Cowley was the kind of critic spurred into action by his sense of some literary injustice having been perpetrated. He'd undertaken *Exile's Return* from the feeling that his particular generational cohort had been scanted in the estimation of its literary accomplishments and importance. A sense of "outrage" at the narrow critical understanding of Hemingway's art animated the depth psychology he applied to it. In Faulkner's case his Mellon grant afforded him the time to reread Faulkner's work, and he came to the conclusion that "among the writers of his generation his public reputation was one most out of line with his extraordinary talent." As a corrective, Cowley's first impulse was to begin, in a compulsive manner, taking ninety single-spaced pages of preparatory notes for a long essay on Faulkner's work. The piece would grow to a length too unwieldly for publication in one magazine, so he would have to, in his words, "beef it"—that is, cut it up in the manner of steaks—into three sections for wider serialization. He was engaged in writing this essay when Viking asked him to edit *The Portable Hemingway* in 1944.

Cowley had been fairly slow in coming around to an appreciation of Faulkner's work. From the late twenties to the early forties, when Faulkner was producing most of his canonical books, Cowley had reviewed just three of his novels, and in distinctly mixed terms. In 1935 he found virtue in the poetic style of Faulkner's aviation barnstorming saga *Pylon*, but he thought that the book "seems to have exerted more emotional power over the author than it exerts over its readers." In 1939 he declared himself puzzled by the way *The Wild Palms* yoked together two wildly different and seemingly unrelated narratives: an almost Elizabethan account of a tragic amour fou and the hallucinatory, near-epic tale of a convict's adventures in the great Mississippi flood of 1927.

His 1936 review of *Absalom, Absalom!*, however, is an altogether deeper and more perceptive take on a novel central to Faulkner's oeuvre. He situates the book, a fevered and multivoiced account of the rise and fall of the South's planter caste, as a modern instance of romantic literature, comparable to Poe's "The Fall of the House of Usher" and Byron's *Manfred*. "One might say," he writes, "that Faulkner is Mississippi's Poe. Poe modernized with techniques and psychological devices imported from Joyce's Dublin and Freud's Vienna." This is a sharp insight that recognizes Faulkner as the Modernist artist he was, though Cowley finally takes strong exception to the book's "strained, involved, ecstatic style" and says that it "falls considerably short of the powerful mood it might have achieved." Still, he'd picked up hints in the book that "the second or hidden subject is the decline of the South after the Civil War."

His responses to the novel *The Hamlet* in 1940 and the story collection *Go Down, Moses* in 1942 were considerably warmer and farther seeing. In reviewing the novel, which is the first installment of what would become a trilogy about the inexorable rise of the Snopes family, a voracious clan of formerly poor whites, Cowley expresses something like a sense of relief. "Reading it, one feels that Faulkner has emerged from his Gothic midnight into the light of day." He notes a sense of friendliness and humor and rural community new to Faulkner's work and once again states that Faulkner's essential subject remains the defeat—in this case economic—of the planter caste, once capable of a certain moral dignity but hobbled by its guilt over the sin of slavery.

Go Down, Moses is a compilation of seven loosely connected stories, an almost-but-not-quite novel centered on the generations of the McCaslin family and its plantation in northern Mississippi and the Native Americans and Blacks who have worked on it and intermarried with them. As a book, Cowley says, its origins in disparate magazine installments mean it does not quite hold together narratively or stylistically, although he does proclaim that the first half of "The Bear" is "almost the best hunting yarn I have ever read." But he now perceives and states plainly for the first time that the book is best judged "simply as another installment of the Mississippi legend on which Faulkner has now been working on for fifteen years." He concludes, "There is no other American writer, and not many novelists anywhere, who have succeeded in presenting the life of a whole neighborhood, with all its social strata, all its personal conflicts, all its humor, and more than its share of violent crimes." In Cowley's view now, Faulkner is, after Hemingway and perhaps Dos Passos, "the most considerable novelist of his generation."

By 1944 this view would have been shared by few other people in the country. Faulkner's literary career had pretty much ground to a halt. No less an authority on such matters than Maxwell Perkins had flatly told Cowley, "Faulkner is finished." He delivered this verdict after Cowley had suggested during an interview for his profile that he take over the publication of Faulkner's book from Random House. As Perkins explained, "He has fallen into a certain position which is not nearly as high as it should be, and once that happens to a writer, it is extremely difficult to change the public's opinion."

A good part of the problem was commercial: Faulkner's books were, in the parlance of the book trade, notoriously hard sells. With the exception of his luridly compelling literary thriller of 1931, *Sanctuary*, which sold around ten thousand copies, none of his books had caught on. Too many readers were put off by the challenges of his elaborate prose, and some by the sensationalistic contents of his books, with their generous lashings of violence, incest, rape, suicide, crime, miscegenation, mental deficiencies, emotional maladjustments of a baroque nature, and even occasional bestiality. Faulkner once admitted to Cowley that he'd written his books and sent them off to New York without giving much thought to the fact that someone would eventually have to read them, and this was a price he paid. As a result, by 1944 every one of Faulkner's seventeen books was out of print, with the exception of *Sanctuary*, and exceedingly difficult to find.

Faulkner had had no trouble getting his books published by firms of high literary repute over his career and he was represented by a super-agent of the day, Harold Ober, who also represented F. Scott Fitzgerald and Pearl Buck. Since the mid-thirties he'd been published by Bennett Cerf's prestigious and powerful imprint Random House, and they dutifully, proudly, if also cautiously, published everything Faulkner sent them. The increasing gap between Faulkner's reputation as an important literary figure and the unfortunate reality of his sales meant that the advances for those books were correspondingly modest and, at a time before paperback reprints gave books a longer shelf life, royalties from backlist sales were nonexistent. In fact, during the war, Random House donated the metal plates used to print many of Faulkner's books to the war effort (the copper was used to make the jackets on bullets). This may have been patriotic, but you can be sure that Random House held on to the plates for John O'Hara's bestselling novels.

Money is a primary source of concern in the life of almost every writer not born into wealth, but it became a considerable and finally almost insoluble problem for Faulkner once it was clear that his books would yield little income. He had generally made more money from the short stories he was able to sell to mass-circulation magazines such as *The Saturday Evening Post*, which would pay a thousand dollars or more for a piece he could knock off in a few days. That source of income, however, began to dry up in the forties. From time to time a windfall in the form of a movie contract for one of his books would arrive, easing the financial anxiety for a period. But he'd earned less than fifteen thousand dollars from the sales of five books he published from 1936 through 1942, nowhere near the five thousand dollars or so he required annually to support his home in Oxford, Mississippi— Rowan Oak, the farm, with tenants, that he'd purchased in a brief flush period—and a considerable extended family that depended on him, including a mother, a wife, a child, his brother's widow and child, and two stepchildren. For a self-described "artist, a sincere one and of the first class, who should be free of even his own economic responsibilities, and with no moral conscience at all," the obligations were crushing. It is dismaying to read his letters to his editor at Random House maneuvering payments of hundreds of dollars necessary to keep his creditors and tax authorities at bay. At one especially low point, his agent had to wire him the hundred dollars he needed to keep the electricity on.

It is always difficult to track the correlation between the critical esteem a writer has attracted and his or her book sales. In Faulkner's case, though, it was clear, particularly to Malcolm Cowley, that part of his problem resided in critical misapprehension and sometimes just plain hostility. It was not that Faulkner's work lacked for attention and admiration in certain circles. In 1939 the critic Robert Cantwell, having moved on from *The New Republic*, profiled Faulkner for a cover story in *Time* on the occasion of the publication of *The Wild Palms*. In terms of author publicity at that time, this was a coup, as the magazine's verdicts on matters of culture held sway with millions of readers. Cantwell visited Faulkner in Oxford and praised the way he had "packed his observation" of the life that revolved around Oxford's courthouse square "into a series of bitter, imaginative, extraordinarily powerful but extremely uneven books." He declared that Faulkner was a "central figure in any investigation of Southern literary life." There were other critics of note in this country, notably Conrad Aiken and a phalanx of Southern Fugitives, who held Faulkner in the highest esteem.

By 1944 the strongest pockets of Faulkner admiration were to be found in France. He'd been recognized there as a major talent and literary innovator by such commanding figures as Jean-Paul Sartre, André Malraux, and André Gide. This Continental enthusiasm accounts for the fact, which would have seemed astonishingly unlikely at the time if known, that by the mid-forties, Faulkner was already under active consideration by the Swedish Academy for the Nobel Prize in Literature.

The central problem was that Faulkner was so poorly understood and so vigorously attacked in his own country by too many other critics. Horrified by what he perceived as the decadent amorality of *Sanctuary*, Henry Seidel Canby had clutched his pearls and delivered a censorious philippic titled "The School of Cruelty" in *The Saturday Review*. He called Faulkner the leading figure of the "sadistic school of fiction" and warned that "no sane reader can doubt that along the path he is following lies the end of all sanity in fiction." Faulkner had

written and published much of his most important work in the thirties, when social and so-called proletarian novels were in vogue. A
class-based Marxist interpretation of his work would of necessity be
tortured and even risible, and leftist critics such as Granville Hicks,
who called him "a Sax Rohmer for the sophisticated," were by and
large hostile. Centrist critics such as Maxwell Geismar, while praising
Faulkner's literary skills, lamented the absence of the kind of progressive uplift to be found in Steinbeck's work to counterbalance the economic misery and psychological deformations that so much of
Faulkner's work abounds in. Bernard DeVoto, always reliably hostile
to Lost Generation writers, went at *Absalom, Absalom!* with hammer
and tongs, claiming that its "tortured prose" showed "a style in the
process of disintegration" from "a quicksand of invertebrate sentences";
deploring "its obsession with pathology, this parade of Grand Guignol
tricks and sensations"; and concluding that in Faulkner's overwrought
and obscurely motivated book "witchcraft [has come] to substitute for
the ordinary concerns of fiction."

The person who did the most damage to Faulkner's broader reputation was Clifton Fadiman, who mounted something like a decades-
long jihad against his work. The word "critic" does little justice to
Fadiman's powerful sway for decades as a tastemaker and influencer.
In the public mind he was *the* middlebrow Designated Intellectual.
He served as *The New Yorker*'s chief book critic and editor from 1933
to 1943, but he became a household name to millions of Americans
when he began moderating the wildly popular radio quiz show *Information Please* in 1938. On top of all this, he helped to found the Book
of the Month Club, the single most powerful commercial force in
American publishing at the time, and he served as one of its judges for
more than fifty years. Clifton Fadiman was not an adversary any novelist would care to have.

One by one, year by year, Fadiman set up Faulkner's novels for examination only to knock them down, often with a facetious tone that is hard to forgive: *The Sound and the Fury* ("The theme and the characters are trivial, unworthy of the enormous and complex craftsmanship expended on them"); *As I Lay Dying* ("Despite the enthusiasm which has greeted Mr. Faulkner's work, it is difficult to believe him an important writer"); *Dr. Martino* ("I have frequently felt that the publishers are missing a sure bet in not arranging to have every emergent Faulknerian met by a brandy-bearing St. Bernard"); *Pylon* ("It has me licked a dozen ways . . . one part repulsion, one part terror, one part admiration, three parts puzzlement, four parts boredom"); and *Absalom, Absalom!* ("I do not comprehend why *Absalom, Absalom!* was written, what the non-Mississippian is supposed to get out of it, or indeed what it is all about. . . . Mr. Faulkner's latest work is the most consistently boring novel by a reputable writer to come my way in the last decade"). This sort of thing had a cumulative effect on readers and even on other critics, who were given permission to avoid grappling with the challenges to taste and syntax and cognition that even Faulkner's admirers admit to. You can sum up Fadiman's overall argument contra Faulkner this way: The smart set is putting one over on you, folks. You don't have to bother.

This was the considerable challenge that faced Malcolm Cowley as he undertook to write a long corrective essay to reverse the negative estimation of Faulkner's worth and achievement. He knew it would be an uphill battle. He understood, probably even better than Faulkner himself, that the voices of his supporters had been "drowned out by a larger chorus of academic critics, almost all contemptuous, and by a deafening frogpond croak of daily and weekly reviewers." Cowley's favorite analogy for the literary marketplace was the stock exchange. This may seem reductive and unrefined to delicate sensibilities, but it is in fact a clarifying way to think about the rise and fall of a writer's reputation. "How could one speak of Faulkner's value on the literary stock exchange?" Cowley asked. "In 1944 his name wasn't even listed there."

Cowley wrote to Faulkner in early 1944, seeking to clarify certain biographical and literary matters. The two men had never met, but they must have had contact in the thirties when Faulkner was contributing some poems and his one review to *The New Republic*. As it happened, Faulkner was in Hollywood for an extended stint of screenwriting, under an onerous contract with Warner Bros. It was his habit to open most of his letters to extract any return postage and then drop them into a desk drawer to be disinterred on some future date. Thus he only replied to Cowley's letter three months later. He pronounced himself pleased at the prospect of the essay: "I would very much like to have the piece done. I think (at 46) that I have worked too hard at my (elected or doomed, I don't know which) trade, with pride but I believe not vanity, with plenty of ego but with humility too (being a poet, of course I give no fart for glory) to leave no better mark on this our pointless chronicle than I seem to be about to leave." Clearly, Faulkner knew that in trading terms at that point he was a penny stock. He demurred only on the matter of biographical content, pleading the desire for privacy and the autonomy of the work. It would emerge that he had other motives.

Thus began a warm, extended, and exceptionally detailed correspondence on all aspects of Faulkner's writing. It seems that no one had ever asked him any serious questions about his methods and intentions. Cowley's next letter gave Faulkner a full and rather brutal summation of his standing with critics and publishers, going so far as to suggest he consider finding a new publisher. Then he got down to literary business, querying Faulkner as to how consciously he intended his fictional creations to be symbols or allegories for the larger story or myth or legend of the South. (The answer: Kind of.)

This was a leisurely process: Faulkner's reply would come four months later. In the interim, Cowley had made enough progress on his essay that he was able to "saw off" a portion of it, which ran in *The New York Times Book Review* on October 29, 1944, under the title "William Faulkner's Human Comedy." The allusion to Balzac's sprawling series of novels was intentional, and Cowley draws an analogy between the way that Balzac divided his many-volumed saga into "Scenes from Parisian Life," "Scenes from Provincial Life," etc., and the way one might categorize Faulkner's novels and stories that deal with "Yocknapatawpha County," as he misspelled it at the time. The piece begins with the blunt forthrightness of a flag being planted—"It is time to make a plea for the work of William Faulkner"—and proceeds to make a closely argued case that "there is no American author of our time who has undertaken and partly completed a more ambitious series of novels and stories." The one-page essay contains, ab ovo, most of the insights and arguments that Cowley would later fully develop.

Faulkner was pleased, and he gave Cowley his blessing to proceed with the longer essay. In the course of his letter, Faulkner delivered a famous explanation and defense of his supposedly obscure style. Citing Thomas Wolfe's overstuffed novels, which attempted to cram everything possible between two book covers, as a contrast to his own method, he declared, "I am trying to say it all in one sentence, between one Cap and one period. I'm still trying to put it all, if possible, on one pinhead." Faulkner also claimed that his real subject was actually not the South itself. The South was simply the raw material that personal circumstances made available to him. His real subject was the wider life of humanity, "the same frantic steeplechase toward nothing everywhere."

All during this time Cowley had been finishing up his work for the Viking Press on *The Portable Hemingway*, and they were well pleased with the results. What Cowley did not tell Faulkner, though, was that he had been urging Viking to follow it up with a *Portable Faulkner*, but the idea had been coolly received. As he later put it, "The proposal elicited some interest but no enthusiasm. I was told that Faulkner's audience was too limited and his critical standing too dubious to justify such a book; it would have no sale." Given the discouraging word on the street in respect to Faulkner, this was a rational decision. There was, however, a somewhat unpleasant irony to it that Cowley would not have known about. In 1940, Viking's Harold Guinzburg had engaged in serious negotiations with Faulkner and with Bennett Cerf of Random House to publish Faulkner's next two books and buy the plates and remaining inventory and publication rights to *The Hamlet*. The deal fell apart over a shortfall of $1,500 (almost $33,000 in current dollars), and he stayed on with Random House. It has been speculated that the demoralizing failure of this deal, which had offered him a financial lifeline in a time of dire need, explains why he would not finish another novel for eight years. It is another index of Faulkner's falling "share price" that in four years Viking's interest in his work had so diminished.

Undaunted, Cowley finished his long critical essay. He placed a longer piece titled "William Faulkner Revisited" in the April 14, 1945, issue of *The Saturday Review*, an easy sale as Harrison Smith, the publication's editor, had been Faulkner's onetime editor and publisher. An even easier sale was made to Allen Tate at *The Sewanee Review*. "William Faulkner's Legend of the South" ran in the Summer 1945 issue and it won an essay contest cosponsored by the magazine and the publisher Prentice-Hall. It suddenly seemed, from Viking's perspective, that quite a flurry of highly positive critical activity had arisen around Faulkner and his work. Something seemed to be brewing out there. The acronym FOMO didn't exist in 1945, of course, but it was as powerful a force then in the literary world and everywhere else as it is today.

In early August, Cowley got a call from Marshall Best, Viking's managing editor, asking him to drop by the office. When he did, Best told him, "It seems to us that Faulkner is receiving a great deal of attention in the magazines." "I modestly agreed," Cowley would dryly remember. "Under the circumstances we feel that a *Portable Faulkner* might have a chance to attract readers. How soon could you have the copy ready?" One of the most underrated of publishing virtues is the ability to alter one's mind when circumstances change. Viking's change of heart enabled a true hinge moment in the history of American literature.

In a jubilant mood, Cowley wrote to Faulkner to share this good news, suggesting that a Portable would juice the sales for his new books and be "a bayonet prick in the ass of Random House to reprint the others." He outlined his already well-formed ideas for the anthology, not a "best of Faulkner" but an integrated selection of short stories and excerpts from novels that would give the reader a sense of the history of the fictional Yoknapatawpha County from Indian times to the beginning of the present war. The larger goal was to create a book of episodes that could be read from beginning to end almost as if a new novel had been fashioned from those episodes. Faulkner replied promptly this time, writing, "By all means let us make a Golden Book of my apocryphal county. I have thought of spending my old age doing something of that nature." At this point what had been a friendly consultation between critic and author shifted gears into a full-on collaboration, Faulkner responding point by point to Cowley's suggestions for inclusion.

The ensuing correspondence is a treasure trove for students of Faulkner and contains, en passant, a fair amount of literary gossip. Cowley wrote that Hemingway, in a glum mood, had written to him that "Faulkner has the most talent of anybody but hard to depend on because he goes on writing when he is tired and seems as though he never threw away anything that is worthless." This is a shrewd take from a very competitive writer. The letters at times take on a faintly comic tone, with Cowley pressing in on inconsistencies of detail over the sprawl of the Yoknapatawpha saga and Faulkner slipping some of the punches. (Cowley would compare himself in this *Information Please* mode to Polonius or J. Alfred Prufrock.) But Faulkner was absolutely serious about the task at hand and gave Cowley almost all the answers he needed to assemble an authoritative book.

One of his lines of inquiry resulted in an important contribution to Faulkner scholarship. Cowley wanted to include a selection from Faulkner's 1929 novel *The Sound and the Fury*, a book whose nonlinear, time-hopping structure and stream-of-consciousness narration mark it as the most radically Modernist of his books. He and Faulkner had first thought the third part of the novel, a monologue by the venal Jason Compson, the youngest of the three children, might work best, as it is comparatively straightforward. But they finally decided on an excerpt from the fourth and final section of the book, the only one that uses an omniscient narrator and that relates the final decline of the Compson family from the point of view of their faithful, long-suffering, and closely observant Black servant, Dilsey. The original intention was for Faulkner to introduce this section with a tight synopsis summarizing preceding events for the reader's benefit. "It must be right, not just a list of facts," he told Cowley. "It should be induction, I think, not a mere directive."

Two weeks later a fat envelope arrived in Sherman containing not simply an "induction" but a thirty-page genealogy of two centuries of the Compson family, beginning with the Battle of Culloden in 1745 and ending with Dilsey and three other Black characters and the final words "They endured." This is no mere listing of characters: It sprawls far beyond the temporal compass of *The Sound and the Fury* and it includes many facts and incidents mentioned nowhere else in Faulkner's fiction. He was obviously delighted by it, declaring, "I should have done this when I wrote the book. Then the whole thing would have fallen into pattern like a jigsaw puzzle when the magician's wand touched it." Cowley believed that it "was an event in [Faulkner's] career as a novelist" and "an integral part of *The Sound and the Fury*." Some critics consider this genealogy to be the fifth and final section of the novel. Faulkner wrote it without even consulting the text of the book, as he did not own a copy of it himself. This accounts for some factual discrepancies, but it also speaks volumes about how real, how vividly *present* his fictional creations remained in his mind years after he imagined them. As Cowley wrote, "The works might disappear from the shelves and even from the second-hand bookstores, but the story lived completely in his mind." This genealogy would serve as the invaluable final appendix to *The Portable Faulkner*, and once *The Sound and the Fury* was reprinted and began to sell in new editions, it would unfailingly be added to them, to the benefit of students and general readers.

There was one final round of close textual back-and-forth letters, mildly mind-numbing to read but necessary from Cowley's punctilious point of view, and by November 11, 1945, he would write to Best, "The Faulkner text is ready to shoot," with his introduction and some short prefaces still to come. In addition to the Compson genealogy, a map of Yoknapatawpha County, "Surveyed & mapped for this volume by WILLIAM FAULKNER," would be reproduced on the hardcover's front and back endpapers. There was some delicate back-and-forth regarding the copy on the front cover of the dust jacket, as Viking wanted to state that the book was actually a new addition to the Faulkner canon without ruffling the feathers of his publisher Random House. The parties finally agreed on this wording: "The saga of Yoknapatawpha County, 1820–1945, being the first chronological picture of Faulkner's mythical county in Mississippi . . . in effect a new work, though selected from his best published novels and stories; with his own account of one of the principal families, written specially for this volume."

Even more delicate, and protracted, were Cowley's attempts to confirm certain biographical facts about Faulkner for his introduction. He'd depended on Hemingway's listing in *Who's Who* for his preceding Portable and been led astray. In Faulkner's case he used his listing in the reference volume *Twentieth Century Authors*, which plainly stated that Faulkner had trained as a pilot with the Royal Air Force in Canada, served in France as a forward air observer, and had two planes shot out from under him. Only the first of these assertions was true; the rest of it had been embroidered by Faulkner himself, but Cowley, not knowing this, repeated the details in his original draft of the introduction. Faulkner, in his own fashion a match for J. D. Salinger in his obsessive protection of his privacy, did not explicitly correct the misstatements so much as elide them. This disappointed Cowley more than a bit, as he was eager to recruit Faulkner into his Lost Generation cohort, but if he had never gone overseas and seen anything of the Great War, that case became harder to make. Cowley persisted in including those putative facts up to the point of page proofs, and when he sent them to Faulkner as a courtesy, things got testy. Faulkner wrote, "You are going to bugger up a fine dignified distinguished book with that war business," and offered to pay to correct the plates to state only that he "was a member of the RAF in 1918." The penny finally dropped for Cowley, and the final text of the introduction begins, "When the war was over—the other war—William Faulkner went back to Oxford, Mississippi. He had served in the Royal Air Force in 1918." An embarrassment for both sides was narrowly averted.

The Portable Faulkner was published in April 1946 and a copy was sent to Faulkner in Oxford, Mississippi. As with Hemingway, Cowley's all-important audience of one was well pleased. Faulkner wrote back to him, "The job is splendid. Damn you to hell anyway. But even if I had beat you to the idea, mine wouldn't have been this good. By God, I didn't know myself what I tried to do, and how much I had succeeded." Unsurprisingly, Cowley would write, "It was the handsomest letter of acknowledgement I had ever received." Perhaps even better, though, was this: Cowley had sent Faulkner on loan his precious copy of *The Sound and the Fury*, as Faulkner did not own one himself. Faulkner sent the book back to him with this inscription: "To Malcolm Cowley—Who beat me to what was to have been the leisurely pleasure of my old age. William Faulkner."

Cowley's editing of *The Portable Faulkner* was a magnificent example of selfless, disinterested generosity on the part of one writer toward another. The book was perfectly designed to make the case for this famous assertion in the introduction: "There in Oxford, Faulkner performed a labor of imagination that has not been equaled in our time, and a double labor: first, to invent a Mississippi county that was like a mythical kingdom, but was complete and living in all its details; second, to make his story of Yoknapatawpha County stand as a parable or legend of all the Deep South." Readers who honored his desire that they read the anthology front to back would be carried along episodically into the broad sweep of that "mythical kingdom," becoming familiar with the Sartoris, Sutpen, Compson, McCaslin, Snopes families, et al., and being given a compact crash course on what they needed to know to enter into Faulkner's sometimes puzzling novels. But even the casual reader inclined to dip in here or there would encounter such works of epic narration as the novella-length stories "The Bear" and "Old Man" (extracted from *The Wild Palms*) and the hilarious classic of frontier humor "Spotted Horses" and be intrigued enough to proceed further in Faulkner's work.

In some ways Cowley's long introduction was even more important to the achievement of his task of literary resurrection. In its quiet, unflashy way it is a masterpiece of critical advocacy and explication, flowing, detailed, persuasive, and adroitly pitched at both the educated general reader and other writers, critics, and scholars. By concentrating on the Yoknapatawpha stories and novels to the exclusion of other of Faulkner's work, he brought his most enduring and original achievement into clear focus for the first time. He reframed Faulkner's essential literary talent as not simply a novelist taking a situation and a set of circumstances and fashioning them into a tight, delimited narrative, but more as a bard, a teller of tales that sprawled across the decades and were available to him at all times for expansion and elaboration. Also as a moralist, sitting in judgment on the decline of his own civilization and its failings in the matter of slavery.

Cowley also did one other thing for Faulkner similar to what he did for Hemingway: He placed him in the larger context of American literature. Cowley argues that "the American author he most resembles is Hawthorne, for all their polar differences." Each of these writers, Faulkner in the South and Hawthorne in New England, "applied himself to creating his moral fables and elaborating its legends, which existed, as it were, in his solitary heart." Each heard the secret voice of his home territory in his mind. One can imagine Hawthorne repeating to himself, like a Salem-born Quentin Compson, "I don't hate New England, I don't hate it."

Cowley had some anxiety that his book might not attract much attention, but in fact the publication of *The Portable Faulkner* went off like a starter's pistol, and its report was heard clearest below the Mason–Dixon Line. The first significant notice was a long and eye-catching review by the Southern novelist Caroline Gordon on the front page of *The New York Times Book Review* on May 5, 1946. You could call this an inside job, as Gordon and her husband, Allen Tate, were two of Cowley's closest friends, and you'd be right. Both Faulkner and Cowley came in for praise in the lead paragraph: "William

Faulkner, alone among contemporary novelists, it seems to me, has the distinguishing mark of the major novelist: the ability to create a variety of characters." She continues, "It is Malcolm Cowley's distinction to have presented in his preface to 'The Portable Faulkner' the first comprehensive survey of Mr. Faulkner's work that takes into account his symbolism." Gordon goes on to echo all of Cowley's insights into Faulkner's work, with emphasis on the Faulkner–Hawthorne comparison. A better review in a more visible place could not have been hoped for, and Gordon's focus on the symbolism in Faulkner's work would have been an unmissable beacon for those symbol hunters, the New Critics.

Gordon's piece soon had a mighty echo three months later when the Southern writer and critic (and friend of Malcolm Cowley's) Robert Penn Warren weighed in at such length in *The New Republic* that his essay ran in two consecutive issues. Warren praises Cowley's efforts on two counts, the editing of the selections and, especially, the introduction, which he calls "one of the few things ever written on Faulkner which is not hag-ridden by prejudice or preconception and which really sheds some light on the subject." Warren has nothing but praise for Cowley's labors on all fronts, but the real aim of his long essay is to make a larger claim for Faulkner's significance than even he does: "It is important, I think, that Faulkner's work be regarded not in terms of the South against the North, but in terms of issues which are common to our modern world. The legend is not merely a legend of the South, but also a legend of our general plight and problem." "The modern world is in moral confusion," Warren declares, and he proceeds to suggest that Faulkner's humanity and humor and feel for the natural world and his rendering of the virtues of the old agrarian order can offer corrective lessons. Few, if any, critics had dared to see Faulkner's often violence-laden chronicles of the defeat, decadence, and decay of a rural, racist, backward, one-crop society that the Industrial

Revolution and the various other revolutions of the twentieth century had largely passed by as having any relevance or moral instruction to offer to the modern world. But Warren made this assertion stick.

Warren ends with this clarion call: "The study of Faulkner is the most challenging single task in contemporary American literature for criticism to undertake." He was heeded. His essay, along with Cowley's introduction, became one of the two foundational pillars of that postwar growth industry, Faulkner Studies. Warren was no mere book reviewer. He was a widely respected novelist, poet, and critic, a founder of the Southern Fugitive movement, and in the academic world already a major figure in the New Critical takeover of literary studies. Two textbooks he coauthored with Cleanth Brooks, *Understanding Poetry* (1938) and *Understanding Fiction* (1943), would inculcate the New Critical gospel to literature students for generations to come.

This mattered, because in the postwar world a new, academically based paradigm in the creation of literary prestige was about to begin. Recall that Malcolm Cowley thirty years earlier at Harvard had not taken a single course in American literature. The aura of greatness was something bestowed outside of the academy by professional critics and other writers in the prestige-bestowing magazines and reviews, and to a certain extent by readers themselves. This was about to change radically, as two related developments took hold. American higher education was expanding exponentially as millions of American soldiers were discharged and resumed their university studies once more or began them anew. The GI Bill of 1944 signed into law by FDR was the super-accelerant here, providing World War II veterans with funds for their college educations. The other was the widespread sense that, if America was now so great a power in the world that the twentieth century itself belonged to it, then its culture and, especially, its literature required renewed and intensive scrutiny. That meant that it wasn't enough for a writer merely to be widely admired and read—

he or she had to be widely *studied*. The Faulkner revival arrived at the perfect moment to benefit from these developments.

Faulkner was delighted to have his achievements recognized, but his feelings were not unmixed. Harold Ober was enabled to sell three of Faulkner's stories to Hollywood, which brought in a welcome ten thousand dollars. But all the attention meant that he also had to surrender a certain amount of his privacy, and this he did not like at all. In May of 1946 the Russian writer Ilya Ehrenburg, a Faulkner admirer who'd read some of his novels in French, had arrived in New York and he'd asked Malcolm Cowley to help arrange a visit to Oxford to meet him. Faulkner's reply was one of dismay at the coming intrusion: "Goddam it I've spent almost fifty years trying to cure myself of the curse of human speech, all for nothing. Last month two damn swedes, two days ago a confounded Chicago reporter, and now this one that cant even speak English. . . . I swear to Christ being in hollywood was better than this where nobody knew me or cared a damn." Ehrenburg did make it to Oxford but he did not manage to meet Faulkner. As for the "two damned swedes," they were journalists who had heard a rumor that the Nobel Prize Committee was actively considering awarding the literature prize to Faulkner and had come to Oxford to secure an exclusive story.

The Nobel Prize arrived in 1950, definitively ending any hope Faulkner might have retained that he could continue to live as a private figure, away from the glare of attention from journalists, critics, academics, biographers, photographers, fellow writers, rabid fans, autograph seekers, and favor-askers. At first Faulkner declined to travel to Stockholm to accept the award, but he supposedly changed his mind when his daughter Jill pleaded that she could go with him and finally see Paris along the way. He ended up giving his famous acceptance speech, with its declaration that "I believe that man will not merely endure; he will prevail." It is tempting to draw a straight or even curved line from the process of reevaluation in Faulkner's own country set off by the publication of *The Portable Faulkner* to the awarding of the Nobel Prize. The most that can be said is that the elders of Stockholm could not have been unaware of the ascent of the value of Faulkner's shares on the literary stock exchange in the United States, and that it may have reinforced an inclination that had already taken hold that Faulkner was in contention for this recognition of his life's work.

The collaboration between Malcolm Cowley and William Faulkner on *The Portable Faulkner* would ripen into a warm, if intermittent, friendship between the two men, with great respect and fondness— Faulkner would sometimes begin his letters with the honorific "Brother Cowley"—on both sides. Most of it was conducted through the mails, with the two writers, both confirmed country squires, often sharing details of hunting, fishing, animal husbandry, and agricultural pursuits. Cowley would sometimes weigh in with his editorial suggestions, generally not taken, for certain of Faulkner's book projects, such as the arrangement of the volume *Collected Stories*. Cowley was also assiduous in keeping Faulkner up to date on his unstoppable takeover of college reading lists. In July of 1948 he wrote, "When you get North you will find that you are not a neglected author any longer, that they're studying you in the colleges, including Yale, where lots of the kids think that 'The Bear' is the greatest story ever written." The next year Cowley wrote, "Have to report that the Faulkner boom continues; some professors and librarians told me in NY, over drinks, that your work was more studied in the colleges than that of any other living American author." Cowley clearly took pleasure in having written the prospectus for Faulkner, Inc.

At about this time, Cowley was deep into his work on one of his most demanding (and lucrative) journalistic assignments, a long profile of Ernest Hemingway for *Life* magazine, the most broadly influential magazine in the country, with a weekly circulation of more than ten million copies. Even before that piece ran on January 10, 1949, his editor at *Life*, Robert Coughlan, asked Cowley if he would undertake a similar profile of Faulkner, a dramatic index of Faulkner's meteoric rise.

The two men met for the first time in October of 1948 when Faulkner came to New York to do publicity chores for the publication of *Intruder in the Dust*, his first book to be published since *Go Down, Moses* in 1942, hence a major publishing event. The Cowleys attended a dinner in Faulkner's honor on October 17 at the Park Avenue apartment of Robert Haas, a partner at Random House. The next week Cowley drove into New York to pick up Faulkner and drive him back to Sherman as his houseguest for an overnight visit, during which the two men talked literature long into the night. One of the subjects broached was the profile for *Life*, which Cowley suggested could be confined for the most part to Faulkner's work, with biographical material limited to such facts as were already in the public record. Faulkner was far from delighted by this prospective intrusion, but after lunch he emitted what Cowley optimistically interpreted as "a sigh of assent." He also felt that for the balance of his visit, Faulkner became even more forthcoming with information, as if helping the profile along.

At least this is the version of the visit that Cowley offers in his little volume *The Faulkner-Cowley File: Letters and Memories 1944–1962*. A darker story is told by Faulkner biographer Jay Parini in *One Matchless Time*. The shy Faulkner was notoriously prone to going on alcoholic binges, especially when he had to attend social functions, and this time, not for the first or last time, he drank himself into a total breakdown. Cowley and Haas had to get the manager of the Algonquin Hotel to let them into Faulkner's room, where they found him barely coherent and unable to stand up. They first checked him into the

Fieldston Sanitarium in the Bronx, and then decided that a visit to the Cowleys' home in Sherman might serve as an improvised rehab. Malcolm's son, Robert, remembers that "my father brought him home in horrible, horrible shape. He was quite literally raving." Having lost much of his clothes, the diminutive Faulkner had to wear some of Rob Cowley's trousers with the bottoms rolled up. In a few days he made a remarkable recovery, "back to normal, like a new penny." It is hard to square this version of the Sherman visit with Cowley's account of a talk-filled sojourn, but one can understand his protectiveness in 1966, less than four years after Faulkner's death. The only hint in *The Faulkner-Cowley File* that the visit had a darker purpose than a simple country sojourn is this sentence from Cowley's note-taking: "This morning [Faulkner] carried only a book, which he asked to borrow and I invited him to keep, a paperback copy of *The Lost Weekend*."

In any case, ever the Southern gentleman, Faulkner ordered twelve long-stemmed roses to be delivered to Muriel after his departure for Oxford. Cowley took notes on their talks to keep all the details fresh and accurate for what he believed would soon be their journalistic use. Not so fast. Shortly after the turn of the year a "perturbed" letter from Faulkner arrived that began, "I have waited two weeks, and am still no nearer getting into the dentist's chair." There is a certain amount of polite, awkward hemming and hawing in the letter about possible ways some kind of piece for *Life* might be done, but the operative sentence is this one: "I still don't want it, I mean me as a private individual, my past, my family, my house." Cowley graciously half accepted this refusal, holding out for some slight chance that the thing might somehow be done. But the final "NO" came after Faulkner cast his eyes on Cowley's long profile of Hemingway in *Life*. What dismayed him was not so much the content of the piece itself but rather the voluminous photographs that *Life*'s art directors had festooned it with. Faulkner wrote Cowley, "But I am more convinced and determined than ever that this is not for me. I will protest to the last: no photographs, no recorded documents. It is my ambition to be, as a private individual, abolished and voided from history, leaving it markless, no refuse save the printed books." (Joseph Blotner, Faulkner's close friend and, after his death, his appointed biographer, annihilated this ambition singlehandedly in 1974 with his 2,115-page, two-volume tome *Faulkner: A Biography*.)

Cowley and Faulkner would meet on other occasions in New York in the years to come. Cowley was in the audience in 1955 when Clifton Fadiman, Faulkner's critical archenemy, was forced in his capacity as the host of the National Book Awards to hand Faulkner the award for his novel *A Fable* as the best work of fiction of 1954. Another notable occasion was when Cowley managed to coax Faulkner into coming to the American Institute and Academy of Arts and Letters in May of 1957 to present the Gold Medal of the Institute for Fiction to John Dos Passos at their annual ceremony and reception on Audubon Terrace in New York. Legend has it that Faulkner, bored stiff by all the verbiage that preceded him, scotched his prepared speech and said, "Here it is, Dos. Take it." In fact he said this: "Oratory can't add anything to John Dos Passos's stature, and if I know anything about writers, he may be grateful for a little less of it."

The last time Cowley and Faulkner met was on his visit to New York in May of 1962 to accept yet another award from the Academy and Institute, the same Gold Medal for Fiction he'd presented to John Dos Passos. He met his early and constant critical supporter Conrad Aiken at the cocktail party and sat next to Kenneth Burke and Muriel Cowley at lunch; he appeared to her to be in rude country health. This time the ceremony was arranged so that Faulkner received his medal early in the proceedings; it was presented to him, with a short speech, by his fellow Mississippian Eudora Welty. His brief, eloquent acceptance speech was his last public statement. Six weeks later, word of

William Faulkner's death in Oxford of a heart attack at age sixty-four raced around the world. If he had died before the publication of *The Portable Faulkner*, his death would have received respectful notice in the usual places, and the odds are that he would have faded into obscurity. Instead, in part as a result of forces that Cowley's anthology set in motion, his demise was a global news story.

Malcolm Cowley became forever identified with Faulkner, all of whose subsequent books he would review and about whom he would write intermittently for the rest of his life. It cemented Cowley's relationship with the Viking Press and led to his being hired by the firm as a consulting editor in 1949.

The Portable Faulkner was the most influential of all the many Viking Portables, and it remains in print today in a Penguin paperback edition. It was far from the bestselling Portable, though. In 1970, Cowley recalled that "it took a long time for the book to reach 20,000." He estimated that the yearly pace in paperback was 20,000 copies, though, and that the sales to that point had been 50,000 in cloth and 100,000 in paper—good but not spectacular.

Its real effect was to be on the sales of Faulkner's other books, which went from tiny and even zero to millions sold worldwide. And numbers tell only part of the tale. The example of Faulkner's work inspired such brilliant Southern writers as Eudora Welty, William Styron, Flannery O'Connor, and Cormac McCarthy. Toni Morrison, from Lorain, Ohio, studied Faulkner as a graduate student and her towering work is clearly indebted to his. And Faulkner powerfully influenced the writing of the Latin American Boom generation. Faulkner made two trips as a literary goodwill ambassador to Latin America under the auspices of the American government in 1954 and 1961, and he established close ties with important intellectuals in the region. His example was crucial to the work of Gabriel García Márquez, Julio Cortázar, Mario Vargas Llosa, and Carlos Fuentes.

William Faulkner belongs to the world as a literary hero, not simply to the South or America.

Over the course of a very long career in letters, Malcolm Cowley had numerous achievements to be proud of. In his many interviews on the subject of Faulkner he was always modest, careful not to take too much credit for the revival, citing the contributions of such critics as Robert Penn Warren, who followed in his wake, and of course pointing out that it was Faulkner's work itself that really mattered. One can't miss, though, the pride suffusing these sentences that begin *The Faulkner–Cowley File*:

> Almost every critic dreams of discovering some great work that has been neglected by other critics. Some day might he come upon an author whose reputation is less than his achievement and in fact is scandalously out of proportion with it, so that other voices will be added to the critic's voice, in a swelling chorus as soon as he has made the discovery? That is the dream.
>
> At least once in my critical career I had the good luck to find it realized.

TWELVE.

THE LITERARY SITUATION

———

In the middle of August of 1948 Malcolm Cowley celebrated his fiftieth birthday at a joint party at his Sherman home with his western Connecticut neighbor Alexander Calder, who, born two days before him on August 22, 1898, was also turning fifty. By the actuarial tables of the day, Cowley had entered late middle age, as the average life span for American males at the time was sixty-five years. In fact, he would live for four more intellectually and physically active decades. The dashing handsomeness that Alfred Kazin had noted in the thirties had faded a bit. He now had a modest bay window and graying hair, and his cheeks were fuller and somewhat rubicund. Invariably photographed with his lifelong mustache, wearing a tie and a tweed jacket and holding a pipe, he looked almost like a caricature of the distinguished man of letters. An eminence—but an eminence still motivated by an unwavering passion for literature.

The deafness that had begun in the late thirties and that an ear operation had failed to correct would progress in severity for the rest of his life. By 1950 or so, he would wear a hearing aid, clearly visible in those pre-transistor days. His already booming voice would become even louder—you always knew when Malcolm Cowley was around—but he was able to function perfectly well in work or classroom settings. His deafness was a mild handicap but not a disability; in fact he would at times treat it as a convenience, discreetly turning off his hearing aid when the proceedings around him became tiresome or contentious. He was "deaf enough *not* to hear remarks made in an undertone, so that in meetings I could preserve the equanimity that is mistaken for benignity or magnanimity." His deafness also contributed to his impressive assiduousness as a correspondent, letters feeling to him like a more direct and intimate means of communication than in-person conversations.

During this period Malcolm Cowley's life assumed the pattern that it would keep for the next forty years. He and Muriel settled into their life in Sherman for good. It now felt like a refuge and a home, not the exiled "hermit kingdom" he'd lamented earlier in the decade. By choice and circumstance alike he'd managed to place the wider world at just the right distance for his liking.

Rural as Sherman was, the town and the neighboring villages in western Connecticut harbored an impressive array of notable cultural figures. Across Church Road lived the painter Peter Blume and his wife, Ebie, the Cowleys' closest friends. Peter Blume was highly regarded enough to have had paintings purchased by the Metropolitan Museum and the Museum of Modern Art; one of his signature works, a surreal tableau called *Parade*, featured a recognizable rendering of Cowley brandishing a suit of armor above his head. Up Church Road a bit were Matthew and Hannah Josephson, as well as Robert Coates, who as the first art critic for *The New Yorker* coined the phrase "abstract expressionism."

By the forties, western Connecticut had attracted a large number of important visual artists. The most famous of these was Alexander Calder, who had his home with his wife, Louisa, and the studio, "an alchemist's laboratory," where he fabricated his wondrous art objects, on Painter Road in Roxbury, thirteen miles from Sherman. Peter

Blume had introduced Cowley to Calder back in the thirties and they'd become fast friends; Calder referred to Blume, Coates, Josephson, and Cowley as "the boys from Sherman."

Calder's genial personality was of a piece with his creations, in contrast to Malcolm Cowley's more phlegmatic affect. Nor was Calder particularly literary or intellectual, though he was often underestimated in those areas and would do illustrations for a number of classic texts. Nevertheless the two men bonded in a close and enduring friendship that lasted decades and never faded. They had in common their shared generational experience and their formative years in Paris, although Calder arrived there later, in 1926, and stayed there until the early thirties, where he refined his unique approach to sculpture and would be accepted as an equal among such innovators as Mondrian, Léger, Arp, and Miró. They were both uxorious as well, Calder's marriage to his beloved Louisa forming an unbreakable partnership as durable as Cowley's to Muriel, in a milieu where adultery and divorce were more the norm.

The Calders became the magnetic center of the social life of western Connecticut. Cowley recalled that "they entertained in a simple, unreckoning fashion: artists met artists at the Calders', laughed and danced and had a glorious time." Cowley and Calder would very often celebrate their birthdays with joint parties, some of them riotous and memorable. One such was a fortieth birthday party in August of 1938 that took place on Painter Road. It featured an elaborately stepped-back birthday cake from an Italian bakery that proclaimed "FORTY, FIT, FAT, AND FARTY" (Calder being known for his girth), people plunging into a pond fully dressed and almost drowning, many missing items, like the eyeglasses of poet John Berryman, and much drinking and misbehavior. Cowley would inscribe a copy of *Blue Juniata* to Calder to mark the occasion with the words "in memory of 1 mad night." The party they held ten years later would be more sedate.

The warmth and closeness of the Cowley–Calder friendship can be gauged by the fact that Calder gifted him a 1941 kinetic sculpture, *The Clangor*, whose suspended elements made a kind of aleatory music when in motion; it was important enough to his oeuvre that Cowley lent it to the Museum of Modern Art for a blockbuster 1944 retrospective that rocketed Calder's fame with the general public. Calder also dedicated the edition he illustrated in 1946 of Coleridge's "The Rime of the Ancient Mariner" to Cowley, with a characteristic line drawing of his friend's face on the dedication page.

Throughout the thirties, there had been a diaspora of European writers and artists who ended up in New York City, and a fair number of them would find their way to leafy western Connecticut, some for temporary respites and some to live there full time. Among the artists who moved to the area and became part of the Calder circle were the painters André Masson and Yves Tanguy, the sculptors Naum Gabo and David Hare, and the filmmaker Hans Richter. Marc Chagall spent the summer of 1941 in nearby New Preston. Marcel Duchamp, the supreme Trickster of twentieth-century art and an energetically social creature, can be spied in many of the pastoral party snapshots of the period.

André Breton, the chief theoretician of Surrealist doctrine, and Max Ernst, one of the school's most gifted practitioners, had both come to New York and colonized the town for their artistic point of view, in the process profoundly influencing American art in the direction of abstraction. One side effect of this takeover was that, as Calder's biographer Jed Perl writes, "Western Connecticut was a refuge for all sorts of dissident Surrealists and ex-Surrealists." Cowley and Josephson, those veterans of the Parisian Dada campaigns and friends of Louis Aragon's, Breton's sometime coconspirator and sometime adversary, felt at home in their company.

A major artist and pioneering first-generation Abstract Expressionist of Surrealist tendencies lived in Sherman, a bit over two miles from Church Road, in the person of the Armenian American painter Arshile Gorky. A survivor of the Armenian genocide as a young boy and a tragic and tormented figure, Gorky was the polar opposite of the sunny Calder. He was a friend of Breton's, who became his chief promoter after Gorky's triumphant show at the Julien Levy Gallery in New York in 1945. He moved with his young family to Sherman, where they took up residence at the Modernist house of the architect Henry Hebbeln and his wife, Jean. The remodeled nineteenth-century structure featured one whole two-story wall of glass that looked out on the verdant Connecticut landscape. A converted barn on the property served as Gorky's studio.

Cowley had first met Gorky in 1942 or so at a party at the Calders'; he recalled Gorky on this occasion "crooning folk songs." His impression of him was of a man of great responsiveness and depth. They saw each other in Sherman only occasionally, but Cowley liked and respected him a great deal.

Circumstances would test Gorky's capacity for tragedy to the limit. The final years of his life brought a series of escalating disasters. In January of 1946 the chimney in the barn where he worked caught fire suddenly. He called Cowley and Blume for help and they came quickly with Rob, but their attempts to douse the flames and rescue some of the artworks were unsuccessful. The local volunteer fire department in Sherman arrived too late. The barn and its contents—many drawings, at least twenty paintings, art books, canvases, and flammable tubes of paint and cans of turpentine that fed the flames—were destroyed in the conflagration. Rob Cowley would vividly recall Gorky "on the ground weeping and banging his head, bang, bang, bang, bang." "All my work is in there! My life's work is burning," he wailed inconsolably.

Gorky would recover his artistic momentum and produce some of his most powerful work over the next couple of years; the paintings he titled *Charred Beloved* alluded to this disaster. But two months later he would be admitted to Mount Sinai Hospital and operated on for intestinal cancer. As a result he had to wear a colostomy bag and experience considerable discomfort and bodily humiliation for the rest of his life. Two years later, on June 24, 1948, Gorky fractured his collarbone and two neck vertebrae in a car accident while being driven home by his gallerist Julien Levy. He was forced to wear a metal-and-leather brace that immobilized his painting arm and made him fear he might never paint with it again. During this period his young wife, Agnes, some years his junior, had begun an affair with the rival Chilean painter Roberto Matta, and in July she took their two young children and flew back to her family's farm in Virginia, abandoning Gorky to almost bottomless despondency.

What happened next was Gothic, and Cowley would describe it in a detailed letter to Ernest Hemingway. In response to an alarmed visit from a friend of Gorky's, who earlier in the day had said to him, "My life is over. I'm not going to live anymore," Peter and Ebie Blume had driven to Hebbeln House to check on him. Shortly after, Malcolm and Muriel arrived on the same mission after another worried phone call. Blume and Cowley searched the house and grounds but found no sign of Gorky. They did discover lengths of rope on the ground by a woodshed and another rope hanging from an apple tree. Blume and Cowley walked half a mile through the woods to a beautiful gorge that had been one of Gorky's favorite spots, but they still did not find him. On the way back, Gorky's dog barked at them from a side road and they followed it to an old abandoned shed, where they found Gorky's body hanging from a rafter. In Cowley's words, "I hadn't expected him to be so waxlike, with his neck stretched until his toes were only an inch from the ground and his eyes wide open and staring down at us contemptuously." Gorky had stepped up on an empty champagne case, removed his shoulder harness, tied the noose around his neck to the rafter, and kicked the case aside. Over by the wall was another case on which, Cowley remembered, Gorky had written the words "Goodbye all my loved." They called the state police.

In Cowley's letter he lays a certain amount of blame on Gorky's beautiful young runaway wife, Agnes, whom he felt Gorky intended to make feel guilty, but he admits that even if he and Blume had managed to stop him in time, Gorky would have killed himself later on. Cowley brooded on this tragedy for a couple of weeks until "at last I don't pity Gorky or condemn Agnes or feel that Gorky's death was anything but a formal spectacle, like a bullfight." These words don't really have the ring of truth; such a ghastly discovery is not so easily expunged.

It may seem a bit odd that Malcolm Cowley would have taken the time to write such a long and detailed account of Gorky's demise to Ernest Hemingway, who would have known nothing of him or his work. At the time, however, Cowley was at work on a journalistic profile of Hemingway for *Life* magazine, and he may have had an impulse to impress his subject with an unflinching, hard-boiled account of an incident he'd been personally involved in. He'd undertaken this assignment for financial reasons: By this time the five-year Mellon grant that had supplied most of his income was almost expired and he had to look about for new sources of support. The immediate financial issue pressing in on Cowley was the need to earn enough money to cover the tuition fees to send his son, Rob, to Phillips Exeter. *Life* paid a $2,500 fee (something like $33,000 in current dollars) plus expenses, enough to substantially underwrite the costs of the school.

At the time, Cowley and Hemingway had entered an era of good feelings. Hemingway had praised Cowley in a letter as "the critic who best understands my work." And he would not have been unaware of the likely multiplier effect of a profile in *Life* on his fame and sales.

He agreed to cooperate with Cowley on the profile. For a while the warm and generous Hemingway was on display. With a plane ticket from *Life*, Cowley, Muriel, and young Rob flew down to Havana in March of 1948 to spend two weeks with Hemingway, now a full-time resident of his legendary compound Finca La Vigía there. He arranged for the Cowleys to stay in the same suite of rooms at the Hotel Ambos Mundos where he had begun his novel *For Whom the Bell Tolls*, so Cowley could get a tactile feel for its place of composition. One day he took the Cowley family out on his fishing boat the *Pilar*. The seas were very high that day, and both Rob and Muriel had to retreat to the cabin from seasickness. Hemingway and Cowley each caught one barracuda on the trip.

Cowley went about his interviewing of Hemingway and his associates with great diligence, and it occasioned no little friction. He admits to Hemingway as being in a state of confusion about his wounds in Italy from a mortar shell that exploded near him in June 1918 on the Piave. Cowley was the first of many scholars and biographers who have tried and failed to disentangle the facts of his wounding and putatively heroic actions that day from Hemingway's subsequent fabulation and his variations on those events in some of his best stories. Cowley put considerably more detail about it all in his profile than the terse description of the event that Hemingway wanted.

Hemingway was also nervous about Cowley's handling of his activities as a combatant in the war. Nominally an accredited correspondent for *Collier's*, he had attached himself to the Twenty-Second Regiment of the Third Army, under the command of General Buck Lanham, who would become a close friend. Under the Geneva Conventions, war correspondents were forbidden to carry arms and were required to wear an identifying insignia on their jackets. Hemingway carried rifles and pistols, and used them on numerous occasions in battle while leading his own band of French irregulars. The other correspondents had registered an official complaint about this, feeling that this behavior put them in danger of German reprisals if captured. Hemingway was forced to testify to an inspector general in a hearing at Rambouillet about these activities and only avoided being sent back to the States by perjuring himself—he denied everything. The matter was touchy, and Hemingway did not want it aired in the pages of *Life*.

A strain of passive-aggressive ambivalence runs through Hemingway's letters to Cowley concerning the profile, before and after its publication. In the same letter he could be candid and open about his private and inner life, helpfully direct Cowley to old friends and associates who were eyewitnesses to key events, and then become harshly minatory about areas of inquiry that are off-limits. He boasts about the sex he had with every woman he ever desired and many he did not, and confesses to temporary bouts of impotence brought on by head trauma. He testifies to the shattering psychic effect that exploding mortar shell had on him, admitting, "In the first war, I now see, I was hurt very badly; in the body, mind and spirit and also morally."

Caught between these strictures and the desires of his editor at *Life* for as much fresh detail about the private Hemingway as possible, Cowley was in a difficult position. Hemingway had put a great deal of trust in him, but in his role, this time, as not simply a critic but a professional journalist, he was required to deliver on the real-world, non-literary facts as he had discovered them. These tensions were never really resolved.

"A Portrait of Mister Papa" appeared in the January 10, 1949, issue of *Life*. It begins with a teaser for the big novel of World War II that Hemingway told people he was working on, Cowley promising that, much as he had accomplished for World War I with *A Farewell to Arms*, "when the smoke has cleared, it will be found that Hemingway, now grizzled and paternal, has written the best novel of this war, too." Time would reveal that he'd done nothing of the sort, but this was what the readers of *Life* and its editors wanted to hear. To support this assertion, Cowley goes into considerable detail about Hemingway's exploits in the waters off Cuba and the battlefields of Europe. The piece segues then into a carefully researched biographical treatment of Hemingway's life and career, from his childhood in Oak Park and Upper Michigan, the beginning of his career in the Paris of the twenties, his four marriages, his working habits, and all the rest, not neglecting his drinking habits and prowess at hunting, fishing, and boxing. All of this might seem a bit stale and overfamiliar to a present-day reader, but at the time, much of it was fresh news. While this piece lacks the sense of discovery of Cowley's Max Perkins profile, it is an honest piece of work.

Life seems to have felt they got their money's worth. Robert Coughlan, his editor, told Cowley that many people felt it was one of the best things ever written about Hemingway, and he tried hard to get him to take more such assignments. The piece moved the editor Harold Strauss of Knopf to suggest that he undertake a full-scale biography of his subject, a notion he seriously entertained but then dropped.

The problem was that Ernest Hemingway disliked the profile. He loathed the selections of photos (including a gallery of his three ex-wives and his current one) and the mildly insipid captions, neither of which were under Cowley's control, and in subsequent letters laid down a drumbeat of complaint. He accused Cowley of a breach of security because he had revealed that the *Pilar* had been carrying high explosives without the Cuban government being so informed. The details of the war correspondent inquest displeased him. A stinging letter from Mary Hemingway arrived, telling Cowley that parts of the profile were absolutely mistaken and questioning whether he really knew enough about her husband as a man to write a biography of him. One passage that seems to have particularly irked Hemingway was one that questioned his football skills and portrayed him as "sometimes the butt of jokes," a lonely boy who had problems getting a date for dances. There was nitpicking on smaller matters, symptoms of a greater discontent.

To other friends, Hemingway was more bluntly critical of Cowley's profile. In 1954, he asked his Boswell and professional celebrity whisperer A. E. Hotchner, "Did you read his piece? Sure is a lot of difference between *Life* and life. . . . I don't think Cowley or Lillian [Ross] know anything about whatever material people like me are made of. All the time I was reading Cowley's piece I felt like I was being formed into his image." He goes on to complain that the piece has him carrying a canteen of gin on one hip and a canteen of vermouth, about which the expert martini mixer snorts, "Can you imagine me wasting a whole canteen on vermouth?"

For all these complaints, the epistolary friendship between Cowley and Hemingway continued until 1952. The letters between the two men are often warm and chatty and on occasion quite intimate and revealing. In 1945, a full-time resident in remote Cuba, he had complained to Cowley, "The trouble is that it is awfully dull not to have anybody you can talk [to] about writing." Cowley became that perfect somebody, an expert judge of literature, a sympathetic ear, and a conduit for news from a literary world he needed to hear about. Hemingway was also a highly competitive man who held grudges, and the letters were an outlet for him to blow off steam, in a fashion that could be funny or vicious or both. He lampoons Thomas Wolfe, by this point ten years dead, as "the overblown Little Abner of literature." In what we would today call concern-troll fashion, he condescends to his putative friend F. Scott Fitzgerald as a writer and a man. Edmund Wilson comes in for repeated vituperation for an essay he'd written on Hemingway, who compares him to a shit-eating Gila monster.

Hemingway felt real fear at the thought of a biography of him during his lifetime. He referred to biographers as carrion eaters, buzzards, and premature grave robbers. Cowley's profile had served as a signal for scholars looking to undertake works with a biographical slant. Both Carlos Baker, his eventual official biographer, at Princeton and Charles Fenton at Yale contacted Hemingway about studies they were engaged in; their books were eventually published, but not before much wrangling over how much biographical material they would contain.

The most tangled and protracted of these affairs concerned a dissertation looking to become a book written by Philip Young of New York University. Cowley, who was asked his opinion of the work by an editor at Rinehart, made the mistake of not just involving himself in the matter but telling Hemingway about it. He thought the book had some merit, but Young had taken the so-called wound theory of Hemingway's work way too far, identifying the author and his fictional surrogates all too mechanically. Hemingway, from what he heard of the book from Cowley, felt reduced to a symptom and labeled a neurotic and a basket case. The whole business devolved into a drawn-out and tiresome four-corner dispute among Young, Cowley, the Rinehart editor, and an increasingly agitated and aggrieved Hemingway. Finally an exasperated Cowley threw up his hands and declared to Hemingway, "I really and truly want to get shut of the business completely . . . This is my last will and testament on this subject signed malcolm cowley so help me god amen."

Young's book was eventually published, with Hemingway's grudging permission to quote from his work, but the damage to his friendship with Cowley had been done. Too much of his antagonism toward snoopy biographers and psychoanalytically inclined critics had spilled in Cowley's direction and their relationship sagged under the strain. There was not any one definitive moment of rupture, but their correspondence petered out to a final Christmas card from Finca La Vigía in 1952.

Malcolm Cowley never faltered in his loyalty to Hemingway and in his critical support of Hemingway's work to the end of his life, standing almost alone in finding some virtues in his badly flawed and widely regretted novel *Across the River and Into the Trees* and calling his late masterpiece *The Old Man and the Sea* "as nearly faultless as any short novel of our times." He offered much useful advice to Hemingway's widow on the proper way to proceed with the posthumous publication of his remaining work, and he would mount a vigorous defense of Hemingway's work and its permanent value against what he felt was a deplorable onslaught of critical revisionism. After Hemingway's death in 1961 he wrote to Conrad Aiken, "I mourn for Hemingway. He could be as mean as cat piss and as sweet as a ministering angel."

———

As Cowley's handsome payday from *Life* indicates, the postwar period was a very good time to be a literary intellectual. The employment opportunities had exploded, as what came to be called the knowledge industries expanded at a rate never before seen. A great deal of those opportunities were academic, thanks to the GI Bill and surging enrollments in higher education. A college degree, once restricted to members of the upper class and the brightest members of the middle and lower classes, would become a necessity for career advancement and upward mobility.

A college education required courses in composition and literature and other so-called liberal arts, and intellectuals who had previously scraped by suddenly found themselves in demand. The intelligentsia had been accustomed to looking down their noses at academics, but the chance of earning a steady paycheck for not overly demanding work proved a stronger attraction than any distaste for marking papers and discoursing before the as yet unlettered. With the right connections and a profile burnished by some success, a writer could become a university teacher without ever having earned a graduate degree. Thus Mary McCarthy (BA, Vassar, 1933) would teach at Sarah Lawrence and then Bard, and Phil Rahv, who never attended college, at Brandeis.

One of the most important developments in postwar American literature was the growth of degree-granting university programs in creative writing, and these proved especially congenial in providing employment to novelists, poets, and short-story writers. The idea that imaginative writing of the literary sort could actually be taught was a new one; novelists had been expected to gather the raw material for their work out in the great wide world, preferably in the school of hard knocks or at least as a witness to events high and low as journalists— as Hemingway, Stephen Crane, Mark Twain, and many other notables once had. American writing, however, had been undergoing a slow but steady process of professionalization and credentialization, and a host of academic critics had, or so they claimed, unearthed the formal techniques through which literature achieved its effects.

These techniques having been discovered, logically they could be recapitulated by other writers, in much the same way the techniques of music and painting had long been taught. The first formal academic writing program was the Iowa Writers' Workshop, begun in 1936 by Wilbur Schramm and later taken over and made famous by Paul Engle. The idea took off after the war, not coincidentally with the increase in college enrollments. Those programs needed professional and at least somewhat plausibly credentialed writers as instructors, even if in private many writers would express skepticism that a classroom was the ideal place to become a novelist or poet.

Malcolm Cowley was well positioned to benefit from these

opportunities for employment. As he would write, "Being a literary historian is a rewarding but not a lucrative profession. After 1948 I supplemented my income by doing a great deal of knockabout teaching and lecturing at various universities." Elsewhere in a letter to Hemingway he makes mildly mocking reference to "the new Chautauqua circuit . . . lecturing at colleges and teaching at writers' conferences for marbles." But teach he did; he confessed to Lillian Hellman that "half the time I've been traveling round the country to writers' conferences." Cowley and many other intellectuals became modern versions of the medieval scholar gypsies, wandering from college town to college town.

He'd dipped his toe in academic waters in 1947 when he delivered two lectures over two days at Syracuse University. The first lecture, titled "Why Teach American Literature?," answered this question by asserting that "certain American books should be required reading in every American college" because, among other reasons, "a national literature . . . has the function of serving as a unifying element in the national culture." The second, titled "Some Notes for Postwar Writers," was a characteristic generational consideration of American literature in the twentieth century, specifically the signal successes of his own interwar cohort, the difficulties faced by the writers who came of age in the thirties, and the possible literary paths that new postwar writers were likely to blaze. Cowley's preoccupation with the formation of an American literary canon informs both lectures.

His first gig as a full-time visiting instructor was a rocky start. Invited in the fall of 1949 by Professor Robert Heilman to take up a ten-week post as a prestigious Walker–Ames Visiting Lecturer at the University of Washington, he was concerned enough by the likely prospect of anti-Communist opposition to his appointment to write him a long just-in-case account of his political activities in the thirties.

That opposition arrived, as his appointment, the United Press reported, "caused a storm of protests from the university's board of regents, a state senator, parent-teacher groups, and some officials of veterans' groups." One especially energetic regent managed somehow to find some putatively "dirty" lines in Cowley's poetry and circulated them to various organizations; he even tried to enlist the nonexistent chapter of the Sherman American Legion to his side. Cowley had the full support of the university's president, though, and he saw it through.

This episode had a quick and unfortunate sequel a year later when he was invited to take over Robert Penn Warren's classes for the winter of 1951 at the University of Minnesota. He had the backing of the English Department, but the president of the university was running scared from the state legislature, so he blocked the appointment. In a letter to Samuel Monk, the English professor with the sorry task of conveying this news, Cowley framed what had happened to him as a blow to academic freedom and a symptom of the "real catastrophe . . . the self-defeat and fragmentation of the liberals," whom he believed were "being picked off one by one." He offered no solution to this crisis of demoralization, however, beyond a vague suggestion: "We have to re-establish the community of minds." He feared the consequences of poking his head out of the political foxhole he'd had to dig.

As with many fevers, the real cure was simply time. The wave of rabid anti-Communist paranoia would gradually abate. This was the last time one of Cowley's academic sojourns occasioned any controversy. Over the next decades he would teach writing and American literature as a visiting writer or lecturer at Cornell, Yale, Berkeley, Michigan, Hollins, and the University of Warwick in Great Britain. He would even end up teaching at the University of Minnesota in 1971, this time without incident. His most consequential appointment would take place when he taught multiple times at the famed Stanford Creative Writing Program to a small galaxy of soon-to-be-famous writers.

Cowley could grouse in private about the longueurs and indignities of teaching and the pettiness and peculiarities of the academic milieu. ("I am sick of teaching. I am sick of teaching. I am sick of teaching," Vladimir Nabokov wrote to Edmund Wilson, driven to plain speaking by his professorial duties.) By 1957, Cowley had logged enough classroom time to advise Kay Boyle sagely, "Have your students talk as much as possible, thus taking the burden off your shoulders." But he took the work seriously and gave excellent value to his literature and writing students; he would mentor many of them and a few would end up being published by him. Evidence of that seriousness can be found in his 1957 Hopwood Lecture, "How Writing Might Be Taught." The essay is at once a pocket history of the teaching of creative writing in an academic setting, a critique of what such courses can and cannot accomplish for aspiring writers, and a detailed practical proposal for a creative writing curriculum that emphasizes craft over art and the practical realities of the writing profession over arty (and often misleading) inspiration.

Opportunities for employment in the print industries and well-paid journalistic assignments were also exploding in the postwar years. The late forties were flush times for the publishers of books, magazines, and newspapers, as the curve of mass literacy shot sharply upward. Millions of people in the service had acquired the habit of reading. The rapid growth of inexpensive mass-market paperbacks, available for purchase at tens of thousands of newsstands, drugstores, commuter hubs, and candy stores nationwide, made satisfying that habit convenient and affordable. And the titles on offer were not simply restricted to pulp and genre fiction; works of real literary merit and even the classics were also being reprinted and sold for a quarter, often with lurid cover art that either amped up or totally misrepresented their content. The income from reprint sales helped to subsidize the hardcover publishers, in a virtuous circle. Then, with the creation at Doubleday of so-called egghead paperbacks in Anchor Books in 1953 by the publishing visionary Jason Epstein, works of considerable literary and intellectual interest would be skillfully commodified through attractive packaging and pricing and made available to the expanding college adoption market and at bookstores nationwide. Other houses took note and created their own similar lines of paperbacks, such as Knopf's Vintage and Viking's Compass editions.

Suddenly the riches of Western and world culture were being released from moribund backlists and dusty library shelves and put on prominent, affordable display. As a result the skills of literary intellectuals were in demand to edit anthologies, introduce new editions of the classics, and serve as editorial advisers to publishers looking to profit from this flourishing new market. Malcolm Cowley availed himself of this demand for his services to the fullest. In the decades after the war he would edit or coedit, among other anthologies, the Viking *Portable Faulkner* and later the *Portable Hawthorne* (1948), *Great Tales of the Deep South* (1955), and *The Lesson of the Masters* (1971); and introduce editions of *The Ordeal of Mark Twain* by Van Wyck Brooks (1955), *Madame Bovary* (1959), *Miss Lonelyhearts* (1959), *Winesburg, Ohio* (1960), *Anna Karenina* (1960), and *Fontamara* by Ignazio Silone (1960). He also made a permanent contribution to the burgeoning Fitzgerald revival in editing for Scribner's in 1951 *The Stories of F. Scott Fitzgerald*; this still canonical collection unearthed several important stories that had pretty much gone missing since their original magazine publications, and Cowley's introduction, subsequently titled "The Romance of Money," is one of the best things ever written on Fitzgerald. Cowley also edited for Scribner's in 1951 a new edition of Fitzgerald's 1934 novel *Tender Is the Night*, which rearranged the sequence of events in the book to conform to the detailed instructions Fitzgerald had left.

In July of 1949, Harold Guinzburg wrote to Malcolm Cowley to offer him a position as an "Advisory Editor," "working a day and a half a week on Viking's affairs [for] a salary of $300 a month." Cowley had just finished his third Portable, on Hawthorne, for the house, and Viking was seeing an uptick in Portable sales to the growing college market. Cowley could offer expert advice on expanding the Portables list to feed this new demand and attract high-profile editors for new ones. The offer came at a convenient time: "the Mellon munificence," as he called it, was expiring, his plans for new books had stalled, and the tuition costs of sending his son, Rob, to Exeter and then to college were weighing on his mind. So, despite some private misgivings about leaving his perch as an independent literary observer, he accepted the offer. He would hold his job as an editorial consultant to the Viking Press almost until his death in 1989, by far the longest and on balance the happiest paid professional association of his life.

Viking had been started in 1925 by Harold Guinzburg and George Oppenheimer, two young publishing veterans, with fifty thousand dollars of capital from family money (nine hundred thousand dollars in current dollars). It was one of the Jewish-owned new firms, like Simon & Schuster, Alfred A. Knopf, the Modern Library, and Boni & Liveright, that shook up the previously WASP-dominated industry in the twenties with their adventurous editorial tastes and innovations in promotion and merchandising. The company got a boost in the year of its founding when it merged with the small but distinguished firm of Ben Huebsch, who brought along a backlist of titles by the likes of James Joyce, D. H. Lawrence, and Sherwood Anderson, among others. Huebsch became the editor in chief and his young assistant, the Harvard graduate and *Advocate* staffer Marshall Best, would become over time the managing director and an important editorial force. In

1938, Pascal Covici joined Viking as an editor after his firm Covici and Friede went under. He lured his friend and author John Steinbeck to the house, and the first book of his they published was *The Grapes of Wrath*—an auspicious start. He would later publish works by Arthur Miller, Shirley Jackson, and Saul Bellow, among many others.

Harold Guinzburg had become one of the true elder statesmen of the publishing industry; he was politically liberal in sentiment and a New Deal insider who served as one of FDR's unofficial media advisers. He did not have the high profile of such flamboyant publishing figures as Alfred A. Knopf and Bennett Cerf, but he was a behind-the-scenes actor of great energy and effectiveness for the causes he cared about. His values, both literary and political, aligned with those of Malcolm Cowley and informed everything that the Viking Press published.

Cowley had known Ben Huebsch from the League of American Writers. He respected Covici and had already dealt with Best on his three notable Viking Portables. He was a good fit. In hiring Malcolm Cowley as an adviser, Viking was adding considerable literary prestige to an already superb editorial team; in associating himself with Viking, Cowley was gaining a regular paycheck, albeit a modest one, and a seat at the publishing industry table.

For the next four decades, he would commute from Sherman to New York City once a week (when not away on a teaching gig) to attend editorial meetings and handle the numerous chores, large and small, of an office job. He served as a scout, an adviser, a reader, and an acquiring editor. His primary duty was to guide the progress of the Viking Portable Library, which he regarded as perhaps the best thing happening in contemporary publishing and whose audience constituted "the 18th century ideal of community of culture in which the average intelligent reader could share." On Tuesdays, he would come into the city for a Portables lunch at the Dogwood Room on East

Fifty-Eighth Street, and he, Best, and Pascal Covici would toss out ideas for new Portables over the corn bread he favored.

The in-house editing of the Portables was a collective activity. Cowley was particularly involved in the publication of *The Portable Walt Whitman* and *The Portable Emerson*, both edited by Mark Van Doren, as these writers were of intense interest to him. Since its beginning, the Viking Portable series has published more than 125 titles, and Cowley's influence and literary acumen can be felt in its excellence and the way the series became a perennial staple of humanities courses. This was one of the important ways that Malcolm Cowley's hidden editorial hand influenced postwar literary studies.

Cowley was also expected and encouraged to recommend and develop and acquire new books as they came to his attention or were submitted by literary agents. This task Cowley took seriously. In the year of his hiring he wrote to Alan Barth, a respected liberal columnist for *The Washington Post*, suggesting that he write a book about the effects of anti-Communist hysteria on freedom of thought and expression. That book was published by Viking as *The Loyalty of Free Men* in 1951. At the same time he wrote to W. H. Auden suggesting that he undertake a guide to the prosody of English poetry for students and poets, but Auden did not bite—a shame as the book would have been a classic. And in two instances Cowley acquired novels for Viking that changed American culture, as well as contributing immensely to the firm's bottom line.

Another novel by a writer of note that Cowley edited for Viking was *The Golden Spur by* Dawn Powell, published in 1962, her last novel and the only one singled out for a major literary award—a nomination for the National Book Award for Fiction. She and Cowley were old friends from their Greenwich Village days; Malcolm and Muriel would sometimes have her up to Sherman for birthday weekends, and he thought that Powell was the cleverest and wittiest writer in New York. *The Golden Spur,* one of Powell's expert satires on the human condition, New York literary subdivision, did not sell many copies as per her usual track record, but it did inspire a long and glowing critical essay by Edmund Wilson in *The New Yorker* that would be much referred to when her posthumous revival began in the nineties.

In time, Cowley found in the Viking Press a publisher as well as an employer. Of the thirteen books of his own he would publish in his lifetime, not including the anthologies, eleven would be published by Viking, if one includes the reissues and revisions of his first two books. He quickly became, to use an antique phrase, one of the great men of Viking, a multipronged asset to the house, respected, cherished, beloved by its employees.

The effect of this industrial-scale explosion in high culture that the writers and intellectuals were benefiting from was not simply quantitative, but qualitative. As Louis Menand puts it in *The Free World,* his cultural history of the Cold War, "Most striking was the nature of the audience: people cared. Ideas mattered. Painting mattered. Movies mattered. Poetry mattered. The way people judged and interpreted painting, movies, and poems mattered." It was a very good time to be a critic. As Randall Jarrell quipped, some people consulted their favorite critic about the conduct of their lives as they had once consulted their clergymen. Critics enjoyed prestige and sway over not just educated but even mass opinion. The flood of cultural production threatened to overwhelm its intended consumers, so they turned to what they felt were the authorities for guidance as to what to read and watch and listen to and what to think and say about it all.

Lionel Trilling's *The Liberal Imagination,* a collection of critical essays on literary and even popular topics—e.g., the *Kinsey Reports* and psychoanalysis—was a conspicuous example of why this period would become known as the Age of Criticism. Trilling wrote with a Jamesian style that was at once erudite and elusive. The book's preface deployed references to the work of Mill, Coleridge, Goethe, Words-worth, and others with the expectation that the reader would know what he was getting at. When *The Liberal Imagination* was published in 1950 it sold an astonishing seventy thousand copies in hardcover and eventually over a hundred thousand copies in its Anchor reprint edition.

The pioneering New American Library began its own line of Sig-net Classics and middle-highbrow nonfiction Mentor paperbacks, tag-lined "Good Reading for the Millions." Their editions became high school and college classroom staples for decades, up until the present day. NAL also published an uncompromising mass-market literary magazine called *New World Writing*, which featured a glittering list of international contributors in fourteen numbers from 1950 to 1961. It was name-checked by Frank O'Hara in his poem "The Day Lady Died," where he buys "an ugly *New World Writing* to see what the po-ets / in Ghana are doing these days." The back ad copy of Number 5 includes the come-on: "Avant Garde Means You! *Avant Garde* may sound stuffy—but it only means a reconnaissance party—adventurous people who willingly enter uncharted territory."

Intellectuals were in demand for other functions besides the USDA-style sorting and grading of cultural output. Menand calls the critic of the day a kind of public health inspector, serving as docent to the eager but still unsure mass audience consuming it. The world had assumed an ominous illegibility that frightened and confused ordi-nary Americans, so they turned to intellectuals for explanations and even moral guidance.

Far from fading away, the Age of the Crisis of Man had only gath-ered momentum in the intellectual class. The prestige that its mem-bers enjoyed depended on the perception that intellectuals saw things more clearly and penetrated into their meaning more deeply. In the postwar years it was largely an article of faith that they did.

No literary intellectuals proved more adept at trading on this prestige than the group of writers who came to be known as the New York intellectuals, and no magazine wielded more power and influence over this group and the people who paid heed to them than *Partisan Review*. Its centrality to the lives of the young and serious of this era is captured in Harvey Swados's bittersweet short story "Nights in the Gardens of Brooklyn." A combat veteran marking time as a census taker looks across a subway car on the sooty Seventh Avenue Local and notices a young woman "deep in *Partisan Review*. That was what first caught my eye, that and her legs." He takes a seat next to her and sees that she is reading something by the then highly regarded writer Isaac Rosenfeld. "What do you make of that Rosenfeld story," he croaks nervously. Certainly not much of a meet-cute icebreaker, but it works: The two end up getting married and raising a family amid the compromises of postwar American life.

The contents of the typical issue of *Partisan Review* bristled with aggressively argued essays, stern and sometimes brutally dismissive reviews, and fiction and poetry written with the tutelary gods of Mann, Kafka, Eliot, Joyce, Pound, and Yeats in mind. (*Kafka Was the Rage* was the way the critic Anatole Broyard titled his memoir of the period.) Dispatches from Europe included Jean-Paul Sartre on existentialism; Albert Camus on the myth of Sisyphus; London letters from George Orwell and Arthur Koestler; symposia on "The State of American Writing" and "Religion and the Intellectuals"; Hannah Arendt on the Nazi concentration camps; and Clement Greenberg laying down the iron laws of the development of modern painting. *Partisan Review* was so ahead of the curve that in December 1948, it ran an essay by Delmore Schwartz asking "Does Existentialism Still Exist?," years before most people had even heard of it.

Partisan Review did not just wear its anti-communism on its sleeve, it waved it as a banner and used it as a club against anyone it saw as an adversary. As early as the summer of 1946 it was taking *The New Republic* and *The Nation* and the short-lived liberal newspaper *P.M.* to task for being soft on communism and the Soviet threat in an editorial titled "The Liberal Fifth Column." "We have in our midst a powerfully vocal lobby willing to override all concerns of international democracy and decency in the interests of a foreign power." This is a sentence that would sit comfortably in the mouth of a HUAC congressman or a Hearst columnist. In a roundup review of little magazines in *The New Republic*, Cowley took sharp exception to the editorial's thesis and especially its heavy-handed style: "The mildest judgment one can pass on such writing is that it seems utterly out of place in a magazine distinguished by its interest in literary values." He was poking a very irritable bear.

The culture of the New York intellectuals was tribal and insular, with a ground note of gossipy spitefulness. They were cocktail party assassins, with an ability to dispatch an enemy with the right poisonous dismissal in the right ear. Their many published memoirs abound in backbiting, feuds, rivalries, long-simmered resentments, score-settling, betrayals, and generalized scorn for opponents. If Cowley had managed to camouflage or expunge his own fellow-traveling with half the skill of the former Trotskyists, he might have been able to join this contentious tribe as an elder statesman and living link to the heroic age of American literature, much as Edmund Wilson, a regular contributor to *Partisan Review*, had. But his enemies in that camp were grudge holders and would never have allowed that.

The result was subtle but real. Malcolm Cowley was not so much written out of literary history as insufficiently written in. He continued to write for a variety of important publications—among them *The New York Times*, *The Saturday Review*, the *New York Herald Tribune*, *New World Writing*, and the influential literary quarterlies *The Kenyon Review* and *The Sewanee Review*. He became an unofficial adviser to the editors of the lively new magazine *The Paris Review*, whose young editors were avid for any Lost Generation connection or lore. But the pages of the publications of the anti-Communist cultural left—*Partisan Review*, and also Irving Howe's *Dissent*, *The New Leader*, and *Commentary*—were closed to him, and if he was ever mentioned in their pages, it was disparagingly.

Malcolm Cowley was well aware that he had a target on his back. In 1967, nervously anticipating the reviews of *Think Back on Us*, a collection of his pieces from the thirties, he wrote to Kenneth Burke that he could "hear the *Partisan* knives on the whetstone." The inheritor of *Partisan Review*'s mantle of intellectual authority ever since its founding in 1963 was *The New York Review of Books*. Malcolm Cowley published several books in the seventies and eighties, some of them important and unique pieces of literary recollection and estimation and personal testimony; those books were widely and, by and large, favorably reviewed in a great many places, but not one of them in *The New York Review of Books*.

In part it was a matter of style. The cocksure and often ad hominem polemical style of the *Partisan Review* critics was entirely alien to Malcolm Cowley's approach. Cowley would sometimes go on the attack himself, but he aimed to correct rather than demolish. His approach as a critic was broadly Emersonian, humanistic, exploratory; he was not dogmatic and he did not come on, as so many of the *Partisan Review* crowd did, as a lawgiver. He carried his learning, which was considerable, lightly. It would never have occurred to Cowley to sort the creators of American literature into two categories, as Philip Rahv did in his famous essay on "Redskins and Palefaces." He knew too many writers too well to be so reductive.

Finally, Malcolm Cowley was a genuine man of the country, and the New York intellectuals were terminally urban. The closest they ever came to catching a trout was reading about it in "Big Two-Hearted

River." Cowley simply didn't fit in; he would recall late in life, "I am and always have been a country boy, a little uneasy in the company of urban intellectuals." This disparity was one of the reasons that Cowley found his true affinity group among the Southern literati Allen Tate, Caroline Gordon, John Crowe Ransom, and Robert Penn Warren, despite their conservative cultural politics.

Two twinned preoccupations of the literary minded in the postwar decade were the revived interest in the American writers of the twenties and the question of how their inheritors, the younger generation of writers, might respond to their achievement and what they might make of their own experience of war and the new conditions of American life. As early as 1947, *Life* magazine profiled a clutch of these relative newcomers, including Robert Lowell, Truman Capote, Gore Vidal, Jean Stafford, Calder Willingham, and Thomas Heggen. Little seemed to link them together as anything resembling a literary generation aside from a reaction against literary Naturalism and the proletarian emphases of the thirties and a fondness for Hawthorne and Kafka as models. A year later *Life* weighed in again with an editorial titled "Fiction in the U.S.: We Need a Novelist to Re-create American Values Instead of Wallowing in the Literary Slums." This scolding critique observed that our best writers were now focusing on the sordid and raffish and demoralizing aspects of American life, to the exclusion of its hardworking and reasonably happy citizenry. The piece captures the sense that the new generation of writers was not quite carrying its weight or up to the still ill-defined task that had been assigned to them.

Cowley was also dissatisfied with the direction American fiction was heading. The first target of his critical scrutiny was the novels by Americans who had participated in the war. By 1948 he would already have dozens of such novels to consider; the best and most successful of them were Norman Mailer's *The Naked and the Dead*, John Horne

Burns's *The Gallery*, James Michener's *Tales of the South Pacific*, and Thomas Heggen's *Mister Roberts*. Weighing their virtues as a group, Cowley granted that these authors had quickly mastered their literary craft, so that "on average they are better written than all but a few of the war novels produced in the 1920s." He also found that they conveyed a great many facts about the experience of Americans at war: the caste tensions between the officer class and enlisted men; their sexual frustrations and behaviors; their often lamentable attitude toward conquered people as occupation troops; and their feeling that the war, for all its happy military outcomes, had been a demoralizing experience.

Cowley's final verdict, though, was this: "The truth is that the books are more impressive as a group than they are as separate works of fiction." Using the works of his Lost Generation comperes as a logical, but perhaps also unfair yardstick, he finds these war novels to be "concerned with using and perfecting the discoveries already made by their predecessors"—specifically Dos Passos, Fitzgerald, Steinbeck, and, inescapably, Hemingway. Cowley makes a distinction between his wartime generation's rebelliousness and its search for new literary forms and styles to express its disgust and its aspirations alike, and what he characterizes as this new generation's "disillusionment" about "the general contrast between our ideals and our performance." This disillusionment, he argues, accounts for the novels' conservatism of literary technique, and their authors' inability to break through and forge a bold new tradition.

Over the next few years, Cowley would extend this negative judgment to the work of many of the postwar American novelists in a series of essays and reviews. In 1949, in the essay "New Tendencies in the Novel: Pure Fiction," he took the measure of recent novels by most of the writers mentioned in the *Life* feature, as well as Eudora Welty (*The Golden Apples*), Saul Bellow (*The Victim*), Shirley Jackson (*The*

Lottery), and Mary McCarthy (*The Oasis*). He found it easier to describe their books in the negative; they were neither idealistic nor experimental nor behavioristic nor socially minded, having very little to say about American society. Cowley amplified this critique in his essay "A Tidy Room in Bedlam: Notes on the 'New' Fiction." Adding the work of Paul Bowles, Frederick Buechner, and Caroline Gordon to his specimen jar, he finds the new fiction to be nonhistorical, nonintellectual, apolitical, temporally vague, aloof and ironic in affect and ambiguous in plot, and peopled with characters who have no real functional relationship with American life. As for the writing itself in these books, "the tone . . . is decorous, subdued, in the best of taste, with every sentence clear in itself." This is not meant as a compliment.

Cowley discovers the culprit behind this, to him, all too neat and tidy fiction in the growth and reach of higher education. He observes, "There has never been a time when so many practicing authors have been attached to the staffs of American universities." As students and then teachers, the new or newish writers had enjoyed full exposure to the canon of Western literature and the paradigm-shifting works of early modernism. The tool kit of fiction was fully opened for them; what was left was to apply those techniques to a given situation in an ever more refined fashion. This almost neoclassical purity and correctness, in Cowley's view, drained away all the robust, felt life and the spirit of adventure and discovery that inform the best fiction. "The result is that we are now reading novels by intellectuals, for intellectuals, about supposedly intellectual, or at least well-educated characters, in which not a single intelligent notion is expressed about the world in which we live." Cowley excludes from this quietly baleful verdict the works of the war novelists and such books as Nelson Algren's *The Man with the Golden Arm*, which won a National Book Award in 1950 with his support, and Ralph Ellison's *Invisible Man*, which won the same award in 1953.

At bottom, Cowley felt that it was the New Criticism and its sway over the college English departments and the sorts of fiction it valued and devalued and just plain ignored that was really to blame for this state of affairs. He admitted that the practice of close reading and analysis of poems and stories and novels that was the New Criticism's core practice strongly resembled the French explication de texte method that he'd had "a brain-and-bellyful of" at the University of Montpelier. As a relatively new teacher himself, he'd found that close textual reading beat the historical background method he'd first tried out in terms of classroom efficacy. The art of close reading was the first and best lesson he could impart to his students. For this he offers due praise.

The problems for Cowley arose outside of the classroom. The New Criticism privileged the literary qualities of irony and ambiguity and was ever in search of symbols and mythic patterns in texts. As Gore Vidal put it with witty malice, "They go about dismantling the text with the same rapture that their simpler brothers experience while taking apart combustion engines." Its canon was severely limited to the duly anointed Modernists whose works were, in a word, teachable. But literature is vast and includes countless works of real value and even greatness that are not suited to this kind of dissection. A method that might work in analyzing a verse by a metaphysical poet would be far less useful applied to long novels.

Meanwhile, their brightest students, the ones most likely to become writers themselves, were being taught that the value of a poem or a work of fiction required the same things that they'd been taught to unearth in the classroom. As Cowley states in a symposium, "It may terrify them; it may stop them from writing at all, or, if they do write, it may cause them to write according to the formulae advanced by whatever New Critic is teaching that year at Princeton or wherever it may be." He felt that American writing faced the danger of becoming a kind of closed circle, with critically trained writers—and critic-writers, of which there were many—producing ultrarefined and airless work for other such people.

With a postwar vogue for the Lost Generation writers now in full flood, and with a receptive new employer publisher handy, Cowley saw the opportunity for a redemptive do-over. He seized the moment and suggested to Viking that it reissue his one full-length prose work, *Exile's Return*. The core of the book, its generational thesis, was still sound, and its firsthand, autobiographical acts of witness were more valuable than ever. As he noted in a letter to Marshall Best, "The book has a sort of subterranean public in the universities and outside of them." Rare-book dealers reported a steady demand for copies and sold the ones they could find at a hefty price, whereas the copies in college libraries were invariably falling apart and needed to be rebound and mended with Scotch tape. The most important revisions he was contemplating were a new introduction setting the book in historical context, and a new final chapter to replace the badly time-bound political one. Other important changes included more material on Hart Crane to balance the Harry Crosby chapter, which was itself revised to cohere more clearly with the rest of the book; a mention of the Sacco and Vanzetti case; the complete text of Cowley's mock-heroic ode to the demise of *Secession*; and a full account of his Parisian visit to Ezra Pound.

These changes made *Exile's Return* a sturdier and sleeker vehicle. The excisions not simply of the final to-the-barricades chapter, but of a fair number of political opinions and asides that had dotted the original text, depoliticized the book, which improved it as a work of literary witness to an essentially apolitical era, and also lessened opportunities for Cowley's adversaries to take potshots at it. Carefully scrubbed clean by its author and reconditioned like a vintage sports car that had been kept in the garage for years, it emerged finally as what it should have been recognized as, faults and all, in 1934: an essential book. It has been continuously in print, first in hardcover and then in various paperback editions, since the Viking republication in 1951, an indispensable first stop for students and general readers seeking to understand how a fabled generation of American writers in our history was formed and what they achieved.

Exile's Return's republication was enthusiastically received. It caught the Fitzgerald revival, coinciding with the Cowley-assembled *The Stories of F. Scott Fitzgerald* and his reedited edition of *Tender Is the Night*, thereby giving editors and reviewers the trend they needed. Arthur Mizener, Fitzgerald's first biographer, in the *Times Book Review* called it "far and away the best book about [the Lost Generation] by a participant, and this was a generation that was crucial not only for American literature but for the whole of American culture in the twentieth century. . . . *Exile's Return* was a good book about this generation in 1934. It is a better book now . . . because like all genuine books, it has improved with age." Perry Miller, one of the founders of American Studies, wrote in *The Nation* that "Malcolm Cowley should be proud that his historico-biographical narrative of the 1920s, published in 1934, can impress us, after only minor revisions, as an even more substantial account than it at first seemed."

———

Even as Cowley had been taking the measure of the new postwar American writing in his essays and reviews, he was also, more than ever before, examining the whole system within which those writers began and conducted their careers and found an audience or not. In the autumn of 1952 he edited an issue of *Perspectives USA*, a literary quarterly published by James Laughlin of New Directions and funded by the

Ford Foundation. Part of a far wider effort in cultural propaganda that one historian has termed "the Cold War modernist project," the magazine was published in English, French, German, and Italian editions and was intended for a European readership in order to "represent the best American writing and thinking on the highest level" and "promote peace by increasing respect for America's non-materialistic achievements among intellectuals abroad." Cowley's opening editorial on the state of American literature asserted that, while the level of American critical writing was high and literary scholarship flourishing, "fiction and poetry seem to be standing still." The best circumstance he could hope for to get things moving again was for a writer of Hemingway's or Faulkner's talent and stature to appear and energize "another great period in American writing." But this was a hope, not a prediction.

Cowley's brief editorial spurred his desire to have his say on contemporary literary matters at greater length and in franker fashion. In August of 1953 he proposed to Viking that he "do a short (50,000–60,000 word) book called *The Literary Situation*, based on articles I have written in the past two or three years. . . . The book would be a survey of the profession of writing in America, from the standpoint of a writer speaking to fellow writers and readers and students of writing. The tone would be popular—for me—and often provocative." The book he proposed and outlined was published by Viking on October 25 of the following year under that title.

The Literary Situation was an ambitious tour d'horizon of the state of American writing and writers, a hybrid work that can best be described as a work of literary sociology. In his foreword Cowley claims that the book is not a collection of his previously published essays, but in fact it often reads as just that, and as a result it is generally stronger in some of its constituent parts than as a unified work. He draws blood in his chapter on the New Criticism, in which he notes the narrow range of works to which these critics apply their method and their abandonment of the critical functions of discovering new works and assessing the value of other works of less than formal—i.e., teachable—perfection. *The Literary Situation* also reveals once more how little sympathy Cowley felt for the work of postwar American writers.

Cowley does provide readings of two of the most important American novels of the fifties, Ralph Ellison's *Invisible Man* and Saul Bellow's *The Adventures of Augie March*, that do justice to their unique strengths while missing their portents for the future of American fiction. These books provided the early models for a new kind of American fiction, picaresque bildungsromans in which the narrator-hero or antihero engages in strenuous self-making in an often absurd or threatening world. Cowley's term for this kind of book, "personalism," falls considerably short. His Lost Generation lenses were actually blinders, preventing him from seeing beneath the surface of some of the best contemporary writing to recognize the development of some things that were fresh and valuable and built to last. Vidal, in a pseudonymous essay in *New World Writing*, tartly observed, "the men of the 1920s are loyal to their time if not to one another: everyone was a genius then, and liquor was cheap abroad . . . For the Cowleys, the novel stopped at *Gatsby*."

The Literary Situation received the respectful and widespread reviews that Viking and Cowley expected, but it was not a commercial success. He was writing against the grain of the literary moment, with a tone of sociological interest, but no real passion, pro or con. "All I've done is make enemies," he lamented to Conrad Aiken.

———

In broad terms, there are two different economies operating in the literary world. One is the usual monetary economy: the ways that writers actually make a living and provide for the necessities of life. Malcolm Cowley's interest in the ways that writers make a living was not simply personal or confined to his own circle of friends. He'd made a considerable study of the matter to write his essay "How Writers Lived" for *Literary History of the United States* in 1948. In its first paragraph he observes, "By the 1940s, a host of serious writers, with the aid of publishers, foundations, universities, and the government, had learned how to make writing a profession, how to make a living at it, and how to get themselves read." Except for those fortunate few—Cowley estimates their number at about two hundred—who could live and even prosper on the royalties from their books, most writers had to get by on "an irregular series of little windfalls": a story sold to a magazine, a literary prize with check attached or a fellowship, a permissions check, a residence at an endowed center for creative work, a paid lecture, a teaching gig at a college or writers' conference, and eventually, they hoped, an advance of some size from a publisher.

These sources of income, Cowley asserted, were made possible by two larger trends in the literary world: "institutionalization and collectivization." The institutionalization had begun in the thirties with the creation of the Federal Writers' Project, which gave paying work to hundreds of literary toilers of all description. Congress had shut it down, though, for political reasons, and into the vacuum had moved the colleges and universities, which hired once-unaffiliated writers to teach creative writing and literature, and the Carnegie and Ford and Mellon and Rockefeller Foundations, et al., that channeled a portion of the surplus resources of capitalism into a variety of grants and subventions for cultural institutions. By collectivization, Cowley meant the organs of the mass media: the broadcast networks, the magazine corporations like Time Life, and the Hollywood studios, who all paid writers, sometimes very well, for their work, but who then owned that work and submitted it to a kind of industrial process, "a vast collective enterprise" completely indifferent to the intentions of the original creator, that resulted in film, a radio or television program, or a magazine on a newsstand.

The point is, in the modern world the sole autonomous creator, "the one man alone in his room with his conscience and a stock of blank paper," in practical terms actually has to live in a complex and highly interconnected environment—what the literary scholar Mark McGurl calls "the social-professional and patronage networks of fiction and poetry." And that brings up the second literary economy, which one might call the prestige economy. The reach and the importance of the prestige economy can be seen in the evolution of that humble artifact, authors' biographies on dust jackets. At one time such squibs were focused on the range of life experiences that the (male) author had amassed, often blue-collar and occasionally dangerous pursuits—brakeman, merchant marine, assembly line worker, platoon leader, short-order cook, ambulance driver, fishing guide, etc. The idea was that the writer had seen plenty of the rougher side of life and was going to share the facts about it with the reader. Over time, though, as the writing profession has become populated almost exclusively by ever more credentialed college graduates, these biographies have become far more focused on information that signifies specifically literary achievement and advancement—undergraduate and graduate degrees, prizes, fellowships, grants, residencies, publication in the "right" places.

Those associations and emoluments don't just happen. Often the writer has to apply for them, but just as often someone has to recommend that the writer be awarded them. Many hundreds of times over the course of his long lifetime Malcolm Cowley was that someone. His biographer Hans Bak uses the descriptive term a "'middleman' of letters," which conveys the way he managed to place himself with strategic adeptness between solo literary actors and the institutions that could benefit them. Cowley was the man to see for a variety of purposes, from job tips to career advice to a timely and persuasive letter. One could say that he functioned as a literary bureaucrat. He belonged to and served on the board of a number of institutions that enjoyed considerable influence over the incomes and careers of writers. By the fifties, Malcolm Cowley was thriving within a complex ecosystem of private foundations, prize-bestowing organizations, for-profit publishing companies, and academic institutions. He was someone almost any writer would want on his or her side.

One of the institutions Cowley had powerful sway with for half a century was the legendary and eccentric writers' colony in Saratoga Springs, Yaddo. The millionaire nineteenth-century financier Spencer Trask and his aristocratic and cultured wife, Katrina, had arranged for their Victorian-era mansion and its four-hundred-acre grounds to be devoted after their deaths to "a permanent home to which shall come from time to time for Rest & Refreshment authors painters sculptors musicians and other men & women few in number and chosen for their Creative Gifts & besides and not less for the power & the will & the purpose to make these gifts useful to the world." Amazingly, Yaddo has succeeded in realizing this impractical notion for a century.

This was largely owing to the leadership of one woman, Elizabeth Ames, a war widow who was named the first executive director in 1924. A combination hostess, booking agent, housemother, concierge, confidante, social psychologist, and headmistress, she ran Yaddo with a facade of genteel manners that hid the steely will and near-genius level of improvisation required to minister to the demanding egos and trip-wired creative temperaments of thousands of "guests" who came there to work and, on many occasions, frolic during her forty-five-year tenure. By her decree the hours between breakfast and four p.m. were sacrosanct and devoted to solitary creative work above all, with no socializing permitted. After that, the guests were generously fed at a joint formal dinner in the spacious dining room and then set about mingling.

One of Elizabeth Ames's first and shrewdest actions before Yaddo formally opened for business in 1926 was to establish a network of confidential advisers, including the social critic Lewis Mumford, the editor Alfred Kreymborg, and the literary power trio Carl, Mark, and Irita Van Doren, to suggest suitable guests. Irita Van Doren in 1928 suggested Malcolm Cowley, as "a young man for whom Yaddo would be perfect . . . poor as a church mouse with no visible means of support." As early as 1930 he had become one of Elizabeth Ames's circle of advisers, an arrangement that would be formalized when he became a board member of the Corporation of Yaddo in 1933, and he would serve on the board, sometimes as the president, until about 1980. He would become a yearly visitor to Yaddo as either a guest or a board member until the last years of his life. Over the decades, Cowley recommended many dozens of guests for residencies to Elizabeth Ames and endorsed the invitations of hundreds of others. John Cheever was the most famous of his recommendations.

Perhaps the most important service Malcolm Cowley performed for Yaddo was his involvement in 1949 in the infamous Lowell Affair, "an epic clash of literary titans" that could have been an extinction event for the institution. Robert Lowell, in residence and at the start of a spectacular manic episode, began a crusade against Elizabeth Ames for having turned Yaddo—or so he claimed—into a haven for Communist subversives. He recruited Elizabeth Hardwick, Flannery O'Connor, and others to his side and convened a stormy hearing to air his charges. Cowley attended that hearing and also a subsequent board meeting in New York where Ames was absolved. His behind-the-scenes advice and adroit ability to keep press coverage to a minimum kept the matter from ballooning into yet another destructive public outbreak of Cold War hysteria.

Of its counterparts in the world of grant-giving foundations, perhaps only the John Simon Guggenheim Memorial Foundation can match Yaddo for the luster of its name. Any writer lucky enough to have "gotten a Guggenheim" will automatically add that fact to his or her author's biography and back-matter acknowledgments. Yaddo and the Guggenheim Foundation are mirror institutions in many ways. Their institutional missions are aligned, although the Guggenheim Foundation spreads its largesse far more widely, to academic scholars in the humanities and the physical and social sciences as well as writers and artists. Both began in the mid-twenties, and they are alike as well in the origins of their endowments in the capitalism of the Gilded Age: The Guggenheims became one of the richest families on earth from their mining interests, chiefly silver and copper, in the American West.

The Guggenheim Foundation has always been at pains to keep their deliberations private, and over the years many theories emerged as to who was tugging the strings and pulling the levers. Delmore Schwartz believed that Malcolm Cowley was one of those people, writing to Allen Tate in 1939 that he "evidently has much to do with the choices in poetry" and asking Tate "to put in a good word for me." Schwartz, the fair-haired boy of the *Partisan Review* set and prone to paranoid thinking, worried that Cowley would be opposed to him on ideological grounds. Schwartz got his fellowship in 1940. He was not wrong about Cowley's influence with the foundation. (He also helped Schwartz win the Bollingen Prize for Poetry in 1959 over Robert Lowell.) From 1931 to 1984 he rendered his opinion on more than a hundred applications. On some occasions he would be asked to rank a batch of four or five supplicants from strongest to weakest; in other years he would write on behalf of individual grants, ranging from brief comments pro or con to page-long assessments.

Obviously, given his fifty-three years of advice rendered to them, the Guggenheim Foundation valued Cowley's services highly. A comparison of his recommendations against the list of people who actually succeeded in securing fellowships reveals an impressive batting average. Among the people he recommended who received grants were Horace Gregory in 1934; Isidor Schneider in 1936; his soon-to-be-adversary James T. Farrell in 1936 ("He has done a lot and will do more"); Elizabeth Hardwick in 1948; John Berryman in 1952, not for his poetry but for a critical biography of Shakespeare; Saul Bellow in 1955 ("To me he is the most interesting of the new novelists who have appeared in this country since World War II"); Wallace Stegner and the Whitman and Emerson scholar Gay Wilson Allen in 1959; John Cheever in 1960 for the book that would become *The Wapshot Scandal*; the critic Cleanth Brooks in 1960 for a critical study of the work of William Faulkner; Yvor Winters in 1961; his student Larry McMurtry and the novelist Ivan Gold in 1964; his student Peter Beagle in 1972; the critic Seymour Krim in 1976; the scholar of American literature Larzer Ziff in 1977; and Page Stegner, Wallace's son, in 1980. One major figure, though, who did not receive a Guggenheim was Malcolm Cowley. His application was turned down on, it seems, the grounds of his age.

Cowley also had a long association with the organization now known as the American Academy and Institute of Letters. The more exclusive Academy, limited to 50 members elected for life, and the Institute, which has had for much of its existence 250 members, were each chartered by acts of Congress at the turn of the twentieth century with the noble but vague mission of promoting "the interests of literature and the fine arts." In fact, neither serves any real function beyond preserving its own high stature and bestowing portions of it upon others. As Saul Steinberg, a member, pithily put it, "The Mafia. But *our* Mafia." It is as pure a manifestation of the prestige economy as exists in American cultural life, although some of the prizes do come with not insignificant amounts of money attached. Like Yaddo and the Guggenheim Foundation, the Academy and the Institute were endowed by a Gilded Age fortune, in this case Huntington railroad money that paid for their building and funds the prize money and administrative costs to this day.

The arc of Cowley's connections to the Academy and Institute nicely describes his ascent to the top of the literary heap. In 1946 he received an Arts and Letters Award in Literature, which came with a much-needed thousand-dollar check. In 1949 he was elected to the Institute. From 1956 to 1959 and then from 1962 to 1965 he served as the president of the Institute, a position that took up a considerable amount of his time and attention. From 1967 to 1976 he served as the chancellor of the Academy ("kind of an honorary vice president," as he described it), to which he had been elevated in 1964, endorsed by, among others, Marianne Moore. In 1981 he received the Academy and Institute's highest award, the Gold Medal for Belles Lettres and Criticism. Kenneth Burke, who'd received the same prize himself, was on the podium with him.

Cowley chaired many dozens of meetings over the decades and was a regular attendee and sometime speaker at the annual prize ceremony. He weighed in on the election of new members and the selection of prize awardees, wrote citations, gave speeches at luncheons memorializing such deceased members as John Dos Passos and Conrad Aiken, made efforts to inform the general public of its existence and history and importance in magazine articles, and was involved in giving grants from a revolving fund for writers and artists in need.

The preceding only scratches the surface of the instances of Malcolm Cowley's interventions in the great game of literary reputation and advancement. From a certain angle, this has the aroma of insider trading and coterie coziness. The world Cowley operated in was overwhelmingly white and male and upper middle class and it took care of its own. But within that, he was scrupulous in his actions and opinions, often moved by charitable impulses, and never acted in a way calculated to benefit himself financially or reputationally. If his particular loyalty to his literary generation and its luminaries shines through, there are worse vices.

What is clear is that Malcolm Cowley had an instinct for where the action was. In its July 1963 issue, *Esquire* created a stir with an article entitled "The Structure of the American Literary Establishment." The editors devised a fantastically detailed "chart of power," a color-coded diagram of hundreds of novelists, poets, critics, academics, agents, publishers, magazines large and "little," writing programs, book reviews, and the like, all organized around what was called "the Hot Center." The closer a person or institution was to the Hot Center, the more powerful or relevant they were meant to be. A great deal of tut-tutting took place over *Esquire*'s putative reduction of something as holy as literature to something as vulgar as mere status, but nobody ever said the chart was not accurate. Malcolm Cowley appears on it twice, in his capacity as an editor for Viking and also as a "Working Critic," both times very near the Hot Center. That was a surprise to no one.

THIRTEEN.

THE COUNTERCULTURE COWLEY

———

Another clear proof of Malcolm Cowey's heat-seeking abilities in that 1963 *Esquire* chart was the prominent presence there of two writers whose novels he would publish at Viking within five years of each other. These two books would alter the brain waves of millions of young Americans and light the fuse of the mass transformation of consciousness that would come to be known as the counterculture. Jack Kerouac appears in the chart five times, under the headings of Viking, as a client of his agent Sterling Lord, as a contributor to Donald Allen's anthology *The New American Poetry*, and twice as an avatar of "the Cool World." Ken Kesey appears twice, under Viking and Sterling Lord, and he should have been listed a third time, under the Stanford Creative Writing Program. He had not yet been deemed "Cool," but that was about to change, spectacularly. In discovering and editing their novels *On the Road* and *One Flew Over the Cuckoo's Nest* and bringing them to market, Cowley showed that even into his sixties his literary tastes were not simply relevant but eerily on target with a far younger literary audience.

As we've seen, Cowley could not summon much enthusiasm for most of the new American fiction of the late forties and early fifties. To him the new writers seemed like a crop of A-plus students determined to impress their elders, the New Critics. He wanted something more, something different, something fresher, nervier, more ambitious. Cowley was looking for a hero, someone like Hemingway or Faulkner, autonomous figures who answered only to themselves, who'd managed to alter the literary landscape and its future direction by genius and force of will. Jack Kerouac and his headlong and ecstatic and all-embracing and fearlessly *un*-self-conscious novel *On the Road* filled the bill, or at least came closer than anyone and anything else did. Cowley would go to extraordinary lengths to persuade his employer to take the book on.

———

No American novel of consequence had a more tortured progress toward publication, nor has been more encrusted by myth and misinformation, than *On the Road*. The one thing everybody knows, or thinks they know, about the book is that Jack Kerouac composed it in a days-long bout of frenzied nonstop typing, feeding a continuous scroll of paper into his typewriter to avoid breaking the flow of inspiration by having to insert a new page of conventional typing paper over and over. As the Kerouac textual scholar Isaac Gewirtz puts it, this is accurate but not true. It neglects the larger context of *On the Road*'s long gestation and its even longer struggle to reach print.

The accurate part is this: On April 2, 1951, Jack Kerouac sat down in his then-wife Joan Haverty's studio apartment in Manhattan to begin that grueling session to bang out the first full draft of *On the Road*. He had on hand several rolls of architectural drafting or tracing paper of just the right size for a Remington manual. The rolls had a rather grisly provenance: Kerouac had found them in the West Twenty-First Street loft apartment of the deceased Bill Cannastra, a hard-partying minor Beat figure who'd been decapitated the year before when he stuck his head out the window of a speeding subway train. In that loft Kerouac had first fed a roll into a typewriter and made the discovery: "It'll save me the trouble of putting in new paper, and it just about guarantees spontaneity."

For twenty straight days, fueled by coffee and pea soup provided by his wife, Kerouac typed so furiously at a 100-words-a-minute, 6,000-words-per-day rate that at the end of each day's session he would have to strip off his sweat-soaked T-shirts and drop them on the floor by his desk. By April 22 he had completed a 125,000-word draft of *On the Road*, the novel that would change his life and, to a certain extent, the world. The book's propulsive, comma-starved prose had been typed in an eye-straining single-spaced format with no paragraphs or page breaks and amazingly few typos. The scroll it was typed on would be 120 feet long. Kerouac had, without intending to, replicated the format of the books of antiquity, before the invention of the codex. When the object itself was displayed at Christie's in 2001 prior to being auctioned, one onlooker whispered reverently, "It's like the Dead Sea Scrolls."

As a prose transcription of his cross-country adventures with his Beat companions—"the mad ones, the ones who are mad to live, mad to talk, mad to be saved, desirous of everything at the same time"—Kerouac's composition of *On the Road* brilliantly married the method to the matter: He wrote it fast because the "road is fast." Elsewhere in his notebooks, he brags, "Meanwhile, On the Road is on the road, that is, moving." Movement and speed were of the essence. *On the Road* reads like a pilgrimage without a shrine at the end, an odyssey without an Ithaca. The journey really *was* the destination. While it was as impressive a feat of memory and cognition as it was of literary athleticism, all of the subsequent talk about Kerouac's "spontaneous bop prosody," a phrase coined by Allen Ginsberg, and the Zeninflected preaching about "first thought, best thought," obscures the fact that *On the Road* took years, not days, to write, and underwent a process of revision longer than its gestation.

The true part is this: On August 23, 1948, Kerouac wrote in his notebook, "I have another novel in mind—'On the Road'—which I'll keep thinking about: about two guys hitch-hiking to California in search of something they don't *really* find, and losing themselves on the road, and coming all the way back hopeful of something *else*." At the time, he was finishing the final chapters of his first novel, *The Town and the City*, an autobiographical work about the life of his French Canadian family in Lowell, Massachusetts, their eventual move to New York City, and the death of his father. It was written under the spell of Thomas Wolfe. And Kerouac seemed to be at the start of a promising, if conventional, literary career. The manuscript would be read by Columbia professor Mark Van Doren and recommended by him to Robert Giroux at Harcourt, Brace, a great editor who worked with T. S. Eliot and who would go on to publish Flannery O'Connor, Walker Percy, Thomas Merton, Robert Lowell, and Bernard Malamud, among many other notables. He signed up the book in early 1949 for an advance of one thousand dollars.

He and Kerouac enjoyed a close and warm working relationship. They spent months together editing and revising the novel, Kerouac occupying an empty office at Harcourt for weeks at a time, and Giroux, eight years his senior, treating his new author to steak dinners with company salesmen and swank cocktail parties and operas that required a rented tux. He'd even gone well beyond the usual editorial duties by traveling all the way out to Denver in July to experience hitchhiking Western-style with Kerouac and to meet some of the unconventional characters he'd been hearing about. Their bond was strengthened by the fact that Giroux was a cradle Catholic and half-French Canadian, which mattered greatly to Kerouac.

Giroux, also like Kerouac, had attended Columbia, though he'd graduated in 1936 while Jack had not. A standout athlete at Lowell High School, Kerouac had been recruited to play football at Columbia, but the school did not agree with him either athletically or academically. After dropping out in his sophomore year in 1942, he'd served for a few months as a merchant marine and then for a brief time in the Naval Reserve until being discharged for psychological reasons. Returning to New York, he began to associate with the colorful circle of people, mostly aspiring young writers but also petty thieves, drug addicts, and unclassifiable reprobates and wild men, who would in time become famous as the Beats and populate the pages of *On the Road* and subsequent novels by Kerouac. Their number included Allen Ginsberg, the slightly older Harvard graduate William S. Burroughs, Lucien Carr, Herbert Huncke, Hal Chase, John Clellon Holmes, and Bill Cannastra. It was Huncke, a heroin-addicted adept of the lower depths, who first introduced the group to the notion of being "beat," as in knocked down and defeated by the harsh conditions of life, and it was Kerouac who would apply the word to this nascent literary movement. Kerouac would subsequently expand this concept to encompass the idea of "beatific," asserting that the Beats were really on a religiously inspired kind of vision quest to break through to a higher plane of existence. They cultivated a bottom-dog kind of spirituality where the path to wisdom ran through abjection and suffering. As Kerouac, who may be better understood as a mystic and aspiring saint than merely as a writer, would later declare to his interviewer John Wingate on the television show *Night Beat*, "I am waiting for God to show me his face."

Cultural critics have expended a great deal of effort interpreting the Beat movement as a response to the grim postwar atmosphere created by the use of the atomic bomb, the discovery of the death camps, the advent of the Cold War, and similar affronts to optimism, and later a revolt against the regime of social conformity, and constant consumption demanded by the new economic order of prosperity. Kerouac claimed that he wasn't interested in politics, he was interested in life, but he also said, "I prophesy that the Beat Generation . . . is going to be the most sensitive generation in the history of America and therefore it can't help but do good." That was considerably later, though, when he was forced into the role of spokesman.

Did the Beats constitute anything like a movement? In the fifties the answer would be yes, as the mass media took notice of and often mocked the striking new instances of what was being called noncon-formism, which it conflated with another worrisome postwar phe-nomenon, juvenile delinquency. But it would be helpful to use our imagination to recapture them in the forties not as a movement, but rather as a bunch of guys, three of them future geniuses, with simpa-tico literary interests who liked one another's company and got off on their rash and aimless adventures together. It is true that they were seekers in their way and, some of them, tortured souls. But it is hard to picture the core group of Beat founding fathers considering them-selves as part of some even lightly organized program, literary or spir-itual. They were too various in their habits of mind and too short of impulse control for that.

Enter Neal Cassady, the charismatic sociopath and motormouthed car thief, con man, and cocksman, whose charm was exceeded only by his amorality. For once myth and reality meet on a level playing field in the person of this cowboy-like figure out of the American West, a Paul Bunyan or Davy Crockett, lean, muscular, wired, fearless, and reckless. Born in 1926, literally on the side of the road, Cassady had been barely raised by his hopelessly alcoholic barber father, growing up in flophouses and fleabag hotels and doing stints in reformatories in the Denver area. By his mid-teens he was reputed to have stolen hundreds of cars, and he could drive an automobile the way Chuck

Yeager flew a fighter jet, all the while unspooling an endless monologue on whatever subjects his perpetually firing neurons lighted on.
He was largely free of any formal education after the eighth grade, but
he'd spent many hours in Denver libraries reading aimlessly and pro-
miscuously, and he would drop names like Nietzsche, Proust, and
Schopenhauer into his onrushing spiel for effect, to gain some credi-
bility from the literary crowd he gravitated toward. Of all the unlikely
things, he wanted to be a writer.

Word of this character had reached the Morningside Heights
crowd by way of Hal Chase, the Denver native who'd passed around
some of his letters from reform school. He'd told Cassady about the
circle of young writer friends back east, and in 1946 he'd driven in a
stolen car to New York City with his near-child bride, LuAnne Hen-
derson, to make their acquaintance. Jack Kerouac finally met Neal
Cassady in December of that year in a cold-water flat in Spanish Harlem. Characteristically, Cassady answered the door in the nude. The
momentous meeting inaugurated a real-life literary friendship to rival
those of the fictional Natty Bumppo and Chingachgook, Ishmael and
Queequeg, Huck Finn and Jim. Kerouac would not only immortalize
Cassady as the folkloric Dean Moriarty, the hero and companion of
On the Road, he would find stylistic inspiration in his monologues
and, even more directly, in the freewheeling letters Cassady wrote.

Over the next five years Jack Kerouac would ping-pong back and
forth across the continent and south of the border to Mexico several
times by bus, train, hitchhiking, and car, usually with Neal Cassady at
the wheel, since he never procured a driver's license and didn't really
like driving himself. It was these trips that provided Kerouac with the
raw material of *On the Road*, and Neal Cassady, fearless to a fault, who
gave him the energy and artistic courage to realize his lyrical and ecstatic vision of American life. Kerouac and Ginsberg were supposed to
be Cassady's tutors in the literary arts, but it was really he who taught

them how to write their masterworks, *On the Road* and *Howl*, which rhapsodized him as the "secret hero of these poems, cocksman and Adonis of Denver."

In the four years between his first embryonic conception of a book to be titled *On the Road* and the day he started typing the scroll, Kerouac struggled to find the right voice and plot elements and angle of approach to encompass his experiences. He would find a good part of the solution in emulating the example of the jazz innovators of bebop, Charlie Parker and Dizzy Gillespie, whose improvisational genius was revolutionizing American music. As he puts it in his notebooks, "I wish to evoke that indescribable sad music of the night in America— for reasons which are never deeper than *the music.* Bop only begins to express that American music. It is the actual inner sound of a country."

When Jack Kerouac began to type the first full draft of *On the Road*, whatever spontaneous bop prosody he practiced was undergirded and guided not simply by years of contemplation and multiple trial runs, but by detailed character sketches and a chapter plot outline. The road to finally writing *On the Road* had been carefully mapped out in advance. A significant amount of the text of the scroll edition is copied either verbatim or very close to, from both the notebooks and the earlier partial drafts of the novel. Kerouac was a highly orderly and conscious literary artist whose discipline and planning have been almost completely obscured by those mythic twenty days of composition. That wasn't typing, that was *writing*.

Soon after finishing the scroll version of *On the Road*, Kerouac went to Robert Giroux's Harcourt office at lunchtime to show him the book. He was both elated and exhausted by what he had achieved. Giroux recalled that "he was in a very funny, excited state. I was too dumb to realize he was drunk or on drugs," although that might not have been the case. Kerouac unfurled the scroll right across the office "like a piece of celebration confetti." Startled by the yards of typescript on his floor, Giroux said the worst possible thing, something like "But, Jack, how are we ever going to edit this?" He really meant how could the words on the impractical and unwieldly scroll ever make their way to a printer, but Kerouac took it the wrong way and was enraged by the question. He retorted, "This book has been dictated by the Holy Ghost! There will be no editing!" He rolled the scroll back up and stormed out of the office. He and Giroux would not speak again, although the editor made every effort to get Kerouac to bring the book back. He finally sent him a pleading telegram, which generated this curt note in response: "You have offended the Holy Ghost. Goodbye."

Thus began another odyssey, the years-long travels of *On the Road* around New York in search of a publisher. Kerouac very quickly retyped *On the Road* as a conventional typescript that could be submitted to publishers and read by them in conventional fashion, presumably double-spaced and broken into paragraphs. That version probably went to Harcourt, Brace, where it was declined; it is not clear how much of a fight Giroux may have put up for it. Over the next couple of years it was also passed on by Little, Brown; E. P. Dutton; Dodd Mead; the down-market paperback publisher Ace Books; and the Viking Press. A response from Joe Fox, a Knopf editor who would turn it down, feels typical: "This is not a well-made novel, nor a saleable one nor even, I think, a good one. His frenetic and scrambling prose perfectly expresses the feverish travels, geographically and mentally, of the Beat Generation. But is that enough? I don't think so."

Here is where Malcolm Cowley enters the story. In a letter dated July 3, 1953, Allen Ginsberg, who was acting as Kerouac's informal agent, wrote to him, saying, "I would like a chance to talk to you, if you are as interested in seeing Jack Kerouac published as I am." Cowley responded encouragingly: "You are right in thinking that I am interested in Kerouac and his work. It seems to me that he is the most interesting writer who is not being published today—and I think it is important that he should be published, or he will run the danger of losing that sense of an audience, which is part of a writer's equipment." His letter reveals that Cowley had already read not only *On the Road*, but also Kerouac's slightly sci-fi novel of his Lowell boyhood, *Doctor Sax*, and what he calls a "second version" of *On the Road* that probably was an early and fragmentary draft of the book that would be posthumously published as *Visions of Cody*. His opinion was that it was only "the first version of *On the Road*" that had a chance of immediate book publication at Viking.

In the late seventies, Cowley remembered that the manuscript of *On the Road* had come to him directly at Viking, recalling that "Allen Ginsberg may have brought it." In fact it was submitted by Phyllis Jackson at MCA; she was John Clellon Holmes's agent and he prevailed on her to represent his friend. Oddly, Cowley would also manage to get his hands on the original scroll. His son, Rob, remembers being home in Sherman from Harvard during the Christmas break of 1953 when his father walked into the house with the scroll in his briefcase. Cowley took out the scroll, said to his son, "Watch this," and rolled it out like a bowling ball onto the living room rug.

Cowley had read *On the Road* "with great interest and enthusiasm," and had gotten others at the house to read it as well, but Viking "was then a rather conservative house, and they thought that this was too much out of the beaten path for our salesmen to place in the bookstores." Here Cowley is being diplomatic. Viking was in no sense a welcoming port for young Turks: The average age of the five editorial principals (Cowley, Covici, Huebsch, Best, and founder Harold Guinzburg) was sixty-two years of age, at a time when that was considered to be *really old*.

Beyond considerations of taste, *On the Road* would have smelled like trouble. The original draft might seem relatively tame today, but for the time, it was sexually explicit, straight and gay, at a time when American culture was brutally homophobic. (There is a vivid description in the original version of Neal Cassady giving a hitchhiking salesman "a monstrous huge banging" in a hotel room while Kerouac watches from the bathroom.) The censors and blue noses were still on high alert and all too eager to prosecute books that offended. In the previous decade a far tamer novel by Edmund Wilson, *Memoirs of Hecate County*, had been banned after a complaint lodged by the New York Society for the Suppression of Vice, and the ban had been upheld by the Supreme Court. Later in the decade, one of the most consequential obscenity trials in American history took place over Grove Press's publication of an unexpurgated edition of *Lady Chatterley's Lover*; the witnesses for Grove included such critics as Alfred Kazin and Malcolm Cowley. Another classic hot-potato novel was making a long and uncertain journey through the publishing industry at much the same time, Vladimir Nabokov's scandalous *Lolita*, collecting a long list of emphatic and horrified rejections, including by Viking.

The potential for the author and publisher of *On the Road* to attract libel suits seemed to hold an even greater risk. The original version used the names of the real characters and included numerous instances of the purchase and sale of controlled substances, drug addiction, sexual license, grand theft auto, homosexuality, bigamy, grand larceny, and even a borderline case of statutory rape. Viking could not have known at the time that the people Kerouac wrote about would have been more likely to sue if they'd been portrayed as responsible, law-abiding citizens, or that figures like Neal Cassady and William Burroughs were essentially libel-proof. There was no such thing as libel insurance at the time, and a run of bad legal luck might hobble and even sink a privately held firm like Viking.

So there was not unreasonable internal resistance at Viking to *On the Road*. Nevertheless, Cowley made a vigorous case for the book against the counsels of the older and grayer heads around the editorial table. One strong naysaying voice was Marshall Best, who was both tightfisted and strongly disinclined toward avant-garde culture. After Viking had published both *On the Road* and its follow-up *The Dharma Bums*, Best wrote to a journalist for *Newsday* who'd sent him a profile he'd written of Kerouac in this fashion: "I have mixed feelings about that character. As you probably know, we have published two of his books and turned down half a dozen others, some of which unfortunately have been published elsewhere."

What did Malcolm Cowley think when he first read Kerouac's *On the Road*? Cowley would always claim that "I knew that Jack wrote well. Jack wrote well naturally . . . *On the Road* was good prose." And *On the Road* was genuinely something *new*. Few people who do not read for a living can grasp how rare this is in an editor's life. You read millions of words and the vast majority of those words, whether skillful words or clumsy ones, are still at bottom very much like all the other ones. Cowley liked the flavor of new that Kerouac was delivering very much. He also liked it because it allowed him to engage his generational sense of the progress of American literature, which his mind intuitively turned to. Proof of this can be found in the first paragraph of the catalogue copy that Cowley would end up writing for *On the Road*:

> After World War I a certain group of restless, searching Americans came to be called "The Lost Generation." This group found its truest voice in the young Hemingway. For a good many of the same reasons after World War II another group, roaming America in a wild, desperate search for identity and purpose, became known as "the Beat

Generation." Jack Kerouac is the voice of this group, and this is his novel.

But not the first voice. Even in 1953 the Beat Generation had already become a visible thing, and much of the credit for that goes to John Clellon Holmes. Of all the original core members of the Beats, Holmes was the one we would today call the adult in the room. A medic in the war, the scion of an old New England family, and married, he'd met Kerouac and Ginsberg in 1948 and the three of them had bonded. It was at Holmes's Lexington Avenue apartment, where he would often crash, that Kerouac coined the phrase "Beat Generation." Those words appeared in print for the first time in Holmes's 1952 roman à clef *Go*, the first novel of the Beat scene, in which Ginsberg, Kerouac, Cassady, Carr, Cannastra, Huncke, and others appear just as he knew them in real life, but with pseudonyms. *Go*, well crafted and observant and full of eye-opening behaviors, was written in the minor key of mid-century emotional realism and had none of the breakthrough energy of *On the Road*. The novel itself generated little attention, but then an editor at *The New York Times Magazine*, Gilbert Millstein, asked Holmes to write what would become a famous essay exploring the temper of his anxious and uncertain cohort. "This Is the Beat Generation" was the subject of Sunday breakfast conversations across the land, and the phrase entered the national conversation.

Holmes, like Cowley, noted the Lost Generation/Beat Generation parallels, but he also pushed back at them. In his view the Lost Generation "was caught up in the romance of disillusionment," playing out a self-conscious "drama of lostness." In contrast, the new postwar generation, raised in a depression and coming of age in a global hot war followed by a twilight cold one, had never been given a set of illusions to lose. "They take these things"—the shattered ideals and moral uncertainties—"frighteningly for granted. They were brought up in these ruins and no longer notice them." Its "wild, desperate search for identity and purpose," in Cowley's words, contained an aspect of a spiritual quest, entirely alien to the Lost Generation figures. An unnerved adult world truly did not know what to make of this coolly detached and apolitical cultural revolt brewing in its midst.

Cowley knew that the generational shift Holmes's essay illustrated would be a strong topical selling point for *On the Road*, if he could manage to get it published. He was decades past his rebelliousness of the twenties and had nothing to prove, but when he felt he was in the right, he could be stubborn, shrewd, and very patient in getting his way. So he commenced a brilliant guerrilla campaign to win Viking to his side, one that would take four years and all the considerable tactics and pulling of strings available to him as a literary insider to succeed. An observer at Viking at the time recalled it as "an example of Malcolm Cowley's perseverance about books that nobody else likes . . . It was really Malcolm who kept going on record to say, 'This is the best unpublished manuscript I have read, and it continues to be the best unpublished manuscript.'"

To get his way, Cowley had to wage a two-pronged effort, on the climate of literary opinion in the outside world, which would then have its effect on the internal weather inside the Viking Press. To accomplish the first he determined to get portions of *On the Road* serialized in places where it, and Kerouac, would be noticed, adapting a variation of the outside game he'd played on behalf of *The Portable Faulkner*. In late 1953 he wrote to Arabel Porter, the editor of *New World Writing*, about "a long autobiographical novel by John [*sic*] Kerouac called *On the Road* (or alternatively *Heroes of the Hip Generation*). It's about the present generation of wild boys on their wild travels between New York, San Francisco, and Mexico City. . . . Of all that beat generation crowd, Kerouac is the only one who *can* write, and about the only one who doesn't get published." Because he was Malcolm Cowley and because he'd just contributed a critical piece himself to the magazine, he was heeded. In April 1955, *New World Writing* Number 7 published an account of a frantic jam session titled "Jazz of the Beat Generation." (That same issue also featured an excerpt of a novel in progress, by Joseph Heller, titled at the time *Catch-18*.) Unfortunately, Cowley's purpose was a bit blunted by Kerouac's insistence that the piece be attributed to "Jean-Louis" because he was worried that his ex-wife would confiscate his fee for child support if his real name appeared.

Next, Cowley did what only Malcolm Cowley among all book editors could have done: Write a public endorsement of Kerouac and his book that would be noticed. In the final chapter of *The Literary Situation*, he assesses the "individual and nihilistic" rebellion of "the beat generation" and then writes, "It was John Kerouac who invented [that] phrase, and his unpublished long narrative, *On the Road*, is the best record of their lives." It takes a special brand of self-confidence to question the editorial judgment of one's employer, in a book published by that employer.

The next year, 1955, he persuaded Peter Matthiessen, then the fiction editor of a lively new literary magazine called *The Paris Review*, to accept an excerpt titled "The Mexican Girl," about a romantic idyll Kerouac had with a woman who was a migrant farmworker. Cowley told Kerouac that "it will be a good thing to get your name back in the public eye, and in a magazine that it's good to appear in," counseling him to use his real name this time. He also cajoled the American Academy and Institute to fork over two hundred dollars to Kerouac from the Artists and Writers Revolving Fund for those in urgent financial need.

That much-needed grant, and the serializations, which would later also include an appearance in *New Directions* Number 16 of "A Billowy Trip in the World" about the trip Kerouac and Cassady took to Mexico, had a feedback loop effect. The fact that three respected magazines thought that *On the Road* was impressive—and safe—enough to publish parts of, and that the prestigious Academy and Institute judged Kerouac to be a writer talented enough to warrant their support, influenced Viking's thinking. One editor, even one as eminent as Malcolm Cowley, standing up for a book at an editorial meeting might well be overruled, but when editors elsewhere start signing on, doubts about the doubts begin to creep in and the familiar dynamic of FOMO takes hold.

Cowley's outside game was a long one and would take years to have its effect. This would test the inner resources of any writer, let alone someone as impatient and anxiety-ridden as Jack Kerouac. There is no torture for a writer like having to wait for a publisher to make up its mind.

Cowley did his best to keep Kerouac's spirts up during this time in the wilderness. Their relationship had gotten off to a rocky start early in 1953 when, at their first lunch, he'd suggested that Kerouac's work could benefit from revision. Kerouac, characteristically, took offense. He described Cowley in a letter to Carolyn Cassady as a "semipedantic Vermont professor type with a hearing aid." They would soon get on a warmer footing. Kerouac and Ginsberg would sometimes bring Cowley down to their Village haunts for a bit of early Beat tourism. Cowley was able to give Kerouac regular shots of good news about the serializations and the grant; the moneys attached—$108 from *New World Writing* and $50 from *The Paris Review*—while modest, were desperately needed, as Kerouac's travails included painful phlebitis, which required penicillin treatments that he could ill afford. Cowley's letters to Kerouac were upbeat and encouraging. Kerouac would tell his agent that Cowley "assured me that better days were coming" and it lifted his spirits.

On top of these torments, other typescripts by him were now making the rounds of publishers, including Cowley and Viking. A torrent of new works would emerge over the next few years. An entry in the "Chronology" at the front of the Viking Critical Edition of *On the Road* tells a painful tale: "1951–1957: Writes twelve books, publishes none." Those books included the novels *Doctor Sax*, *Maggie Cassidy*, *The Subterraneans*, *Tristessa*, *Visions of Gerard*, *The Dharma Bums*, and *Visions of Cody*, all of which would appear after the publication of *On the Road* in 1957 created a demand for new works by Kerouac. He had acquired the services of a new and highly competent agent, Sterling Lord, in 1954, and Lord tirelessly kept those typescripts in circulation with publishers, but the whole experience was like a maddening years-long bad run of fishing—some nibbles, no bites. It is likely that some of those publishers, whatever they made of any of the individual works, were waiting to see what the fate of *On the Road* would be. The book had become somewhat legendary on the publishing circuit, and it would have been known that Viking was teetering on the fence.

It fell to Malcolm Cowley to decline to publish some of the new work that Sterling Lord was circulating. He turned down *Doctor Sax*, the proto–*Visions of Cody*, *Desolation Angels*, and one or two other novels. He had to. To go to bat for another, and lesser, novel by Kerouac while maneuvering to be allowed to publish a book that he had so vigorously and publicly praised would have confused the issue. Besides that, Cowley did not really connect with Kerouac's other works; he would turn them down with comments like they did not have enough people in them or that what Kerouac needed to do was to concentrate on telling a story. He did not see that these new works were the early building blocks of a large, Proustian, self-mythologizing edifice that he would call the Duluoz Legend. In time, Cowley would particularly come to regret that he had not found a way to get Viking to publish *Doctor Sax*.

The effect of all this on Kerouac was demoralizing. At one low point in January of 1955 he asked Lord to retract his manuscripts from submission, declaring that "publishing to me . . . is like a threat over my head." Perhaps the most poignant expression of Kerouac's frame of mind came almost two years later in 1956 when he wrote to Lord that "no rejection or acceptance by publishers can alter that awful final feeling of death—of life-which-is death." In that same letter Kerouac instructed his agent to pull *Beat Generation*, as it was then being called, back from Cowley: "Tell him I respect his sincerity, but I'm not sure about the others at Viking and tell him *I don't care*." The letter had a second-thought PS that absolved Cowley of blame and called him "a good friend."

In fact by this time Cowley had made progress in bringing Viking to the brink of actually publishing *On the Road*. He had garnered the support of some younger staffers in reaching that point. One of them was a man named Keith Jennison, who had arrived at Viking in 1953. He was more of a promotion director than editor, but his opinion about books, especially their commercial viability, was taken seriously by higher-ups. He and Cowley formed an alliance and the two of them would sometimes take Kerouac out to lunch for morale-boosting and strategizing.

Another supporter was an in-house editor named Helen Taylor. She was a cautious and strict copybook editor of the old school, but in her report on the book she said that she'd been "stirred" by Kerouac's "bold writing talent," which she found both "lavish" and "reckless." She suggested that the book needed cutting, but that all that was required was a "lightly touching pencil, for refinement has no place in this prose."

The real key to the changing climate at Viking was the arrival at the house of Thomas Guinzburg, the son of the founder Harold Guinzburg and the heir apparent to the firm. After graduating from Hotchkiss he'd enlisted in the Marine Corps and saw combat in the invasion of Iwo Jima. He'd attended Yale after the war, coediting the *Yale Daily News* with William F. Buckley, and then gone to France and helped to found *The Paris Review* with George Plimpton, Peter Matthiessen, and others. He arrived back in the States in 1953 to join the family business, where he first worked in sales and marketing, his father knowing that once he got involved in editorial matters he could never be dislodged. A visible figure on the New York social scene, Tom Guinzburg had style and taste and would prove to be a more than able inheritor of the publisher's mantle when his father died in 1961. He would remember that "when I got there I helped to get that one [*On the Road*] published because I was at the right age to, and my father was perhaps more tolerant or perhaps respected my conviction that it was a book that was worth it." He connected with the book on a personal level: "I was of that generation. I hadn't done all that stuff, but I wished I had, and I understood it . . . I understood better than some of the older people what he was talking about." Tom Guinzburg brought new verve and relevance to the house.

In September of 1955, Cowley finally had the at least partial break-through he'd been hoping for at Viking. He wrote to Kerouac a hedged-about "acceptance" letter: "*On the Road . . .* is now being seriously considered, or reconsidered, by Viking, and there is quite a good chance that we will publish it, depending on three *ifs*: *if* we can figure out what the right changes will be (cuts and rearrangements); *if* we can be sure that the book won't be suppressed for immorality; and *if* it won't get us into libel suits. The libel question is important because I take it that you're dealing with actual persons." Cowley also said that he'd write a short introduction to the book if it could be published, something that had some internal sway at Viking. Kerouac replied swiftly and pronounced himself the most cooperative of authors. He assured Cowley that he had already made changes to guard against the possibility of suits by changing the names of real characters and identifying details. In regard to the editing, time and the publishing industry's indifference had defeated Kerouac's initial stance that his text was inviolable. "Any changes you want to make okay with me," he declared. On the immorality question, Kerouac was flippant. But he would cooperate. Kerouac was terribly poor and a lot of the fight had been taken out of him.

The word "acceptance" is in quotes for a reason. Some of Kerouac's biographers have used the word to imply a stronger level of intent or obligation on Viking's side than was really there. In most cases a publisher that has decided to publish a book will have agreed upon an advance and other terms with the author and agent beforehand and will then draft a contract for signing. None of these necessary formalities were discussed at all in this instance. All of the obligations were on Kerouac's side, to clear the hurdles represented by those italicized "*ifs*," the clearance of which was solely in the judgment of the Viking Press. Nothing was ever signed by the two parties, not even an option contract, a fairly common interim sort of agreement at the time, and no money changed hands, despite Kerouac's occasional pleas for a monthly stipend to support him during the revision process. Kerouac had moved from purgatory to limbo in regard to the publication of his book.

The first two "*ifs*" were dealt with in a comparatively painless fashion. Cowley's editorial changes mostly concerned the compression of the second and third cross-country trips in the original text into one trip, for the sake of narrative economy. The sex scenes were toned down to the point that it is sometimes hard to figure out whether the characters are copulating or wrestling, and the homosexual material removed. The "monstrous huge banging" in the back seat was excised, and there is no suggestion of an affair between Allen Ginsberg and Carlo Marx or Neal Cassady and Dean Moriarty, only much soulful philosophizing.

The vetting process for libel, however, was painful and prolonged. It is the job of the lawyer to see every detail in a book, whether fiction or nonfiction, in the aspect of a worst-case legal scenario and scare the author and editor with dire hypotheticals. *On the Road* was studded with libel land mines. So off the manuscript went to Viking's outside counsel, Nathaniel Whitehorn, for close legal examination.

The report that came back from him on November 1, 1955, was a detailed and sobering document: a nine-page memo with a page-and-a-half cover letter identifying hazards and suggesting changes and excisions that could minimize the risk of libel suits. In his letter Whitehorn points out that even though the names had been changed, the characters were easily identifiable, at least within their own circle. Kerouac had also been tasked with securing signed releases from the major characters, including Cassady, Ginsberg, and Gary Snyder, saying they would not sue for libel, and he had dutifully done so. But Whitehorn points out that these releases might not hold up in court in some jurisdictions.

Over the next year or so, Cowley worked with Kerouac to revise *On the Road* to conform to the lawyer's suggestions and make it safer for publication. Increasingly, though, the editorial responsibilities for the book devolved on the in-house Viking editor, Helen Taylor. Malcolm Cowley was a consulting editor at Viking, not a full-time staffer. He went into the office once a week, and he was regularly absent from there for months at a time while in residence at this or that university as a visiting instructor. Getting a book into the world is a complex procedure, and someone has to be in the office to get down in the weeds and stay there. That person was Helen Taylor.

The impression one gets from Helen Taylor's letters and memos is of a high-functioning and extremely professional mid-century American editor: brisk, detail-oriented, devoted to clarity of language and the meeting of deadlines. She had to accomplish three crucial tasks: to make sure that all the legal corrections in the typescript of *On the Road* were made in order to satisfy the lawyer Whitehorn; to do the close-in line-editing of the book to bring Kerouac's idiosyncratic prose nearer to the standard usage of the day; and, once a publication date had been set, to keep the book's production on schedule to meet that date. The latter two tasks would lead to friction.

Jack Kerouac wrote to please his ear. "As it comes, so it flows, and that's literature at its purest," he proclaimed to Sterling Lord. He didn't like commas much, especially ones that slowed down the flow of his sentences, and rarely resorted to semicolons. Helen Taylor liked commas and semicolons a lot. They gave structure and clarity to sentences. It was her line-editing of *On the Road* that imposed the style and usage of the time on the book. Kerouac's characters behave just as wildly and irresponsibly as before, but they do so in a regularized prose that for the most part resembled the prose of most other contemporary American novels. There is no doubt that the eventual Viking version of *On the Road* is more readable, at least to the average reader, than the scroll edition, but that readability was accomplished with the loss of quite some energy and immediacy of effect.

On March 21, 1957, Helen Taylor wrote an interoffice memo to Harold Guinzburg and Marshall Best to inform them that "Whitehorn called this morning to say that the book was clean now, in his opinion." He still had some reservations about two of Cassady's wives, but Taylor dismissed that concern in this fashion: "If the women are respectable now (dubious), they would hardly sue. If they are not, they are hopheads or otherwise so unrespectable that they would not sue." Ahem. This is the point at which the real line-editing and then the even closer-in copyediting of *On the Road* would have taken place, and a tentative future pub date scheduled. And here is where Viking broke faith with its author in a shocking fashion.

After the copyediting stage, *On the Road* would have been sent to the compositor to be set in type and made into galleys. Galleys are long and as yet unpaginated strips of type that serve two functions. They are cut into book-page lengths and assembled into what are called bound galleys: bound-up proto-versions of the eventual book that are sent out some months in advance of the pub date to book reviewers and publicity outlets. The other function is for the author to be able to read his or her book freshly set in type to both catch any mistakes the compositor may have inadvertently made, and, for the last time, make sure that what is going out into the world conforms to his or her intentions. Authors are routinely advised not to make too many changes in galleys, because incorporating those changes costs money and can delay the book's production. Nevertheless, it is a near-sacred principle that the author must be given the chance to read the galleys.

Viking violated that principle. Jack Kerouac was never sent his galleys for reading and correction. There is no paper trail to trace the thinking behind this decision, so we are left to speculate as to why. There was a distinct air of in-house condescension and mild distaste toward Kerouac and his Beat companions on Viking's part, although not Malcolm Cowley's. Kerouac was nervous and excitable and almost certainly would have grumbled about many of the changes to his book that were being forced on him. He was also someone unacquainted with a fixed address, and Viking may not have been entirely sure where he was at the time that the galleys came in. He'd traveled to Tangier in early February and was there until the end of March, occupied with the typing of a book by William Burroughs that would become his masterpiece *Naked Lunch*. In April he'd traveled north to Paris and then to London; by the end of that month he'd made it back to New York for a short stay, and by mid-May he had settled into an apartment in Berkeley, California, where he anxiously awaited the galley proofs of *On the Road*. They never came.

At some point an executive decision must have been made to keep

Kerouac out of the loop on his own book. Viking may have feared that Kerouac would, upon seeing *On the Road* in type, decide to rethink what had gone before and restore so many edits and add so much new material by hand to the galleys that the bound book date would be lost. The turnaround time for galleys is usually two or at most three weeks; even if Viking knew where Kerouac had landed, he might well move again. The galleys might not reach him at all. Whatever the reasoning or the justification, Jack Kerouac never got to read *On the Road* in type until he received the printed book, and he would be justly aggrieved by this breach of publishing protocol.

At least Kerouac had finally signed a publishing contract with Viking for an advance of one thousand dollars, or nine hundred dollars after his agent's 10 percent commission, which was to be paid out in monthly hundred-dollar increments. Even with a contract and a September pub date, Kerouac experienced anxiety that Viking might get cold feet at the last minute and cancel his book. Allen Ginsberg's *Howl and Other Poems* (dedicated to Kerouac) had been published as a pamphlet by the City Lights bookshop in San Francisco's North Beach, and in May its owner Lawrence Ferlinghetti and the store manager had been arrested and charged with the distribution of lewd material. It had been some time since Kerouac had heard from Cowley or anyone else at Viking, and the silence about the galleys became increasingly ominous to him. He would write to the poet Gary Snyder that he feared the prosecution of *Howl* would cause Viking to postpone his own novel. Of course it had the precise opposite reaction, fueling even greater anticipation for the already legendary chronicle of the Beat Generation's adventures.

For more than a year leading up to the publication of *On the Road*, Jack Kerouac and Malcolm Cowley were in sporadic contact. They were supposed to have met up in the Bay Area in the spring of 1956 to work together when Cowley was teaching at Stanford, but Kerouac had left before Cowley arrived, and then Cowley departed before Kerouac, crossing the continent, arrived. Missed connections like this drew out the editing process painfully. The slow pace so rattled Kerouac that he sent Cowley a famously economical expression of impatience: a postcard with the single word "BOO" in large red letters. Finally, though, on April 8, 1957, Cowley could write a genuine "Manuscript Acceptance Report" for *On the Road* and share the fruits of Kerouac's and his and everyone else's labor with the company:

> The characters are always on wheels. They buy cars and wreck them, steal cars and leave them standing in fields, undertake to drive cars from one city to another, sharing the gas; then for variety they go hitch-hiking or sometimes ride a bus. In cities they go on wild parties or sit in joints listening to hot trumpets. They seem a little like machines themselves, machines gone haywire, always wound to the last pitch, always nervously moving, drinking, making love, with hardly any emotions except a determination to say Yes to any new experience. The writing at its best is deeply felt, poetic, and extremely moving. Again at its best this book is a celebration of the American scene in the manner of a latter-day Wolfe or Sandburg. The story itself has a steady, fast, unflagging movement that carries the reader along with it, always into new towns and madder adventures, and with only one tender interlude, that of the Mexican girl. It is real, honest, fascinating, everything for kicks, the voice of a new age.

Cowley goes on to summarize something of Kerouac's own history and that of his book, including its serializations and its having been defanged for libel risk. His final paragraph provides a look into the crystal ball: "The book, I prophesy, will get mixed but *interested* reviews, it will have a good sale (perhaps a very good one), and I don't think there is any doubt that it will be reprinted as a paperback. Moreover it will stand for a long time as the honest record of another way of life."

Cowley got back in touch with Kerouac on July 16. He'd been teaching at the University of Michigan that spring and he had not written the introduction to *On the Road* that had been planned, which was just as well. He comments on the book's cover, which Kerouac had not seen before the finished book arrived: "The Viking edition of *On the Road* is very handsome—don't you think? And very chaste." Instead of taking a paperback-like approach of illustrating the Beats at their revels, the cover featured a small, semi-abstract cityscape within a full-bleed black background. Cowley was not consulted on this design, nor was Kerouac. He then raises "the old question of what we should work on next." He expresses the opinion that *Doctor Sax* was the most promising of the several manuscripts he'd considered and suggested that Kerouac write more scenes of his boyhood in Lowell and send the results to him in the fall. Clearly, Cowley felt that Kerouac and Viking had a future together, with him in the editorial cockpit.

There was something both miraculous and somehow inevitable about the way *On the Road* would be launched. The book was scheduled for review at *The New York Times* in the first week in September. As luck would have it, the paper's main book reviewer, Orville Prescott, was on vacation that week. He was a notorious curmudgeon and would have been sure to write a negative review of this offense against decency and literary standards. Instead the review assignment fell to Gilbert Millstein, the same person who years earlier had gotten John Clellon Holmes to write his famous "This Is the Beat Generation" essay for the paper's magazine. And he delivered.

Millstein's ecstatic and exceptionally smart review calls the publication of *On the Road* "a historic occasion"; praises the novel as "the most beautifully executed, the clearest and the most important utterance yet made by the generation Kerouac himself named years ago as 'beat'"; and compares it to *The Sun Also Rises* as the same kind of testament and behavioral guide for the Beat Generation as Hemingway's was for his. It continues on in this vein, essentially a six-hundred-word-long pull quote, ending emphatically "*On the Road* is a major novel." This was a spectacular curtain-raiser. In its effect the review was the literary equivalent of Elvis Presley's appearance the year before on *The Ed Sullivan Show*. Presley delivered an electrifying jolt of sexual energy to the somnolent culture of the fifties; Kerouac's book, the review asserted, offered an irresistible new model of freedom and spiritual questing to a younger generation chafing under the decade's cultural constraints.

The editor and novelist Joyce Johnson has described what happened then in her classic memoir *Minor Characters*. She was Kerouac's girlfriend at the time, and he was staying with her in her Upper West Side apartment the day before the review ran. Alerted by Viking, she and Kerouac had gone down to a newsstand on Broadway at midnight to get a copy of the next day's paper, fresh off the truck. They both scanned the review eagerly and warily. Kerouac asked her uncertainly, hardly believing his luck, "It's good, isn't it?" "Yes," she replied, "it's very, very good." She'd worked in publishing for two years after Barnard and she knew what it meant. She was thrilled, but also a bit frightened by what this kind of anointing of a writer as a generational prophet might mean for Kerouac. He was more pensive than elated.

Lord Byron remarked, "I awoke one morning and found myself famous," after his poem *Childe Harold's Pilgrimage*—a kind of Romantic Era road novel in verse—sold out in three days. The same thing happened to Jack Kerouac the next day. The phone in Johnson's apartment never stopped ringing with demands for interviews and appearances. Keith Jennison arrived that morning with half a case of celebratory champagne, three bottles of which were quickly dispatched. The first newspaper interviewer showed up that afternoon and Kerouac, now excited and champagne-fueled, had to explain for the first of hundreds of times in his life the beatific meaning of "Beat" to an ill-informed journalist angling for a quick personality feature.

The publication of *On the Road* was the making of Jack Kerouac and his eventual undoing. Saul Bellow once compared the management of fame to the way snake-handling preachers have to control poisonous serpents without getting fatally bitten. Kerouac was totally unprepared and temperamentally unfit to handle the kind of fame that descended upon him. The torrent of attention found the cracks in his fragile psyche as surely as a heavy rain finds the entry points in a roof. He was shy and he drank to manage that shyness, which led to a familiar downward spiral as he found himself for the first time before audiences and radio microphones and television cameras. He got thrown into the deep end of a treacherous pool.

The head of Viking publicity, Patricia McManus, was hardworking and inventive and a total pro who moreover liked Kerouac a great deal and took care of him as well as a publicist could. She sent advance copies of *On the Road* to such pertinent public figures as Marlon Brando and Dave Brubeck; booked Kerouac on *The Mike Wallace Interview*, *The Steve Allen Show* (Allen played a jazz piano accompaniment as Kerouac soulfully if unsteadily read from his novel), and *Night Beat*, at a time when authors rarely made it onto television; and tirelessly kept book review and feature editors of newspapers and magazines up to date on the book's upward trajectory with a drumbeat of letters and press releases. She even helped to set up a week's residency for Kerouac at the famed jazz club the Village Vanguard, where he read his prose and poetry to the accompaniment of the jazz pianist Ellis Larkin and, again, Steve Allen. *On the Road* would hit the bestseller list for five weeks, and it became the focus of heated debate, in literary circles and in the culture at large.

Malcolm Cowley was not involved in any of these publication activities and had left the States for an academic appointment abroad in October. But he followed the critical response to *On the Road* with keen interest. As he had predicted, opinions were mixed and sometimes sharply divided. There were some good, appreciative reviews in magazines and newspapers across the country—nothing as lyrical and joyous as Millstein's, though, and most of these reviewers felt the need to point out Kerouac's shortcomings.

A good many reviewers and columnists manifested the American tendency to resort to mockery and moral panic when something challenging and unconventional comes their way. An example of this barrage of scoffing condescension would be Robert Ruark, a sub-Hemingway novelist of the manly man variety and a powerful syndicated columnist. Donning the I'm-just-a-regular-Joe costume so useful to a certain type of scribe, he wrote that "what I am by the beat generation is just that—beat. If 'beat' means defeated, I don't know what they are defeated by, or for what reason. All I gather is that they are mad about something." Ruark sneers that *On the Road* was "not much more than a candid admission that [Kerouac] had been on the bum for six years" and concludes, "It's a good word—'kick.' And where the whole sniveling lot needs a kick is right in the pants." No wonder young people hate adults.

Of greater consequence were the attacks that came from the literary intellectuals, the ones who really understood what was at stake in the rise of the outlaw sensibility Kerouac and Ginsberg and the other Beats were expressing. At the front of the pack was *Partisan Review*, which grasped that this new crowd, which hadn't read any Marx and didn't worship at the shrine of T. S. Eliot and made no apologies about it, was muscling in on the avant-garde territory that it considered its turf. Their designated attack dog was Norman Podhoretz, who'd made it from Brooklyn across the river to Columbia, where he studied with Ginsberg and Kerouac's old professor Lionel Trilling, and across the Atlantic to Cambridge, where he studied with F. R. Leavis, and then back to New York, where he quickly became a made man among the New York intellectuals, aka the Family.

His piece in the Spring 1958 issue, "The Know-Nothing Bohemians," was such a durable attack on Beat writing that it was included in the Viking Critical Edition of *On the Road*. In Podhoretz's view the older Bohemianism of the teens and twenties was a repudiation of the provincialism and hypocrisy of American life and "a movement created in the name of civilization: its ideals were intelligence, civilization, spiritual refinement." The Bohemians of the fifties, in contrast, he sees as primitives in thrall to pure instinct, spontaneity, irrationalism, woolly mysticism, crank philosophies, and unearned sentimentality about the supposed simple happiness of the darker races and white rural Americans. Norman Mailer's notorious ode to hipsterism, "The White Negro," and the phenomenon of switchblade-toting juvenile delinquents are dragged in as if they were somehow the peace-loving and completely nonviolent Ginsberg and Kerouac's fault.

Podhoretz's piece is a literary sophisticate's assault on *On the Road* that manages to score points while missing the biggest point of all: the sadness and sweetness and thwartedness at the heart of the book, and the openness and masculine vulnerability of Kerouac's writing. Louis Menand calls attacks of this sort "a crude misreading." "The Beats weren't rebels," he observes. "They were misfits." On a regular basis in American literary history, the misfits end up having their say. As Menand writes, *On the Road* is "exuberant, hopeful, sad, nostalgic; it is never naturalistic. Most of all, it is emotionally uninhibited. . . . The Beats were men who wrote about their feelings." Jack Kerouac was a man who had lots of feelings, far more than the ordinary American male, and he courageously committed them to paper for the world to see. "Life is holy, and every moment is precious"—no American writer since Whitman had risked writing anything this direct. This, and not the go-man-go caricatures of the book, is what brings tens of thousands of new readers to *On the Road* every year and fuels the still flourishing literary cult of Jack Kerouac.

Malcolm Cowley was not in touch with Kerouac much if at all after the publication of the novel, and he had very little to contribute editorially in Kerouac's future dealings with Viking. Cowley had spent years as a middleman between Kerouac and Viking, conducting a kind of editorial shuttle diplomacy between a writer and a company with scant sympathy for each other's needs. Kerouac had jumped through every hoop that Cowley had required, while receiving rejections from him, some of them curt, for new novel after new novel. His first editorial experience with Robert Giroux had been something like an idyll; this one, in contrast, had been a protracted slog. Perhaps they'd had enough of each other.

Viking, with a paradigm-shifting commercial success on its hands, now wanted another book from Kerouac as quickly as possible. Novels that Sterling Lord had been frustratingly unable to place were now being sold with ease. Grove Press had quickly picked up *The Subterraneans*, which it published in 1958, and *Doctor Sax*, which it put out in 1959; Avon, a mass-market publisher, would bring out *Maggie Cassidy* as a paperback original in 1959. Suddenly the market for work by Jack Kerouac—now that there was such a thing—was about to be flooded with books by him of, it seemed, lesser quality than *On the Road*. Luckily, Viking had on submission one of Kerouac's best novels, *The Dharma Bums*, and they signed it up with dispatch. Like all of his fiction, it was autobiographical and concerned the time Kerouac spent in 1956 with the poet, outdoorsman, and student of Zen and Native American cultures Gary Snyder. *The Dharma Bums* was another exercise in male bonding, this time with far fewer kicks and far more spiritual questing, with Snyder/Japhy Ryder in the Dean Moriarty role, moving about in hiking boots instead of hot cars, and spouting koans instead of monologues.

The Dharma Bums was both different from and similar enough to *On the Road* to suit Viking's purposes perfectly, and it found immediate and enthusiastic favor with in-house readers. Keith Jennison, probably Kerouac's closest friend there, enthused that "this new book by Jack Kerouac seems to me to be a great advance over ON THE ROAD. . . . this time Jack comes much closer to swimming in the sea of language (his phrase) than drowning in it." Catharine Carver, newly arrived from *Partisan Review*, wrote, "I think this is miles and even worlds ahead of ON THE ROAD; in fact, I'm quite overboard about it. . . . We ought to be proud and delighted to publish this book." Which Viking did, bringing it out in October 1958, a brisk seven months from submission. Helen Taylor once again did the editing. Kerouac was stuck with a bill for $519.45 in author's alterations when she added or restored many dozens of dozens of commas and other changes to the galleys without asking his permission. Cowley never saw the manuscript. When he did finally read *The Dharma Bums* he didn't like it much; he thought it was underpopulated and short on story.

The Dharma Bums received, on balance, more favorable reviews than *On the Road*. The shock of the new, however, had worn off Kerouac and the Beats, and the book sold modestly in hardcover. It was the last book by Jack Kerouac that Viking would publish for almost half a century. Tom Guinzburg had become his main point of contact at Viking, and he had every reason to want to continue publishing Kerouac's work into the future. But his editors kept writing negative and sometimes scathing reports on the books he and his agent were submitting. By February 1959, all of the submissions were sent back to Sterling Lord, and Viking and Jack Kerouac were quits.

In the years to come, Malcolm Cowley would in certain circles, particularly among Kerouac's friends and loyalists, be seen less as the hero of the saga of *On the Road*'s long march to publication than as Jack Kerouac's nemesis and underminer. The source of a lot of this will be found in the rollicking and more than a little drunken "Writers at Work" interview that Kerouac did with the poets Ted Berrigan and Aram Saroyan, the year before his death. Kerouac states, "In the days of Malcolm Cowley, with *On the Road* and *The Dharma Bums*, I had no power to stand by my style for better or for worse. When Malcolm Cowley made endless revisions and inserted thousands of needless commas . . . why, I spent five hundred dollars making a complete restitution of the *Bums* manuscript and got a bill from Viking Press called 'Revisions.' Ha ho ho." Later he makes much the same claim about Cowley's having fiddled without permission with the text of *On the Road*, the same claim he made to Allen Ginsberg in a letter written the day he first received his finished books, declaring, "Oh shame! shame on American Business!"

Some of Kerouac's biographers and commentators have carelessly taken complaints like these about Cowley's putative actions at face value, but they are not true. It was Helen Taylor who put the clamps on Kerouac's prose for Viking in both books. In later years Cowley would become more than a little defensive about all this, responding in *Jack's Book* that "Jack and his memory are very, very unfair to me. Blaming me for putting or taking out commas or caps and what-not in *On the Road*. I really didn't give much of a damn about that." He would always be a Viking loyalist, though, and he would never try to divert blame to anyone else.

To sort out the instances where Cowley stood tall as Kerouac's editor and where he failed him requires an understanding of Cowley's position vis-à-vis the Viking Press. In the years between the time he read the earliest typescript of *On the Road* and the day it was genuinely accepted, he had to play a double game if he was ever going to get it published. If he'd done what Maxwell Perkins had famously done when Scribner's was balking at Fitzgerald's *This Side of Paradise*— essentially threatening to quit if he could not sign it up—he would have fatally undercut his own position at Viking and possibly not had his consultant's contract renewed. Cunning was called for, not bluster. That strategy caused Jack Kerouac a lot of pain. If Cowley had been in the Viking offices full-time, it is certain that he would have insisted that Kerouac have the chance to read and correct the galleys of *On the Road*. But he wasn't. There is no getting around the fact that Viking as a house pushed Kerouac around and at times condescended to him and his friends and his book. The divisions in the house expressed themselves in its behavior. But Malcolm Cowley himself never ever did anything like that. His caring for Kerouac might on occasion have been avuncular and paternalistic and even intermittent, but he really did care.

Malcolm Cowley was the perfect editor for *On the Road*, but the wrong editor for Jack Kerouac. His sometimes blunt and impatient rejections of other Kerouac novels prove that he could never be for him what Max Perkins had been for Thomas Wolfe. He had no interest whatsoever in Kerouac's interest in Buddhism, and he never took the enterprise of the Legend of Duluoz seriously. (He referred to it as "interminable" in one of his in-house Viking memos.) Cowley was a man whose own credo as a writer was that he hated to write and loved to rewrite; Kerouac could be brought to revise, but at heart he fiercely trusted his first thoughts and initial inspirations. Cowley was also a man who'd written his master's thesis on Racine; Kerouac's temperament was Romantic, privileging perception and feeling over form.

Still, on this one occasion, these two figures went to war against the forces of conventional opinion and won a great victory. Nothing else Malcolm Cowley did had anything like the effect that his advocacy for *On the Road* had, not even his revival of Faulkner's career. Once *On the Road* came out in its Signet paperback editions, the book would be read by millions of people, and for a high percentage of the younger ones it lodged in their hearts and minds as a gateway to at least the possibility of another life. There is a very bright straight line of influence between Kerouac's book and soulful troubadours such as Bob Dylan and Tom Waits and Bruce Springsteen. Jack Kerouac was and remains a conductor of that core American value, freedom.

———

And then Malcolm Cowley did it again.

The story of how Ken Kesey's first novel, *One Flew Over the Cuck-oo's Nest*, came to be published is a shorter, simpler, and happier tale. It began in a classroom in Palo Alto. The Stanford Creative Writing Program was one of Malcolm Cowley's most reliable academic employers and something of a happy hunting ground and second home for him. In the first real flush of what Mark McGurl would term "the Program Era" in American fiction, the Stanford MFA program ran neck and neck with the Iowa Writers' Workshop in prestige and output of talent. The program had been inaugurated in 1945 by the novelist and teacher Wallace Stegner, who would make the claim that he was one of the inventors of creative writing as a formal field of study. He himself had been one of the first people to earn a master's degree in creative writing from Iowa. He'd moved west to Stanford from teaching jobs at Harvard and the Bread Loaf Writers' Conference in Middlebury, Vermont, and he found that many of his students were older veterans studying on the GI Bill, married with children and domestic responsibilities. His wife, Mary Stegner, recalled that "he said they needed a place where they could write and talk, like a coffee house in Europe." So he devised the creative writing workshop, where fledgling writers would read and critique one another's work in a spirit of sometimes competitive camaraderie. The seminar table would become the formalized academic stand-in for the literary café society that had previously been the seedbed of movements and writers.

The Stanford program was generously supported from its inception by E. H. Jones, a rich Texas oilman with a love of literature, and the brother of a Stanford English professor. His endowment made possible the Stegner Fellowships, which provide living stipends for promising candidates in fiction, poetry, and playwriting to study for their degree. Many Stegner Fellows have become marquee names in American literature over the decades. Wallace Stegner was not only an innovator in the field of creative writing, he was a very able administrator and academic politician, and his program flourished. One of his assets was his own stature as a highly regarded novelist of the American West, which helped him hire the sort of high-profile instructors who would in turn attract the most talented and promising of the aspiring writers. Malcolm Cowley was just the kind of teacher Stegner wanted.

Cowley first came to Palo Alto at Stegner's invitation to teach in 1956. The two men quickly became close friends, and Cowley would return to Stanford for repeat appointments in 1958 and 1959, becoming a fixture there. He taught writing diligently, if less formally than a credentialed academic might. He modeled his classroom efforts on the way Archibald MacLeish was doing it with Harvard students, including his son, Rob. As he wrote to Stegner, "Archie's great trick is to make the students feel that they are a *very* selected group, entitled to meet the great men [*sic*] of literature. That sets them up, and they become very serious about their writing and about tearing apart one another's work." This was a trick easy for him to pull off himself. His student at Stanford, Larry McMurtry, recalled that "gossip about the great does as much as anything else to pull young writers into the great stream of literary endeavor."

Cowley was also on duty as a literary scout for the Viking Press. For an ambitious young novelist, admission to Cowley's classroom would not only be the opportunity to rub shoulders with a legendary editor and Lost Generation personage and hear firsthand tales of literary gossip and glory, it was also like buying a lottery ticket to a Viking contract. In 1958 one of his students, Dennis Murphy, had won that lottery when Viking published, very successfully, his first novel, *The Sergeant*.

In the fall of 1960, Cowley returned to Stanford, where the now legendary roster of fellows and MFA students was so starry that a Paris–Palo Alto comparison becomes almost obligatory. They included Ernest Gaines; Peter Beagle; Larry McMurtry; Robert Stone; the young Australian Christopher Koch, future author of *The Year of Living Dangerously*; Wendell Berry; and Tillie Olsen. (Cowley had published a piece by Olsen back in 1934 in *The New Republic*, "Thousand Dollar Vagrant," and he had had her in his first class at Stanford in 1956. She would at his behest sign a contract with Viking for a novel, but the famously blocked Olsen never finished it.) The talent in the room was just tremendous, even if you don't include the most famous—some would say infamous—fellow of them all, Ken Kesey.

Ken Kesey at the time was a rough-hewn, heavily muscled young man who presented as something of a hick. He'd grown up on a dairy farm in Oregon, and a lot of that muscle was the result of the strenuous chores he'd had to do growing up, like wheeling heavy cans of milk and cream around and lifting them onto trucks and picking beans at six cents a pound. He understood and relished physical labor more than most writers. In 1958 Kesey and his wife and high school sweetheart, Faye, had moved into a cottage on woodsy Perry Lane, the home of what passed for the cultural avant-garde at Stanford in the late fifties. Larry McMurtry called it "a hotbed of low-rent revolt." In his classic Kesey chronicle *The Electric Kool-Aid Acid Test*, Tom

Wolfe has great fun sending up the social set there, people appalled by America's grotesque tail fin civilization, enviously smitten by those civilized Europeans who had so clearly, they'd solemnly intone, "mastered the art of living." Naturally, the sandal-and-natural-fabric-wearing Perry Lane sophisticates found Kesey, who used words like "bub" and "caint" in conversation like a displaced Okie, charmingly in need of polishing and condescended to him and Faye at every communal occasion. Little did they know that they had a true cultural visionary in their midst who would take over the scene and remake it in his image.

Ken Kesey may have grown up on a farm, but he was not really a hick. Wolfe describes him as the beau ideal of the young American male at the height of our postwar/pre-Vietnam imperium—a member of "the first wave of the most extraordinary kids in the history of the world . . . Superkids!" Kesey's father, Fred, had built the Eugene Farmers Cooperative into the biggest dairy operation in the Willamette Valley. The Kesey family was prosperous and lived in a low-slung new house in the suburbs, with powerboats and gas-guzzling cars with V-8 engines, and Ken Kesey himself, in terms of achievement, fully qualified for Superkid status. He'd been voted "most likely to succeed" at Springfield High School and attended the University of Oregon, where he was a champion college wrestler in the 174-pound class, just missing out on qualifying for the American Olympic team because of an injury. He'd joined a fraternity and been a star actor in college plays. He had drive and talent and presence and ambition, and he was a young white American male when that was just about the most favored thing in the world you could possibly be. As his friend and fellow novelist Robert Stone put it, Kesey "personally embodied the winning side on every historical struggle that had served to create the colossus that was nineteen-sixties America."

Ken Kesey's first love was not literature per se, but comic books.

He would tell an interviewer in 1963 that "a single *Batman* comic is more honest than a whole volume of *Time* magazine." The comic book strain of his aesthetic and worldview would remain strong throughout his career. His college major was in speech and communications, which required him to write plays and television scripts, but he gradually shifted over to fiction writing. An epiphany took place for him in a class on the short story taught by the novelist James B. Hall when they were studying Hemingway's story "Soldier's Home." Hall focused the students' attention on the line in the story where the forlorn veteran Krebs sits down to a meal of bacon and eggs prepared by his mother: "Krebs looked at the bacon fat hardening on his plate." It felt like a kind of magic trick, and Kesey would recall that "a door opened for me and it's never been closed." He saw how this one mundane detail could lodge itself inside the reader unconsciously and go off inside him "like a bomb. At the very end of the story you find yourself affected and you can't put your finger on why." Kesey would later send some of his early work to Hemingway and receive a letter of encouragement. He was also quite excited when none other than William Faulkner arrived at the University of Oregon for a reading.

In his senior year, Ken Kesey wrote a novel about college football titled *The End of Autumn*, which was never published. After graduating in June in 1957, he spent some months in Los Angeles trying to kick-start a career as a screenwriter and even as an actor, with little result or encouragement. He placed his first published work of fiction, "First Sunday of September," in the Fall 1957 issue of the *Northwest Review*, and on the strength of that and with the encouragement of James Hall, he applied for a Woodrow Wilson Fellowship to attend Wallace Stegner's already famed creative writing program at Stanford and was accepted. That was how he found himself in a seminar room with Malcolm Cowley in the fall of 1960. His fellowship had run out and he was no longer formally part of the program, but former fellows were extended the courtesy of attending classes as they wished without enrollment.

From the very beginning of his entrance into the Jones Room, Ken Kesey asserted his propensity for what his lifelong friend Larry McMurtry would call "stud-duckery"—the will to assert himself in a group and hold court with a kind of rowdy self-confidence that tended to put off those not won over by his brash charm. There were a dozen writers in the class, all but one of them young males and competitive—"Like stoats in a henhouse, we were poised to rend and tear," McMurtry recalled. Kesey was behind most of the other writers at the table in career terms. McMurtry himself was about to publish his first novel, *Horseman, Pass By*, with Harper, inaugurating a very productive and successful career. Peter Beagle, a nephew of the painters Raphael and Moses Soyer, was already a Viking author with a couple of books published. Others were well along with books.

Kesey, in McMurtry's telling, was unfazed. He took out some pages and began to read the first chapters of the novel that would become *One Flew Over the Cuckoo's Nest*. McMurtry's novelistic account feels a bit too convenient to be entirely true—would Kesey really have commandeered the very first class being taught by the very eminent Cowley in such a bold fashion and without permission? But at whatever point in the semester that Cowley encountered the boisterous Ken Kesey and his novel, they certainly caught and held his attention.

In his 1977 reminiscence "Ken Kesey at Stanford," Cowley could not recall any specific classroom comments Kesey made, but he paints him as "stolid and self-assured," with "the build of a plunging halfback, with big shoulders and a neck like the stump of a Douglas fir." Cowley saw his main task at the head of the table was "to get the class working together." His entire career had consisted, in a sense, of fieldwork in studying the behavior of writers in groups. He believed that the writers would learn more from one another than from him *if* he could manage the opposed impulses in the class of aggression—to put down one's rivals and assert one's ego—and agape—"to advance the cause of good writing in an unselfish fashion by making useful suggestions." Cowley remembers that class as one in which agape won out and writing was improved.

Cowley was excited by the chapters of *Cuckoo's Nest* that Kesey read in class, and later he read the whole of the half-finished manuscript and they talked it over in private sessions. Kesey would have been excited himself to be engaged in talks with Jack Kerouac's editor; "like all the other young candidates for beatitude," he'd prowled San Francisco's North Beach hoping for a glimpse of Neal Cassady and even written a (not terribly good) Beat novel himself. In December, Cowley would write two letters to Pat Covici back in the home office by way of scouting reports on the work of his students, including Ernest Gaines, Tillie Olsen, and Peter Beagle. It was Ken Kesey's work in progress, though, that took up the most space. "I'm interested in the work of a rough bird in the class named *Ken Kesey*," he announced. Cowley found Kesey's novel, set in a mental hospital, to be full of promise. He told Covici, "The narrator is a loony [Cowley's language here and elsewhere grates to contemporary ears] who pretends to be deaf & dumb, so that he is allowed to hear all sorts private conversations . . . One tough customer, not loony at all, comes into the hospital and tries to disrupt the system. The plot of the novel is this tough customer's battle with the head nurse, in which the reader feels certain he'll be defeated. I suspect, but I'm not at all certain, that the book may turn out to be something rather powerful." Under Cowley's guidance over the next year, conveyed more in conversation than editorial work, the book emerged just as he'd hoped and predicted.

The origins of *Cuckoo's Nest* are almost as mythic as those of *On the Road*. Kesey found the subject matter and the inspiration for his novel in two jobs he took to support himself and his wife when his fellow-ship lapsed. The first was as an orderly in the psych wards of a local VA hospital in Menlo Park, where he was employed for nine months, from the summer of 1960 to the spring of 1961. He mostly worked the red-eye shift, from midnight to eight a.m., relatively easy duty: "I had nothing to do but a little mopping and buffing, check the wards every forty-five minutes with a flashlight, be coherent to the night nurse stopping by on her hourly rounds, write my novel, and talk to the sleepless nuts." Kesey's sympathies were with the patients, whom he saw being mistreated, sometimes cruelly, by some of the aides. In fact he would be fired for picking up one such coworker and throwing him through a shower door. Mostly, though, Kesey occupied himself by sitting at his typewriter five or six hours a night and writing the book that would become *Cuckoo's Nest*. His book's sense of place and con-finement is always powerfully palpable, as is his empathy for the in-mates. "I could see the suffering and anguish in the faces of the mental patients as if it were written there in black and white," he'd recall. He even made crude but powerful pencil sketches of them.

Kesey's empathetic reaction was being mediated by the powerful hallucinogens that he was taking, courtesy of his second "job." Six months earlier his friend Vic Lovell, a graduate student in psychology and one of the Perry Lane insurgents, had told Kesey of his experi-ences as a test patient in drug trials being conducted at that VA hospi-tal, for which one could be paid. The money was good, twenty dollars per session for beginners and up to seventy-five dollars for experi-enced psychic travelers. It sounded like easy work and Kesey looked like a perfect subject, young, healthy, and with no mental health is-sues, as was required by these carefully "scientific" experiments. Thus quite accidentally and ironically, Ken Kesey became a kind of psy-chonaut or inner space monkey, "taking a ride to the land inside," as the Amboy Dukes sang, courtesy of the United States government. What he found in there changed the trajectory of his life, and then quite a few other lives.

It was the Central Intelligence Agency that was interested in the possible uses of psychedelic drugs like LSD as potential Cold War weapons for mind control and interrogation and other purposes. Ken Kesey's participation as a test subject and what would transpire from it represent a spectacular example of blowback. Starting early in 1960, Kesey would show up at the VA every Tuesday to an antiseptic room, equipped with only a Wollensak tape recorder to capture what he would think and feel and see, with a wire window looking out on the psychiatric ward, to be dosed with LSD-25, psilocybin, mescaline, and other chemical compounds. Various tests would be performed on him to assess his motor functions and cognitive and perceptual abilities. Questioned by a nurse after one trip, Kesey replied blissfully, "I think it's a good experience. . . . I think any time you see more, especially if you have a basic inherent love among people, the more you see of them, of the real person, the more you like." A bunch of sober doctors in white lab coats had helped Ken Kesey blast open the doors of perception.

Soon enough, a lot of those drugs were finding their way over to Perry Lane, and the character of the parties there would change drastically. Malcolm Cowley and his wife, Muriel, would sometimes have Ken Kesey and Faye over to their home for drinks and dinner with visiting literary royalty like C. P. Snow and Stephen Spender. One night Kesey returned the favor by inviting the Cowleys to a big party at their house where most of the writing class was in attendance. "On the table by the window was a huge bowl of green punch from which clouds of mist or steam kept rising," he recalled. Kesey told him that the punch was Kool-Aid with dry ice, and he handed half a cupful to Cowley, who remarked, "It looks like the sort of punch that Satan would serve." He never did take a sip of that electric Kool-Aid; he put the cup down and went into the kitchen, where Kesey's visiting grand-mother gave him a pull from a bottle of Arkansas bootleg whiskey. The party got noisier from there.

Another door opened for Kesey as a result of his psychedelic ex-periments, a literary one. In particular they helped him to handle the schizophrenic inner visions of the half–Native American Broom Bromden, the narrator, and Nick Carraway of *Cuckoo's Nest* to Mc-Murphy's Gatsby. The famous opening scene of the book, and possi-bly the idea of the story being told from the Chief's point of view itself, came to Kesey after gobbling some peyote buttons. The Chief's sudden vision of the Big Nurse swelling to monstrous proportions—"she blows up bigger and bigger, big as a tractor"—and his belief in a mys-terious and all-powerful Combine in shadowy control of all that hap-pens in the ward, have a hallucinatory power that owes a debt to the effects of the peyote. According to Tom Wolfe, Kesey even had some-one clandestinely administer a shock treatment to him so he could accurately render the Chief's state of mind when one is given to him.

In July of 1961, Ken Kesey sent off the finished typescript of *One Flew Over the Cuckoo's Nest* to his old teacher. It found immediate favor with Cowley and the younger staffers at Viking, so with some grum-bling from "the gaffers," it was quickly signed up for an advance of $1,500. Shortly thereafter, Kesey took on Kerouac's agent, Sterling Lord, as his agent. Cowley's report on "the loony bin novel I've been talking about" was positive, but also frank about what he saw as it faults, mostly taking issue with the book's ending and some of the un-convincing speeches that Kesey puts in Broom Bromden's mouth. A bit of final editing took place, and then Viking got to work.

The appeal of the book to a young audience was crucial to Viking's publishing strategy and to its immense cultural resonance. The cata-logue copy invokes George Orwell in its first line and asserts that

"Ken Kesey is concerned with man's battle to be himself in a world of increasing controls, the battle of joy and freedom against a society which fosters guilt and shame." That framing was largely the way the book has been read, and as the sixties gathered momentum, it and Joseph Heller's *Catch-22*, another cry of protest against institutional evil and idiocy, became required generational reading. Today the intensely male and more than a little misogynistic attitudes of the book, the borderline racist use of "the black boys" orderlies as villains, and the cultural appropriation inherent in the figure of Chief Bromden, all strike us as problematic. But at the time, and for decades after, Kesey's novel was taken straight as a powerful and tragic story, an archetypal parable about the struggle to assert one's freedom against the forces of coercion and control. That message is still relevant.

One Flew Over the Cuckoo's Nest was published on February 1, 1962. Although it did not make the list of the top ten bestselling works of fiction of 1962, it was still an immediate hit and it made Ken Kesey a genuine literary star. Much like *On the Road*, the book really took off and reached a readership of millions in the paperback edition that came out a year later. Unlike Jack Kerouac, fame suited Ken Kesey perfectly. His subsequent adventures as the Pied Piper of Psychedelia and a fugitive from justice can be read about with tremendous pleasure in Tom Wolfe's *The Electric Kool-Aid Acid Test*. *Cuckoo's Nest* was adapted into a Broadway play with Kirk Douglas as McMurphy that had a three-month run and was considered a financial and artistic failure. In 1975, though, its film adaptation, directed by Milos Forman and starring Jack Nicholson as McMurphy, would win five Academy Awards and join the short list of film adaptations of classic novels that have been judged to be worthy of their source material. The effect of the novel and film on ideas about mental illness and how sufferers should be treated has been profound.

Two years later Viking would publish Ken Kesey's second novel,

Sometimes a Great Notion, the Faulknerian saga of the brawling Stamper family of Oregon loggers and their epic struggle to bring its timber to market. While a success, it had neither the impact nor the sales of its predecessor. Some people, this writer included, think it the better book. Malcolm Cowley, however, had nothing to do with its publication. There was no breach between them. Cowley just seems to have been otherwise engaged, and Tom Guinzburg and other in-house staffers at Viking took over the publication and the care and feeding of its author, now a celebrity. Kesey would always speak in the warmest terms about his first editor. In a 1963 interview with Gordon Lish, he stated that "Cowley taught me how good a writer *I* could be," and when Lish asked, "Cowley believed in you?" he replied, "More than most." In a 1986 radio interview, Kesey had this to say about his famous writing class at Stanford: "All the people that came out of it have done well, and I've tried to understand why a number of times, and I think it goes back to Malcolm Cowley. Malcolm Cowley taught us something about writing which has to do with more than writing. It has to do with respect for writing, and respect for people who have written. And whenever I do a writing seminar, the first thing I tell them is that it's just as hard to write a bad novel as it is a good novel, and that you don't ever want to hurt anybody." That is a piece of wisdom to cherish in a literary world that is more often cutthroat and competitive.

In 1964, Ken Kesey and his crew of Merry Pranksters piled into a wildly painted old school bus tagged "Furthur," fully wired up with tape recorders and cameras and speakers for maximum sensory overload, for the most famous and certainly the druggiest long bus trip in American history. At the wheel, as God had surely planned it, was none other than Neal "Speed Limit" Cassady, who'd gotten wind of some wild goings-on on Perry Lane, showed up one day in a burnt-out Willys Jeep, speed-rapped his way into Kesey's circle, and never left. They were headed to New York City to see the World's Fair in Queens and to be in the Big Apple for the publication of *Sometimes a Great Notion*. One of the most powerful endorsements of *Cuckoo's Nest* had come from none other than Jack Kerouac. Tom Guinzburg had sent him an advance copy of the book and Kerouac had replied enthusiastically, "A GREAT MAN AND A GREAT NEW AMERICAN NOVELIST . . . tell him not to be ashamed of the dignity of his experience as a man in the world, the hell with the rest." Kesey was thrilled, and one of his ambitions was to finally meet Kerouac when he was in New York. "An epochal summit conference of literary hip" was in the offing.

Neal Cassady was just as eager to bring together his old Beat world and his new drug-fueled milieu. It did not work out that way. Wired on speed, he drove out to Northport, Long Island, to fetch his old friend back to a Prankster party in Manhattan. They were staying in a vacant apartment on Madison and Eighty-Ninth owned by a relative of the group.

When they got back to the party, everybody but Kerouac was tripping and the crazed environment of tape loops and movie cameras and floodlights and distorting mirrors and cavorting nutjobs put off the half-drunk and aging Beat. Kerouac was well into his rightward Barry Goldwater–William F. Buckley phase, and when he saw an American flag draped over a sofa, he walked over to it, folded the flag carefully, and asked if these people were Communists. Robert Stone asked him for a cigarette, and Kerouac angrily told him to buy his own smokes. Shortly thereafter he left. Kesey would always regret that they hadn't just made a quiet and respectful visit to Kerouac's home. The two men never even spoke to each other. "I was disappointed in myself for not going up to him and sincerely expressing how much his work meant to me."

Tom Guinzburg would call *On the Road* and *One Flew Over the Cuckoo's Nest* two of the books, along with *The Grapes of Wrath* and

Death of a Salesman, that would define the history of the Viking Press over the decades. Jack Kerouac and Ken Kesey were as influential in defining the culture of the sixties as F. Scott Fitzgerald and Ernest Hemingway were in the twenties. For one man to have discovered, championed, edited, and published two such books in such a short period of time is a remarkable achievement.

FOURTEEN.

THE LONG RETROSPECTIVE

———

The broad pattern of Malcolm Cowley's life in his last quarter of a century on earth did not differ greatly from the one he had established in the years following the war. He continued his work as a consulting editor for Viking, focusing for the most part on the Portable Library and the Viking Critical Editions. As late as the early eighties, when *he* was in his early eighties, he would come into the offices on Madison Avenue every month from Sherman for a Portables meeting and to transact other business. To many of the younger staffers, he was a kind of curiosity; to others he felt like a visitor from a bygone era, to be regarded with awe. The late distinguished Viking editor in chief Elisabeth Sifton recalled that, despite the challenges of his increasing deafness, he was alert, fully on top of the trends in academia and literaria as they might affect the sale of current and prospective Portables, and a hard-headed judge of market realities.

Cowley was wont to boast that he'd published more books after the age of seventy than he'd done before. The arithmetic backs him up on this claim, if just: By 1967 he'd published six books—actually five and a half, as one of them was a collaboration: *Black Cargoes: A History of the Atlantic Slave Trade, 1518–1865*, published in 1962 with the journalist Daniel Mannix.

From there on, he would publish eight more books, if one includes the Cowley–Burke correspondence. Admittedly a number of these latter books were either collections of previously published essays and reviews, or drawn from earlier writings that he repurposed. But two of them, *The Dream of the Golden Mountains* and *The View from 80*, were original works, and *A Second Flowering*, his prose portrait gallery of Lost Generation figures, while drawn in good part from earlier writing, flows beautifully as a unified work.

The two major themes of Cowley's final decades were these: to offer a retrospective on the works and days of his heroic literary generation, and sometimes, when needed, a vigorous defense; and to come to terms, finally, with his political misjudgments of the thirties, and what kind of guilt he should feel about them. The former task was one of the pleasures of his old age, even if it involved the melancholy duty of memorializing the honored dead, many of them his friends, as he outlived almost all of them. The latter was the internal work of his own conscience, but it was often summoned by attacks from his enemies and critics, which continued to his death in 1989.

Though Cowley had published two books that were vital to the culture of what we call the sixties, a good deal of the excitements of that decade passed him by. He describes himself in that period as "a detached observer, a deaf man gardening in the country and writing about books." Much of what contact he had with younger Americans was in the somewhat artificial milieu of the college classroom. He did recognize that the sixties generation was indeed "a real generation," but they were not really his people and their fights were not his fights. In 1977 he would publish an essay titled "Reconsiderations—the '60s," which proved that he'd been reading the work of the newer writers, but he concluded that the whole project of the sixties had run out of energy and would have little effect on American culture going forward. This was not his opinion alone, of course. He'd been quite alienated by the behaviors of the student radicals, writing this to Wallace Stegner in 1969 about "the great unwashed, unbarbered proletariat of graduate students": "And to think that these jerks, with their ignorance of everything that isn't 'relevant,'—i.e., that happened more than ten years ago—will soon be on the faculties of American universities!"

Unsurprisingly, then, Cowley would soon absent himself from the college campus. His last formal and longish-term teaching engagement was in 1973, when he taught American literature at the University of Warwick for a semester. The students didn't know him from Malcolm Bradbury or Malcolm X, he recalled. From that time forward, although he would still do one-off lectures and panels at various colleges for pay, his teaching career was over.

For a time, Cowley gamely kept up with the new writing, maybe more out of habit than genuine interest. He did pick out Cormac McCarthy early on in his career as a writer to watch, writing to his editor Albert Erskine about his first novel, *The Orchard Keeper*, that "he tells a story marvelously, with a sort of baresark joy as he rushes into scenes of violence. . . . he also loves language, in the way that Faulkner did." (Erskine had been Faulkner's last editor at Random House.) He was not at all enchanted by what he called "the American black-humor-and-catastrophe novelists," with the exception of Thomas Pynchon, whom he deemed "brilliant." He also saw merit in the work of Joyce Carol Oates, Thomas McGuane, Harry Crews, Reynolds Price, and Robert Coover. One writer, though, who loomed large over American fiction in the sixties and seventies whom Cowley could not abide was John Barth, writing to Bernard Bergonzi that "I bogged down night after night in *Giles Goat-Boy* till I said to myself, 'This is spinach and to hell with it.'"

The truth was, Malcolm Cowley was never going to sign on to Barth's theory and practice of "The Literature of Exhaustion." Cowley's critical approach was entirely alien to postmodernism, post-structuralism, self-referential metafiction, the death of the author, the antinovel, and anything whatsoever to do with the new French literary theory. He was finally, he confessed to one correspondent, "unable to read the new fiction," and to another, "It's a new world in which the books themselves seem long-haired and bearded, and I don't know that I feel at home in it." As far as Malcolm Cowley was concerned, the future of literature would have to take care of itself. Time's arrow was pointed backward.

The lengthy list of deaths of Cowley's friends and associates in this period began on July 2, 1961, with the shocking death of Ernest Hemingway at the age of sixty-one. The obituaries stated that he'd accidentally shot himself while cleaning a shotgun, but he'd actually turned the gun on himself to commit suicide, a fact that his wife, Mary Hemingway, would confirm only years later. This hit Malcolm Cowley with particular force. The man who was synonymous with the Lost Generation, the first American to have become the most famous writer on earth, left an absence that Cowley struggled to comprehend. In public, though, he was unflagging in his loyalty and critical advocacy. He served for years as one of Mary Hemingway's most trusted advisers in the matter of which of Hemingway's unpublished works should see the light of print and in what order. In 1967, Cowley, with his keen scent for the literary winds, picked up that Hemingway's stock was falling, and he wrote one of his most impassioned pieces, "Papa and the Parricides," in his defense.

Death had not been good for Hemingway's career. Without his living presence in the world, scholars and critics felt free to say some things about his work that they'd probably been thinking to themselves for years: that a lot of it had been overvalued. Cowley notes that respected critics like Leslie Fiedler and Stanley Edgar Hyman had whittled down the canon of Hemingway's work genuinely worth reading to *The Sun Also Rises* and an indeterminate number of stories, mostly the early ones. Dwight Macdonald had excluded even the novels from serious consideration, asserting that Hemingway was essentially a short-story writer and really just that. Out the window went *A Farewell to Arms* and *For Whom the Bell Tolls* and *The Old Man and the Sea.* Something similar was happening in academia, where the stories alone were being assigned and seriously studied. Cowley frames this as the result of a kind of critical one-upmanship—"I am even more discerning than you are because I exclude even more than you do."

Taking in the larger picture of determined attempts to shrink Hemingway and his work down to size, he resorts to the metaphors of jackals circling around the carcass of a dead lion, and the primal Freudian ritual murder of the literary fathers. This latter process he believed was happening not just to Hemingway but to other Lost Generation figures. He concludes, "My protest is simply in defense of American literature. This is vastly richer now than it was when Hemingway started writing, but it is not yet so rich that it can afford to disown and devalue one of its lasting treasures."

The deaths of his friends and colleagues in his last decades came in blows: William Faulkner and E. E. Cummings in 1962; Van Wyck Brooks in 1963; John Dos Passos in 1970; Edmund Wilson in 1971; Ezra Pound in 1972; Conrad Aiken in 1973; Thornton Wilder in 1975; Alexander Calder in 1976; Bruce Bliven in 1977; Matthew Josephson in 1978; Allen Tate in 1979; and Marshall Best and Archibald MacLeish in 1982. With each death a part of his literary, intellectual, and emotional life was leaving him. As he would put it in 1977 in a letter to his old classmate Jacob Davis, "My address book reads like a necrology."

Some of these deaths he would mourn privately; others he took as the occasion to memorialize the departed figure in print, including Cummings, Wilson, Aiken, and Bliven. Edmund Wilson was a special and complicated case. Their careers had mirrored and intersected with each other's in so many ways. In their generation, Wilson had clearly been the dominant critical figure, and Cowley, while never competitive with Wilson precisely, was always aware of who stood where in the literary pecking order. Cowley would write about Wilson twice after his death, once for *The New Republic* in an obituary of sorts, and once for *The Saturday Review* in 1977, a review of his posthumous *Letters on Literature and Politics*. Both pieces hit all the right notes, tick off all the pertinent facts, tell all the right stories, deliver all the appropriate superlatives, but they lack one conspicuous quality that Cowley was skilled at summoning when he felt it: affection.

Cowley may have been a bit short of warmth for Edmund Wilson, but the older critic provided him with a good example to follow in the matter of tending to his literary legacy. Wilson was an orderly and assiduous self-curator, and he left a mighty shelf of books behind, the majority of them collections of the essays, reviews, journalism, poems, parodies, and plays that he'd written. Cowley began his own self-curation later in life, but he would make up for lost time in his own assemblage of a substantial shelf of books.

The publishing part of the long retrospective began in 1966 with the Viking publication of *The Faulkner-Cowley File*, a deft assemblage of letters and interstitial narration that tells the tale of how the *Portable Faulkner* volume came into the world and the effect it was to have on Faulkner's career and the resulting friendship between the two men. In 1967 came the publication of the collection *Think Back on Us: A Contemporary Chronicle of the 1930s*, edited and introduced by the scholar of American literature Henry Dan Piper. Piper had the idea for the book because he needed some kind of sourcebook for college reading on the intellectual, social, and literary history of the thirties, just then coming back into view. Cowley's work from the decade, almost all of it published in *The New Republic* and divided into "The

Social Record" and "The Literary Record," filled the bill splendidly. Its publication was well received and proved that Cowley's work could survive the passage of thirty years. Cowley also deserves credit for allowing Piper to reprint some political pieces from the decade that place his overenthusiasm for the revolutionary cause and his shortsightedness about Stalinist Russia on display—something Wilson was not willing to do. Piper followed up that book in 1970 with a companion volume titled *A Many-Windowed House: Collected Essays on American Writers and American Writing*. A collection of fifteen critical essays on American writers ranging from Hawthorne, Whitman, and James to Frost, Brooks, Pound, and O'Neill, the book demonstrates Cowley's gifts as an Americanist.

The collecting of Cowley was taken up by Viking later in the decade, at his suggestion and by his own editorial hand, with the publication of —*And I Worked at the Writer's Trade: Chapters of Literary History, 1918–1978*. The book manages to hang together as an episodic sort of survey of the American literary enterprise from the First World War to the present. The book's opening essay, "'And Jesse Begat . . . ': A Note on Literary Generations," is Cowley's fullest explanation of his core idée fixe about the generational progression of American literature.

The *Times Book Review* gave it a splashy send-off, and an equally long and prominent interview with George Plimpton ran in the same issue. By this point, Malcolm Cowley was in certain circles regarded as a national literary treasure and attention was being paid. Seven years later, Viking would publish a similar volume, *The Flower and the Leaf*, compiled and introduced by Donald Faulkner, filled with essays and reviews and reminiscences.

Cowley's 1973 book *A Second Flowering: Works and Days of the Lost Generation* might have been published as another collection, consisting as it does, for the most part, of previously published work. But he applied himself with great skill to creating a seamless reading experience, a warm and often magical book. The idea for the book dated back to the early fifties, with the same cast of Lost Generation subjects, save Hart Crane: Hemingway, Fitzgerald, Faulkner, Cummings, Wilder, Wolfe, and Dos Passos. Cowley's introduction, "The Other War," about the effect the experience of the Great War had on his generation, is arguably the most moving piece of writing he ever did.

The reviewers greeted the book rapturously. William Styron put it eloquently in the *Times Book Review*: "It is unthinkable that this beautiful, honest book will not be read as an indispensable companion piece to the work of Hemingway, Fitzgerald, Faulkner, Wolfe, and all the rest, as long as they are read and have bearing upon men's common experience. *Ave atque vale!*" Vincent Sheean, a distinguished member of Cowley's generation himself, asked, "How many generations ever had a true chronicler at the deep heart's core?" Even Cowley's old critical adversary Clifton Fadiman wrote him an enthusiastic letter of praise. It is a book that deserves rediscovery.

One of the dubious honors that attend literary longevity is that the survivor can become regarded as something like a vending machine of anecdotes and facts about the distinguished departed by biographers, scholars, graduate students, and the merely curious and intrusive. Cowley took on this burden diligently and for the most part with good humor, with the occasional complaint registered. In 1978 he wrote to Allen Tate, "People come round here with tape recorders to tap, tap, tape my memories as if I were a National Scholarly Resource. The National Endowment for the Humanities ought to provide me with a secretary."

The interviewing had actually begun a little ominously in 1955 when a Yale graduate student in American Studies by the name of Thomas Kennerly Wolfe questioned him, along with James T. Farrell and Archibald MacLeish, for his PhD thesis titled "The League of American Writers: Communist Organizational Activity Among American Writers, 1929–1942." We know that author today as the swashbuckling, white-suited New Journalist Tom Wolfe. The thesis of his thesis is that the League was a front organization of the Communist Party, whose aim it was to manipulate the system of status and other career rewards to keep the literati in line and inside the big ideological tent that was the People's Front. He was not wrong. About the last thing Malcolm Cowley would have wanted to talk about on the record in 1955 was his fellow-traveling past, and his testimony is cautious and quite hedged about.

Wolfe would be succeeded in the next decades by dozens of other interviewers, and Cowley's cooperation with them, sometimes willing and sometimes weary, is testified to by his prominence in the pages— text, acknowledgments, and indexes—of unnumbered biographies, cultural histories, literary studies, journal articles, and long unread graduate theses. Of particular note is his almost ubiquitous presence in the pages of Daniel Aaron's classic 1961 history of the literary politics of the thirties, *Writers on the Left*.

The most painstaking, most halting, and most painful work of Malcolm Cowley's last decades, however, was really internal: arriving at some sort of self-understanding about his political positions and miscalculations of the thirties. In 1982, he would write with blunt frankness to Kenneth Burke, "God, how blind we were in the 1930s." The difficult problem he faced was how to say something as straightforward as this in public without being pilloried yet again. "Now I'll have to face up to my own errors, and that without encouraging the Cold Warriors." Those two conflicting imperatives lend a note of ambivalence to everything he would write on this subject.

This process began in earnest in 1965 with the publication of an essay suggestively titled "The Sense of Guilt" in *The Kenyon Review*.

This was an essay that was as much about a feeling as it was about actions. It flirted with becoming a confessional, but always pulled back.

Cowley reached an important inflection point in 1968 when he read the historian Robert Conquest's definitive history of Stalin's murderous purges, *The Great Terror*, and wrote an almost anguished review of it for *The Washington Post Book World*. He concedes that Conquest proves beyond any doubt that Stalin's trials were rigged and that their victims were innocent of the crimes for which they were convicted and executed. This forces him to reflect on his own past and that of the other "men of good will" in that crucial period. He concludes that, even if their influence on Stalin would have been negligible, "most of us did nothing" and their "silence . . . now seems close to complicity." In his review, he accuses himself and his fellow liberals in the period of a middle-class naivete about the ways of tyranny, and offers a personal confession "to what might be called my astute gullibility." "Astute," he means, in his careful reading of the trial record, but "gullible in the sense that I missed the telltale signs of fraud and coercion." This was an apology, but with an excuse and an odd adjective attached.

Cowley had been contemplating and working on and avoiding working on his memoir of the thirties almost as soon as the decade ended. Fifty years later he finally got around to it, or at least its first half, and *The Dream of the Golden Mountains: Remembering the 1930s* was published in 1980. The title alludes to "The Big Rock Candy Mountain," the 1928 folk song about a hobo's idea of heaven. In this case "The Golden Mountain" was the writer's idea of social heaven, a world where they would help to overthrow the capitalist system and march shoulder to shoulder with the workers into "a dream of revolutionary brotherhood." The events it relates from 1930 to 1936, most of them ones that Cowley either witnessed or participated in, have been fully covered earlier. It was published as a major literary event.

Observers from all points of the political compass, from Cowley's most fervent supporters to his most devoted foes, had been awaiting it for a long time, and they all wanted to have their say. It was a beacon and a target.

The *Times Book Review* made the obvious choice of Alfred Kazin to review it. Kazin was a nurser of resentments, but he put those aside to produce a warm and appreciative review. Daniel Aaron and R. W. B. Lewis weighed in with praise, and many other such effusions were registered across the country.

The most predictable naysayer was Cowley's devoted adversary Sidney Hook, who begins his review in *The American Scholar* by calling the book well written and absorbing before going full *Partisan Review*: "With respect to all this"—i.e., the radical intellectual movement of the thirties—"and particularly Malcolm Cowley's own activity during the decade, this book is from first to last a self-serving exercise in apologetics." Even when he was right, or even sort of right, Hook managed to be as tiresome and bombastic as when he was wrong, and he put Cowley in the dock for his show trial sins, even though the book ends before any news of them had emerged from the Soviet Union. An even more vicious, this-time-it's-personal review appeared in *The American Spectator* by a Harvard academic historian, Kenneth Lynn.

Cowley would work on the second half of his memoirs of the thirties for the next four years and publish four long installments. The first excerpt, "No Homage to Catalonia," came out in January 1982. The second, "Echoes from Moscow: 1937–38," in January 1984, describes the confusion and disarray on the left as word of Stalin's show trials began to emerge and offers up contrition for his own "blind credulity" about them. The third, "Lament for the Abraham Lincoln Battalion," came out in summer 1984. The final excerpt, "A Time of Resignations," appeared in November 1984 and evokes the incoherent responses of the Western radicals and liberals when the Nazi-Soviet Non-Aggression Pact of 1939 was signed, and it offers some haunting vignettes of the pinched lives of the European émigrés who'd made it to New York. After that, despite this impressive burst of productivity, he published nothing more on the subject—his health was failing and his energy seeping away.

To the end of his life, Malcolm Cowley remained in an unquiet state on these political matters. John Leonard, at the conclusion of his review of —*And I Worked at the Writer's Trade*, asks himself what accounts for the sense of uneasy qualm that suffuses that book. He decides that "I suspect that Stalin bothers him the most . . . he won't forgive himself for a confusion of politics and literature." He finishes this way: "If I am right about Mr. Cowley, then he is wrong about himself. It was a century for mistakes. He is still a hero of the culture we breathe."

There was one last battle to fight, at the advanced age of eighty-six. His adversary was the literary historian Kenneth Lynn, who'd made a reputation as a truculent, sharp-elbowed contrarian of a conservative bent. Lynn's assault on Cowley began in 1978 in *Commentary* with his review of A. Scott Berg's widely beloved biography *Max Perkins: Editor of Genius*. Lynn explains that Berg had gotten everything wrong, not just about Perkins, but also about publishing, American literature, and human nature. The review begins with a long attack on *Exile's Return*, which, Lynn claims, has clouded our minds and prevented a clear and accurate understanding of the Lost Generation giants that Perkins published. The assault gained momentum in 1980 with his ugly review of *The Dream of the Golden Mountains*. It culminated in July 1981, again in *Commentary*, with Lynn's review of Hemingway's selected letters, which he used as the occasion for a comprehensive attack on Cowley as a literary critic, a political malefactor, and, when you came right down to it, an enemy of the people.

Lynn's thesis was that, as the political thirties ended, the radicals Edmund Wilson and Malcolm Cowley were casting about for some new "non-Marxist modes of continuing [their] assault on the moral credentials of capitalist society." First Wilson and then Cowley found it, he asserts, in a politically motivated misreading of Hemingway's haunting story "Big Two-Hearted River." Lynn maintains that the story is nothing more than an unshadowed idyll of trout fishing and wilderness renewal in Michigan's north country. The two critics, however, Wilson in his 1939 essay on Hemingway and Cowley in his introduction to *The Portable Hemingway*, recast Nick Adams not as a happy latter-day Huck Finn, but as a man holding on psychically for dear life against the trauma of his disastrous experience of war. It was, Lynn argues, the first instance of a larger intellectual postwar trend of "anti-American interpretations of American literature [that] sprang up like poisonous weeds."

This was inaccurate, and frankly ridiculous. Lynn was accusing Cowley of bad faith, of perverting the thing he cared about most in the world to a base political end. Cowley responded, as he had to, in 1984 with one of the best essays he ever wrote, "Hemingway's Wound—and Its Consequences for American Literature."

Cowley's first riposte is that Lynn is reasoning from incomplete evidence—a volume of *selected* letters. In fact, in the course of writing his profile for *Life* and for some time afterward, he and Hemingway had had a long exchange of letters and in one of those Hemingway explicitly says, "In the first war, I now see I was hurt very badly, in the body, mind and spirit, and also morally . . . Big Two Hearted River is a story about a man who is home from the war. But the war is not mentioned." Hemingway goes on to admit that Nick Adams is really he, and that "I was still hurt badly in that story."

After showing how other key Hemingway stories also deal with the effects of what we now recognize as post-traumatic stress disorder,

Cowley goes on to answer Lynn's political libel. His introduction to the Portable was written in 1944, at the height of World War II, a struggle he supported with every fiber of his being. Demoralizing his fellow citizens was the absolute last thing he would have intended to do. More than that, he decides that, now being under attack, "it is time for me to break a self-imposed political silence and state my position. I am a little American." What he means by that is that he loves his country chiefly for its people, its freedoms, and its remaining rural spaces and cohesive communities. What he doesn't like are the big abstractions like Progress and Prosperity and their outsize manifestations, and the kind of saber-rattling jingoism that characterized America during the Reagan years. He concludes with a three-page description of the triumphant rise of American literature in the twentieth century to world stature, and the part that critics such as Edmund Wilson, and by implication, he himself, played in that rise. His defense against Lynn's attack becomes something like a closing statement on everything that has mattered to him in his long life. Malcolm Cowley took his stand, and he went out swinging. "Hemingway's Wound" was one of the last pieces he published.

By 1984 he and Muriel had entered the country of the Old Old. At the age of eighty-six, the challenges to their health and mobility were becoming considerable, and they were forced to move their bedroom to the ground floor. The stairs were no longer negotiable, and a home health aide had become a necessity.

As it happened, Cowley had written about these things five years earlier, and it had earned him a pretty decent payday, by his modest standards. In 1978, *Life* magazine had resumed publication as an illustrated monthly magazine, and its editor, Byron Dobell, had written to him to see if he would be interested in contributing something on the realities of aging. Cowley's essay "The View from 80," tagged "Facing old age with wit and even a measure of joy," ran in the December

1978 issue. It garnered a fair amount of positive attention, won a National Magazine Award in the essay category, and got Cowley on *The Dick Cavett Show* as a guest, along with Lillian Gish, the pioneering film actress then aged eighty-six—one of his few times before a television camera.

Viking had the idea to capitalize on this opportunity, and in 1980 it published a slim, seventy-four-page expansion of Cowley's essay under the same title. The book possesses humor, charm, and a measure of true, hard-won wisdom. Cowley captures the doubleness of old age beautifully: It is "only a costume assumed for others; the true, the essential self is timeless. In a moment he will rise and go for a ramble in the woods, taking a gun along, or a fishing rod, if it is spring. Then he creaks to his feet, bending forward to keep his balance, and realizes that he will do nothing of the sort." It became a modest bestseller and remained in print for many years in its Penguin paperback edition.

A piece of advice that Cowley offers at the end of the book is this: "Poet or housewife, businessman or teacher, every old person needs a work project if he wants to keep himself alive." He cites Grandma Moses, who traded needlework for oil painting at age seventy-eight; Carl Sandburg, who took to raising goats in his eighties; and *New Yorker* editor Katharine White, who retired with her husband, E. B. White, to garden in Maine. Gardening had been one of his and Muriel's passions, but as the years passed, that activity became too strenuous for them. Cowley continues, "One project among many, one that tempts me and might be tempting to others, is trying to find a shape or pattern in our lives."

To finish a story, it is necessary also to look back at its beginnings. A trip he took, probably his last from Sherman, in 1986, helped him do that. He and his son, Rob, had not been estranged precisely, but there had been coolness and a distance. That began to change in the early eighties when Rob visited for a weekend and his car broke down, so he had to stay a couple more days while it was being repaired. As he recalls, "So my father and I started talking, and something happened." He took to visiting every other weekend from Newport, Rhode Island, and father and son would usually end up talking all through the night. On one of those weekends, Malcolm Cowley asked his son to drive him back to Belsano, the place of his birth.

In Belsano, they went in search of some of his boyhood friends who were still alive. One of them was the widow of his best boyhood friend, Doss Paul. They drove up to a house where an elderly woman was sitting on the porch. Cowley said, "Hello!" and called out to her, and she replied, "Well, Mal, I thought you'd never come!" They sat down together for a good long chat. Whenever Cowley would ask after an old friend, Mrs. Paul would say, "Well, he's ailin' some." There was a lot of "ailin'" going on among his still living old friends and acquaintances in Belsano.

The next stop was the first house that his family had owned, which had been turned into a roadhouse tavern, the White Mill. They went in and Cowley asked the owner if he could look around because he'd been born there. The owner replied, "Well, I think that is worth a beer, pal!" and they sat and had another long jaw with him and his son, a long-haul trucker. The journalism students at Indiana University had actually produced a plaque for the White Mill stating the Malcolm Cowley, the distinguished writer, had been born in that very building. Cowley was pleased to see the plaque but amused that it had been relegated to a place among the liquor bottles at the back of the bar. A last stop down the road was the old stone house that Cowley's parents had later built. The lintel over the doorway still had "Doctor Cowley" carved into it.

The years after that trip were progressively more difficult for Malcolm and Muriel, as the ravages of old age got the upper hand. Details of that struggle and decline can be gleaned from an essay Cowley wrote for the About Men column of *The New York Times Magazine* of May 26, 1985, "Being Old Old." He observes that the infirmities accumulate, and the once simple and easy things, like getting into bed and out, pulling on pants, standing up, and walking (or in his case a sort of waddling sideways shuffle), are now "problems to be solved" if any independence is to be maintained. Help should be gratefully accepted from any quarter.

The essay was the last piece Malcolm Cowley was to publish. He either couldn't write anymore or just plain didn't want to, and the next year he declared himself finished. Rob had set up a workspace for his father on the ground floor with his books and filing cabinets and manual typewriter all handy, but nothing doing. Kenneth Burke came up to Sherman at that time, driven by his son Mike, ostensibly for a party at the Blumes' across Church Road. His real purpose was to try to get his old friend writing again. Burke spent an hour with Cowley alone in the house, but when he finally finished and left, he was in tears. He told Rob, "I tried to do everything to persuade your father to start writing again, and he refuses. He says he's written his last words." Remembering this, Rob Cowley shook his head and said, "Oh Jesus, it was a tough moment." Tough for his father too—"It's a torture to be useless," Cowley would lament.

I had the honor of attending Malcolm Cowley's ninetieth-birthday party in the house in Sherman on August 24, 1988. Elisabeth Sifton had left Viking, and I had become Cowley's editorial contact there. When Donald Faulkner and I arrived, a small crowd of well-wishers had gathered in the kitchen-dining area of the house, with a birthday cake and the usual balloons and presents on hand. I remember that the distinguished Edith Wharton biographer R. W. B. Lewis and his wife, Nancy, were there; Peter and Ebie Blume from across the road; and Rob Cowley and his wife, Didi Lorillard, as well. Then the health aide wheeled Malcolm and Muriel out in their wheelchairs. This was my own first close-up view of the really old old, and I found it shocking to see how physically reduced they were. Still, everyone soldiered on cheerfully, the candles were lit and somehow blown out, the slices of cake were distributed, and we all fell to making party chat, until . . . a startlingly loud voice boomed out, "I'M BORED!!!" Then a pause. Then at a slightly lower volume, "With myself!" Malcolm was telling us that all his energy had been used up and we all needed to leave, which we did, with polite dispatch.

The end was not all that far away. In December 1988, the letters volume, the final book by Malcolm Cowley, was published to great acclaim for its astonishing riches; it would be nominated for a National Book Critics Circle Award in Biography/Autobiography for 1988. Three months later, on March 27, 1989, at nearby New Milford Hospital, Malcolm Cowley died of a heart attack.

The obituaries were quick in coming. He made the front page of *The New York Times* with his picture in the lower right-hand corner; inside, Albin Krebs provided a highly respectful précis of Cowley's greatest hits—his intimate Lost Generation associations and the writing of *Exile's Return*, the publication of *On the Road* and *One Flew Over the Cuckoo's Nest*, the rescue mission of William Faulkner, the discovery and nurturing of John Cheever, all of it.

Other newspapers followed suit—hundreds of them from the great cities to the small ones. The political controversies were not mentioned at all or only in passing.

One particularly gracious tribute came from John Updike, who'd become friendly with Cowley through American Academy business. He said, "Cowley was a living bridge, both in his genial person and his engaging, shrewd criticism, with the generation that was young in the twenties. His reactions to and perceptions of Hemingway, Fitzgerald, Faulkner and Dos Passos are invaluable. He was an energetic and gregarious man who lived the life of the mind with gusto and good nature."

Malcolm Cowley was buried in North Cemetery, a few hundred yards away from his home on Church Road. Muriel Maurer Cowley would join him there a year later. He was the last significant member of the heroic literary generation of the twenties to die, save his friend from childhood Kenneth Burke.

EPILOGUE:

POLITICS AND MEMORY

———

Two months after his death, on May 22, 1989, a memorial service was held for Malcolm Cowley at the Century Association, the club he'd belonged to for many years. The service took place in the billiards room in the basement. Attendance was modest, perhaps twenty-five or so people, including this writer. In the audience were Altie Karper, who'd served as Malcolm's assistant at Viking with cheerful efficiency, and several other Viking staffers; Donald Faulkner; Scott Donaldson, whose Hemingway biography Cowley had edited; Kenneth Burke; and Eudora Welty, who was seated and whom we all looked at sideways in abashed admiration. Rob Cowley performed the emcee's duties gracefully and with warm humor.

There were three speakers. Alan Williams, who'd been Cowley's editor for many years, spoke of him eloquently and wittily as a colleague at Viking, a peerless editor himself, and a sagacious and sometimes tart judge of literary talent. Claude Rawson of the University of Warwick, where Cowley had taught for a semester, remembered him as a dedicated teacher, a very good friend of his family's, and somewhat unnervingly accident prone. Dan Aaron, the leading academic scholar of the political thirties, memorialized him as the unmatched chronicler of his literary generation, one who "subordinated the over-weening 'I' to the inclusive 'we,' and appeared rather as an open-eyed, sophisticated rustic, recounting bemusedly the antics and tragedies and triumphs of his more assertive contemporaries."

Rob Cowley had invited anyone else to speak who wished to do so. A stooped-over and tiny Kenneth Burke stepped up to the dais, wearing Converse All-Star basketball sneakers and looking like Leon Trotsky on a bad hair day. Every person in the room was aware of the extraordinary personal and literary history that the Cowley–Burke friendship represented, so we prepared to listen with keen anticipation. Burke began to talk in a high-pitched voice, but none of us could make out a word of what he was trying to say. Then he gave up on words entirely and let out the single most heart-rending wail of grief I have ever heard, a keening noise that hurt the heart. It sounded like something you would have heard from the stage at the end of a Greek tragedy. We all understood what Kenneth Burke was saying. Rob Cowley gently led him away from the dais.

The subject of politics would, however, not go away. A year later, Donald Faulkner's *The Portable Malcolm Cowley* was published, and it was reviewed in *The New Republic* by Irving Howe. After a couple of throat-clearing paragraphs about Cowley's stature as a critic, Howe launched into his real theme, which was how inadequately Faulkner had acknowledged his political mistakes of the thirties. Howe then devoted fully half of the long review to a stinging rehashing of the political sins of Malcolm Cowley. Ouch. Really?

By the time the book was published, I had left Viking Penguin for another job, but I still read this review with great dismay. Irving Howe was an important and sometimes even great critic, but he enjoyed "arguing the world" entirely too much, as his famous extended feuds with Philip Roth and the radical students of the New Left showed. Did he really think that the editor of an anthology meant to demonstrate

Malcolm Cowley at his best should go into his subject's worst and most painful moments at great length? Would that have been either appropriate or necessary? That this review ran in, of all places, *The New Republic* made Howe's performance even more upsetting.

Sad to relate, Howe's piece was a harbinger. In 2014, Harvard University Press published Hans Bak's voluminous assemblage of Cowley's selected letters, *The Long Voyage*. The book occasioned a good deal of renewed and positive attention to Cowley and many of the reviews were respectful and full of praise for Bak's heroic job of research, collation, editing, and annotation. The book in no way attempts to hide or minimize his politics; they are on full display, and Bak registers unambiguous judgment on them.

Here, however, are the headlines of two of the reviews by noted critics: "What's Left of Malcolm Cowley" (Adam Kirsch in *City Journal*); and "Malcolm Cowley Was One of the Best Literary Tastemakers of the Twentieth Century. Why Were His Politics So Awful?" (Christopher Benfey in *The New Republic*). Cowley for years served as a convenient political punching bag for neoconservative critics like Robert Alter, Sidney Hook, and Fred Siegel. Joseph Epstein's line "Nearly every one of the printed literary opinions of Malcolm Cowley . . . needs to be fumigated for possible political motive" is much quoted and palpably untrue. Sigh. No wonder Cowley once remarked peevishly to his granddaughter, "I sometimes say I must be a lion because I have so many fleas on my rump."

I am of the party of Malcolm Cowley, obviously, and I think he deserves to be remembered in a fuller, deeper, and kinder fashion. If I were to say to his critics, as I am tempted to, that they should give it a rest and lay off, it would be understandable. But I don't want to say that. I fully stipulate, as the lawyers say, that the political behavior of the American literary left in the thirties was in so many respects foolish and reckless and blind to political realities, and that the "sense of guilt" that Malcolm Cowley wrote about in his sixties and later had been fully earned. All too often in the course of researching this book, I found myself wanting to yell when he was heading badly astray, like the narrator of Delmore Schwartz's story about the courtship of his parents, "Nothing good will come of it!" In no way am I suggesting that his politics should be forgotten or hidden away, or that he doesn't deserve some blame for what he said and did—and didn't say or do. What I am saying is that the critics and literary historians of the future need to widen their apertures and expand their timelines and take him in as a writer in full. Not to do so is to miss great literary riches and distort our sense of an important and immensely attractive and likable figure in our literature. He is a good voice to have in your head. To continue to excoriate Cowley so single-mindedly is to indulge in a tired, over-repeated trope.

There is one thing about Cowley's career that is almost impossible to encapsulate, and that is the intricacy and the tensile strength of the web of associations he wove over many decades. To really appreciate this, you need to get to the reading room of the Newberry Library, where his papers reside, and spend day after day after day (as I have) going through the more than one hundred fifty boxes containing almost five thousand folders of his correspondence, some of them bulging. The letters to and from him include many, even most, of the marquee names of American literature of the past century, even more names of significant figures of lesser wattage, and even *more* names of people little known or not known at all. Early in their careers, major figures such as Kurt Vonnegut and Philip Roth wrote to him soliciting his review attention; sixties cult writers such as Richard Fariña and Richard Brautigan sought his advice.

This epistolary word horde is even more astonishing when you consider that there are significant gaps in the correspondence—chiefly the files of *The New Republic*, which the office manager had purged during the war for scrap paper—and many of Cowley's letters reside in other archives in the United States and in Europe. After a while you get the sense that Malcolm Cowley managed to insert himself in just about every literary development that mattered and was a one-man favor bank, recommending this one, urging on that one, advising another one, day after day, year after year without pause. He did all this and he wrote those thousands of reviews and essays and letters and his books, and edited the reviews and essays and books of other writers too, and tended his garden and supported his family and had a very active social life as well.

This web of associations is the real reason why Hans Bak's otherwise eyebrow-raising claim that Cowley "reached a larger audience, and so in the end did perhaps more for American literature, than such luminaries as Alfred Kazin and Edmund Wilson" holds up. Wilson was the greater critic and Kazin the more graceful and lyrical writer, but neither of them engaged in anything like the heroic, ceaseless activity on behalf of American writers and writing that Malcolm Cowley did. This is why I stand by the conclusion I came to in the review of *The Long Voyage* that initiated this book: If you don't reckon with Malcolm Cowley's life and work, you can't really understand how American literature ascended to its rightful place among the great literatures of the world, or how it was made.

ACKNOWLEDGMENTS

I have many people to thank for the existence of this book.

Bill Thomas, the brilliant publisher of Doubleday and my onetime boss and forever good friend, allowed me to work at home for a period when I began writing (well, not writing, but at least reading a lot and thinking about writing) *The Insider.*

I really do not know how I could have written this book without the heroic efforts of Hans Bak, the very great Malcolm Cowley scholar. In his two books, *Malcolm Cowley: The Formative Years* and *The Long Voyage: Selected Letters of Malcolm Cowley,* he blazed the path to comprehending Cowley's life in ways large and small. He is admirable and exemplary and a master of the endnote. He is the giant upon whose shoulders I have perched.

Robert Cowley, Malcolm's son and a considerable editor and writer himself, has been consistently encouraging of my book over the years and helpful in dozens of ways. Probably my best day as a researcher took place at his home in Newport, Rhode Island, where he submitted to my questions with good grace and impressive acuity. I will never forget it. His devotion to the cause of getting his father the attention he deserves is inspiring.

I am also grateful to his daughter, the novelist Miranda Cowley Heller, for sharing memories of her beloved grandparents in emails and at lunch at Mac's Shack in Wellfleet. She helped me with a couple of phenomenal quotes.

My friend André Bernard, formerly of the Guggenheim Foundation, opened up for me a treasure trove of Malcolm Cowley's reports and recommendations spanning decades. It was like having the curtain pulled back to reveal the operating system of American literary prestige.

Alison Hinderliter of the Newberry Library was endlessly helpful to me as I explored the vast Cowley archive that they own and have so scrupulously put in order. Special thanks to Isabella Strazzabosco and Megan Ryan, who kept those boxes coming.

Thanks to the Berg Collection of the New York Public Library, the Tamiment Library, and the Columbia Library and Columbia's Oral History Project for getting me what I needed.

A big no-thanks to the sloppy bureaucrats of the Federal Bureau of Investigation for either ignoring my requests for Cowley's files or, for God's sake, telling me that no such files exist. Luckily, I found that file at the Newberry. Anyway, thanks for nothing.

I owe a debt of gratitude to the late Donald Faulkner, who was Cowley's friend and anthologizer when he was a professor of literature at Yale. Don and I cooked up *The Portable Malcolm Cowley* and, in general, joined in mutual support when I worked at Viking Penguin.

A very special and heartfelt thank-you to Paul Slovak, the legendary Tall Literary Dude and one of my closest friends. Paul used his insider savvy as a Viking editor of forty years to get me the Cowley, Kerouac, and Kesey files, which were simply invaluable in telling the story I needed to tell.

Thank you to my Viking Penguin colleague Altie Karper, who was Cowley's assistant for a few years and who remembers everything. Altie, a distinguished publisher herself, was great and energizing company as my book made its stately way to completion.

I am blessed beyond measure by what I call Team Cowley. Eric Simonoff, my onetime assistant and now my agent—my agent!—at William Morris Endeavor, is perhaps the ultimate grown-up in the current publishing scene. That he is always calm and sage and reassuring does not hide the fact that he is also very brilliant. I am humbled to be part of his client list, perhaps the most impressive in the business.

What to say about my editor, Scott Moyers? He has been there literally from the beginning, encouraging, advising, prodding, cautioning, and then, oh yeah, editing. A *lot* of editing. He was patient too, more than I may have deserved as I dithered. Scott ranks at the very tip-top of those practicing the craft and art of book editing, a master practitioner—and I really know what I am talking about. He's the best. The *best*.

Helen Rouner, editor at Penguin Press, has been a joy to work with as I have learned the difficult skill of becoming an author (insert ironic horse laugh here). She has guided me with kindness and patience and skill, and I am so grateful for her ministrations. Elijah Matos, Sunset Park's finest, took over for Helen in the latter stages of this process and did so with identical efficiency and good humor.

Heartfelt thanks as well to the other total professionals at Penguin Press: publicist Gail Brussel, marketer Jessie Stratton, cover designer Tom Etherington, interior designer Christina Nguyen, and others there. It takes a village, or rather an imprint. I am deeply grateful to Caitlin Van Dusen for saving me from dozens and dozens of mistakes, some of them truly embarrassing in nature. I now know that whatever talents I may possess, transcribing written material is glaringly not one of them.

Finally, Susanne K. Williams, my wife, my love, my everything, lost her husband to his study for years while I researched and wrote this book. She never complained once. Words are inadequate to express my gratitude to the universe for bringing us together, and to her for making my life a thing of joy.

SOURCES

Books written or edited by Malcolm Cowley

Abbreviations that begin these listings are used in the endnotes:

AGT—After the Genteel Tradition: American Writers Since 1910, W. W. Norton, 1937

BJ—Blue Juniata: Poems, Jonathan Cape & Harrison Smith, 1929

BJCP—Blue Juniata: Collected Poems, Viking Press, 1968

CWMC—Conversations with Malcolm Cowley, edited by Thomas Daniel Young, University Press of Mississippi, 1986

DGM—The Dream of the Golden Mountains: Remembering the 1930s, Viking Press, 1980

ER—Exile's Return: A Narrative of Ideas, W. W. Norton, 1934

ERr—Exile's Return: A Literary Odyssey of the 1920s (revised edition), Viking Press, 1951

F&L—The Flower and the Leaf: A Contemporary Record of American Writing Since 1941, edited by Donald W. Faulkner, Viking Press, 1985

FCF—The Faulkner-Cowley File: Letters and Memories, 1944–1962, Viking Press, 1966

SC—The Selected Correspondence of Kenneth Burke and Malcolm Cowley, 1915–1981, edited by Paul Jay, Viking Press, 1988

SF—A Second Flowering: Works and Days of the Lost Generation, Viking Press, 1973

TBOU—Think Back on Us: A Contemporary Chronicle of the 1930s, edited by Henry Dan Piper, Southern Illinois University Press, 1967

TLS—The Literary Situation, Viking Press, 1954

TLV—The Long Voyage: Selected Letters of Malcolm Cowley, 1915–1987, edited by
   Hans Bak, Harvard University Press, 2014
TPF—The Portable Faulkner, Viking Press, 1946
TPH—The Portable Hemingway, Viking Press, 1944
V80—The View from 80, Viking Press, 1980
WT—And I Worked at the Writer's Trade: Chapters of Literary History, 1918–1978,
   Viking Press, 1978

Books by Malcolm Cowley without abbreviations for endnotes:

Books That Changed Our Minds, edited with Bernard Smith, Kelmscott
   Editions, 1939
The Dry Season, New Directions, 1942
The Complete Poetry and Prose of Walt Whitman, Farrar, Straus and Young, 1947
The Portable Hawthorne, Viking Press, 1947
Black Cargoes: A History of the Atlantic Slave Trade, 1518–1865, cowritten with
   Daniel P. Mannix, Viking Press, 1962
*A Many-Windowed House: Collected Essays on American Writing and American
   Writers*, edited by Henry Dan Piper, Southern Illinois University Press, 1970
Unshaken Friend: A Profile of Maxwell Perkins, Roberts Rinehart, 1985
The Portable Malcolm Cowley, edited by Donald W. Faulkner, Viking Press, 1990

Further abbreviations used in endnotes:

AK—Alfred Kazin
AT—Allen Tate
Bak—Hans Bak, *Malcolm Cowley: The Formative Years*, University of Georgia
   Press, 1993
BS—Isaac Gewirtz, *Beatific Soul: Jack Kerouac on the Road*, New York Public
   Library with Scala Publishers, 2007
HA—*Harvard Advocate*
HC—Hart Crane
HC/LOA—*Hart Crane: Complete Poems and Selected Letters*, Library of Amer-
   ica, 2006
EH—Ernest Hemingway
EW—Edmund Wilson
GM—Gorham Munson

JB—Barry Gifford and Lawrence Lee, *Jack's Book: An Oral Biography of Jack Kerouac*, St. Martin's Press, 1978

JB/EH—Notes taken by James Brasch on the Hemingway–Cowley correspondence

JK—Jack Kerouac

KB—Kenneth Burke

KK—Ken Kesey

LATS—Matthew Josephson, *Life Among the Surrealists: A Memoir*, Holt Rinehart and Winston, 1962

LLP—Edmund Wilson, *Letters on Literature and Politics, 1912–1972*, edited by Elena Wilson, Farrar, Straus and Giroux, 1977

LM—Larry McMurtry

MC—Malcolm Cowley

MCC—Diane U. Eisenberg, *Malcolm Cowley: A Checklist of His Writings, 1916–1973*, Southern Illinois University Press, 1975

MJ—Matthew Josephson

NL—Newberry Library, Malcolm Cowley papers

NYHT—*New York Herald Tribune*

NYJ—Alfred Kazin, *New York Jew*, Alfred A. Knopf, 1978

NYT—*New York Times*

NYTBR—*New York Times Book Review*

ONG—Alfred Kazin, *On Native Grounds: An Interpretation of Modern American Prose Literature*, Reynal & Hitchcock, 1942

OTR—Jack Kerouac, *On the Road*, Viking Press, 1957

OTRS—Jack Kerouac, *On the Road: The Original Scroll*, Viking Press, 2007

RC—Robert Cowley, interview with the author

RR—Susan Jenkins Brown, *Robber Rocks: Letters and Memories of Hart Crane, 1923–1932*, Wesleyan University Press, 1969

SOT—Alfred Kazin, *Starting Out in the Thirties*, Atlantic Monthly Press, 1965

TNR—*The New Republic*

TWIW—Harold Loeb, *The Way It Was*, Criterion Books, 1959

VEF—Viking editorial files

WF—William Faulkner

WOTL—Daniel Aaron, *Writers on the Left: Episodes in American Literary Communism*, Harcourt Brace and World, 1961

WW—*Windblown World: The Journals of Jack Kerouac, 1947–1954*, edited by Douglas Brinkley, Penguin Books, 2004

NOTES

With certain exceptions these endnotes cite sources only for quoted material in the text of the book. Where the text proper provides all the necessary information to find the original source of the quoted material, there is no endnote. Page numbers are provided when available; many online sources do not provide them.

INTRODUCTION: THE COWLEY ERA

2 Scribner's editor Maxwell Perkins had declared: *FCF*, 100.

7 review in *Bookforum*: Gerald Howard, "The Making of American Literature," *Bookforum*, December/January 2014.

9 a pioneering history: *Black Cargoes: A History of the Atlantic Slave Trade 1518–1865*, coauthored with Daniel P. Mannix, Viking Press, 1962.

9 "Oh, Mister Cowley": Quoted by Alan D. Williams at MC's memorial service, the Century Association, May 22, 1989.

ONE. BOY IN SUNLIGHT

11 pastoral poem "Boy in Sunlight": *BJCP*, 3–4.

12 recall this moment: Quoted in Bak, 494.

12 "the essential me": "Looking for the Essential Me," *NYTBR*, June 17, 1984.

12 "the real beginning of the Midwest": MC to Wallace Stegner, *TLV*, 660–61.

12 "been to Paris": *DGM*, xi.

12 "whenever you crossed": *SOT*, 19.

13 exceptionally difficult birth: This description and much that follows about Cowley's mother and father are taken from "Mother and Son," *American Heritage*, February/March 1983.

17 "prosperous, semi-suburban area": MC to AK, *TLV*, 562.

18 "strange, if harmless": MC to AK, *TLV*, 562.

19 "God-awfulest mining camp": Letter to Denise Weber, undated but probably mid-1982.

19 "thousands of acres": Letter to Denise Weber.

20 skill at reading: *TLS*, 144.

20 "We started out": William Cahill, "'Always Keep Watching for Terms': Visits with Kenneth Burke, 1989–1990," *KB Journal* 7, no. 2 (Spring 2011), kbjournal.org/cahill.

21 **He remembers them:** *ERr*, 16.

21 **model themselves on:** *ERr*, 20.

22 **"a new world was being":** "Wowsers on the Run," *Brentano's Book Chat*, January/February 1927, 30–33.

22 **"rather slender diet":** Quoted in Bak.

22 **"greatest existing menace":** "Wowsers on the Run."

23 **"Victorianism, transplanted to America":** *AGT*, 18.

23 **"The whole territory":** *A Many-Windowed House*, 117.

26 **a somber poem:** *Sewanee Review*, Fall 1978, 653–55.

TWO. SCHOLARSHIP BOY

29 **with appalling candor:** Samuel Eliot Morison, *Three Centuries of Harvard*, Harvard University Press, 1936, 423.

29 **"You don't know":** MC to KB, *SC*, 33.

30 **"not defective specialists":** A. Lawrence Lowell, "Inaugural Address of the President of Harvard University," *Science*, October 15, 1909, 499.

30 **"Cockpit of Learning":** Bliss Perry, *And Gladly Teach: Reminiscences*, Houghton Mifflin, 1935, 222.

30 **"a brilliant array":** Perry, *And Gladly Teach*, 243.

31 **As definitively documented:** Jerome Karabel, *The Chosen: The Hidden History of Admission and Exclusion at Harvard, Yale, and Princeton*, Houghton Mifflin Harcourt, 2005.

32 **anti-Semitism manifested itself:** Quoted in Bak, 54.

32 **"ill-bred grinds":** Quoted in Bak, 55.

32 **"I hadn't forgotten":** MC to Jacob Davis, *TLV*, 598.

33 **"in short, to be a man of letters":** MC interview with Miranda Cowley.

33 **Wendell put it:** Henry May, *The End of American Innocence: A Study of First Years of Our Time, 1912–1917*, Alfred A. Knopf, 1959, 76.

34 **"seemed to us":** *ERr*, 28.

35 **"the clan includes":** *NYT*, May 7, 1916.

35 **"nursemaid of genius":** *Harvard Advocate Anthology*, edited by Donald Hall, Twayne Publishers, 1950, 13.

36 **"pacifists, or worse":** "Midsummer Medley," *TNR*, August 15, 1934, 24.

36 **"The 'Advocate' is":** MC to KB, *SC*, 10.

37 **"Wherever the *Advocate*":** Hall, *Harvard Advocate Anthology*, 21–22.

37 **Cowley captures them:** *ERr*, 35.

39 **the quality of "externality":** Amy Lowell, "The New Manner in Modern Poetry," *TNR*, March 14, 1916, 124.

39 **moved the *Advocate*:** "The Externalists," *HA*, April 14, 1916.

39 **"nothing to say?":** Morison, *Three Centuries of Harvard*, 438.

39 **bragging to Burke:** MC to KB, *TLV*, 8.

40 **"the warmth inside":** "Poem for Amy Lowell," *TNR*, January 8, 1936, 258–59.

41 **to his diary:** Alan Seeger, *Letters and Diary of Alan Seeger*, Charles Scribner's Sons, 1917, 163.

42 **speech in Philadelphia:** Quoted in *World War I and America*, edited by A. Scott Berg, Library of America, 2017, 105.

42 **"worse than war":** Quoted in *World War I and America*, 109.

44 **"Germany, often called":** *HA*, May 14, 1917.

44 **"I was anxious":** "John Dos Passos: The Art of Fiction No. 44," *Paris Review*, Spring 1969, 7.

44 **"Copey" presented him:** MC to KB, *SC*, 35.

46 **his camion-driving duties:** MC to KB, *SC*, 43.

47 **titled "On the Road with":** A. Piatt Andrew, *History of the American Field Service,* vol. 3, Houghton Mifflin, 1920, 72–77.

48 **Wolfe would remember:** Letter dated October 30, 1968, to the American Academy, NL.

48 **"might almost say":** *ERr*, 38.

48 **"moments in France":** *ERr*, 42.

49 **even sold a piece:** *Pittsburgh Gazette Times*, January 6, 1918.

49 **"sketches and poems":** Charles Fenton, "Ambulance Drivers in France and Italy: 1914–1918," *American Quarterly*, Winter 1951, 339–40.

49 **"a real attack":** *HA*, January 1918, 240–42.

50 **an instant expert:** MC to KB, *TLV*, 26–27.

51 **"I may find the old life":** MC to KB, *SC*, 55.

51 **"commanded by strangers":** *ERr*, 46.

52 **"seizing the vitality":** *ONG*, 191.

THREE. THE LONG FURLOUGH

55 **"a little frightened":** *WT*, 232–33, along with subsequent quotes re Aiken.

56 **clever literary hoax:** The details and quotes that follow are taken from two sources: William Jay Smith, *The Spectra Hoax*, Wesleyan University Press, 1961; and Malcolm Cowley's "The Real Earl Roppel," *New York Evening Post*, July 7, 1920.

56 **group of poets:** Witter Bynner, "The Spectric Poets," *TNR*, November 11, 1916, 11.

60 **"the Long Furlough," Cowley implied:** *ERr*, 48.

60 **"a vast unconcern":** *ERr*, 49.

60 **the southern reaches:** *ERr*, 47.

61 **espoused by *The Saturday Evening Post*:** *ERr*, 61.

61 **"years from 1917":** Quoted in Adam Hochschild, *American Midnight: The Great War, a Violent Peace, and Democracy's Forgotten Crisis*, Mariner Books, 2022, 132.

62 **"a real-life version":** John Loughery and Blythe Randolph, *Dorothy Day: Dissenting Voice of the American Century*, Simon & Schuster, 2020, 53.

63 **who regarded sex:** Jim Forest, *Love Is the Measure: A Biography of Dorothy Day*, Paulist Press, 1986, 30.

63 **living in sin:** Quoted in Bak, 125.

63 **"dreadful, dark hole":** MC interview with William Miller, August 5, 1976, Papers of William D. Miller, Marquette University, Raynor Library.

64 **"Try reviewing these":** *MCC*, xi.

64 **"big, red-faced Irishman":** *MCC*, xiii.

65 **"three good dinners":** MC address to the Signet Society, April 10, 1976.

65 **"I was paid ten dollars":** "A Weekend with Eugene O'Neill," *The Reporter*, September 5, 1957, 33–36.

65 **a delirious state:** Interview with MC, August 5, 1976, Papers of William D. Miller.

66 **"Some drizzly morning":** *ERr*, 50.

67 **infuses "Free Clinic":** "Free Clinic," *BJ*, 41–43.

67 **"into sudden hysteria":** Quoted in Bak, 143.

68 **a letter to Jacob Davis:** MC to Jacob Davis, *TLV*, 598–99.

69 **"I went through Harvard":** MC to AK, *TLV*, 562.

69 **from his beloved:** J. Donald Adams, *Copey of Harvard: A Biography of Charles Townsend Copeland*, Houghton Mifflin, 1960, 266.

70 **The piece held:** "The Woman of Thornden," *The Dial*, February 1920, 259–62.

71 **the prose interludes:** *BJ*, 33–34.
71 **poems as "Interment":** "Interment," *BJ*, 45.
72 **"cast of mind":** *WT*, 56.

FOUR. LOST AND FOUND

74 **Even fifty years ago:** William Styron, "That Extraordinary Company of Writers Known Ironically as the Lost Generation," *NYTBR*, May 6, 1973, 426.
74 **a French garage owner:** James R. Mellow, *Charmed Circle: Gertrude Stein and Company*, Praeger Publishers, 1974, 273.
75 **As told to Matthew Josephson:** *LATS*, 7–9.
76 **exchange rate prevailing:** Frederick Hoffman, *The Twenties: American Writing in the Postwar Decade*, Free Press, 1965, 46.
76 **"and nervous system":** *SF*, 57–58.
77 **"going abroad":** MC to KB, *TLV*, 48.
77 **noted the presence:** *LATS*, 78.
77 **"a great migration":** *ERr*, 79.
77 **"the 'Lost Battalion'":** GM, "The Fledgling Years: 1916–1924," *Sewanee Review*, January–March 1932, 27.
77 **"of stampeding Herefords":** Quoted by MC in review of William Shirer's *20th Century Journey*, *NYTBR*, October 10, 1976.
78 **Cowley would explain:** *ERr*, 79.
79 **Josephson writes acidulously:** *LATS*, 10.
80 **"no ordinary departure":** *ERr*, 79.
82 **conducive to productivity:** MC to John Brooks Wheelwright, *TLV*, 36.
82 **which he described as:** MC to KB, *SC*, 136.
82 **"amusing satirical voyage":** Quoted in Bak, 181.
82 **This little exercise:** "The Journey to Paris," *Gargoyle*, October 1921, 8–12.
82 **his literary peers:** "This Youngest Generation," *Literary Review of the New York Evening Post*, October 15, 1921, 81–82.
82 **at the age of twenty-three:** *ERr*, 98.
83 **"expressed clearly enough":** *ERr*, 97.
83 **"passage of the generations":** Harriet Monroe, "Renewal of Youth," *Poetry*, December 1921, 146–49.
83 **a scolding piece:** Van Wyck Brooks, "The Illusion of the Critics," *The Freeman*, November 9, 1921, 174–76.
83 **Cowley threatened:** MC to KB, *TLV*, 56.
84 **"he attended sixteen":** Bak, 190.
85 **"home in the seventeenth century":** MC to KB, *SC*, 108.
86 **the stinging rebuke:** "A Brief History of Bohemia," *The Freeman*, August 19, 1922, 439–40.
87 **"not a novelist":** "André Salmon and His Generation," *The Bookman*, February 1923, 714–17.
87 **The seventh profile:** "James Joyce," *The Bookman*, July 1924, 518–21.
87 **Cowley was so taken aback:** *ERr*, 118.
88 **"cold, wet-marble fingers":** *ERr*, 119.
88 **collect his thoughts:** "A Monument to Proust," *The Dial*, March 1923, 234–40.
89 **"elated or sunk":** MC to KB, *TLV*, 74.
90 **"Dada! *Dada!* Dada!":** Tom Stoppard, *Travesties*, Grove Press, 1975, 41.
91 **Tzara's manifestos proclaimed:** *LATS*, 112.
93 **"birth of *Secession*":** GM, "The Fledgling Years," 32.

93 against *The Dial*: "Expose No. 1," *Secession* no. 1, Spring 1922, 22–24.

94 a doubtful compliment: Quoted in Bak, 207.

94 "hope of making": KB to MC, *SC*, 124.

95 attacked the magazine: *Secession* no. 2, July 1922, 31.

96 a critical trend-piece: Louis Untermeyer, "The New Patricians," *TNR*, December 6, 1922, 41–42.

96 "bad writing, Dada": MC to KB, *SC*, 126.

97 "wanted more from": *TWIW*, 98.

97 "like a cross": *TWIW*, 130–31.

98 he saw, opportunistically: MC to KB, *TLV*, 80.

98 of a convert: MC to Harold Loeb, *TLV*, 83.

99 "The general atmosphere": "Louis Aragon," *TNR*, October 7, 1936, 258.

99 a "Dadaist extraordinaire": *WOTL*, 76.

100 "Paris! You leaped": *ERr*, 135.

101 "the most amusing": *ERr*, 135.

101 "one climactic scene": *LATS*, 132.

102 and vivid account of: "Locus Solus," *Broom*, March 1923, 281.

102 "right about faced": MC to KB, *SC*, 150.

103 "There is, for instance": KB to MC, *SC*, 131–32.

103 Cowley's retort was: MC to KB, *SC*, 134–36.

104 archly incoherent statement: The whole "Jilted Moon" episode is covered in *LATS*, 235–38.

105 Giverny in June: This account is drawn largely from *ERr*, 158–59, and *TWIW*, 167–69.

106 One version of this event: Phelps Putnam, *Paris Was Our Mistress: Memoirs of a Lost and Found Generation*, Viking Press, 1947, 184.

106 the sentence read: Quoted in Bak, 537.

107 "a big young man": *ERr*, 120.

109 Nathan Asch remembered: "One Man's Hemingway," *NYHT*, July 9, 1961, 3, 15.

109 a strange poem: Lines quoted in Bak, 254.

109 fracas in question: Unless otherwise noted, this account is drawn from *ERr*, "Significant Gesture," 164–70.

112 Another version of events: Robert McAlmon and Kay Boyle, *Being Geniuses Together: 1920–1930*, North Point Press, 1984, 35–38.

112 return the disfavor: "Those Paris Years," *NYTBR*, June 9, 1968, 1.

112 "performed an act": *ERr*, 169.

113 Cowley's reading had shifted: Bak, 262.

113 "the monumental Racine": MC to KB, *TLV*, 105.

113 potential to develop: MC had his thesis on Racine privately printed in Paris in an edition of two hundred copies, of which only fifteen are known to survive. Also reprinted in *The Freeman* in the October 10 and October 1, 1923, issues.

113 he told Burke: MC to KB, *TLV*, 105.

114 "famous two years": MC to KB, *TLV*, 107.

FIVE. HOME AGAIN, HOME AGAIN

116 "almost in the shadow": *ERr*, 172–74.

116 "to one returning": *ER*, 210.

117 "excitement and inflation": *ERr*, 175.

118 "business was booming": *ERr*, 178.

118 to remain united: *ERr*, 178.

119 "a literary entertainment": *ERr*, 180.

121 **for attracting attention:** *LATS*, 255.

121 **Broomists "skyscraper primitives":** "Comment," *The Dial*, September 1923. The writer attributes the coinage to Gorham Munson but does not cite any source.

121 **"had the effect of a few people":** *LATS*, 261.

121 **"time to think":** The account that follows of the literary conclave on Prince Street is drawn from *ERr*, 178–85, except where otherwise indicated.

123 **coup de grâce:** Two versions of this event can be found in *LATS*, 265–67, and in GM, "The Fledgling Years," 51–52. They differ considerably, especially on the matter of who "won."

124 **at some length:** "'Broom' Is Barred from Use of Mails," *NYT*, January 15, 1924.

124 **a disconsolate letter:** Quoted in Bak, 293.

125 **"re-create the atmosphere":** *ERr*, 196.

125 **"been more fantastic?":** *LATS*, 291.

126 **this more bitterly:** *ERr*, 196.

126 **"Aesthete: Model 1924" by the:** *American Mercury*, January 1924, 51–56.

127 **"the intense satisfaction":** *Time*, January 5, 1924.

127 **"the early careers":** *ERr*, 191.

127 **an agitated Cowley:** *ERr*, 192.

127 **rage in Cowley:** Ernest Boyd, *Portraits: Real and Imaginary*, Geroge H. Doran, 1924, 155.

128 **"excelled us all":** *LATS*, 269.

128 **"behind his books":** Boyd, *Portraits: Real and Imaginary*, 161.

129 **confused and demoralized:** *ERr*, 196.

130 **"city where every one":** MC to EW, *TLV*, 159.

130 **"the topic changes":** MC to KB, *SC*, 158–59.

130 **"New York in the 1920s":** Ann Douglas, *Terrible Honesty: Mongrel Manhattan in the 1920s*, Farrar, Straus and Giroux, 1995, 26.

131 **"College girls in New York":** *ERr*, 225–26.

132 **"The Dada movement":** "Literary Calendar," *TNR*, February 4, 1937, 78–80.

132 **"I utterly hate":** Quoted in Bak, 301.

132 **"the disgusting feature":** MC to Harold Loeb, *TLV*, 120.

133 **"There is no one":** Quoted in Bak, 358–59.

133 **"and a lyric singer":** "Paul Valéry's Essays in an English Translation," *NYTBR*, March 20, 1927, 5.

134 **"all very funny":** *LLP*, 119.

134 **Wilson called him:** Quoted in Bak, 396.

134 **"'Style and Fashion'":** *LLP*, 143.

135 **remember her fondly:** *MCC*, 25.

135 **memorable private nickname:** Linda Leavell, *Holding On Upside Down: The Life and Work of Marianne Moore*, Farrar, Straus and Giroux, 227–28.

135 **"no one writing":** Leavell, *Holding On*, 339.

136 **"Suddenly I felt":** *SF*, 194.

136 **a long essay on Poe:** EW, "Poe at Home and Abroad," *TNR*, December 8, 1926, 78–80.

136 **Wilson's unseemly haste:** Quoted in Bak, 385.

SIX. ROARING BOY

140 **"Their real exile":** *ERr*, 214.

140 **"This was the beginning":** *SF*, 198.

140 **his "cannibal dance":** *SF*, 198.

142 **rented a farmhouse:** *WT*, 62.

NOTES

142 **Cowley waxed rhapsodic:** MC to Harriet Monroe, *TLV*, 139.

142 **a down payment:** Quoted in *RR*, 102.

142 **leaving him "completely":** Quoted in Bak, 424.

142 **One of his color pieces:** "Connecticut Valley," *TNR*, January 28, 1931, 297–99.

143 **"There is nothing facile":** Harriet Monroe, "Man-Size Poems," *Poetry*, October 1929, 35.

144 **"I ricochet-ed":** HC to GM, HC/LOA, 306.

146 **wrote Crane to say so:** *RR*, 10.

146 **a memorable trip:** This trip is described in "A Weekend with Eugene O'Neill," *The Reporter*, September 5, 1957, 33–36.

146 **"a roisterous time!":** HC to Jean Toomer, HC/LOA, 356.

147 **Cowley's preferred epithet:** "The Roaring Boy," *TNR*, June 9, 1937, 134, including subsequent quotes.

148 **"the passionate pulchritude":** HC to MC, HC/LOA, 601.

149 **"ecstasy of walking":** HC to Waldo Frank, HC/LOA, 384.

150 **list of six:** These projects are all described in Bak, 366.

150 **"get [Malcolm's] poems accepted":** HC to Isidor Schneider, quoted in John Unterecker, *Voyager: A Life of Hart Crane*, Farrar, Straus and Giroux, 1969, 561.

151 **"I rather preferred":** *WT*, 66.

151 **a "secret arbiter":** Quoted in Bak, 428.

152 **"'beholden' to anyone":** *WT*, 67.

152 **some commercial oomph:** MC to Harriet Monroe, *TLV*, 157.

152 **the "high life":** *WT*, 68.

152 **"certain that the book":** *WT*, 68.

153 **"The little victories":** *WT*, 68.

154 **"Wilson will see":** MC to AT, *TLV*, 160.

154 **"Like all of his writing":** AT, "A Regional Poet," *TNR*, August 28, 1929, 51–52.

154 **"You're a lucky boy!":** *RR*, 18.

155 **not publish another:** Bak, 413.

155 **he would cite Fitzgerald:** *ER*, 237.

155 **quotes the passage:** From "Echoes of the Jazz Age" in F. Scott Fitzgerald, *The Crack-Up*, New Directions, 1945, 19–20.

156 **"the simple contagion":** "1930: The Year That Was New Year's Eve," *Commentary*, June 1951.

156 **"caravans of taxicabs":** *ERr*, 307.

157 **The first piece:** "Our Own Generation," *NYHT*, June 23, 1929.

157 **follow-up piece:** "The New Primitives," *NYHT*, June 30, 1929.

158 **his review of *A Farewell*:** "Not Yet Demobilized," *NYHT*, October 6, 1929.

158 **three review-essays:** All in *NYHT*: "Machine-Made America," November 3, 1929; "The Escape from America," November 10, 1929; and "The Business of Being a Poet," November 17, 1929.

160 **"[Wilson] had persuaded":** "A Reminiscence: Edmund Wilson on *The New Republic*," *TNR*, July 1, 1972, 25–28.

160 **"the uneasy feeling of having perhaps belonged":** *ER*, 240.

161 **"that doesn't bear":** MC to Morton Dauwen Zabel, *TLV*, 185.

161 **He'd conceived of this:** HC to GM, HC/LOA 321.

162 **"a social whirl":** HC to Charlotte and Richard Rychtarik, HC/LOA, 611.

163 **Crane had been:** "The Roaring Boy," 134.

163 **"The faults of":** "A Preface to Hart Crane," *TNR*, April 23, 1930, 276–77.

164 **"anxiety is wearing":** HC to Wilbur Underwood, HC/LOA, 653.

165 **feeling was mutual:** Peggy Baird Cowley, "The Last Days of Hart Crane," reprinted in *RR*, 147–73. Peggy's eyewitness account is the one Crane's many biographers have relied on.

165 **"The old beauty":** HC to Wilbur Underwood, HC/LOA, 720.

165 **slowly from disingenuousness:** HC to MC, HC/LOA, 711.

165 **coy, oblique cheerfulness:** HC to MC, *The Letters of Hart Crane: 1916–1932*, edited by Brom Weber, University of California Press, 1954, 406.

166 **"What place is there":** Quoted in *SF*, 210–11.

167 **"I'm not going to make it":** *RR*, 172.

168 **a heartsick letter:** MC to AT, *TLV*, 185.

169 **"like a crash":** "1930: The Year That Was Like New Year's Eve."

SEVEN. TO THE BARRICADES

170 **a comprehensive anthology:** *Years of Protest: A Collection of American Writings of the 1930's*, edited by Jack Salzman, Pegasus, 1967.

174 **"Advertisers were tolerated":** *DGM*, 10.

175 **"less to inform":** Quoted in David Seideman, *The New Republic: A Voice of Modern Liberalism*, Praeger, 1986, 68.

176 **"I was appalled":** *DGM*, 12.

176 **"Bryn Mawr girl":** *DGM*, 13.

176 **"like most writers":** *DGM*, 13.

177 **"last great historian":** EW, *Axel's Castle: A Study of the Imaginative Literature of 1870–1930*, Charles Scribner's Sons, 1930, 190.

177 **the following sentiments:** EW, *Axel's Castle*, 293.

179 **To quote a historian:** Seideman, *The New Republic*, 102.

179 **the prescient exhortation:** Mike Gold, "Go Left, Young Writers!," *The New Masses*, January 1929, 3.

180 **"a beautifully rouged":** Mike Gold, *The New Masses*, April 1930, 4.

180 **"Gold-Wilder case marks":** EW, "The Literary Class War I," *TNR*, May 4, 1932, 320.

181 **"sometimes only four":** Bruce Bliven, *Five Million Words Later*, John Day Company, 1970, 206.

181 **as an aerie:** *DGM*, 14.

182 **"the moral atmosphere":** *DGM*, 2.

182 **Bliven would state:** Bliven, *Five Million Words Later*, 207.

182 **"curiously close to":** *DGM*, 3.

183 **"we listened to":** *DGM*, 7.

184 **"Wilson came out":** MC to Katherine Anne Porter, *TLV*, 172.

184 **"I sometimes felt":** "Edmund Wilson on *The New Republic*," *TNR*, July 1, 1972, 26.

186 **"my own class-war":** Mary McCarthy, *Intellectual Memoirs: New York 1936–1938*, Harcourt Brace and Company, 1992, 6.

186 **Smith College graduate:** Mary McCarthy, "I Went to Pit College," *TNR*, May 2, 1934, 343.

186 **"with the result, of course":** McCarthy, *Intellectual Memoirs*, 9.

187 **"heavy Brownsville voice":** *DGM*, 265.

187 **clutching a handwritten introduction:** AK, *SOT*, 10.

188 **"the immense spread":** AK, *SOT*, 15ff.

188 **"the longest journeys":** Norman Podhoretz, *Making It*, Random House, 1967, 3.

188 **"strenuously on the make":** MC to AK, *TLV*, 561.

189 **"surly and worse":** Richard Cook, *Alfred Kazin: A Biography*, Yale University Press, 2008, 32.

189 **Kazin titled the section:** AK, *SOT*, 139.

189 **"that he had been at Harvard"**: These words from an *Atlantic Monthly* serialization do not appear in the eventual published book *SOT*.

189 **"Once or twice"**: *DGM*, 262.

190 **"I had felt that I was hearing"**: Quoted in Blake Bailey, *Cheever: A Life*, Alfred A. Knopf, 2009, 47.

190 **"lest anyone think"**: Quoted in *F&L*, 361.

191 **"During the last year"**: MC to Elizabeth Ames, *TLV*, 206.

192 **"if I can't"**: *F&L*, 362.

193 **"everyone in the literary world"**: *DGM*, 55ff.

196 **"maybe not enough"**: *DGM*, 67ff.

197 **"fixing to keep"**: *DGM*, 69ff.

198 **"We must not talk"**: *DGM*, 70.

198 **"Malcolm Cowley, particularly"**: John Hammond, *On Record: An Autobiography*, Summit Books, 1977, 79.

198 **"Malcolm . . . held it"**: EW, *The Thirties*, Farrar, Straus and Giroux, 1980, 171.

198 **"Of course, Malcolm Cowley"**: Hammond, *On Record*.

199 **"a sinister old buzzard"**: EW, "Class War Exhibits," *The New Masses*, April 1932, 7.

200 **"like a patient"**: *DGM*, 73ff.

203 **"bleak homespun music"**: Described in Albert Halper, *Union Square*, Viking Press, 1933, 274–75.

203 **"I found myself committed"**: *DGM*, 75.

204 **he would write angrily**: "The Flight of the Bonus Army," *TNR*, August 17, 1932, 13–15.

204 **famous two-part article**: EW, "The Literary Class War I," 319–23; and "The Literary Class War II," May 11, 1932, 347–49.

205 **a piece in *The New Republic***: "Leftbound Local," *TNR*, August 17, 1932.

206 **"pleasant man who"**: Walter Lippmann, *NYHT*, April 28, 1932.

206 **the hard-boiled manner he affected**: John Dos Passos, "Out of the Red with Roosevelt," *TNR*, July 13, 1932, 232.

207 **write a pamphlet**: *Culture and the Crisis*, League of Professional Groups for Foster and Ford, 1932.

207 **"a collection, gritty as crushed limestone"**: *DGM*, 114.

209 **"wasn't the depression"**: *Daily Worker*, October 14, 1932.

210 **Cowley would watch**: "A Remembrance of the Red Romance," *Esquire*, March 1964, 124–31.

212 **"a convoy of wheezing"**: *DGM*, 127.

213 **issued a statement**: "Hunger Marchers Arrive at Capital," *NYT*, 3.

213 **"Tax the rich!"**: Quoted in William Manchester, *The Glory and the Dream: A Narrative History of America, 1932–1972*, Little, Brown, 1974, 54.

213 **Cowley ends his *TNR* piece**: "Red Day in Washington," *TNR*, December 21, 1932, 153–55.

214 **"in those days, however"**: *DGM*, 133.

214 **"the literary history"**: George Orwell, "Inside the Whale," *A Collection of Essays*, Harcourt Brace and Company, 240.

EIGHT. LITERARY POLITICS

215 **the Fish–Dies Bill**: *Daily Worker*, July 11, 1932.

215 **signed a letter to the governor**: *Pittsburgh Courier*, September 10, 1932.

215 **one of ninety-eight**: *NYT*, March 1, 1937.

216 **support of the Federal Writers' Project**: *NYHT*, July 28, 1937, 14.

216 signed "A Statement by American": *Daily Worker*, April 18, 1935.

216 "shown these capitalists": *Daily Worker*, February 7, 1933.

216 an anti-Hitler rally: *NYT*, April 6, 1933.

216 Communist publishing house: *Daily Worker*, December 18, 1934.

216 Twentieth Soviet Anniversary: *Daily Worker*, November 4, 1937.

216 Mother Bloor Celebration: *Daily Worker*, June 28, 137.

216 "a Communist Society": *New York Evening Post*, May 31, 1933.

217 "The American Literary Scene": *Daily Worker*, December 29, 1930.

217 "A Frank and Open": *Daily Worker*, March 18, 1937.

217 "in Defense of Freedom": *Daily Worker*, February 10, 1937.

217 "Lenin's Contribution to Modern Thought": *Daily Worker*, January 1–25, 1938.

218 "never be more": "A Remembrance of the Red Romance," *Esquire*, March 1964, 125.

218 an uncharacteristic rapture: *DGM*, 118.

219 "they had ideas": *DGM*, 116ff.

219 "actually a Communist": MC interview with Miranda Cowley.

221 of W. W. Norton: Unless otherwise indicated, the quotes regarding *ER* are from the editorial file of its publisher, W. W. Norton, whose files are held by the Columbia University Rare Book and Manuscript Library.

222 "Mr. Matthew Josephson": MC to Ellizabeth Ames, *TLV*, 175.

222 "a high old time": Quoted in Bak, 465.

223 with Scott and Zelda: "A Ghost Story of the Jazz Age," *Saturday Review of Literature*, January 25, 1964, 20–21.

225 an idyllic reprieve: *DGM*, Chapter 17, "The Meriwether Connection," 192–206.

228 "I couldn't yet bear": *DGM*, 221.

228 "I was trying to pick": MC to Caresse Crosby, *TLV*, 199.

229 "doing my part": *DGM*, 223.

229 "And now you turn": *ER*, 299–303.

229 "as the high summit": *DGM*, 224.

230 "who showed less than": *DGM*, 224.

230 "a pretentious phrase": *ER*, 55.

230 "the exiles invented": *ER*,106.

230 "the first true generation": *ER*, 7.

230 "I might even point": *CWMC*, 103.

231 were "almost pilgrimage[s]": *ER*, 113.

231 "under a feeling": *ERr*, 217.

233 "I had taken the risk": *DGM*, 228.

233 "When future Parringtons": John Chamberlain, *NYT*, May 28, 1934.

233 "has written the Odyssey": John K. Sherman, *Minneapolis Tribune*, June 9, 1934, 22.

233 "a stimulating book": Alfred McEwen, *Roanoke Times*, June 17, 1934, 6.

234 Cowley's fellow fellow traveler: Bernard Smith, "The Lost Generation," *The New Masses*, July 3, 1934, 38.

234 "Arrested emotional development": Ludwig Lewisohn, "Perpetual Adolescence," *The Nation*, July 4, 1934, 23.

235 scoffed at the exiles: Lewis Gannett, *NYHT*, May 28, 1934, 13.

235 Bernard DeVoto's piece: Bernard DeVoto, "Exiles from Reality," *Saturday Review of Literature*, June 2, 1934, 1–2.

235 "the worst review": MC to John Brooks Wheelwright, *TLV*, 198–99.

236 "a swell run-around": MC to F. Scott Fitzgerald, *TLV*, 198.

236 "ton of brickbats": MC to John Brooks Wheelwright, *TLV*, 198–99.

237 "amusing in retrospect": *DGM*, 230.

237 **"the most argued-about book":** John Chamberlain, *NYT,* June 7, 1934.
238 **"my petit-bourgeois illusions":** "A Remembrance of the Red Romance II," *Esquire,* April 1964.
238 **"The radical artists":** *The New Masses,* November 1929, 21.
239 **"they were the least":** *DGM,* 136.
239 **"the Thirties in literature":** AK, *SOT,* 12–13.
240 **of political disillusion:** Richard Wright, *The God That Failed,* edited by Richard H. Crossman, Gateway Editions, 1987, 136.
241 **"After recklessly finding enemies":** *DGM,* 268.
242 **Cowley interpreted this:** *DGM,* 272.
243 **"In my mind, it was one":** *CWMC,* 56.
243 **"four thousand people":** Ruth McKenney, "U.S. Writers Quite Ivory Towers at Congress," *New York Post,* April 27, 1935.
243 **"the overwhelming number":** "Text of Speech by Browder at American Writers' Congress," *Daily Worker,* April 29, 1935.
244 **the red meat they craved:** Quoted in *Daily Worker,* April 29, 1935.
244 **Malcolm Cowley's contribution:** "What the Revolutionary Movement Can Do for the Writer," *American Writers' Congress,* International Publishers, 1935, 59–65.
246 **politically naive Burke:** "Revolutionary Symbolism in America," *American Writers' Congress,* 87–93.
246 **"throbbing like a locomotive":** *CWMC,* 72–74.
246 **Burke felt "slain":** "Thirty Years Later: Memories of the First American Writers' Conference," *American Scholar,* Summer 1966, 495–516.
248 **the best speech:** "The Short Story," *American Writers' Congress,* 103–13.
248 **"They'll say the writers":** James T. Farrell, *Yet Other Waters,* Vanguard Press, 1952, 128.
249 **A national council:** "The League of American Writers," *The New Masses,* May 7, 1935, 7.
250 **"I still had my dream":** *DGM,* 294.
251 **"one of the comic episodes":** Mark Schorer, *Sinclair Lewis: An American Life,* McGraw-Hill, 1961, 611.
251 **"no uninvited persons":** *DGM,* 296ff.
252 **Cowley would review the book favorably:** "American Tragedy," *TNR,* May 3, 1939, 382–83.
253 **The move of *The New Republic*:** "The New Republic Moves Uptown," *TNR,* February 11, 1978, 27–29.
253 **Cowley wrote a glowing letter:** *DGM,* 290.
254 **"to find myself possessed":** *DGM,* 306–7.
255 **Tout le monde:** *DGM,* 307.
256 **"Hurry, the printer is waiting":** *BJCP,* 88.
256 **One of his best poems:** "The Long Voyage," *BJCP,* 93.

NINE. THE BITTEREST THIRTIES

259 **by Marquis Childs:** "They Still Hate Roosevelt," *TNR,* September 14, 1938, 147–49.
261 **"In effect," he writes:** "Adventures of a Book Reviewer," *TBOU,* 386.
261 **"The lead review":** AK, *SOT,* 190.
262 **"for a scheme of values":** *TBOU,* 387.
262 **"In running a book department":** MC to KB, *TLV,* 180.
262 **"I am not":** "Yeats and O'Faolain," *TNR,* February 15, 1939, 49–50.
263 **His review of the Socialist:** "Donkey Town," *TNR,* October 10, 193, 247–48.
263 **the literary action hero:** "Man's Solitude," *TNR,* July 4, 1934, 214–15.

263 **1933 group review:** "Panorama," *TNR*, December 20, 1933, 172–73.

263 **He takes issue:** *DGM*, 247–49.

264 **offered this sarcastic précis:** 1982 interview with MC, videotape, Tamiment Library, New York University.

264 **In his reviews of:** "The Poet and the World," *TNR*, April 27, 1932, 303–5; "The End of the Trilogy," *TNR*, August 12, 1936, 79–80.

265 **June 4, 1937:** This description of the event is largely taken from Mary Dearborn, *Ernest Hemingway: A Biography*, 380–81.

265 **acerbic words of Dawn Powell:** Dawn Powell to John Dos Passos, *Selected Letters of Dawn Powell: 1913–1965*, edited by Tim Page, Henry Holt, 1999, 97–98.

266 **"A National Congress of":** *TNR*, 390.

267 **somewhat slapdash talk:** "The Seven Years of Crisis," *The Writer in a Changing World*, edited by Henry Hart, Equinox Cooperative Press, 1937, 44–46.

267 **Earl Browder again:** "The Writer and Politics," *The Writer in a Changing World*, 48–55.

268 **would write in his report:** "A Congress in Madrid," *The New Masses*, August 10, 1937, 16.

268 **arrived in Paris in early June:** Unless otherwise noted, the details of MC's trip to Spain to attend the international writers' conference are taken from a series of articles that appeared in five issues of *TNR*: "To Madrid I," August 25; "To Madrid II," September 1; "To Madrid III: Offensive on Two Fronts," September 15; "To Madrid IV: Three Spanish Kids," September 22; and "To Madrid V: The International Brigade," October 6, 1937.

269 **One historian estimates:** Robert S. Thornberry, "Writers Take Sides, Stalinists Take Control," *The Historian*, Spring 2000, 594.

270 **"there is no doubt whatever":** George Orwell, "Spilling the Spanish Beans," *New English Weekly*, July 29, 1937.

277 **take him until 1982:** "No Homage to Catalonia: A Memory of the Spanish Civil War," *Southern Review*, January 1982, 131–40.

278 **an unfortunate conflict:** The fullest and clearest narrative of this distressing episode can be found in Stephen Koch's *The Breaking Point: Hemingway, Dos Passos, and the Murder of José Robles*, Counterpoint, 2005. I am indebted to Koch and his superb book.

278 **in strict confidence:** Josephine Herbst, "The Starched Blue Sky of Spain," *The Noble Savage I*, Meridian Books, 96–97.

280 **"You do that and":** *The Fourteenth Chronicle: Letters and Diaries of John Dos Passos*, edited by Townsend Ludington, Gambit, 1973, 496.

280 **inverted *Pilgrim's Progress*:** John Dos Passos, *Adventures of a Young Man*, Harcourt, Brace and Company, 1939.

281 **"Trotskyist agit-prop":** Samuel Sillen, "Misadventures of John Dos Passos," *The New Masses*, July 4, 1939, 21–22.

281 **Clifton Fadiman's verdict:** Clifton Fadiman, "Rebels and Ants," *New Yorker*, June 3, 1939.

281 **and most honest critique:** Mary McCarthy, "Two in Our Time," *Partisan Review*, Summer 1939, 111–14.

281 **Malcolm Cowley's review:** "Disillusionment," *TNR*, June 14, 1939, 163.

282 **the tone of the letter:** John Dos Passos, "The Death of José Robles," *TNR*, July 19, 1939, 308–9.

282 **a rave review:** "Death of a Hero," *TNR*, January 20, 1941, 89–90.

283 **review is devoted to applying:** "The Art of Insurrection," *TNR*, April 12, 1933, 248–50.

284 **Cowley next took aim:** "Comrade Trotsky," *TNR*, April 6, 1936, 254.

284 **five-thousand-word screed:** Felix Morrow, "Malcolm Cowley: Portrait of a Stalinist Intellectual," *New Militant*, April 18, 1936, 2–3.

285 **As James T. Farrell would:** Quoted in Alan Wald, *The New York Intellectuals: The Rise and Decline of the Anti-Stalinist Left from the 1930s to the 1980s*, University of North Carolina Press, 130.

285 **to discredit Trotsky:** "The Trial of the Trotskyites in Russia," *TNR*, September 2, 1936, 88–89.

285 **"the most exciting book":** "The Record of a Trial," *TNR*, April 7, 1937, 267–70.

286 **A long private letter:** EW to MC, *LLP*, 286–87.

286 **Cowley's response to this:** MC to EW, *TLV*, 231.

287 **"Imagine Robespierre or Cromwell":** James T. Farrell, quoted in Alan Wald, "Memories of the John Dewey Commission," *Antioch Review*, Autumn 1977, 435.

288 **Cowley did admit in private:** MC to EW, *TLV*, 243.

288 **fell the task:** MC to John Dewey, *TLV*, 233–35.

291 **a peevish broadside:** "Partisan Review," *TNR*, October 19, 1938, 311–12.

291 **printed in full:** "A Letter to the New Republic," Fall 1938, 124–27.

292 **a low point:** "There Have to Be Censors," *TNR*, April 27, 1938, 364–65.

292 **"a doctrine of salvation":** "Red Ivory Tower," *TNR*, November 9, 1938, 22–23.

292 **Wilson decries the comparison:** EW to MC, *LLP*, 309–10.

293 **could in a long reply:** MC to EW, *TLV*, 242–45.

293 **His notebook for the year begins:** "Echoes from Moscow: 1937–1938," *Southern Review*, Winter 1984.

294 **"I did my job":** "The Sense of Guilt," *Kenyon Review*, Spring 1965, 264.

294 **To Kenneth Burke he lamented:** MC to KB, *SC*, 223–24.

294 **"was becoming not so much":** "The Sense of Guilt," 264.

295 **would later sniffily observe:** *CWMC*, 84.

295 **"I could easier imagine myself":** Quoted in William Manchester, *The Glory and the Dream: A Narrative History of America, 1932–1972*, Little, Brown, 1974, 243.

296 **"Since the Soviet Union has never intended":** "Why the Pact Was Signed," *The New Masses*, September 5, 1939, 10.

296 **extraordinary two-part article:** Vincent Sheean, "Brumaire: The Soviet Union as Fascist State," *TNR*, November 8 and 11, 1939.

297 **"that I knew nothing":** "Echoes from Moscow."

297 **The closest Cowley ever:** "Krivitsky," *TNR*, January 22, 1940, 120–22.

298 **"more and more puzzled":** EW to MC, *LLP*, 357–58.

298 **the most heartfelt:** MC to EW, *TLV*, 258.

299 **letter of resignation:** MC to Franklin Folsom, Executive Secretary, League of American Writers, *TLV*, 267–71.

TEN. PASTS, USABLE AND NOT

302 **"The retreat from Moscow":** *WOTL*, 378.

302 **a ripe bouquet:** *WOTL*, 378–79.

303 **Gold, whose series of articles:** Mike Gold, *The Hollow Men*, International Publishers, 1941.

303 **Wilson's former climbing:** Quoted in *WOTL*, 380.

303 **July 1941 article:** "The Michael Golden Legend," *Decision*, July 1941, 40–45.

303 **for an olive branch:** John Chamberlain, "Soak the Idle Rich, *TNR*, January 22, 1940, 118.

303 **"After all, what does Joseph Stalin":** James T. Farrell, "The Cultural Front," *Partisan Review* 7, no. 2, 1940, 139–42.

304 **This distinctly chastened piece:** "Sixteen Propositions," *TNR*, February 26, 1940, 264–65.

306 **"she nearly died":** Robert Cowley, Foreword to *TLV*, xi.

306 **"a great shake-up":** MC to KB, *TLV*, 281ff.

306 **as he would later confess:** *NYJ*, 30.

308 **"It will cost me":** Quoted in Sam Tanenhaus, *Whittaker Chambers: A Biography*, Random House, 1997, 166.

309 **Robert Cowley recalls:** Foreword to *TLV*, xiv–xv.

310 **His review of Arthur Koestler's *Darkness at Noon*:** "Punishment and Crime," *TNR*, June 2, 1941, 766–67.

310 **nature of communism:** "Faith and the Future," in *Whose Revolution?: A Study of the Future Course of Liberalism in the United States*, edited by Irving DeWitt Talmadge, Howell, Soskin, Publishers, 1941, 146–65.

310 **sourly writing to Burke:** MC to KB, *TLV*, 294.

310 **"of not doing enough":** MC to Archibald MacLeish, *TLV*, 297.

312 **salary was a "lordly":** MC to KB, *TLV*, 298.

313 **"I regret to say that the flow":** Martin Dies, *Congressional Record—House*, January 15, 1942, 409–10.

314 **repeated and amplified:** Westbrook Pegler, *Los Angeles Times*, January 31, 1942, 3.

314 **took up once again:** Westbrook Pegler, *Minneapolis Star*, January 20, 1942.

315 **"Most inopportune book":** Whittaker Chambers (unsigned), "Inopportune," *Time*, February 16, 1942.

315 **in a letter to *Time*:** *Time*, March 16, 1942.

316 **"It was the 'seventy-two'":** *New Yorker*, January 31, 1942.

316 **his fealty to America:** MC to Archibald MacLeish, *TLV*, 301.

316 **"If it were now decided":** MC to George J. Gould, *TLV*, 306.

318 ***New Republic* decried:** "Justice for Federal Workers," *TNR*, May 4, 1942, 592–93.

318 **"After my exposure":** "Quotations from Dies' Letter to Henry Wallace," *Palladium-Item*, March 31, 1942, 11C.

319 **He later calculated:** MC to Benjamin DeMott, *TLV*, 667.

320 **"I wouldn't convict":** RC.

320 **One paper characterized:** "Hiss Tells of Mystery Man in Office," *Washington Evening Star*, June 24, 1949, 3.

320 **"booming, ponderous voice":** "Hiss on Stand Denies Being a Red or Taking Papers," *NYT*, June 24, 1949.

320 **Stryker told reporters:** *Washington Evening Star*, June 14, 1939.

321 **His son heard:** Robert Cowley, *TLV*, xxii.

322 **the "Hermit Kingdom":** *TLV*, xiv.

322 **"a state of estivation":** MC to Archibald MacLeish, *TLV*, 321.

322 **a full-throated defense:** "The Sorrows of Elmer Davis," *TNR*, May 3, 1943, 591–93.

323 **sharply observed piece:** "Town Report: 1942," *TNR*, November 23, 1942, 674–76.

323 **his friend Otis:** "For Otis," *TNR*, November 23, 1942, 625–26.

323 **surveyed the various experiments:** "Books by the Millions," *TNR*, October 11, 1943, 417–19.

325 **anecdotes about Perkins:** "Unshaken Friend," *New Yorker*, April 1 and April 8, 1944.

326 **"The flow of manuscripts":** Berg, *Max Perkins: Editor of Genius*, E. P. Dutton 1978, 427.

326 **"dreamed of being adopted":** *Unshaken Friend*, xiii.

326 **"being like that fellow":** Berg, *Max Perkins*, 427.

327 **"I began thinking about projects":** MC to Stanley Young, *TLV*, 335.

328 **"Conceiving the book":** MC to Thomas Costain, Doubleday, Doran and Company, *TLV*, 330.

329 **coined in 1918:** Van Wyck Brooks, "On Creating a Usable Past," *The Dial*, April 11, 1918, 337–41.

NOTES

329 in this fashion discover: "Brooks and the 'Usable Past,'" *TNR*, November 10, 1947, 25–27.

329 critic Mark Greif: Mark Greif, *The Age of the Crisis of Man: Thought and Fiction in America 1933–1973*, Princeton University Press, 2015, 20.

330 "I doubt that there was ever": "The Book of Martyrs," *TNR*, March 22, 1943, 386–87.

330 "Surely there was never": "Louis Aragon: Poet of the French Resistance," *Salute*, May 1946, 11.

331 "most influential book": Greif, *The Age of the Crisis of Man*, 110.

331 "no American critic": MC to F. O. Matthiessen, *TLV*, 348.

332 "is an extraordinary mixture": Introduction, *The Complete Poetry and Prose of Walt Whitman*, Farrar, Straus and Young, 3.

332 "Studs Lonigan of letters": "Why So Hot?," *Time*, April 24, 1944.

332 "culture may be understood": Bernard DeVoto, *The Literary Fallacy*, Kennikat Press, 43.

333 Sinclair Lewis erupted: Sinclair Lewis, "Fools, Liars, and Mr. Devoto: A Reply to 'The Literary Fallacy,'" *Saturday Review of Literature*, 9–12.

333 Cowley unburdened himself: MC to KB, *TLV*, 357.

333 a mournful letter: MC to KB, *SC*, 268–69.

334 "work I love now": MC to Mary Mellon, *TLV*, 119.

334 that the agreement between: Quoted in William McGuire, *Bollingen: An Adventure in Collecting the Past*, Princeton University Press, 1982, 119.

334 "120 articles and reviews": McGuire, *Bollingen*, 80.

335 "For the records of your office": McGuire, *Bollingen*, 81.

ELEVEN. THE PORTABLE MALCOLM COWLEY

337 "the first great experiment": Quoted in John Cole, *Books in Action: The Armed Services Editions*, Library of Congress, 1984, 10.

338 "designed (without profit": Alexander Woollcott to Sophie Rosenberger, *The Letters of Alexander Woollcott*, edited by Beatrice Kaufman and Joseph Hennessey, Viking Press, 1944, 384.

338 "of their stopping": Marshall Best, memo, VEF, Viking Portable Library, 1946.

339 "No complete son of a": *WT*, 266.

339 "the bad habit": *CWMC*, 7.

339 "twirp like Malcolm": EH to John Dos Passos, *Ernest Hemingway: Selected Letters, 1917–1961*, edited by Carlos Baker, Charles Scribner's Sons, 1981.

340 "I was outraged": "Hemingway's Wound—and Its Consequences for American Literature," *Georgia Review*, Summer 1984.

341 "back to Hemingway's": *TPH*, vii–xii.

342 a warm letter: EH to MC, *Ernest Hemingway: Selected Letters 1917–1961*, 603.

Malcolm Cowley saved forty-three letters to him from Ernest Hemingway from 1937 to 1952. These letters are now in the hands of a private collector and unavailable for examination. However, the scholar James Brasch was allowed access to them in the early eighties in order to write his paper "Invention from Knowledge: The Hemingway-Cowley Correspondence." Brasch took 151 pages of typed notes, which I have had access to. These notes quote many passages verbatim and paraphrase others. I use the citation "JB's notes," as below, when I quote, sparingly, from those letters.

342 In another letter: Quoted in "Hemingway's Wound."

343 "five major influences": James Jones, *Some Came Running*, Charles Scribner's Sons, 1957, 12–13.

344 "among the writers": *CWMC*, 12.

345 aviation barnstorming saga: "Voodoo Dance," *TNR*, April 10, 1935, 254–55.

345 His 1936 review: "Poe in Mississippi," *TNR*, November 4, 1936, 22.

346 **"feels that Faulkner":** "Faulkner by Daylight," *TNR*, April 15, 1940, 510.

346 **"the best hunting":** "Go Down to Faulkner's Land," *TNR*, June 29, 1942, 900.

347 **told Cowley, "Faulkner is finished":** A. Scott Berg, *Max Perkins: Editor of Genius*, E. P. Dutton, 1978, 421–22.

347 **Faulkner once admitted:** *FCF*, 80.

348 **"a sincere one":** WF to Robert K. Haas, *Selected Letters of William Faulkner*, edited by Joseph Blotner, Random House, 1977, 122.

349 **story in *Time*:** "When the Dam Breaks," *Time*, January 23, 1939, 45–48.

349 **He called Faulkner:** Henry Seidel Canby, "The School of Cruelty," *Saturday Review of Literature*, March 21, 1931, 1–2.

350 **"a Sax Rohmer":** *CWMC*, 44.

350 **always reliably hostile:** Bernard DeVoto, "Witchcraft in Mississippi," *Saturday Review of Literature*, October 31, 1936, 1.

350 **Fadiman set up:** These review quotes can all be found in the chapter on Faulkner in Clifton Fadiman, *Party of One: The Selected Writings of Clifton Fadiman*, World Publishing Company, 1955, 98–125.

351 **"a larger chorus":** *FCF*, 5.

352 **"would very much like":** *FCF*, 7.

353 **"say it all":** *FCF*, 7.

355 **"seems to us":** *FCF*, 21.

355 **"a bayonet prick":** *FCF*, 22.

355 **"By all means":** *FCF*, 25.

356 **"must be right":** *FCF*, 35.

357 **"have done this":** *FCF*, 36.

357 **"an event in [Faulkner's] career":** *FCF*, 37.

357 **on this wording:** Front cover copy, *TPF*, Viking Press, 1946.

358 **"You are going":** *FCF*, 82.

359 **"The job is splendid":** *FCF*, 91.

359 **"There in Oxford":** *TPF*, 1–2.

360 **"he most resembles":** *TPF*, 3.

361 **essay ran in two consecutive issues:** Robert Penn Warren, "Cowley's Faulkner," *TNR*, August 12 and 26, 1946.

363 **"nobody knew me":** *FCF*, 96.

364 **"you get North":** *FCF*, 100.

365 **A darker story:** Jay Parini, *One Matchless Time: A Life of William Faulkner*, HarperCollins, 2004, 100–101.

366 **The only hint:** *FCF*, 114.

366 **"waited two weeks":** *FCF*, 121.

366 **"convinced and determined":** *FCF*, 126.

368 **"it took a long time":** *CWMC*, 178.

TWELVE. THE LITERARY SITUATION

370 **Alexander Calder, who, born:** Although Calder's actual birth certificate says that his date of birth was July 22, 1898, Calder's family was quite certain that this was a mistake and he was born in August.

371 **"deaf enough *not* to hear remarks":** MC to Louise Bogan, *TLV*, 500.

371 **"an alchemist's laboratory":** Eugene Jolas, quoted in Jed Perl, *Calder: The Conquest of Space: The Later Years, 1940–1976*, Alfred A. Knopf, 2020, 35.

372 **"simple, unreckoning fashion":** Introduction, Margaret Calder Hayes, *Three Alexander Calders: A Family Memoir*, Paul S. Eriksson, 1977 xviii.

372 **fortieth birthday party:** Jed Perl, *Calder: The Conquest of Time: The Early Years, 1898–1940*, Alfred A. Knopf, 2017, 554–56.

373 **"refuge for all sorts":** Perl, *Calder: The Conquest of Space*.

374 **"crooning folk songs":** Karlen Mooradian, *The Many Worlds of Arshile Gorky*, Gilgamesh Press Limited, 1980, 121–22.

374 **"bang, bang, bang":** Nouritza Matossian, *Black Angel: The Life of Arshile Gorky*, Chatto and Windus, 1998, 403.

375 **"be so waxlike":** MC to EH, *TLV*, 386.

376 **"understands my work":** The original source of this assertion has proved hard to pinpoint, but it is repeated widely in Hemingway biographies and studies, including the 2004 Sotheby's catalogue for some Hemingway letters on auction.

378 **admitting, "In the first war I now see":** EH to MC, 8/25/48, quoted in the essay "Hemingway's Wound," which in turn is quoting from the Sotheby's catalogue for the auction of Hemingway's letters to him.

380 **"read his piece?":** A. E. Hotchner, *Papa Hemingway: A Personal Memoir*, Random House, 1966, 107.

380 **"The trouble is":** EH to MC, September 3, 1945, JB's notes.

380 **"Abner of Literature":** EH to MC, October 11, 1949, JB's notes.

381 **an exasperated Cowley:** MC to EH, *TLV*, 441.

382 **widely regretted novel:** "Hemingway's Portrait of an Old Soldier Preparing to Die," *NYHT*, September 10, 1950, 1, 16.

382 **"as nearly faultless":** "Hemingway's Novel Has the Rich Simplicity of a Classic," *NYHT*, September 7, 1952, 1, 17.

382 **"mourn for Hemingway":** MC to Conrad Aiken, *TLV*, 552.

384 **"Being a literary historian":** *WT*, 159.

384 **mildly mocking reference:** MC to EH, September 24, 1949, JB/EH.

384 **The first lecture:** "Why Teach American Literature," lecture delivered at Syracuse University, June 9, 1947.

385 **United Press reported:** "Former Communist on Washington U. Staff," *Medford Mail Tribune*, January 3, 1950.

385 **what had happened:** MC to Samuel Monk, *TLV*, 423–24.

386 **"I am sick of teaching. I am":** Quoted in Mark McGurl, *The Program Era: Postwar Fiction and the Rise of Creative Writing*, Harvard University Press, 2009, 1.

386 **"your students talk":** MC to Kay Boyle, February 25, 1957, VEF.

386 **1957 Hopwood Lecture:** "How Writing Might Be Taught," *The Portable Malcolm Cowley*, 554–69.

388 **"working a day":** Harold Guinzburg to MC, July 9, 1949, VEF.

389 **"the 18th century ideal":** "The Greene-ing of the Portables," *Washington Post Book World*, April 29, 1973.

390 **undertake a guide:** MC to W. H. Auden, *TLV*, 37.

391 **"was the nature":** Louis Menand, *The Free World: Art and Thought in the Cold War*, Farrar, Straus and Giroux, 2021, xii.

391 **Randall Jarrell quipped:** Quoted in Anatole Broyard, *Kafka Was the Rage: A Greenwich Village Memoir*, Vintage Books, 1997, 31.

393 **bittersweet short story:** Harvey Swados, "Nights in the Gardens of Brooklyn," reprinted in *Nights in the Gardens of Brooklyn: The Collected Stories of Harvey Swados*, Viking Press, 1986, 1–39.

394 "in our midst a powerfully vocal": "The Liberal Fifth Column," *Partisan Review*, Summer 1946, 279–93.

394 took sharp exception: "Ten Little Magazines," *TNR*, March 31, 1947, 30–33.

395 closed to him: With one exception: "1930: The Year That Was New Year's Eve," *Commentary*, June 1951.

395 "the *Partisan* knives": MC to KB, *TLV*, 585.

396 would recall late in life: MC to Christopher Lasch, *TLV*, 686.

396 *Life* magazine profiled: "Young U.S. Writers," *Life*, June 2, 1947, 71–78.

396 *Life* weighed in: "Fiction in the U.S.," *Life*, August 16, 1948, 24.

397 "they are better written": "American Novels Since the War," *TNR*, December 28, 1953, 16–18.

397 series of essays and reviews: "New Tendencies in the Novel: Pure Fiction," *TNR*, November 28, 1949, 32–35.

398 amplified this critique: Gore Vidal writing as "Libra," "Ladders to Heaven: Novelists and Critics of the Forties," *New World Writing* 4, October 1953.

399 in a symposium: "American Scholar Forum: The New Criticism," *American Scholar* 20, 1950–1951, 98.

400 As he noted: MC to Marshall Best, *TLV*, 426–27.

401 "the best book": Arthur Mizener, "Home Was the Stranger," *NYTBR*, June 10, 1951.

401 "should be proud": Perry Miller, "Departure and Return," *The Nation*, October 27, 1951, 356–57.

402 historian has termed: Greg Barnhisel, *Cold War Modernists: Art, Literature, and American Diplomacy*, Columbia University Press, 2015.

402 "best American writing": Barnhisel, *Cold War Modernists*, 186–87.

402 "(50,000–60,000 word) book": MC to Marshall Best, August 12, 1953, VEF, *TLS*.

403 "men of the 1920s": Vidal as "Libra," "Ladders to Heaven."

403 "I've done is make enemies": MC to Conrad Aiken, *TLV*, 479.

404 essay "How Writers Lived": "How Writers Lived," *Literary History of the United States* (3rd edition, revised), edited by Robert E. Spiller et. al, Macmillan, 1963, 1263–72.

405 Mark McGurl calls: McGurl, *The Program Era*, 29.

407 "would be perfect": *Yaddo: Making American Culture*, edited by Micki McGee, New York Public Library/Columbia University Press, 4.

407 infamous Lowell Affair: The two best accounts of this episode are Ruth Price's "The Longest Stay," in *Yaddo*, and Ben Alexander's comprehensive "The Lowell Affair," *New England Quarterly*, December 2007, 545–87.

407 "an epic clash": Price, "The Longest Stay."

408 Delmore Schwartz believed: Delmore Schwartz to AT, *The Letters of Delmore Schwartz*, edited by Robert Phillips, Ontario Review Press, 1984, 77.

409 comparison of his recommendations: The citations of and quotations from Cowley's reports are all to be found in the files of the Guggenheim Foundation, access to which was kindly granted to me by André Bernard, former vice president and secretary of the foundation.

409 As Saul Steinberg: Geoffrey Hellman, "Some Splendid and Admirable People," *New Yorker*, February 15, 1976, 44.

THIRTEEN. THE COUNTERCULTURE COWLEY

413 accurate but not: *BS*, 8.

414 "It'll save me": Joan Haverty Kerouac, *Nobody's Wife: The Smart Aleck and the King of the Beats*, Creative Arts Book Company, 1990, 141.

414 onlooker whispered reverently: Joyce Johnson, "Kerouac Unbound," *Vanity Fair Hive*, August 20, 2007.

414 "road is fast": *WW*, xxv.

415 another novel in mind: *WW*, 123.

415 final chapters of his first: *TLS*, 241.

417 "prophesy that the Beat Generation": JK, "Lamb, No Lion," *Pageant*, February 1958, 161.

419 "indescribable sad music": *WW*, 262.

419 Giroux recalled that: The story of what actually happened and was said in Robert Giroux's office has been told numerous times by many biographers, with certain variations; this one hews to Joyce Johnson's in her *Vanity Fair* article.

420 "a well-made novel": Quoted in Sterling Lord, *Lord of Publishing: A Memoir*, Open Road, 2013, 4.

420 "I would like a chance": Allen Ginsberg to MC, July 3, 1953, VEF, *OTR*.

420 Cowley responded encouragingly: MC to Allen Ginsberg, July 14, 1953, VEF, *OTR*.

421 Cowley had already read: *JB*, 187.

421 Oddly, Cowley would: RC. Even more oddly, Marshall Best testifies that Kerouac "threw the manuscript off in front of Pat Covici" in the Viking offices. Page 33 of Best's interview in the Oral History Archives, Columbia University.

422 "monstrous huge banging": *OTRS*, 307.

423 journalist for *Newsday*: Marshall Best to Bill McIlwain, May 18, 1959, VEF, *OTR*.

423 "Jack wrote well naturally": *JB*, 206.

423 the catalogue copy: VEF, *OTR*.

424 a famous essay: John Clellon Holmes, "This Is the Beat Generation," *NYT Magazine*, November 16, 1952.

425 "Malcolm Cowley's perseverance": Thomas Guinzburg, Oral History Archives, Columbia University, 258.

425 "long autobiographical novel": MC to Arabel Porter, *TLV*, 484–85.

427 "Vermont professor type": JK to Carolyn Cassady, February 1953, *Jack Kerouac: Selected Letters, 1940–1956*, edited by Ann Charters, Penguin Books, 1996.

427 tell his agent: JK to Sterling Lord, *Jack Kerouac: Selected Letters, 1940–1956*, 50.

429 "publishing to me": JK to Sterling Lord, *Jack Kerouac: Selected Letters, 1940–1956*, 466.

429 "a good friend": JK to Sterling Lord, *Jack Kerouac: Selected Letters, 1940–1956*, 588–89.

429 "bold writing talent": Paul Maher Jr., *Kerouac: The Definitive Biography*, Taylor Trade Publishing, 2004, 280.

430 "there I helped": Guinzburg, Oral History Archives, Columbia University, 3–137.

430 "of that generation": Guinzburg, Oral History Archives, Columbia University, 4–223.

430 "being seriously considered": MC to JK, *TLV*, 518.

431 "okay with me": JK to MC, *Jack Kerouac: Selected Letters, 1957–1969*, edited by Ann Charters Penguin Books, 2000, 518–19.

432 back from him: Nathaniel Whitehorn to Helen Taylor of Viking, November 1, 1955, VEF, *OTR*.

433 "so it flows": JK to Sterling Lord, October 7, 1956, *Jack Kerouac: Selected Letters 1940–1956*, 589.

433 an interoffice memo: Helen Taylor to Harold Guinzburg and Marshall Best, March 21, 1957, VEF, *OTR*.

435 he feared the prosecution: JK to Gary Snyder, June 14, 1957, *Jack Kerouac: Selected Letters, 1957–1969*, 52.

436 single word "BOO": JK to MC, April 18, 1956, NL.

436 "Manuscript Acceptance Report": MC memo to Viking staff, April 18, 1957, VEF, *OTR*, also *TLV*, 488–89.

437 **"The Viking edition":** MC to JK, *TLV*, 490.

437 **exceptionally smart review:** Gilbert Millstein, *NYT*, September 5, 1957.

438 **scanned the review:** Joyce Johnson, *Minor Characters*, Washington Square Press, 1984, 195–96.

441 **a durable attack:** Norman Podhoretz, "The Know-Nothing Bohemians," *Partisan Review*, Spring 1958, 305–18. It is either curious or ironic or both that the preceding issue of the magazine includes the poem "Ready to Roll" by Allen Ginsberg, who comes in for a drubbing in Podhoretz's essay.

441 **ode to hipsterism:** Norman Mailer, "The White Negro," *Dissent*, Fall 1957.

441 **Menand calls attacks:** Louis Menand, *The Free World: Art and Thought in the Cold War*, Farrar, Straus and Giroux, 2021, 487.

441 **"Life is holy":** *OTRS*, 159.

443 **Kerouac's closest friend:** Report by Keith Jennison, undated, VEF, *The Dharma Bums*.

443 **"I think this is miles":** Report by Catherine Carver, February 25, 1958, VEF, *The Dharma Bums*.

443 **Kerouac was stuck:** Publishing contracts of the period required authors to repay any amount above 10 percent of the total cost of composition for the cost incurred by changes in galleys. The Viking files indicate that Taylor had overridden a considerable number of Kerouac's desired changes that he made in the copyedited manuscript, which then made it into galleys, which she then changed back. Or so it appears—everybody has their own story. Kerouac's lasting bitterness about the bill is unambiguous, though.

444 **"days of Malcolm":** JK, "The Art of Fiction 41," *Paris Review*.

444 **"Oh shame, shame":** JK to Allen Ginsberg, July 21, 1957, *Jack Kerouac and Allen Ginsberg: The Letters*, edited by Bill Morgan and David Stanford, Viking Press, 2010, 352.

444 **"and his memory":** *JB*, 206.

446 **"needed a place":** Mark McGurl, *The Program Era: Postwar Fiction and the Rise of Creative Writing*, Harvard University Press, 2009, 184.

447 **"Archie's great trick":** MC to Wallace Stegner, *TLV*, 495.

447 **"about the great":** LM, *Walter Benjamin at the Dairy Queen: Reflections at Sixty and Beyond*, Simon and Schuster, 1999, 134.

448 **"low-rent revolt":** LM, "On the Road," *New York Review of Books*, December 5, 2001.

449 **"most extraordinary kids":** Tom Wolfe, *The Electric Kool-Aid Acid Test*, Farrar, Straus and Giroux, 1968, 41.

449 **"the winning side":** Robert Stone, "The Prince of Possibility," *New Yorker*, June 14, 2004.

450 **"A single *Batman*":** Gordon Lish, "What the Hell You Looking in Here for, Daisy Mae?," *Genesis West*, Fall 1963.

450 **epiphany took place:** Rick Dodgson, *It's All a Kind of Magic: The Young Ken Kesey*, University of Wisconsin Press, 2013, 64.

451 **would call "stud-duckery":** McMurtry, "On the Road."

451 **his 1977 reminiscence:** "Ken Kesey at Stanford," *F&L*, 324–28.

452 **"candidates for beatitude":** KK, *Demon Box*, Viking Press, 1986, 78.

452 **"a rough bird":** MC to Pascal Covici, *TLV*, 547.

452 **"narrator is a loony":** MC to Pascal Covici, *TLV*, 547.

453 **"I had nothing to do":** KK, *Kesey's Garage Sale*, Viking Press, 1973, 7.

453 **"see the suffering":** Dodgson, *It's All a Kind of Magic*, 136.

454 **"a good experience":** *Conversations with Ken Kesey*, edited by Scott F. Parker, University Press of Mississippi, 2014, 14.

454 **"On the table by the window":** *F&L*, 327–28.

456 **"Kesey is concerned":** Catalogue copy, VEF, *One Flew Over the Cuckoo's Nest*.

457 **"Cowley taught me"**: Lish, "What the Hell You Looking in Here for, Daisy Mae?"

457 **"came out of it"**: *Conversations with Ken Kesey*, 107.

458 **"GREAT NEW AMERICAN NOVELIST"**: Dodgson, *It's All a Kind of Magic*, 126.

458 **"An epochal summit"**: Dennis McNally, *Desolate Angel: Jack Kerouac, the Beat Generation, and America*, Da Capo Press, 200, 315.

458 **"I was disappointed in myself"**: McNally, *Desolate Angel*, 315.

459 **that would define:** Guinzburg, Oral History Archives, Columbia University, 3–139.

FOURTEEN. THE LONG RETROSPECTIVE

461 **"a deaf man"**: "Reconsiderations: The Sixties," *TNR*, August 20, 1977, 37–40.

462 **"unwashed, unbarbered proletariat"**: MC to Wallace Stegner, *TLV*, 616.

462 **didn't know him:** MC to KB, *TLV*, 637.

462 **Cormac McCarthy early:** MC to Albert Erskine, *TLV*, 581.

462 **"American black-humor-and-catastrophe novelists"**: MC to Bernard Bergonzi, *TLV*, 629.

463 **"to read the new fiction"**: MC to KB, *TLV*, 586.

463 **"a new world"**: MC to Conrad Aiken, *TLV*, 586.

463 **most impassioned pieces:** "Papa and the Parricides," *Esquire*, June 1967.

464 **"My address book"**: MC to Jacob Davis, *TLV*, 599.

465 **about Wilson twice:** "A Reminiscence: Edmund Wilson at *The New Republic*," *TNR*, July 1, 1972, 25–28; and "Old Doc Wilson," *Saturday Review of Literature*, October 29, 1977, 36–39.

466 **a splashy send-off:** Benjamin DeMott, "Malcolm Cowley, Writing and Talking," *NYTBR*, April 30, 1978.

467 **"beautiful, honest book"**: William Styron, *NYTBR*, May 6, 1973.

467 **"a true chronicler"**: Vincent Sheean, "A Mature, Eloquent Appraisal of 'The Lost Generation,'" *Chicago Tribune*, May 6, 1973.

467 **old critical adversary:** Clifton Fadiman to MC, January 19, 1973, VEF, *SF*.

467 **"People come round"**: MC to AT, *TLV*, 663.

468 **"God, how blind"**: MC to KB, *TLV*, 684.

468 **essay suggestively titled:** "The Sense of Guilt," *Kenyon Review*, Spring 1965.

469 **almost anguished review:** "The Soviet Socialist Republic of the Dead," *Washington Post Book World*, September 22, 1968.

470 **the obvious choice:** AK, "Writers in the Radical Years," *NYTBR*, March 23, 1980.

470 **most predictable naysayer:** Sidney Hook, "Disremembering the Thirties," *American Scholar*, Autumn 1980, 556–60.

470 **vicious, this-time-it's-personal review:** Kenneth S. Lynn, "Malcolm Cowley Forgets," *American Spectator*, October 1980, 14–17.

470 **The first excerpt:** "No Homage to Catalonia: A Memory of the Spanish Civil War," *Southern Review*, January 1982, 131–40.

470 **confusion and disarray:** "Echoes from Moscow: 1937–1938," *Southern Review*, January 1984.

470 **the third, "Lament . . .":** "Lament for the Abraham Lincoln Battalion," *Sewanee Review*, Summer 1984.

470 **The final excerpt:** "A Time of Resignations," *Yale Review*, November 1984.

471 **at the conclusion of his review:** John Leonard, *NYT*, April 28, 1978, C25.

471 **assault on Cowley:** Kenneth S. Lynn, "The Strange Unhappy Life of Max Perkins," *Commentary*, December 1978.

471 **with Lynn's review:** Kenneth S. Lynn, "Hemingway's Private War," *Commentary*, July 1981.

472 **the best essays:** "Hemingway's Wound—and Its Consequences for American Literature," *Georgia Review*, Summer 1984.

474 **captures the doubleness:** *V80*, 3.

474 **"project among many":** *V80*, 71.

476 **"everything to persuade":** RC.

476 **"to be useless":** MC to Ruth Nuzum, *TLV*, 695.

477 **He made the front page:** Albin Krebs, "Malcolm Cowley, Writer, Is Dead at 90," *NYT*, March 29, 1989.

477 **"a living bridge":** John Updike, quoted in "Malcolm Cowley, Critic, Dies," *Washington Post*, March 29, 1989.

EPILOGUE: POLITICS AND MEMORY

479 **a memorial service:** The details that follow are taken from a transcript of the remarks made by the speakers, provided to the author by Robert Cowley, and my own memories of the event.

480 **launched into his real theme:** Irving Howe, "Critics Return," *TNR*, April 30, 1990, 42–44.

481 **"What's Left of . . .":** Adam Kirsch, *City Journal*, Spring 2014.

481 **"Politics So Awful?":** Christopher Benfey, *TNR*, February 28, 2014.

481 **Joseph Epstein's line:** Joseph Epstein, "The Literary Life Today," *New Criterion*, September 1982, 13.

481 **"I sometimes say":** MC interview with Miranda Cowley.

483 **otherwise eyebrow-raising claim:** Hans Bak, Editor's Preface, *TLV*, xxxvii.

483 **initiated this book:** Gerald Howard, "The Making of American Literature," *Bookforum*, December-January 2014.

INDEX

World War I (*cont.*)
  Cowley's ambulance-driving service
    in, 4, 37, 41, 43–50, 56, 58–80,
    158, 223
  France in, 4, 37, 40–41, 43–50
  Harvard and, 41–45, 60
World War II, 4, 295–96, 305, 307,
    309–12, 315, 322, 323, 333,
    378, 473
  publishing industry and, 336–38
  veterans of, 362
Wright, Richard, 239, 240, 242,
    299, 300
Wright, Willard Huntington, 22
writing programs, 383,
    446–47

Iowa, 383, 446
Stanford, 386, 412, 446–48,
    450–51, 457
Wylie, Elinor, 121

Yaddo, 191, 221–22, 406–8, 410
Years of Protest (Salzman, ed.), 170, 202
Yeats, William Butler, 70, 393
Young, Art, 175
Young, Philip, 381
Young, Stanley, 327, 328
Young, Stark, 171, 181, 182

Zabel, Morton Dauwen, 154, 166, 169
Ziff, Larzer, 409
Zola, Émile, 23, 90v